WILLIAM LOVETT.

THE
LIFE AND STRUGGLES

OF

WILLIAM LOVETT,

IN HIS PURSUIT OF

BREAD, KNOWLEDGE, AND FREEDOM;

WITH SOME SHORT ACCOUNT OF THE DIFFERENT
ASSOCIATIONS HE BELONGED TO, AND OF THE
OPINIONS HE ENTERTAINED.

"Onward! while a wrong remains
To be conquered by the right;
While oppression lifts a finger
To affront us by his might;
While an error clouds the reason
Of the universal heart,
Or a Slave awaits his freedom,
Action is the wise man's part."—
CHARLES MACKAY.

LONDON:
PUBLISHED BY TRÜBNER & Co.,
57 AND 59, LUDGATE HILL.

1876.

PREFACE.

THE commencement of the following pages I must attribute to the solicitations of some of my radical friends, who, when I had been talking of some of the events of my life, of the different associations I have been connected with, and of the various political struggles in which I have been engaged, have urged me to write the facts down; so that the working classes of a future day may know something of the early struggles of some of those who contended for the political rights they may be then enjoying; and of those who aided in establishing a free and cheap press, and in the diffusion of that knowledge which may have brought peace, plenty, and happiness around their dwellings. I shall offer no apology to the reader for the manner in which I have executed my task; as I have done it, as I best could, in those intervals of time not devoted to my labours for bread. It may, perhaps, be objected, that I ought not to have introduced the Addresses and Documents of the Associations I have belonged to into my own history. To this I reply that I have introduced nothing but my own writings, unless acknowledged; and I think that those who desire to know anything of me, would like to know what my opinions and sentiments were—(as well as great numbers who thought with me)—regarding the great questions of human right, social progress, and political reform; and these, in fact, constitute a great part of my own history. Moreover, most of the principles and opinions enunciated in those Addresses are as important now as when they were first written; the opinions given are as true now as then; and the advice in them is as necessary, as most of the reforms aimed at are yet to be achieved. The Working Classes are still compelled to pay and obey at the mandates of exclusive legislators—Catholics, Jews, and Dissenters, —are in England still compelled to support a Church whose rule they hate, and whose doctrines they abhor. Education is still regarded by vast numbers as a means of filling Churches and Chapels, instead of a glorious instrument of human elevation—vast revenues are still squandered on armies and warriors—and a privileged few still maintain an ascendancy for evil, in court, camp, navy, and senate-house. The Working Classes are still to a vast extent following blind guides, and trusting to leaders and orators, outside their own ranks, to achieve that for them which their own efforts, self-sacrifices, and organization can alone effect. They still, unhappily, undervalue *mental and moral effort* for raising their class and advancing the welfare of their country, and therefore the advice given to them from thirty to forty years ago may still be found useful. I have yet another reason for adding the documents of the Associations I have taken part in, and for giving a brief account of their proceedings; and it is this—That hitherto, little is found in history, or in our public papers, that present a fair and accurate account of the public proceedings of the Working Classes; for if the Whig and Tory papers of the day ever condescend to notice them, it is rather to garble and distort facts, to magnify faults and follies, and to ridicule their objects and intentions; the pleasing of their patrons being more important with them than a truthful record. In consequence of this unjust system the historians and writers of a future day will have only garbled tales to guide them—as those of past history have—and hence a caricature is oftener given of the industrious millions than a truthful portrait.

It is very probable that, in reading the following pages, some ease-enjoying, pious believer in the excellence and purity of our social and political institutions, may be led to think that I have been a busy, restless, discontented fellow. In forming such opinion of me he will be politically correct; and which disposition—unfavourable as it may appear to him—I am prepared to justify. For it is one of the items of my political creed, that the man who sees the rights of the industrious many withheld by a privileged, idle, and incompetent few; who sees one law for the rich and another for the poor; and perceives injustice, corruption and extravagance daily sapping the vitals of his country, and remains a silent, passive, and contented spectator, is a soulless participator in the wrongs inflicted on his country and his kind. In thus stating this, others again, may be led to think me self-consequential and conceited; which, if they do so, I shall think—with all deference to their opinions—that they will do me an injustice, for the older I get the more I am finding out my great deficiencies, and perceive how lamentably ignorant I am on a great variety of very important subjects with which I ought to be acquainted; and to think how much more useful I might have been, in my humble sphere, if I·had had that early education which I hope, at no distant period, will be realized for the rising generation, and which I have hitherto, and will in future do my best to promote. But whatever may be the political or religious opinions of those who differ from me, I would ask them—ought the great battle and struggles of life to be *for the multitude, such as they are?* Seeing that the great author of our being has placed us in a world fitted with abundant means to secure the happiness of all, if justly administered, ought these means to be monopolized and applied to secure *an excess of luxuries for the few,* while the mass of the people are not only compelled to toil and labour to secure it, but to be very frequently destitute of the necessary means of subsistence for themselves and families? Justice, I think, will cause them in their conscience to say they should not ; for, though toil and natural evils are the conditions of life, they ought not to be augmented by social and political injustice.

To account for any repetitions that may be found in the work—and which may have escaped me—I may state that it was begun in 1840, and has been added to from time to time up to the year 1874.

THE
LIFE & STRUGGLES OF WILLIAM LOVETT.

CHAPTER I.

IN resolving to string together the events of my life I am hopeful that they may be of interest to my working-class brethren, with whom and for whom I have laboured for the last forty-five years, in the hopes of improving our social and political condition. The success of our efforts has not been to the extent of my wishes, although I believe great progress has been effected; and if the following pages may in any way serve to stimulate younger and wiser men to continue the contest, earnestly but discreetly, till the victory is won over political injustice, social oppression, ignorance and wrong, I shall not have written them in vain. I am conscious of my inability to make my story interesting by style or force of language, and therefore I shall tell it right on as I best can. I was born on the 8th of May, in the year 1800, in the little fishing town of Newlyn, situated about a mile westward of Penzance, in the county of Cornwall. My mother's maiden name was Kezia Green; she descended from a family of that name, well known in the west of the county for their skill as blacksmiths, and their strength and dexterity as wrestlers, trophies won by my grandmother's brother being still in the family. My father was a native of Hull, of the same name as myself, and the captain of a small trading vessel, often entering

the port of Falmouth, where he met with my mother. He
was, however, unhappily drowned in his last voyage home
before I was born, so I can say nothing further respecting
him. My mother, however, in her lonely position, was
relieved and taken care of by an affectionate brother, one
who possessed great goodness of heart. Soon after this
he commenced business as a ropemaker, and, being successful in the beginning, was able to render her ample assistance while I was an infant. He possessed an amiable
disposition and a well-informed mind, which he had been
assiduous in cultivating, and was always held up to me as
an example by my grandmother. He died, however, of a
decline, in his 32nd year, and when I was very young.
My mother being thus thrown entirely on her own resources, fortunately possessed a vigorous constitution and a
persevering spirit, so that, by labouring industriously in
the usual avocations of a fishing town, as well as by selling
fish in Penzance market, she was enabled to bring me up
in some degree of comfort, as well as to support for the
most part her aged mother, who became greatly dependent
on her. Among my earliest recollections was that of
being taken in my grandmother's arms to see the illumina-
tions for the short peace of 1803, was that of seeing a
plentiful supply of raisins in the town, occasioned by the
wreck of the fig-man—as she was called—the vessel that,
I think, knocked down the works of the wherry mine in a
storm ; and was my being driven home by an old shop-
keeper of the town for having run down street in my
night-clothes after my mother. I have also deeply
engraven on the memory of my boyhood the apprehensions
and alarms that were experienced amongst the inhabitants
of our town regarding the press-gang during the war.
The cry that "the press-gang was coming" was sufficient
to cause all the young and eligible men of the town to
flock up to the hills and away to the country as fast as
possible, and to hide themselves in all manner of places till
the danger was supposed to be over. It was not always,
however, that the road to the country was open to them,
for the authorities sometimes arranged that a troop of
light horse should be at hand to cut off their retreat when

the press-gang landed. Then might the soldiers be seen, with drawn cutlasses, riding down the poor fishermen, often through fields of standing corn where they had sought to hide themselves, while the press-gang were engaged in diligently searching every house in order to secure their victims. In this way, as well as out of their boats at sea, were great numbers taken away, and many of them never more heard of by their relations. On one of those exciting occasions, it so happened that an old man and his daughter were out at one end of the town, beside a small stream cleansing fish. The daughter was a woman between thirty and forty, and her father, I should think upwards of sixty, though he looked younger. Being thus engaged when the press-gang landed, and she being deaf, one of the gang had been and seized her father, and was bearing him off before she was aware of it. On raising her head, and seeing her father borne off a prisoner, she snatched up one of the dog-fishes she was opening, and running up to the man she asked him what he was going to do with her daddy. Pointing to the man-of-war at a distance, he told her he was going to take him aboard that big ship. The words had scarcely passed his lips before she fetched him a blow across his face with the rough dog-fish, that made him relinquish his hold. Then seizing her father with one hand, and resolutely defending him with the dog-fish in the other, she kept her opponent at bay till other women and boys came to her assistance. Thus was Honour Hitchens, by her courage, enabled to bear off her daddy in triumph amid the cheers and rejoicings of half the women and boys of the neighbourhood.

Like most children, when very young, my love of play was far greater than that of learning, for I was sent to all the dame-schools of the town before I could master the alphabet. Of my first school I remember being sent home at midsummer with a slip of paper round my hat with my name on it in red ink, given as a holiday present. Of my second school was the being put in the coal-cellar for bad conduct, on the second and last day of my being there. Eventually, however, I was instructed to read by my great grandmother, who lived in the village of St. Creed, about three miles from our town, she being at that period about eighty years of age. A circumstance I remember in connection with this kind old lady induces me to believe that I had a good memory when a child. My mother, who generally paid me a visit once a week to bring me clean linen, on one occasion made me a present of Dr. Watt's Divine Songs, saying at the same time, "William, when you have learnt them all, I will make you a present of a new Bible." This promise so far stimulated me to my task, that I had learnt to repeat them all from memory in a fortnight's time; and I eagerly sent home word by a neighbour to tell my mother to bring the present she promised me as I had learnt all the songs. On going to meet her a portion of the way, as I usually did, I mounted on a large rock to await her coming, and as soon as she saw me at a distance, she held up the Bible to assure me that my request had not been forgotten. I soon, however, got too troublesome for my poor great grandmother, and was taken home; and I remember that the day after I nearly cut off the top of a finger in playing with a knife. My grandmother's sister then took me to live with her for a short time. She was a kind-hearted woman, but fond of drink at times, and I, having accidentally broken one of her windows, one day was sent home in a tiff. I was then sent to a boys' school to learn "to write and cypher," thought at that time to be all the education required for poor people. It was the only school in the town at that time, and I had two masters while there. The first master was a severe one, and the second was somewhat worse. Custises on the palm of the hand and very severe canings were punishments for not recollecting our tasks, and on one occasion I saw him hang up a boy by the two thumbs with his toes just touching the ground for playing truant. Here, too, I caught the small-pox from seeing a little girl brought into the school in her grandmother's arms; she having her little face and arms thickly beset with the dark-scabbed pustules, caused a strange shivering sensation to come over me at the moment, and in a short time I was taken ill with the disease. I think that fear had much to do with it, though the germs must undoubtedly have been wafted towards me. I must here state that the disease at that time being greatly dreaded, I was constantly cautioned by my friends to avoid all children that had had it recently, and being thus brought suddenly face to face with it, with no means of escape, I naturally felt alarmed. And what a terrible disease it was I can well remember, for I think I was seven or eight years old. But bad as I had it I was not marked with it as numbers of my schoolfellows were; for so terrible were its ravages at that period, that I can vividly remember the number of seamed and scarred faces among them. Vaccination at that time had not been introduced into our town, though inoculation for the small-pox was occasionally resorted to; but it was looked upon as sinful and a doubting of providence, although about that period one in every fourteen persons born died from its ravages. Having made but little progress at this school, when I got well I was sent to another about a mile from the town and near the parish church. Here I learned to write tolerably well, and to know a little of arithmetic and the catechism, and this formed the extent of my scholastic acquirements. I remember being once flogged severely by the master, and I think I deserved it. It was in the winter time, and his little boy had set a trap in the garden for catching birds, when myself and another boy seeing some birds in the trap pulled down the opening and caught them. We then wrung their necks, brought them into the school, and put them into our school bags unobserved. Not having however wrung their necks effectually, in a short time they began to flutter, and this led to our detection and punishment. This master was, however, a very clever and ingenious person, and I think also a bit of a wit; for he being too busy on one occasion to set me a copy requested me to write one for myself. From some curious notions I had formed of royalty, I wrote for my copy—" All Kings have long heads," which when my master saw, he wrote on the opposite page, " All horses have longer heads." To prove how anxious my poor mother was to check the least deviation from what she believed to be right and just in my conduct, I will relate the following: "Having returned from school one winter evening, and finding my mother not returned from market, I went to meet her. On crossing a beach leading to the next village, I saw two persons at a little distance from me seeking for something with a lantern. Before I came to them, seeing something shining upon the beach, I stooped down and found it to be a shilling. I accordingly made my way towards the parties, believing them to be seeking for it. But on enquiring what they had lost, I was replied to with a buffet on the head, and bidden to go my way. Taking this in dudgeon, I went on and took the shilling with me. Not meeting with my mother on the road I turned back, and found that she had got home before me. To her I told my story about the shilling, half believing that I had acted rightly, after the treatment I had received, until I saw the frown gathering on my mother's countenance, and the rod being sought for, by a few strokes of which I soon became enlightened to the contrary. She then took me back to the owner of the shilling, to apologize to him for not having given it to him as soon as I found it; and on my way back I received from her a lecture on honesty, which I never afterwards forgot. This old gentleman, to whom I took back the shilling, was a man of some little property in our town, and had, I believe, a large spice of humour in his composition as the following anecdote shows:—He having an orchard at the upper end of the street he lived in, from which he found it difficult to gather much of its fruit, by reason of repeated thefts, got an old man, who lived in a cottage at the bottom of it, to rent it from him. This old man was a journeyman miller, and made a great profession of religion; but was withal a very curious specimen of a religious man, as he could never be induced to say grace over fish and potatoes, a very common dinner in a fishing town. The first question when he came home at noon, was to ask his mistress what she had got for dinner. If it happened to be baked potatoes, pork, and pie-crust—a favourite dinner with him—Uncle Jemmy would kneel down and make a long grace over it; but if it was a dinner of fish and potatoes, Uncle Jemmy could never be induced to say grace; for he always persisted that "God Almighty never ordained fish and potatoes for a working man's dinner." But to return to my story about the orchard. When the bargain had been concluded about the rent, mode of payment, &c., Uncle Jemmy turned to the proprietor and said, "Now, Mr. Pollard, if you have no objection, I'll say a few words of prayer over our bargain?" No objection having been made, Uncle Jemmy knelt down and began his prayer, praying that God would send sunshine and showers, that he would protect the trees from blight, that he would give him abundant fruit, and that when the apples were ripe, he would prevent the boys from stealing them. At this point in his prayer, Mr. Pollard, who was standing up near him, tapped him on the shoulder and humorously said, "Uncle Jemmy, do you remember the time when I caught you in the orchard with your pockets full of apples?" Upon which Uncle Jemmy turned angrily round and said, "Oh, Mr. Pollard, you should never interrupt a man in his prayers, for those you know were only eating articles, and now you have spoiled my prayer." He, evidently conceiving that in his case there was no sin to steal " eating articles," though he had earnestly prayed that the boys might be prevented from doing the same thing.

My mother, belonging to the Methodist Connexion, enforced on me very rigidly a regular attendance at chapel or church, and the reading of texts, prayers, and portions of Scripture, in the interval between the hours of attendance, so much so indeed, as to materially lessen the good she sought to confer; for though I could seldom evade her vigilance, I began to think the duties imposed on me more irksome than profitable. The being obliged to frequent a place of worship three times of a Sunday, strictly prohibited all books but the Bible and Prayer-book, and not being allowed to enjoy a walk, unless to chapel, or recreation of any description, are sufficient to account for those boyish feelings. My poor mother, like too many serious persons of the present day, thought that the great power that has formed the numerous gay, sportive,

singing things of earth and air, must above all things be
gratified with the solemn faces, prim clothes, and half
sleepy demeanour of human beings; and that true religion consists in listening to the reiterated story of man's
fall, of God's anger for his doing so, of man's sinful nature, of the redemption, and of other questionable matters,
instead of the wonders and glories of the universe; of the
wondrous laws that govern it; of trying to understand and
live in accordance with those laws; of performing our moral
and religious duties; of trying to improve ourselves and
to elevate our race; and of striving to make earth more in
accordance with heaven. But although my mother was
strict in the particulars I have referred to, she was very
kind and indulgent to me in other respects. She took
great pains in keeping me scrupulously clean and respectable in my person, and—what I then thought a very
superfluous duty—great pains to keep me from playing
with the boys of the town; for as I delighted in all kinds
of boyish amusements, her mandates in this particular
gave me much mental pain, as well as frequently involved
me in many scrapes. But what enabled her, more than
threats or promises, to keep me from vicious associates,
was the encouragement she gave, and the inducements
and means she afforded me for amusing myself at home.
She laboured to convince me that good of some description was always to be realized from my cutting, carving,
drawing, digging, or writing at home; but that nothing
but vice, mischief, or folly could be gained by associating
with the ignorant, idle, and vicious boys with which the
streets abounded. One of my amusements after school
hours, was the enclosing, digging, and cultivating a very
small flower garden, which I had formed partly out of an
old ruin adjoining our house. Another was what I then
designated "drawing," being very rough sketches of birds,
and flowers, more showy than natural. My first colours,
however, were only bits of different coloured stones, which
I found on the beach, or dug out of the rocks when the
tide was out, and which I rubbed down on another stone.
But having copied out some bills for a German quack
doctor, who lodged in the neighbourhood for a short time,

he gave me some information about the names, and the mixing of water colours, as well as the place and mode of purchasing better drawing materials at the market town. With a few pence, given to me by my indulgent mother, I went and bought a few brilliant sorts, and the very showy productions these enabled me to make, soon met with a ready market among the neighbours, whose walls in a short time were very gaily, if not very tastefully, ornamented. I also possessed some skill in the use of my knife; and boats, carved birds, and the making of bird-cages, afforded me much amusement, as well as often provided me with capital for new projects. It must not be supposed, however, that these home amusements, nor my mother's good advice, were so far effective as to keep me altogether from play; for the love of it is so natural in youth, that the more it is sought to be restrained, the more it is craved after, and the buoyancy of feeling at times breaks through all restraints, especially when any great temptation presents itself. Such a temptation presented itself to me one fine moonlight night—and of a Sunday too—when a number of boys were assembled on the sands at play. My mother, I knew, had gone off to chapel, in the belief that I was safe at my aunt's taking tea, and as my aunt was not very particular in her enquiries when I went out, I bounded off as soon as I could to join in the fun. When I got down, however, I found the sands wetter than I expected, and having on a new jacket and trowsers, I began to think it would be better to look on than join in the play. Before long however, a mischievous fellow slyly suggested to another that it would be good fun to push me down and spoil my new clothes. The idea was no sooner suggested than it was acted on, for one of them came upon me suddenly and pushed me backwards, but in falling one of my legs caught under in some way, and produced a terrible sprain in my ankle, said by the doctor to be far worse than a broken bone. I was carried home by the boys; my mother was sent for from chapel, who pronounced it to be a judgment inflicted upon me for breaking the Sabbath, but notwithstanding sent for the doctor. I suffered great pain with it, and it took many weeks' doctoring before I had the use of it again. I had, however, scarcely got ovet this trouble when I got into another, though not so painful nor expensive. It happened that a very large basking shark was found floating on the ocean, by some of the fishermen of the town, and towed on shore. It was of course a favourable opportunity for an assemblage of boys; and while the fishermen were busy in cutting it open, and taking out the great quantity of liver and oil found in it, the boys were busy in their way in extracting amusement out of it. The mouth of the fish having been propped open by means of handspikes, some boys—myself among the number—had got into its mouth cutting away a black stiff bristly fringe, that lined a part of it, and which bore a comb-like appearance. While we were thus busily employed, other mischievous fellows were busy in kicking the bottom of the handspikes on one side, which brought the jaws plop together and laid us sprawling at the bottom. Our cries soon brought assistance, and the mouth of the fish was opened, but the plight we were in from the oil and slime into which we were tumbled, can be better imagined than described. I remember it was some days before I got over my fright.

The time, however, had now arrived when it was necessary that I should learn some useful employment, and as my Uncle had been prosperous in his business of rope-making, it was resolved that I should be apprenticed to that trade. I was accordingly bound to a firm of three persons, for the term of seven years. But very soon after I was bound the partnership was dissolved, and I was transferred for the remainder of my time to the acting partner. I may here observe that the division of labour, which is generally carried on in London, and other large towns, is not pursued in that part of the country, as far as ropemaking is concerned, so that an apprentice has to learn as many different branches of the trade as would take as many different apprenticeships to acquire in London and other places. This causes the country business to be a laborious one, and so I found it to be. Our rope-yard, being some distance from town, I had, in common with others, to

carry to it heavy loads of hemp for our daily supply of
spinning ; and it being an open yard, nor far from the sea-
cliff, and very much exposed to the weather, caused me to
feel the cold severely at first. I was also a mere strip-
ling, very thin and tall, and no way fitted by my constitution for that laborious business. My master was also
a very unfit person, at that time, for the instruction of
youth, he being given to drink, very passionate, and
scrupled not to relate in our presence many anecdotes of
his dissipations among the women in early life. He was
also very unreasonable at times, for he very frequently
sent me with a heavy load of rope to the adjoining towns
after I had done a hard day's work, so that when I returned home, my extreme fatigue has often taken away
my appetite for food. But what I felt more severely than the
labour inflicted on me, was the coming and going some of
these lonely roads by night, for popular credulity had peopled particular spots with ghosts and appearances of
various kinds, and in which I was a firm believer. For
the numerous stories regarding those nocturnal visitants, told
to me in infancy, reiterated in boyhood, and authenticated
and confirmed by one neighbour after another, who had
witnessed, they said, their existence in a variety of forms,
riveted the belief in them so firmly in my brain, that it
was many years after I came to London before I became a
sceptic in ghosts. Nor was the belief in them confined to
the young, for my master was so fearful of walking these
lonely roads after dark,—when he went to neighbouring
villages to collect his debts, or to obtain orders,—that he
mostly ordered me or my fellow apprentice, to come to
meet him, and accompany him home. I remember one
dark winter evening going to meet him, in company with
a young fellow I had induced to be my companion, and
not finding my master at the place appointed, we had to
follow him to the next village. Our road to this was up
through a long dark lane, in a part of which a monu-
mental stone was erected, on account of a murder having
been committed there. Previous to our approach to this
dreaded spot our fears had subdued our tongues and
quickened our pulse ; but conceive our feelings, when

we saw through the darkness a monster ghost of about three feet high, with erect horns, and large eyes glaring at us, from immediately opposite the monument. We shrunk back for a moment in great terror, but our presence seems to have alarmed the monster also, for it rose up and proved to be a farmer's heifer, which had quietly laid itself down in front of this murderer's monument— which folly had erected in a public highway—doubtless without ever suspecting it would be taken for a demon. On another occasion, when we were making a cable for a large Indiaman, I saw another of those supposed ghosts. It was of a Sunday evening, and all the ropemakers of the town had assembled to help us with our large job, the consent of the parson having been first obtained, an essential requisite at that period, for working on a Sunday. About midnight my master found out that his stock of brandy was exhausted, and as the men on such occasions expected brandy, or other spirits, and as two well-known women lived at Mousehold, a village about a mile off, who dealt in the smuggled article, he thought the night time very opportune for obtaining it. I was accordingly sent off with a large bottle to procure some. I went with a very sorrowful heart; for it was a solitary way along the edge of the cliff, it was a ghostly hour, and many were the ghosts and goblins that had been seen on that road. It was, however, a bright moonlight night, and I had scarcely proceeded a quarter of a mile before I saw in the distance before me what appeared to be the outline of a woman all in white. It being such a solitary road, and such a lone hour of night, that it never once entered my head to think it a being of flesh and blood. No, it must be a ghost, but there was one consolation, which I drew from the ghost stories I had heard, it must be good and not evil, for all good spirits were said to be white. Thus encouraged I went on, but with strange fears and curious imaginings notwithstanding, to overtake this good ghost; for though I was on the search after spirits, they were not of this complexion. The nearer I approached the better it seemed, as far as regards colour, for it was white from top to toe. When I got within a few yards of this stately slow walking figure I made a little noise with my feet, when lo! my ghost turned round and waited my approach. Alas! she was of the earth most earthly, for she proved to be the kept mistress of a lawyer of Penzance, and was returning home at this unseemly hour. Soon after my apprenticeship our home was broken up by my mother marrying a man with whom my grandmother and myself could not be comfortable; we therefore took a small house and went to live together, our subsistence depending for the most part on the five shillings per week which I received as wages, eked out by the little which my grandmother could earn in the fishing season. Our food consisted of barley-bread, fish and potatoes, with a bit of pork on Sundays. In fact, barley-bread was the common food in my boyhood, excepting that the fishermen mostly took a wheaten loaf to sea with them. I have also heard my mother say that so scarce and dear was corn of all kinds the year I was born in, that she could not get bread enough to satisfy her hunger, although she travelled many miles round about to seek to purchase it. It so happened that my bedroom window in this house was exactly opposite the window of a house having the reputation of being haunted. It was not, however, a deserted house, although most of its inmates had been frightened at different times by the ghost; the particulars of which, and the forms it assumed, have often been told me by mother, son, and daughter, with whom I was well acquainted. Whether an indigestible supper had anything to do with their fright, I had not the sense then to enquire. For me to pass this house, when visiting a neighbour at night, required what Mrs. Chick would call "on effort." But to avoid seeing the ghost from my bedroom window, I adopted the expedient of shutting my eyes whenever I entered the room. I mention these silly things to show that superstition of one kind or another was the curse of my boyhood, and I have reasons for believing that such notions are still firmly believed by thousands of our people. And those rulers, who by a wise system of education can succeed in enlightening the rising generation, so that they may laugh down such absurdities, will render to society a benefit none can estimate so well as those who have been the victims of such superstitious delusions; for, notwithstanding the progress of knowledge among our people, by means of the press, the school, and the rail, the belief in ghosts is still widely entertained. The last time but one when I visited my native place, there was quite a sensation there about a ghost that had been seen walking about without a head. For having laughed at the notion in presence of an old acquaintance of mine, a baker of the town, I was very seriously reprimanded, and told that I could not believe the Bible, for was it not said in it, that the Witch of Endor raised up the spirit or ghost of Samuel, and then he quoted other passages in favour of spirits. So deeply seated are these superstitious teachings, and so difficult are they to eradicate, that it is very much to be regretted that our sensational tale-writers still continue to foster the absurd notions of ghosts and goblins; for though some may laugh at them, they have a very prejudicial effect on the minds of others, and more especially on children. Being, as I have already said, fond of tools from a boy, I employed most of my leisure hours during my apprenticeship in making something ornamental or useful. I became an adept in the making of bird-cages, boxes of various descriptions, and, as my grandmother designated them, gimcracks of every kind. I had also a turn for mechanism, and succeeded in making a small machine, similar to those used in factories for the spinning of twine, which pleased my master so well when he saw it, that he wished me to take it to the rope-yard, by means of which we might all learn to spin twine. But this spinning machine turned out to be an experiment productive of many disagreeables to me and my fellow apprentices; for after my master had taught himself and two of us boys to spin twine, he took it into his head to make set-nets, crab-nets, and eventually a foot-seine, and then requested us to go to sea with him of an evening to catch fish with him. To this I had a great aversion on account of sea-sickness, a malady I could never get over; indeed, on one occasion during these fishing excursions I narrowly escaped drowning. On another occasion during my apprenticeship I had another narrow escape from the kick of a horse. It occurred in this manner: a poor young fellow of the town, who had recently lost both father and mother, was dependent for his own and his brother's and sister's support, on any little jobs which he could obtain by the employment of a horse and cart, left him by his father. Not having means for the support of his horse, he was obliged to turn it about the lanes to shift for itself. Seeing the poor horse feeding on the scanty herbage in the road below our rope-yard, it struck my fellow apprentice and myself that it might procure better food for a short time at one end of our yard, where there was a good crop of grass. We accordingly drove the horse up, where it revelled for a good bit on its good fare, and when we thought it had got its belly full, we thought it well to drive it down again, lest our master might come out and find fault with us. But on my approaching him to drive him down he threw out his two hind legs with great force, which, hitting me in the abdomen, sent me a great distance, and nearly struck the life out of me, the blow causing me to feel its painful effects for some time, thus exhibiting a sorry example of horse ingratitude.

When I was about sixteen or seventeen, I had, among my female acquaintances, two or three straw-hat makers, to please whom I was induced to try the experiment of making for them some steel straw-splitters, which at that time were very difficult to procure, as well as expensive. These are small steel-pointed instruments with circular heads, divided into equal sharp-cutting divisions for splitting the straws into equal portions of various degrees of fineness, the same being fixed into ivory or bone stocks. Having succeeded in my attempt, I had several orders to execute for others in the same business, for at that period straw-hat making was a female mania in our neighbourhood. But what rendered my instruments of less value than those sold in the market town, was the inferiority of the stocks, they being made of wood carved with the penknife, instead of being turned out of ivory or bone. To remedy this defect I was induced to direct my attention to the making of a turning lathe, from the description of one I had met with in the fragment of an old book, and, after a great deal of scheming and contriving, I made one that answered my purpose. This opened up to me a new field of amusement as well as some little profit, for I not only succeeded in setting off my straw-splitters with bone stocks, turned out of the nicely bleached bone I met with on the beach, but in a short time I acquired some skill in common turning. By this new contrivance my female friends were also provided with straw mills for the pressing of their plat, as well as with hat and bonnet blocks, and implements of various kinds. With the aid of my lathe I was also enabled to make spinning wheels for the spinning of twine for fishing lines, of which I made several. About this time I was also fortunate enough to get access to a carpenter's shop, in which cabinet work was occasionally executed. Here in my leisure hours and on holidays, I acquired some proficiency in the use of carpenters' tools, and by purchasing of the proprietor such bits of wood as I needed, I was permitted to plane and work them up upon a spare bench. Near the end of my apprenticeship I was permitted to visit a great uncle of mine, at a place called Porthleven, on the eastern coast of Mountsbay, and to have a week's holiday; my uncle being then the huer of a pilchard seine at that place. At that time they were building Porthleven Pier, and during my stay I was witness of the immense power of the sea on that coast during a gale of wind. The end of the pier is built of immense stones dovetailed into one another, and secured by iron clamps along the edges. One of these layers had been put in its place before the gale came on, but had not been secured at the edges, and so powerful was the sea during the storm that the whole layer of these immense stones was driven out of its place, as if it had been a slice of bread. An old fisherman of the place took me round the coast, and, among other places, to the Loo Bar, where he gave me a graphic description of the different wrecks he had witnessed on that coast. He told me that he had seen an Indiaman completely wrecked by the force of two waves, the one driving her on shore, and the other shattering her to pieces. He showed me the graves of many wrecked seamen he had helped to bury, one of which, he said, had thirty men in it. The young and most active, he said, were generally drowned first, as they dropped over the sides as soon as the vessel struck ground, believing the sand to be hard, and, as the waves receded very far, they thought they might save themselves by a run. But, unhappily, instead of solid sand they dropped on, it was quicksand, or sand and water, and which carried them out to sea like a rushing river. At this village I saw two remarkable persons. One was a poor demented creature, who preferred being out in all weather, and in gleaning her food from the dung-hills rather than enter the home provided for her, and it was with great difficulty she could be brought home to get a meal, or a change of clothing. When, however, she could be induced to eat at home she ate most voraciously, for I was witness, on one occasion, to her eating a large, heaped-up dish of potatoes that, I think, could not be far short of a gallon. I have seen her sitting down on a hill, during a drenching shower of rain, as unconcerned as if of no consequence. As her petticoats were ragged at the bottom, all round, as if torn in some curious way, I asked her who tore them so ; she told me it was the wind and the rain, but I afterwards learnt that they were torn by the dogs ; for, as she was exceedingly troublesome to the neighbours in begging for snuff, the dogs were often allowed to molest her. This poor creature, I was informed, was reduced to this sad condition in a singular way. She was, I was told, a few years previously a sprightly young woman, living as servant at a public-house in the village. It happened that, on one occasion, when she was up-stairs making the beds, that a deserter entered the house, and, calling for some drink, went into the parlour, where he was speedily followed by an officer of his regiment, and, a moment after, the report of a pistol was heard, and, when the room was entered, the deserter was found dead. The officer said that the soldier had resisted his arrest, which was the cause of his firing, though he only thought of wounding him.

As, however, the officer was known to be the soldier's enemy, a trial took place, and, from the evidence given, the case was going very strong against the former. At this juncture the servant girl, Betty, was called to give her evidence. She said that she was up-stairs making the beds, and, hearing a *scuffle* below, and then the sound of a gun, she ran down to the parlour and saw the man dead, and the officer standing over him. The word *scuffle*, in Betty's evidence, is said to have saved the officer's life, and as she was much blamed for using this word—for, it seems, there was no scuffle—and she, greatly troubling about it, became in a few days a helpless lunatic. She was at first kept in confinement, but, soon proving harmless, she was consigned to the care of an old couple in the village, and great trouble she seemed to have given them. The other singular person I have alluded to was an old lady, who was reputed to be a *white witch*, one who, from the ill she was believed able to inflict, was regarded by some with superstitious dread. She generally carried a basket about with her, containing all kinds of odds and ends, as well as food, and anything that Aunt Tammy took a fancy to, few who feared her, dared to refuse. I was witness myself to the power of her nimble and abusive tongue on two occasions, and can readily believe that few would like to come under its lash. The first occasion was on Porthleven Pier, where a crowd was assembled in consequence of a poor horse having fallen into the sea. A young man present happened to say to some one near him, "there is the old witch coming," which Aunt Tammy happening to hear, at once gave him a bit of her mind in a manner few, I think, could match, for it was so droll and laughable. Among other drolleries she told him that his mother was such a fool that she hung a pound of butter out in the sun to dry. That the reason of his being such a poor doodle was that his mother fed him on flies and potato peelings, and much more of a like kind that I cannot now recollect. The second time that I heard some of her abusive drolleries, was when I went into Helston Courthouse one day to hear the trials. The reason, I found, of Aunt Tammy being there was on account of her daughter and another girl, being charged with stealing apples. Before the magistrates made their appearance, Aunt Tammy had stationed herself in the place allotted to delinquents, and on one of the officials telling her she must move to some other place, she opened out upon him in her peculiar style. She seemed to have known his pedigree for generations back, and depicted them and him in a manner that convulsed every one present with laughter. When the magistrates came they were informed of what had taken place, but as she insisted that she had business there, and as they seemingly knew her capability of tongue, she was allowed to remain till her daughter's case was brought on, notwithstanding some curious remarks she made on a previous case. As soon as her daughter was brought in and placed beside her, the old lady gave her such a smacking on the back as to nearly take away her breath. Then, turning to the magistrates, and familiarly calling them by name, she said, " Now, before you begin business, I have something very nice in my basket for you," and, opening it, she presented, in a clean white cloth, a large piece of apple-cake, nicely spread over with clotted cream. The piece of cake was then conveyed, amid much fun and laughter, and presented to the parson, who, very graciously refusing, passed it on to another, and so to all the gentlemen on the bench, and on its being returned back to Aunt Tammy, she very bluntly said, " Well, if you are all too proud to taste an old woman's cake I must eat it myself." Her daughter's case then proceeded, not without numerous observations of Aunt Tammy, and when the two girls had been found guilty, and condemned to pay the fine of a pound, she, after a few extra slaps on her girl's back, turned round to the magistrates and said, " Well, I have no money to pay the fine, and I tell you what I shall do ; I shall come round to you to-morrow, to see what you are going to give me towards it. I shall first call on Parson Rogers, and I know I shall get something from him, and I believe, after that, none of you will be shabby enough to send me away empty-handed," and, having thus said her say, Aunt Tammy left the court.

I must here state that within a few months of the time I

was bound for, I found great difficulty in getting from my master the wages due to me, and was eventually obliged to summon him before the magistrates of Penzance to obtain them. Having succeeded, but knowing it would be equally difficult to obtain them in future, as trade was very bad with my master, my friends got him to give up my indentures. Thus free and my own master, the next question was what was I to do for a living? The trade of ropemaking was at that time very bad, owing, among other causes, to the introduction of chain as a substitute for rope for a great variety of purposes. Thus, it was very difficult to obtain employment at my trade, unless for a few weeks in the winter when vessels came into the bay disabled and wanting ropes. I was therefore induced by my great uncle to turn my attention to the fishery as the next alternative; and obtaining a berth on a pilchard seine I pursued it during the season. But unhappily I could never get over my sea-sickness if the weather was the least rough; in fact I have been ill at times before I had got on the boat—ill from the apprehension of the evil—and this more especially if there was an easterly wind, for that wind produced on our shore short cross loping waves, the movements of which seemed to turn your intestines over your stomach, and your stomach inside out, and to extract gall enough from your liver to embitter your whole existence. It was, however, owing to this malady that I was obliged to give up the fishery, or otherwise I might have become a fisherman for life; for my uncle, having a large boat and nets of his own, and no child to inherit them, and he getting up in years, was very desirous of myself becoming qualified to take his place. But this was not to be, and hence the career I am about to record. The seining season being over, I chanced to meet with a carpenter belonging to a village a short distance off, and he knowing me and knowing my mechanical habits made me a favourable offer to come to work with him, which I did for a short time, helping him to saw some wood with the pit-saw, and to do the woodwork of a cottage which he was then erecting. But two or three young carpenters, who were serving their apprenticeship at

Penzance, were so exasperated to find that a ropemaker could find employment as a carpenter, that they called upon my employer, and talked of legal consequences, and he, being timidly apprehensive of what might take place, told me that he was sorry in being compelled to break his engagement with me. Thus was I again out of employment. I then made a walking tour of many miles to different towns (going as far as Falmouth) to see if I could get work as a ropemaker, but I was unsuccessful.

Having said thus much of my ropemaking, of my mechanical and other pursuits, it may be necessary to state that I was also fond of reading from a boy, but found great difficulty in procuring instructive books. There was no bookshop in the town—scarcely a newspaper taken in, unless among the few gentry—and there was at that period a considerable number of the adult population who could not read. To the best of my recollection there was only one bookseller's shop in the market town, and, with the exception of bibles and prayer-books, spelling-books, and a few religious works, the only books in circulation for the masses were a few story-books and romances, filled with absurdities about giants, spirits, goblins, and supernatural horrors. The price of these, however, precluded me from purchasing any, although I was sometimes enabled to borrow one from an acquaintance. Therefore the Bible, and prayer and hymn book, and a few religious tracts, together with fragments of an old magazine, and occasionally one of the nonsensical pamphlets described, were all the books I ever read till I was upwards of twenty-one years of age. As I could write tolerably well, I had to write love letters for many young neighbours, and some I voluntarily undertook to teach to write, and this helped in some degree my own improvement. But in looking back upon this period of my youth, and contrasting it with the present, and the advantages that young people have in the present age—in the multiplicity of cheap books, newspapers, lectures, and other numerous means of instruction—I cannot help regretting that I was so unfortunately placed; for, with a desire for knowledge, I had neither books to enlighten nor a teacher to instruct.

A young man of my own age was my companion of an evening very frequently during my apprenticeship, but he too like myself was ignorant. Of the causes of day and night, of the seasons, and of the common phenomena of nature we knew nothing, and curious were our speculations regarding them. We had heard of "the sun ruling by day, and the moon by night," but how or in what way they ruled was a mystery we could never solve. With minds thus ignorant, persons need not be surprised that we were very superstitious.

I have already stated that I was brought up to attend very regularly the methodist chapel, but I never joined their connection, although I was induced to join for a short time a sect called the Bryanites. I think it was the novelty of their female preachers that first induced me and a young man—my companion—to visit their place of worship; and being there the persuasive eloquence of two young women caused us to be impressed with the general religious enthusiasm that prevailed among the congregation. We afterwards went to hear them a few times, and became what they called "converted members." But though my companion seems to have acquired in a short time the conviction that his sins were forgiven him, I could never work my imagination up to that point. I was, however, very penitent and sincere in my devotions; I attended their prayer-meetings and class-meetings very earnestly, and it was only when we learnt that our young female preachers had been turned out of the body—they having fallen from their saintly position by being with child—that I left the connection. In my frequent visits to the carpenter's shop I have alluded to, I met with an old sea captain of the town, who was there having some work executed, and having often seen me there, entered into conversation with me. He asked me many questions regarding my trade, and eventually pointed out to me the great improbability of the trade of ropemaking ever again affording me constant employment in that part of the country. He told me also of the far greater chances I should meet with in such a place as London; "for," said he, "if you fail of getting work as a ropemaker, there is every opportunity of your getting a berth as a ropemaker aboard an Indiaman, or other large ship, and a rope-maker is at once considered an able seaman." For some time previous to this my home had been rendered un-comfortable to me; for my scanty means of subsistence, my poor mother's very unhappy marriage, and the diffi-culty of getting employment, all tended to cause the conversation of this old gentleman to make a greater impression on my mind. A consideration therefore of the evil of wasting my youthful days at home in a state of half-starving idleness, and the youthful hope that something advantageous might turn out for me abroad, soon determined me to leave home whenever a favourable opportunity presented itself. But there were two great difficulties to be surmounted. In the first place I had to obtain the consent of my friends, who were very much opposed at first to my leaving home; and I felt a great reluctance to leave in opposition to the wishes of my mother, aunt, and grandmother. In the next place I had no money for such a journey; my friends were too poor to assist me, and the prospect of earning any by my trade was as gloomy as could well be. However, after some weeks had transpired, I obtained from my friends a half-reluctant consent; for the conviction of my poor old grandmother that she should never see me again, bound me the closer to her heart; and though her sister gave her a room on her premises to live in, and promised other-wise to assist her in my absence, it was with great pain that we eventually parted. I regret to add, that I never saw her again, for she died soon after I left. To raise the pecuniary means for my journey, I went to the next town and, with a few shillings I had raised, I purchased some mahogany veneers and other requisites for making a lady's work-box, with secret drawers, together with a pair of tea-caddies. These I got up in the best style I was master of, and being fortunate enough to dispose of them, together with two or three little trinkets I had by me, I increased by these means my stock of money to about fifty shillings. Having got so much towards my voyage,

I commenced another work-box which, when I set out for London, the captain of a small trading vessel agreed to take as part payment of my passage money. Previous to leaving home I had procured two or three letters of recommendation to master ropemakers in London; and with these, and a stout heart, I set out on my voyage of adventure. I left home on the 23rd of June, 1821, and in the course of a few days, I forget how many, for we were becalmed a portion of the time, I arrived in the great city, with the clear sum of thirty shillings in my pocket; knowing no one, nor being known to any. Having heard a great many curious stories in the country, about London crimping-houses, and London thieves, I thought it best to lodge near the wharf at first, till I had become a little acquainted with the place. I was therefore induced to put up at a public-house near the wharf, where the Cornish vessels generally land; and early the next morning I set out with my recommendatory letters. In passing the Borough end of the old London Bridge I recollect being forcibly struck with the number of blackened eyes, and scratched and battered faces, that I met with among the labourers going to their employments; the result, I afterwards learnt, of their Saturday evening and Sunday sprees. Owing, however, to the general slackness of the ropemaking business at that period, my recommendatory letters failed of procuring me employment; although I found them useful in enabling me to extend the circle of my enquiries, which, to a stranger in London, is no trifling advantage. After canvassing about for nearly a fortnight among all the rope-yards I could hear of and, failing of success, I began to think myself very unfortunate. However, I fared very hard and sought about for work in every direction, as I had made up my mind to accept of any kind of honest employment, rather than go home again without any. One evening on my return to my lodgings I met with three countrymen, carpenters by trade. They were, however, strangers to me, but coming from the same county, we soon became acquainted. In the course of conversation with them I said that I had picked up some slight knowledge of their trade, and that

I thought I might be useful in a short time if I could get employment in a shop, or building, at low wages. As they were themselves out of employment, they readily agreed that I should go round with them to seek for some; and that if we were fortunate enough to get work together in some building, I should do what I could of the roughest part of it, and should allow them half-a-crown each weekly, in consideration of my not having served any time to the business. To this proposition I readily consented, as I was very anxious to learn the trade, and the following morning we went round together. Two of my companions, however, were fortunate enough to get work in a few days, and I was left with my other partner to shift for ourselves as we best could. My companion was a young man just out of his time, he also had recently come to London, and like myself had very little money. Indeed my own purse was so scanty that I was necessitated to economize so far as to be content with a penny loaf a day and a drink from the most convenient pump for several weeks in succession. We generally got up at five o'clock and walked about enquiring at different shops and buildings till about nine; we then bought one penny loaf and divided it between us; then walked about again till four or five in the afternoon, when we finished our day's work with another divided loaf; and very early retired to bed footsore and hungry. My health at that time, however, enabled me to put up with those privations tolerably well, although my stomach often rebelled against them. At that period too, the water at the public-house we lodged at was very bad; the Thames water, being then pumped up by means of large water works at the end of old London Bridge, had all kinds of impurities in it when first pumped up, and the smell and taste of it was abominable; and this to me was a disagreeable worse even than hunger. Our landlady, too, had little compassion for those of her lodgers who did not drink, for she would not allow us to cook even a meal of potatoes. One day, however, as we were passing down Drury-lane together, on seeing some carpenters at work I went up to one of them who appeared to be the foreman, to ask if he could give me a job. He said he would, as he wanted some flooring laid in a hurry, and requested me to bring my tools next morning. Having so far succeeded I was anxious to introduce my companion, the person who was to have been my instructor in the business, but from his boyish appearance or some other cause, the foreman would not engage him. This to me was a sad misfortune, to be deprived of the only person who could render me any assistance in this new occupation, for I had never seen any flooring laid, nor, indeed, much work done in the building line. But my low purse and gloomy prospects emboldened me to prepare for the morrow. I had brought from home a hammer, a chisel or two, and a few other trifling tools : to these I added a few more bought at a secondhand tool shop, and a few others borrowed from my companion. I passed a very anxious and sleepless night, and early in the morning away I went to my new occupation, wondering what would be the result. It so happened, however, that fortune favoured me in this instance. I had a very joyous fellow for my partner, and when he took up one end of the board I took up the other, and by watching very carefully all his movements I soon got hold of the method of laying flooring. I was also fortunate enough to continue in this place till I had replenished my purse to the extent of about fifty shillings. This job having been concluded I was presumptuous enough to go round by myself and seek for another ; and in a few days was offered some small staircases to make by the piece, provided I could get a partner to assist me. My young companion, however, had got work in the interim ; but meeting at my lodgings with another countryman, who had just arrived in town, we went and took the work together ; I agreeing, at the same time, to give my partner half-a-crown a week out of my earnings, and to do the roughest and hardest part of the work. In about a fortnight's time, however, my fellow countryman got sick of London and went home again, leaving me in the midst of my staircase work, and this being one of the most difficult branches of the business, I was obliged to relinquish it, and at a great sacrifice. Having again sought about for employment for a number of weeks, and having failed to secure any, and being at the same time in a half-starved condition, I began to despair of ever learning the business of a carpenter, and at last, very reluctantly, made up my mind to seek for a rope-maker's situation on board some large vessel. Some of the sailors at the wharf having referred me to an old retired sea captain, who made it his business to look out for berths for seamen; he readily engaged to procure me a situation on board an Indiaman for the fee of a few shillings. Within the week I received a note stating that he had been successful, and that I was to meet him and others at a stated place about the final arrangement. Before, however, I went to engage myself, I thought I would go to see two of my fellow townsmen, who had very recently come to London; one of them being the very person whose shop I was in the habit of frequenting at home. He had failed in his business as a master and had come to town to work as a journeyman, and had, in conjunction with another countryman, been fortunate enough to obtain work the first week of their arrival in a small shop in Cromer Street, Somers Town. Being, therefore, well acquainted with one of those persons, I was desirous of consulting him before I engaged myself as a sailor; for, as I had a great dislike to the sea, I was hopeful that he might have heard of some kind of employment for me. I accordingly went to see him at his place of work, and when I mentioned to him my intention of going to sea he did all he could to dissuade me from it, telling me that it would break my mother's and grand-mother's hearts. I informed him how I was situated, and the doubts I entertained of ever getting work at my trade, or of ever getting an opportunity of learning another. The master of the workshop happening to be present, and hearing our conversation, asked me if I thought I could do cabinet work if he employed me. While I was hesitating as to the answer I could give him, my countryman expressed his opinion in the affirmative, and having explained to him what he knew of me, and what work he had seen me do, I was requested to come the following morning and to bring what tools I had with me.

This person, being what is called "a trade-working master," gave me at first a portion of his own job to execute, and being fortunate enough to please him he next gave me work on my own account. With this master I continued to work for several months, during which time I acquired some proficiency in making such kinds of furniture as he manufactured; being chiefly cabinets, commodes, loo-tables, and card-tables for the London brokers. We worked by the piece, and the price was low; but long hours, industry and economy, helped me along tolerably well. I was now enabled to provide myself with a few clothes which I was much in want of, a coat in particular: for my dress hitherto was that of a sailor (like most of the young men of my native town at that time), and operated, I believe, very much to my disadvantage in obtaining work in London. During this period I also made myself a tool-chest, and had begun to accumulate a few tools, and should have added others had I been paid my wages regularly; but my employer generally paid us something short of our money every week, and at last got into my debt to the amount of between six or seven pounds and nearly similar amounts to my two countrymen. One Saturday evening, when pay-time came, he astounded us all by informing us that he should have to go into the Fleet prison the following week for debt. He assured us, however, that he would pay us all the money he owed us when the work was finished which was then in hand, especially if we would go and help to finish it in a workshop which he had taken *within the rules of the prison;* and as some sort of security he gave me one of his beds to take care of, and to the others other articles of furniture. We accordingly went to work for him the following week in a little shop in one of the lanes near the Fleet prison; my old acquaintance, however, did little work, he being a little too fond of drink, my employer otherwise engaged with the view of eventually cheating us all. When the work on hand was completed the two youngest of us received a message from our employer, stating that he wanted to speak with us in the prison. When we went, he very coolly told us that he had no further need of our services. I then very quietly asked him how we were to be paid the money he owed us, on which he gave me a backward push and bade me not insult him in a prison. This, being a little too much for my Cornish blood, was repaid by a blow that sent him to a respectful distance, which led to the interference of an officer, who when he heard how we had been imposed upon, seemed to sympathize with us. My other old countryman he subsequently served still worse, for having sent him some distance into the country, under the plea of collecting money, he not only got the shop cleared of all the furniture made during his absence, but of the old man's tools also; and he not getting any money, was obliged to travel to town as he best could. I have mentioned that a bed was left in my possession by my employer before he went into prison: this he soon sent a person to demand, but my landlady, in my absence, refused to give it up. Threats having been used respecting it, I deemed it necessary to apply to a magistrate; who, when he heard the case, told me to refer the parties to him. This I was induced to do, as my employer had sent an old watchman, a friend of his, the night before, to try and capture me after I had gone to bed, and to take me to the watch-house, with a view of frightening me, and causing me to give up the bed. When I heard him however, I dressed myself quietly, and slipped over the garden wall into the fields at the back, then occupied by Smith's large dust-heaps, and into a soft portion of which I plunged halfway up the body in my hurry to escape. On examining the bed, however, it turned out to be a paltry wool one instead of a feather one, and worth but the merest trifle. Being thus once more out of employment, and without money—for I had to keep myself while I was helping to finish the work referred to—I felt myself worse off in a pecuniary sense than ever, for I owed my landlady a trifle for rent. She, however, soon devised the means of payment, for she caused wood to be purchased, and got me to make her up some furniture, for a mere subsistence, in a back kitchen; which served me both for bedroom and workshop. This place, being wretchedly damp and unhealthy, soon laid me up with a

severe fit of illness, which was so far aggravated by the
want of proper food and comforts, as to materially injure
my constitution. Having recovered a little from my illness, I procured the loan of a few shillings from a kind old
schoolmaster who lodged in the same house, and with these
I purchased wood and made up some trifling articles of
furniture, which I hawked about to dispose of among the
brokers. But I found this a wretched life ; for the working and sleeping in my miserable kitchen, and the difficulty
of selling what articles I made up at a price to enable me
to live, soon caused me to abandon that speculation. With
the little knowledge and experience I had now acquired of
cabinet-making I resolved to go round and seek work in
that line, instead of my former ones of ropemaking and car-
pentry. After walking about for some days I got employment in a small shop in Castle Street, Oxford Market, a place
where repairs of buhl-work, marquetry, and antique furniture were principally executed. Here I was fortunate enough
to meet with a journeyman of the name of David Todd, a
native of Peebles, one of the most intelligent, kind-hearted
and best disposed men I ever met with. He, finding that
I had not served an apprenticeship to the business, not
only gave me every assistance and information I required
in my work, but advised me as to my best mode of proceeding, with all the benevolence and anxiety of a father.
By his advice I was induced to offer myself as a member
of the Cabinet Makers' Society, he having kindly pointed
out to me the extreme difficulty I should have of ever obtaining employment in any respectable shop unless I belonged to
them. But as I had not " worked or served five years to the
business " (as their rules required), and as a jealous
countryman of mine had informed them that I had served
my time to a ropemaker and not to a cabinet-maker, they
refused to admit me. Failing in this object, my kind
friend got me a situation at Messrs. ——— cabinet manufactory, where I entered into an agreement to work for
them for twelve months for a guinea a-week. They were
at that time cabinet-makers to the King, and consequently
executed a great variety of work. At the time I am
speaking of, this was not a Society shop, and a number of

persons were employed there of very drunken and dissipated habits. When I first went among them they talked of " setting Mother Shorney at me " ; this is a cant term in the trade, and meant the putting away of your tools, the injuring of your work, and annoying you in such a way as to drive you out of the shop. This feeling against me was occasioned by my coming there to work without having served an apprenticeship to the business. As soon, therefore, as I was made acquainted with their feelings and intentions towards me, I thought it best to call a shop-meeting, and lay my case before them. To call a meeting of this description the first requisite was to send for a quantity of drink (generally a gallon of ale), and then to strike your hammer and holdfast together, which, making a bell-like sound, is a summons causing all in the shop to assemble around your bench. A chairman is then appointed, and you are called upon to state your business. In my case, I briefly told them that the reason of my calling them together was on account of the feeling they manifested towards me, which I hoped would be removed when they had heard my story. I then went on to describe how I had wasted the prime of my life in learning a trade which I found comparatively useless ; and appealed to their sense of justice to determine whether it was right to prevent me from learning another. By thus appealing to them in time the majority of them took my part, and others were eventually won over and induced to be friendly. But the demands made upon me for drink by individuals among them, for being shown the manner of doing any particular kind of work, together with fines and shop scores, often amounted to seven or eight shillings a week out of my guinea. However, by taking particular notice of every description of work I saw done in the shop, I became tolerably well acquainted with the general run of work by the expiration of my time. Soon after I was engaged I remember that I had to make a work-table, the top of which was made out of what was called " The Wellington Tree of the field of Waterloo." that under the shelter of which the Duke is said to have stood during the early part of the battle. My little table had a silver plate let into the top stating this. When the expiration of my apprenticeship took place I thought myself entitled to an advance of wages; but the answer to my request being delayed from time to time, and an opportunity presenting itself of obtaining work in another shop in Catherine Street, Strand, at full wages, I thought it wise to embrace it. I may here mention that a great improvement, mentally and morally, has taken place among the working classes of London since that period. There were then comparatively few coffee-houses and eating-houses frequented by working men; workmen, who worked at a distance from their homes, mostly getting their meals at public-houses. And this great inducement to drink was still further increased by the temptation those places held out, to the young and thoughtless, by the establishment of Singing Clubs and Free and Easies—places that I have known to be the destruction of many of my shopmates—not from the musical attractions they afforded, but from the habits of drunkenness and dissipation they engendered. Pugilism also, at this period, was patronized by numbers of the nobility and gentry as "a glorious art of self-defence," and those who had acquired the " science !" as it was called, were very prone to display their pugilistic prowess in the public streets, and regular concerted contests might be often witnessed in the fields surrounding London on Sunday mornings, without much danger of interruption from the Bow Street officers. In fact I have seen three pitched battles carried on at one time of a Sunday morning, in Broad Street, St. Giles's, without any one interfering or striving to part them, except their wives, and these occasionally fought with one another. After I had worked for about twelve months at two other shops, I was fortunate enough to obtain employment at another cabinet-maker's at Castle Street, Oxford Market— at a place where I worked a sufficient number of years to qualify me for joining the Cabinet Makers' Society, of which body I was soon after elected a member, and subsequently president. This society is composed of a very respectable body of journeymen, and had then been established for nearly seventy years, an important object of their union, worthy of imitation by others, being the affording of subsistence to their members when out of employment. I may here notice, too, the great improvement that has taken place in cabinet-making during my time, both in English and French furniture. When I first came to London, English-made furniture was generally substantial and well made, but the design was far from elegant and the finish by no means attractive, as most of it was polished with wax or oil; very little French polish being then used. The French furniture—which I had a good opportunity of seeing in the first cabinet shop I worked at — was tastefully designed and elegantly polished, but the work in most cases was very roughly done and far from being substantial. I have repaired cabinets that were veneered with tortoise shell inlaid with silver, the drawers of which were *nailed together* instead of being dove-tailed, and which were so loosely and badly fitting that you might pitch them in at a distance. The intercourse since then, however, between the two countries has led to the mutual improvement of both, as our English furniture has greatly improved in design and finish, while that of the French is far more substantial and made in a more workmanlike manner.

CHAPTER II.

OWING to the many difficulties I had met with in the
way of learning a trade by which to earn my bread, I had
hitherto made very little intellectual progress. My pro-
vincialisms and bad English being often corrected by the
kind old schoolmaster I have referred to, I was induced by
his advice to study Lindley Murray's Grammar, and by
making it my pocket companion for a few months, and
studying it in all my leisure hours, I was enabled to correct
some of my glaring imperfections in speaking. That
which first stimulated me to intellectual enquiry, and which
laid the foundation of what little knowledge I possess, was
my being introduced to a small literary association,
entitled "The Liberals," which met in Gerrard Street,
Newport Market. It was composed chiefly of working
men, who paid a small weekly subscription towards the
formation of a select library of books for circulation
among one another. They met together, if I remember
rightly, on two evenings in the week, on one of which
occasions they had generally some question for discussion,
either literary, political, or metaphysical. It was by the
merest accident that I was introduced to one of their discussions by a member, and you may judge of its effects on
me when I state that it was the first time that I had ever
heard impromptu speaking out of the pulpit—my notions
then being that such speaking was a kind of inspiration
from God—and also that the question discussed that evening
was a metaphysical one respecting the soul. There were
very excellent speeches made on that occasion which
riveted my most earnest attention, and from what I heard
on that evening I felt for the first time in my life how
very ignorant I was and how very deficient in being able

to give a reason for the opinions and the hopes I entertained. Seeing that their library contained the works of Paley and other authors that I had often heard cited from the pulpit as the great champions of Christianity, I felt an ardent wish to read and study them. From my friend Mr. Todd, who was present, I received an invitation to attend their next meeting, and being subsequently proposed by him I was very shortly after elected a member. I now became seized with an enthusiastic desire to read and treasure up all I could meet with on the subject of Christianity, and in a short time was induced to join my voice to that of others in its defence whenever the question became the subject of debate; and often have I sat up till morning dawned reading and preparing myself with arguments in support of its principles. Political questions being also often discussed in our association, caused me to turn my attention to political works, and eventually to take a great interest in the parliamentary debates and questions of the day. In short, my mind seemed to be awakened to a new mental existence; new feelings, hopes, and aspirations sprang up within me, and every spare moment was devoted to the acquisition of some kind of useful knowledge. I now joined several other associations in its pursuit, and for a number of years seldom took a meal without a book of some description beside me, and to this day relish my meals the better for such an accompaniment. I joined also the Mechanics' Institute, which was just started, and before the present building was erected, and attended its lectures very regularly. I remember being forcibly struck on one occasion, when Dr. Birkbeck was giving some lectures on the senses, on hearing *several dumb boys speak*, which I looked upon for the moment as something miraculous. But the explanation of the doctor soon dissipated the miracle; for he told us that they were taught by the eye instead of the ear; first by noticing the action of the mouth and outward movements of the larynx during the pronunciation of vowels and consonants, and trying to imitate the sounds, and then proceeding to words and sentences. They had in this way made such proficiency that they could readily answer any question asked of them; indeed, one of them repeated a portion of Gray's Elegy, and that very distinctly, the only defect being in the modulation of the voice, as they could not be brought to distinguish the various tones of it. I remember that on leaving the lecture-room on that occasion I got into conversation with Sir Richard Phillips, the author, and walked with him round and round St. Paul's church-yard, Newgate Street, and the old Bailey for several hours, it being a bright moonlight night, while he explained to me many of his scientific theories, among others one which he entertained in opposition to Sir Isaac Newton's theory of gravitation, Sir Richard illustrating his theory by diagrams made with a piece of chalk on the walls and window shutters. About this time, too, I was very fond of attending debating places, especially Tom's Coffee House, in Holborn, and Lunt's Coffee House, on Clerkenwell Green, where, among other celebrities who took part in the discussions, I heard Gale Jones, the Rev. Robert Taylor, C. Whenman, Richard Carlisle, and others. It was at Lunt's that I first saw George Thompson, the eloquent anti-slavery advocate, and where I think he made his first attempt at public speaking. I commenced also about this time the collection of a small library of my own, the shelves of which were often supplied by cheating the stomach with bread and cheese dinners. But in the midst of these pursuits after knowledge my attention was arrested by a new object, by her who for the last forty-nine years has been my kind and affectionate wife. And regarding that meeting as one of the most fortunate events in my life, I think it well to give its brief history.

My wife is a native of Kent, the daughter of a car-penter formerly in a small way of business at Pegwell, near Ramsgate. Her brother at that period being in business at Boulogne, she went over to be his housekeeper, but on his subsequent marriage she engaged herself as lady's maid in an English family. Having come over to London on a short visit with her mistress, she was in the habit of frequenting Marylebone Church, where she first attracted my attention on my going there to hear on one ocacsion the celebrated Dr. Busfield. In a short time I introduced myself to her notice, and, though repulsed at first, was eventully permitted to visit the house and accepted as her future husband. All things now seemed bright and prosperous with me, but a circumstance soon transpired which for a time withered up all my hopes of happiness. This was a difference in our religious views and opinions; one of the universal causes of dissension throughout the world instead of union. My intended wife, having been brought up in the views of the Established Church, regarded its forms and ceremonies with the greatest veneration. I, on the other hand, had been led from my recent studies to look upon practical Christianity as a union for the promotion of brotherly kindness and good deeds to one another, and not a thing of form and profession for mercenary idlers to profit by, who in their miserable interpretations of it too often cause men to neglect the improvement of the present in their aspirations of the future. The explanation of my religious views was called forth by her soliciting me to go with her on the following Sunday to take the sacrament, which, from conscientious motives, I was obliged to refuse. This, as may be supposed, led to some further explanation regarding my religious opinions, for I was resolved to be candid and explicit at all risks, and not subject myself hereafter to the charge of subterfuge and hypocrisy. My Mary, having been brought up to regard the sacrament as one of the great essentials of religion, after hearing my opinion, at once candidly declared that she could not conscientiously unite her destinies with any man whose opinions so widely differed from her own. This avowal I felt with the severest anguish; and our parting that evening was to me like the parting of the mental and bodily powers. I tried to summon some little philosophy to my aid, but philosophy I believe has little control over this strong and powerful passion; and months elapsed before I recovered sufficiently from the shock to resume quietly my usual avocations. In order, however, to divert my mind as much as possible from the object that so affected me, I went and joined several associations; literary, scientific, and political. At one or other of these I spent my evenings, and in this way I believe profited to some extent; although I have since regretted I never went through a regular course of study. And this means of diverting the mind from the object that preys upon it, I would venture to recommend to all those who may experience a similar heart-rending disappointment; for such pursuits serve to excite and strengthen one set of faculties to enable them to overcome the force of another. At all events, between active labour by day, and a variety of intellectual pursuits of an evening, I had so far subdued my feelings in the course of twelve months, that I began to plan out for myself the life of a bachelor. On returning from my work, however, one evening I found a little letter which soon dissipated that notion. It informed me that the writer, having again arrived at Dover with her mistress for a few days, had presumed to send me the compliments of the season (it being Christmas time), and at the same time hoped that my opinions on the subject of the sacrament had undergone a change. This opened up between us a kind of controversial correspondence on the subject—she having shortly after gone back to Boulogne—the result of which was that our religious opinions became perfectly satisfactory to one another, and terminated by her coming over to England and accepting me as her husband, we being married on the 3rd of June, 1826.* In the interim, however, I had provided for this event as far as possible, by making my own furniture, and by otherwise providing for her a comfortable home. I need scarcely say that on my marriage I gave up the different associations I had been connected with; as well from motives of economy as from a desire to make my home a place of happiness. Perceiving also that much of the bickerings and dissensions often found in the domestic circle had their origin in the wife's not understanding and appreciating her husband's political or literary pursuits; too often coupled with his carelessness and indifference in enlightening and instructing her regarding them; I

* This correspondence we thought it well to burn when I was drawn for the militia, fearing it might get into strange hands.

resolved, if possible, to avoid this evil by pursuing an opposite course of conduct. My chief recreation at this period was in reading; my meal hours and my evenings being earnestly devoted to the attainment of some description of knowledge. Soon after my marriage I began also my first attempts in writing short pieces for the press. In all these matters I sought to interest my wife, by reading and explaining to her the various subjects that came before us, as well as the political topics of the day. I sought also to convince her that, beyond the pleasure knowledge conferred on ourselves, we had a duty to perform in endeavouring to use it wisely for others. I endeavoured to make her understand how much of our social improvement and political progress had depended on past sacrifices and sufferings on the part of our forefathers, and how much the happiness of the future will depend on each and all of us doing our duty in the present as our brave old forefathers had done. And in looking back upon this period how often have I found cause for satisfaction that I pursued this course, as my wife's appreciation of my humble exertions has ever been the chief hope to cheer, and best aid to sustain me, under the many difficulties and trials I have encountered in my political career. She has ever been to me

> " A guardian angel o'er my life presiding,
>   Doubling my pleasure and my cares dividing."

When I married her she was a tall, handsome, fresh coloured girl; but she, having received a push in the back from her sister when young, received an injury to her spine. The appearance of it was scarcely perceptible for many years, but when she began to have children her spine began to give way, so that now in her old age she is about a head shorter than when I married her. For two years after my marriage I was in good employment, at a cabinet maker's in St. Paul's Churchyard. Having now got all our little household comforts about us, and a few pounds in our possession, my wife was desirous of getting into some small way of business that she herself could manage; in the hopes of making some little provision for the sickness that might happen, and for the old age and infirmities sooner or later almost sure to overtake us. An acquaintance of mine, having recently commenced the business of a pastry-cook and confectioner, proposed to us that if we would take a small shop in some thorough-fare, and commence that line of business he would serve us on very advantageous terms. Thinking his terms favourable we agreed to try the experiment. We accordingly took a small shop in May's Buildings, St. Martins Lane, which we fitted up and stocked to the extent of our means. Our sale, however, not being such as my friend of large promise expected, he very soon refused to supply our small demands for his goods. This disappointment at the commencement of our speculation entailed on us a great inconvenience as well as loss; for we had to look out for others to serve us on less favourable terms. To still further help us down the hill I was laid up soon after our opening with the ague; a disease which I caught by lodging near the marshes at Plumstead, having been working at a gentleman's house in that neighbourhood. In the midst of it also my poor wife was put to bed with her second child; and, what with care, anxiety, and bad living, was soon laid up on a bed of sickness. We left this wretched place as soon as we conveniently could, but not before we had exhausted all our own little means, and had involved ourselves in debt; the hopes of its improvement having allured us on.

A short time before I had embarked in the business referred to, I was induced to join the First London Co-operative Trading Association; a society first established in the premises of the Co-operative Society, Red Lion Square, and subsequently removed to Jerusalem Passage, Clerkenwell. I think it was about the close of the year 1828 that the first of those trading associations was established at Brighton, by a person of the name of Bryan; and its success was such that between four and five hundred similar associations were very soon established in different parts of the country. The members of those societies subscribed a small weekly sum for the raising of a common fund, with which they opened a general store, containing such articles of food, clothing, books, &c., as were most in request among working men; the profits of which were added to the common stock. As their funds increased some of them employed their members; such as shoemakers, tailors, and other domestic trades: paying them journeymen's wages, and adding the profits to their funds. Many of them were also enabled by these means to raise sufficient capital to commence manufactures on a small scale; such as broadcloths, silk, linen and worsted goods, shoes, hats, cutlery, furniture, &c. Some few months after I had given up my shop in May's Buildings, I was induced to accept the situation of storekeeper to the "First London Association," the late storekeeper, Mr. James Watson, having resigned. In taking this step I made some little sacrifice, as the salary they offered was less than I could earn at my trade. But, like many others, I was sanguine that those associations formed the first step towards the social independence of the labouring classes, and I was disposed to exert all my energies to aid in the work. I was induced to believe that the gradual accumulation of capital by these means would enable the working classes to form themselves into joint stock associations of labour, by which (with industry, skill, and knowledge) they might ultimately have the trade, manufactures, and commerce of the country in their own hands. But I failed to perceive that the great majority of them lacked the self sacrifices and economy necessary for procuring capital, the discrimination to place the right men in the right position for managing, the plodding industry, skill, and knowledge necessary for successful management, the moral disposition to labour earnestly for the general good, and the brotherly fellowship and confidence in one another for making their association effective.

I had not, however, been in the situation of storekeeper many months before a reduction in my salary took place, the business not answering the expectation of members. My wife was next requested to attend to the store at half the salary I had engaged for. Being thus out of employment myself, and my own trade being exceedingly dull, I employed myself for some months in making a model of an industrial village for the late J. Minter Morgan, author of the "Revolt of the Bees," the "Reproof of Brutus," &c. A shop of work, however, being offered me before it was in any way finished, the model was never completed.

At this period, too, our troubles were further increased by the death of my second child, my little Kezia, from an accident. My eldest child also became so weakly that we were necessitated to send her into the country, to her grandfather's, for about two years.

In returning, however, to the formation of those societies I must mention that, as our association was the first formed in London, it was looked up to for information and advice from all parts of the country. This, entailing much labour, led to the formation of another society, entitled "The British Association for Promoting Co-operative Knowledge." As, also, several of those societies had commenced manufactures on a small scale, they were anxious for some depôt, or place in London, where their productions might be deposited for sale to the public, or for exchange with one another. This desire induced the British Association to take a large house in 19, Greville Street, Hatton Garden, the first floor of which was fitted up as a co-operative bazaar, the lower portion being occupied by our First London Association.

The first secretary of the British Association was Mr. George Skene, and, subsequently, on his resignation, I became its honorary secretary. This association kept up the necessary correspondence with the country, held public meetings from time to time, and published several reports of its proceedings. Lady Byron (who took a great interest in these associations), having placed at the disposal of the British Association a small capital—£100—for helping some of the Spitalfields weavers, who were out of work, to manufacture some silk handkerchiefs. This, also, was managed by the secretary, Mr. Skene. Those societies, from the establishment of which so much had been expected, were, however, in the course of three or four years mostly all broken up, and with them the British Association. The chief, or, at least, the most prominent causes of their failure were religious differences, the want of legal security, and the dislike which the women had to confine their dealings to one shop. The question of *religion* was not productive of much dissension until Mr. Owen's return from America, when his "Sunday Morning Lectures" excited the alarm of the religious portion of their members, and caused great numbers to secede from them. The want of *legal security* was also the cause of failure, as they could not obtain the ordinary legal redress when their officers, or servants, robbed, or defrauded them, the magistrates refusing to interfere on the ground of their not being legalized, or *enrolled societies*. The prejudice of the members' wives against their stores was, no doubt, another cause of failure. Whether it was their love of shopping, or their dislike that their husbands should be made acquainted with the exact extent of their dealings, which were booked against them I know not, but certain it was that they often left the unadulterated and genuine article in search of that which was often questionable. When Mr. Owen first came over from America he looked somewhat coolly on those "Trading Associations," and very candidly declared that their mere buying and selling formed no part of his grand co-operative scheme;" but when he found that great numbers among them were disposed to entertain many of his views, he took them more into favour, and ultimately took an active part among them. And here I think it is necessary to state that I entertain the highest respect for Mr. Owen's warm benevolence and generous intentions, however I may differ from many of his views; and this respect, I think, most people will be disposed to accord to him, who know that he devoted a large fortune and a long life in reiterated efforts to improve the condition of his fellow men. I must confess, also, that I was one of those who, at one time, was favourably impressed with many of Mr. Owen's views, and, more especially, with those of a *community of property*. This notion has a peculiar attraction for the plodding, toiling, ill-remunerated sons and daughters of labour. The idea of all the powers of machinery, of all the arts and inventions of men, being applied for the benefit of all in common, to the lightening of their toil and the increase of their comforts, is one the most captivating to those who accept the idea without investigation. The prospect of having spacious halls, gardens, libraries, and museums at their command; of having light alternate labour in field or factory; of seeing their children educated, provided and cared for at the public expense; of having no fear or care of poverty themselves; nor for wife, children, or friends they might leave behind them; is one the most cheering and consolatory to an enthusiastic mind. I was one who accepted this grand idea of machinery working for the benefit of all, without considering that those powers and inventions have been chiefly called forth, and industriously and efficiently applied by the stimulus *our industrial system has afforded,* and that the benefits to the originators and successful workers of them—though large in some instances—have been few and trifling, compared to the benefits *which the millions now enjoy from their general application.* Those great results, too, have hitherto been realized by the hope of wealth, fame, or station, *keeping up man's energies to the tension point.* But who can foresee what human beings may become when the *individualism* in their nature is checked by education, and endeavoured to be crushed out of them by the mandate of a majority— and, it may be, that majority not always a reasonable and enlightened one. What may become of man's inventions when some plodding, persevering schemer (content to starve in his closet in hopes of perfecting a project that may win him fame and benefit his country) is peremptorily called upon to abandon his hopes and yield to the bidding of authority? What even may become of the best portion of man's nature (of his industrial, skilful, persevering, saving energies), when some aspiring, hopeful individual, resolving to labour and to save while youth and vigour favour him, in hopes of realizing leisure and independence, or to procure some cherished object of his heart, is constrained to abandon his resolution, to conform to the routine of the majority, and to make their aspirations the standard of his own? Of what advantage the splendour and enjoyment of all art and nature *if man has no choice of enjoyment?* And what to him would be spacious halls, and luxurious apartments, and all the promised blessings of a community, if he must rise, work, dress, occupy, and enjoy, not as he himself desires, *but as the fiat of the majority wills it?* Surely the poorest labourer, bowed down with toil and poverty, would have reason to bless the *individualism* that gave him some freedom of choice, and a chance of improving his lot, compared with a fellowship that so bound him in bondage. But we shall be told of the perfect and wise arrangements that are so to perfect human character, that no man "shall ever need to be blamed for his conduct," nor men ever have occasion to make their fellows "responsible for their actions." Unfortunately, the great obstacle to the realization of this perfect state of things is, that the perfect and wise arrangements are to depend *on imperfect men and women.* And though much is to be expected from an improved system of teaching and training, it is very doubtful, even by these helps, if they will so far succeed in perfecting human organizations that no ill balanced ones shall be found among them to mar the general welfare ; to need not the enactment of laws to deter and control them, and the necessity for some tribunal to make them responsible for their conduct. But though mature reflection has caused me to have lost faith in "*a Community of Property,*" I have not lost faith in the great benefits that may yet be realised by a wise and judicious system of *Co-operation in the Production of Wealth.* The former I believe to be unjust, unnatural, and despotic in its tendency, a sacrificing of the intellectual energies and moral virtues of the few, to the indolence, ignorance and despotism of the many. The latter I believe to be in accordance with wisdom and justice, an arrangement by which small means and united efforts may yet be made the instruments for upraising the multitude in knowledge, prosperity, and freedom.*

I am satisfied, however, that much good resulted from the formation of those co-operative trading associations, notwithstanding their failure. Their being able to purchase pure and unadulterated articles of food ; their

---

* Since this was written numerous co-operative associations have been started on the old plan.

manufacturing and exchanging with one another various articles which they were induced to make up in their leisure hours, or when out of employment; the mental and moral improvement derived from their various meetings and discussions, were among the advantages that resulted from them.

And while speaking of the failure of our co-operative trading associations at that period, I think it may be interesting to some if I give them a brief account of the failure of the Community of New Harmony as communicated to me by M. D'Arusment, Fanny Wright's husband—on one occasion when he took tea with me. He stated that the chief cause of failure was bad management; persons being appointed to superintend or manage different departments, of which they had no practical knowledge; and chiefly because they professed to believe in Mr. Owen's views. That instead of first seeking to raise the substantial necessaries and comforts of life, on which their success would mainly depend, the members were more intent on hearing lectures on the New System, or in reading, dancing and amusement. Among the illustrations of bad management, he gave me the following. He said that the Rappists, the former proprietors, who had shown themselves to be very successful farmers, had very conveniently divided the land into necessary portions very carefully fenced. These divisions, however, in Mr. Owen's opinion, looked too much like the old world's system, and he ordered the fences to be removed. The consequence of this was that the pigs of the neighbourhood, which were allowed to roam the lanes and forests, had only to get through one fence to be able to rove over a great portion of the estate, and to obtain their choice of the crops, instead of being restricted to a small field if they broke in. Persons, he said, were put to manage agricultural operations who had no practical knowledge of them; and so in like manner in many other departments. Many intelligent members saw this folly, and greatly lamented it; but the generality of them had such faith in Mr. Owen's knowledge of the system, that nothing was done to check the evil till it was too late. He said, if you spoke to any of those blind disciples about this bad management, the reply generally was: "Ah! we see only a link or two in the great chain, whereas Mr. Owen comprehends the whole. The system is his, and he has so much knowledge, and so much experience, that we have best have faith in him, and wait for the result." One of these men, he said, a warm-hearted enthusiast, to whom he had often spoken about the management, and who had the fullest faith in Mr. Owen, was so stunned and heart-broken when the truth of failure and insolvency was made known to him, that he went into the woods and hung himself. I must state, however, that Mr. D'Arusment told me these matters with regretful feelings, and at the same time avowed his belief, that they would have got on very well if the affair had been so managed as to provide them with food and clothing.

About 1832 Mr. William King put forth a proposal for the establishing of exchange bazaars upon a different and more extended plan than that of Greville Street, and subsequently by the co-operation of his friends succeeded in establishing one in Portland Road, and another at the Gothic Hall, New Road. By this plan, *Exchange or Labour Notes* were issued to the depositor of any article in the Bazaar to the extent of its value, which notes were again taken for any article the depositor wanted out of it. This plan was eminently successful for a short period, until in fact the amount of the ornamental, and comparatively useless articles which had accumulated in the bazaar, preponderated greatly over the useful; then it was that the notes that had been issued *began to be depreciated*, and useful articles soon ceased to be deposited. Before, however, this cause of failure was discovered, Mr. Owen's friends and supporters were very anxious that he also should form one of those exchange bazaars upon a large scale. To facilitate the project, the proprietor of some very extensive premises in Gray's Inn Road, offered the use of them gratuitously to Mr. Owen for one year, to try the experiment; which, if successful, they were to be purchased for a stipulated sum. The proposal being accepted the place was opened as "The Institution of the Industrious Classes." A very influential council was also appointed to co-operate with Mr. Owen in the management and a sum of money subscribed towards the objects contemplated; namely, an exchange bazaar, an infant school, and an incipient community. Great assistance being anticipated from the various trading associations, established throughout the country, the use of the premises was offered to them for the holding of their third congress; they having previously held one at Manchester, and another at Huddersfield. This congress was subsequently held there, and was attended by delegates from between sixty and seventy different societies, among whom I was one. We held two very crowded public meetings, and continued the business of the congress for six consecutive days. We had much talk, but did very little business; the chief object of interest to many (that of forming an incipient community upon the plan of Mr. Thompson, of Cork) being stoutly opposed and finally marred by our friend Mr. Owen. The Exchange Bazaar was ultimately opened by Mr. Owen and his council, and for a time promised success, until in fact " the labour notes " began to be depreciated. Its failure was also accelerated by bad management; and finally by a rupture between the proprietor of the building and Mr Owen.

And here I must give a couple of anecdotes regarding Mr. Owen, showing how anti-democratic he was notwithstanding the extreme doctrines he advocated. We, having resolved to call the Co-operative Congress referred to, issued, among other invitations, a circular inviting the attendance of Members of Parliament. Mr. Owen, having seen a copy of the circular drawn up, conceived that it did not sufficiently express his peculiar views. He therefore sent an amendment, which he wished added to it, on to our meeting by Mr. J. D. Styles. The committee having discussed the amendment, rejected it, and then sent the circular on to Mr. Hetherington's to be printed. When Mr. Owen heard of this, he sent Mr. Bromley, the proprietor of the Exchange Bazaar, to tell Mr. Hetherington that his amendment must be added. This at first Mr. Hetherington refused to do, but on Bromley swearing that the Congress should not meet at his place unless he did add it, he began to think it a very serious affair, as the meeting was to take place in a few days ; we had incurred great expenses, and had no means of taking another place. He therefore told Bromley, that if Mr. Owen sent him a letter authorising him to insert it, and took the blame on himself, he would add the amendment. Judge, therefore, of our great surprise when the circulars were brought to our meeting, embodying the rejected amendment. After Hetherington's explanation, it was resolved that a deputation, consisting of Messrs. Lovett, Flather, and Powell, be appointed to go and expostulate with Mr. Owen. We went, and were shown into Mr. Owen's room at the bazaar, and after briefly introducing our business, he told us to be seated, as he had something very important to read to us. This something was the *proof* of a publication just started, called the *Crisis*. After he had read to us a large portion of what he had written in it, I found my patience giving way, and at the next pause I took the opportunity of asking him what that had to do with the business we had come about ? I began by telling him of his having submitted an amendment to our circular, of the committee rejecting it by a large majority, and of his taking upon himself to authorise its insertion in the circular notwithstanding ; and concluded by asking him whether such conduct was not highly despotic ? With the greatest composure he answered that it evidently was despotic ; but as we, as well as the committee that sent us, were all ignorant of his plans, and of the objects he had in view, we must consent to be ruled by despots till we had acquired sufficient knowledge to govern ourselves. After such vain glorious avowal, what could we say but to report—in the phraseology of one of the deputation— that we had been flabbergasted by him ?

In a previous page I have stated that the proposal to establish an incipient community upon Mr. Thompson's plan, was opposed and marred by Mr. Owen. It was in this curious manner. After the proposal was discussed for some time, for commencing a community upon the small scale proposed by Mr. Thompson, instead of waiting for the grand plan of Mr. Owen, we retired for dinner.

When we came back our friend Owen told us very solemnly, in the course of a long speech, that if we were resolved to go into a community upon Mr. Thompson's plan, we must make up our minds *to dissolve our present marriage connections, and go into it as single men and women.* This was like the bursting of a bomb-shell in the midst of us. One after another, who had been ardently anxious for this proposal of a community, began to express doubts, or to flatly declare that they could never consent to it; while others declared that the living in a community need not interfere in any way with the marriage question. One poor fellow, Mr. Petrie, an enthusiast in his way, quite agreed with his brother Owen, and made a speech which many blushed to hear, and contended that it would make no difference, as he and his wife were concerned, for she would follow him anywhere. He then little thought, poor man, that her virtue and his philosophy would so soon be put to the test, and that his mental powers would give way before it, for so it happened soon after. However, nothing could have been better devised than this speech of Mr. Owen to sow the seeds of doubt, and to cause the scheme to be abortive; and when we retired Mr. Thompson expressed himself very strongly against his conduct. I may add that the reporter of our proceedings, Mr. Wm. Carpenter, thought it wise not to embody this discussion in our printed report.

At the time that I held the situation of store-keeper at Greville Street, I was (in conjunction with two other persons) served with an exchequer writ, for selling, in ignorance of our "knowledge restricting laws," a small pamphlet on which *the duty had not been paid.* And as our aristocratic rulers and their tools have often recourse to very round-about ways for entrapping their victims, it may be well to state the way in which we were nearly caught in the meshes of this paltry law; a law, I believe, devised by old Sidmouth, of knowledge-gagging memory. Among the customers who visited our bazaar and store, was a portly old farmer looking gentleman, who manifested a great anxiety to know every thing relating to our co-operative trading associations. He told us that he had already heard enough about them to make him desirous of opening a store in his own village for the benefit of his labourers, and others living in the vicinity; but still he wanted further information respecting their proceedings. As a member of the "British Association for Promoting Co-operative Knowledge," I thought it my duty to give so benevolent an individual all the information I could, and as we sold in our store a great variety of books and pamphlets on the subject of co-operation, I showed him our assortment. From among them he selected two or three copies of our *quarterly reports* and a few other pamphlets, and went away, as we thought, brimful of zeal in the cause. In a few days he called on us again, and informed us that he had been reading our reports and pamphlets, and found from them that some of our members were very great radicals, more especially Lovett, Fosket, and some others whom he named. When I informed him that I was one of the radicals he referred to, he affected great surprise, and said that he believed I should find it very difficult to defend some of the extreme opinions I entertained before a jury. I told him that I thought radicalism, as well as all principles based on justice, were very easily defended, the difficulties being on the other side of the question; for when political inequality, hereditary privilege, unjust possessions, and injustice in law and government, had to be defended in the face of justice, honesty, and common sense, there might be some difficulty in substantiating their claims, and more especially if there was an honest jury in the box. Some further discussion took place between us, and on leaving he told us that he should have something further to say to us in a few days. This something appeared in the form of *an exchequer writ* from Somerset House, which on his information had been forwarded to us. It seemed to set forth some great offence committed against the state, yet noways enlightening us regarding the precise nature of that offence, the mystery or enigma being left for offenders to solve as they best could, generally done through the instrumentality of their legal advisers. In our ignorance of the offence we had committed, we began to examine the different commodities in our store to see if we had been guilty of selling anything without the proper licence; but we found that for all things requiring it we had the proper document. During our investigation Mr Hetherington chanced to come into our store, and he joined with us in trying to find out the cause of our offence, and but for him we should probably have remained ignorant; for in looking over our stock of books, he found out that one of the *quarterly reports* of the British Association was on a sheet and a quarter of paper, and on which *quarter of a sheet* the law required a pamphlet duty of *one shilling* to be paid, which duty the printer in his ignorance or neglect had forgotten. Having found out what we thought to be the cause of the information laid against us, Mr. Hetherington and myself walked down to Somerset House to see if we were right in our surmises. The right department in this great taxing machinery having been found, we presented our slip of paper, and requested the person in attendance to inform us what had induced them to send us that document. He referred to a file of papers, and told us that an information had been laid against us for having published a pamphlet without having paid the required duty. We then informed him that the parties named in the writ were not the publishers of the pamphlet, and that he had consequently sent it to the wrong parties. The fact was it was published for the British Association, a distinct body from the First London Co-operative Association, whose trustees they had sent the writ to, the informer having seen their names over the shop door; but this information we did not think it necessary to give him. He then wanted to know the nature of the First London Society, and the kind of articles we sold. On which Mr. Hetherington began to reckon up the miscellaneous articles we dealt in, rather humorously contrasting bacon with snuff, butter with books, mustard with raisins, &c., which could not but excite the risible faculties of his questioner. This person then very authoritatively declared that we were liable to a heavy penalty for having vended the pamphlet. We then called his attention to the fact, that we bought a variety of books and pamphlets from different persons, and that there was nothing printed on them to indicate whether the duty was paid or not; and, as it was the business of the printer to pay the pamphlet duty, it was evidently a great injustice to visit his offence upon the vendor. He concluded that as the writ had been issued nothing could be done in our favour unless we laid our case before *the Board*. We accordingly drew up a statement for these gentlemen, in which we informed them that as their clerks had made a great mistake in issuing out a writ against us instead of some other persons, we hoped that they would rectify the error, so that we should be subject to no loss. In a few days we received a letter from them, stating that they had considered our *petition*, and had mitigated the penalties against us to ten pounds! To this we replied that the board had made a very great mistake in supposing our explanation about their clerks to be " a petition." That not having committed any offence we had not petitioned, and that consequently we should pay no penalties. After this we heard no more of the affair; but we frequently saw our farmer friend about the Stamp Office and Court of Exchequer, and on enquiry learnt that he was one of their common informers.

CHAPTER III.

ABOUT the same period that I joined the Co-operative Trading Associations I became acquainted with Messrs. Cleave, Hetherington, and Watson, three men with whom I laboured politically and socially for a period of nearly twenty years; some account of these labours in various ways will be met with as I proceed with my story.*   A

---

* Mr. Henry Hetherington, the great champion of the unstamped press, was a native of London, and born in Compton-street, Soho, in the year 1792.   I became acquainted with him some time before he commenced the publication of the "Poor Man's Guardian," an event which gave rise to the unstamped warfare, and which gave birth to the cheap literature we so much enjoy.   It was his firm determination and unflinching courage, that no punishment could daunt, that caused that warfare to be successful, though many others helped, and suffered in the fray.

Mr. James Watson, a seller of the unstamped, and publisher of many liberal works, was a native of New Malton, in Yorkshire, and was born on the 21st September, 1799.   I first met with him at the Old Co-operative Society Rooms, Red Lion Square.   He first came to town to take charge of Richard Carlisle's shop in Fleet Street, when the government prosecution was so hot against him for selling Pain's works.   I have taken part in many associations with him, and I know of no politician I could better repose confidence in.   Independent of his efforts and sacrifices in the cause of the unstamped, he rendered good service to the cause of progress by the great number of political and other useful works which he printed and published.

Mr. John Cleave, bookseller and publisher, was I think about the same age as Hetherington, but the place of his birth I cannot now recollect. He had been, I think, a sailor in early life, and had much of the sailor in his bearing.   He was also rude and bluff in his manner at times, but he had a warm and generous heart; always ready to aid the good cause, and to lend a helping hand to the extent of his means.   He laboured hard, and made great sacrifices in freeing the press from the stamps that fettered it.

le before this time, however, I was introduced to **Mr.**
nry Hunt and a number of other radicals, who were
n united with him in seeking to effect a reform in
:liament. Soon after I became acquainted with him,
. Hetherington, myself, and some other friends sought
:ffect a reconciliation between him and the celebrated
. W. Cobbett; but the feud between them was too
mg for us to be successful. Mr. Cobbett denounced
despotism of Mr. Hunt, and Mr. Hunt spoke bitterly
:he cowardice of Mr. Cobbett. The memory, however,
:hose two earnest men I strongly cherish; for, without
king to extenuate the failings of either, I regard them
:wo noble champions of the rights of the millions; men
o by speaking, writing, and suffering, stamped the
essity *for reform* so deeply into the heart and mind
England, that no effort of corruption will ever again be
e to eradicate it, until all our institutions have been
·ged and reformed even to the very roots. How few of
politicians of the present day are able to estimate how
ch of their own views and opinions they owe to Mr.
)bett's long teaching of the multitude, and how many
the reforms that have been effected in England since
days of Castlereagh and Sidmouth, are justly to be
:ibuted to the public opinion he helped to create.
1en Henry Hunt, too, first stood forward as the champion
·eform, it needed a man of his nerve and moral daring
ace the formidable phalanx of corruption everywhere
ed against every one who presumed to talk of the
hts of man. But he went nobly onward with his work
appealing to the good sense and sound feeling of the
ple, being deterred not by the sabres of Peterloo, nor
threats, sneers, nor imprisonment, till he finally
ained the verdict of his country against the corruptions
assailed. The Whig Reform Bill was that verdict, a
1sure, the enactment of which, admitted the corruptions
our representative system, though its provisions went
her to palliate than to effectually remove them; and
atly is it to be regretted that Mr. Hunt, in contending
1tly for an efficient measure of reform, in opposition to
short-comings of that Bill, found himself abused and

deserted by the great majority of those whom he sought to enfranchise. And from the last conversation I had with this warm-hearted friend of the millions, I am induced to believe that it was this injustice and ingratitude that struck him to the heart.* For some years, however, previous to this event, I continued to take part in the reform exertions of Mr. Hunt and his friends, and was among those who assisted in getting up the large public meeting at the Eagle Tavern, City Road, in March, 1830, for the formation of " the Metropolitan Political Union." Mr. O'Connell was in the chair on that occasion, and the meeting was, I believe, the first public meeting he ever addressed in London. The chief object of that union was " to obtain by every just, legal, constitutional, and peaceful means, an effectual and radical reform in the Commons House of Parliament." I was one of the council of that body, and continued to take an active part in it until what was called " the three glorious days " of the French revolution ; but having taken part at a public meeting at the Rotunda in celebration of that event, in conjunction with Mr. Hetherington, Gale Jones, George Thompson, and others, our proceedings were thought, in the opinion of some members of our council, to savour of sedition. The subject being brought before them on the following evening, Mr. Hetherington and myself contended that the spirit of the meeting was such as an oppressed and tax-ridden people should exhibit when they hear of despots

---

* The following sketch, drawn by an opponent—Blackwood's Magazine—will give some idea of Henry Hunt's treatment in the House of Commons :—" A comely, tall, rosy, white-headed mean-looking, well-gartered tradesman of, I take it, 60 ; nothing about him could detain the eye for a second, if one did not know who he was. His only merits are his impudence and his voice, the former certainly first rate, the latter, as far as power goes, unique. In vain do all sides of the house unite, cough, and shuffle, and groan, and Door, door ! and Bar, bar ! to drown him ; in vain Spoke, spoke ! Mr. Speaker ! Order there ! I rise ! Spoke ! Question, question ! Chair, chair ! In vain is it all ; he pauses for a moment, until the unanimous clamour of disgust is at its height, and then, re-pitching his notes, apparently without an effort, lifts his halloo as clear and distinct above the storm, as ever ye heard a minster bell tolling over the racket of a village wake."

being hurled from their pinnacle of power. This caused our chairman, for the time being,* to declare that he could not continue to be a member with men capable of entertaining such sentiments; and we on our part, not approving of such timidity, thought it well to withdraw from among them.

Shortly before this affair I became greatly interested in the temperance question, and did what I could in various ways to promote it. Among other modes I drew up, as early as 1829, a petition for the opening of the British Museum, and other exhibitions of Art and Nature, on Sundays. The petition was signed by many thousand persons, and was presented to Parliament by Mr. Hume. A few extracts from it will convey its spirit and intent: "Your petitioners consider that one of the principal causes of drunkenness and dissipation on the Sabbath is the want of recreation and amusement. Sunday being the only leisure day for working men, they are naturally induced on that day to seek that recreation and enjoyment from which they are precluded during the week. So far, however, from there being facilities provided for the rational enjoyment of working men on that day, even their most innocent pleasures (from mistaken feelings of religion) are rigorously prohibited; there is no place of public resort in this metropolis (open on Sundays) where amusement and instruction are blended, or where working men could be led to admire and comprehend the wonderful combinations of nature and art. It is therefore not surprising that the injunctions delivered from the pulpit are often disregarded, or that labouring men seek relief from religious instruction in the oblivious and demoralizing sociality of the ale-house, which, unfortunately, too often terminates in drunkenness. Your petitioners are further convinced that many of their labouring fellow countrymen who frequent those haunts of vice and dissipation on Sundays, are tempted to spend their leisure hours in this objectionable manner, more from a desire of participating in agreeable pastime than from a love of drink; thus they

---

* Mr. George Rogers, a well-intentioned man, notwithstanding.

imperceptibly contract bad habits, and from merely sipping in the first instance the intoxicating poison, they ultimately become actively vicious, and often to fall a prey to pauperism and crime. Your petitioners suggest to your Honourable House that the best remedy for drunkenness at all times, is to divert and inform the mind, and to circulate sound knowledge among the people, so that their minds may be profitably engaged, and a public opinion in favour of sobriety may be generated. That attention to those suggestions would do more towards wiping from our national character the stain of drunkenness than prohibitory laws or coercive measures. That if useful knowledge was extensively disseminated among the industrious classes, if they were encouraged to admire the beauties of nature, to cultivate a taste for the arts and sciences, to seek for rational instruction and amusement, it would soon be found that their vicious habits would yield to more rational pursuits; man would become the friend and lover of his species, his mind would be strengthened and fortified against the allurements of vice; he would become a better citizen in this world, and be better qualified to enjoy happiness in any future state of existence. In other countries in Europe every facility is afforded on Sundays for the rational recreation of the industrious population. Music, the museums, and public libraries, all display their attractions, and so far from the innocent diversions and gaiety of the people leading to vice and immorality, the mass of the working population of those countries are confessedly more sober and moral than the same class of persons in our own religious country." I may now add that the forty-six years that have elapsed since the foregoing was written, have only tended to strengthen my conviction that no more effectual means for the removal of drunkenness could be provided than the opening of our museums, our mechanic and scientific institutions, our libraries, and all our exhibitions of art and nature on Sunday, the only day our working population have to enjoy them, and by giving every facility and encouragement for persons delivering scientific, historical, and every description of instructive lectures to the mass of the people on that day.

In 1830 I became connected with the "Unstamped Agitation," one of the most important political movements that I was ever associated with. This unstamped warfare had its commencement in the publication of *The Poor Man's Guardian*, by Mr. Henry Hetherington; although the idea of publishing a substitute for a newspaper, in such a manner as to evade Castlereagh's Act, first originated with Mr. William Carpenter. This last gentleman, a well-known author and editor who has been connected with most of the political movements of the last twenty years or more, believed that he could evade this infamous Act (the 38th of Geo. 3, &c., passed to put down Mr. Cobbett's two-penny publications) by issuing weekly what he called his "Political Letters." Before, however, any of these were published Mr. Hetherington brought out a series of *Penny daily* papers, in a letter form, addressed to different individuals with the view of evading the Act of Parliament, and at the same time to provide cheap political information for the people. After a short time, however, they were published *weekly*, each having the title of a "*Penny Paper for the People* by the Poor Man's Guardian"; and after Mr. Hetherington's first conviction he changed the title to *The Poor Man's Guardian*, published in defiance of law to try the power of right against might.* This publication was first edited by Mr. Mayhew, a brother, I believe, of the author of "London Labour and the Poor," and subsequently by Mr. James Bronterre O'Brien, a writer and politician of some celebrity. It was not started long, however, before the Stamp Office authorities commenced a fierce warfare against it, first against the publisher, and then against the book-sellers who sold it. This having deterred many from selling it, caused some few of us to volunteer the supplying of it to persons at their own houses within any reasonable

---

* The first of the "Penny Papers for the People" was addressed to the People of England, and dated October 1st, 1830. This was followed by papers of a larger form addressed to the Duke of Wellington; to the King; the Archbishop of Canterbury, &c. The first number of the "Poor Man's Guardian" was dated December 25th, 1830, and the last December 20th, 1835.

distance ; and subsequently to organize a general fund for
the support of those who were suffering or likely to suffer
for striving to disseminate cheap political information
amongst the people. This fund was called the "*Victim
Fund*"; it was kept up by small weekly subscriptions
during the many years the contest lasted, and contributed
in no small degree to the success of that contest. The
Committee of Management consisted for the most part of
Messrs Cleave, Watson, Warden, Russell, Petrie, Mansell
and Devonshire Saul : Julian Hibbert was our treasurer ; I
was the sub-treasurer, and acted also as secretary during the
greater part of the time and Mr. Russell the remaining portion. We met weekly in an upstair room at the Hope Coffee
House, King Street, Smithfield, then kept by Mr. John
Cleave, and subsequently at his house in Shoe Lane.
Finding that the booksellers refused to sell the *Poor
Man's Guardian*, and some few other radical publications
subsequently started, we advertised for persons to sell them
in the streets and from house to house, and met with many
volunteers ; some of them from a sincere desire to serve the
cause, and others for the mere trifling benefit we held out
to them, which was generally a stock of papers to begin
with, and a pound in money for every month (or shorter
time) they might suffer imprisonment.

When Mr. Hetherington first commenced the publication of the *Guardian* he was established in Kings-
gate Street, Holborn, as a printer, with a fair run of
business, which for a time was nearly ruined by the
resolute course he pursued. For his name as a radical
became so obnoxious to many of his customers that
they withdrew their printing from him. One of his
most useful apprentices, too, refused to work on such a
radical publication, and was sanctioned in his disobedience
by the magistrates, who very readily cancelled his
indentures. I remember being present on one occasion
when one of Mr. Hetherington's customers, in a large way
of business, offered to give him as much printing as he
could do on his premises, provided he would give up his
radical publications ; but this splendid offer (in a pecuniary
sense) he very nobly refused ; although, to my know-

ledge, his shelves were then filled with thousands of his unsold and returned publications, and all his relations and connections were loudly condemning him for his folly. Mr. Hetherington, however, was not the kind of character to yield under such circumstances. The first time he appeared at Bow Street to answer to the charge of printing and publishing the *Guardian* and *Republican* he honestly told the magistrates that he was determined to resist the efforts of a corrupt government to suppress the voice of the people. His conviction having been confirmed at the next session, he in the interim set off for a tour through the country, and was greatly instrumental in calling up the spirit of the people in opposition to the persecution the Whigs were then waging against the press. Finding also that many of the old established booksellers were fearful of selling his publications, he and his friends succeeded in inducing many other persons to commence the sale of them.* Many of those were prosecuted and imprisoned; but such proceedings only served to enlist public sympathy in their favour, and to increase their business; many of whom are now the largest booksellers for cheap literature in the kingdom. In this tour the police pursued Mr. Hetherington in all directions, but by the help of friends he succeeded in eluding their vigilance until his return to town. This he was induced to do in hopes of seeing the last of his dying mother; but the police (who were on the watch) captured him at his own door, and inhumanly refused him his request of taking a last farewell of his fond parent, or of even letting his wife know of his being taken off to prison. But the details of injustice and cruelty on the part of the authorities, and of the self-sacrifices and patriotic devotedness on the part of many individuals engaged in this unstamped warfare would take a larger space than I can devote to it. Suffice it to say that the contest lasted upwards of five years; during which time upwards of five hundred persons in different parts of the kingdom suffered imprisonment for the publi-

* Among others Mr. Abel Heywood, since then a Mayor of Manchester.

cation, or sale, of the *Poor Man's Guardian*, the *Political Letters*, the *Republican*, the *Police Gazette*, and other radical publications. Among those persons, Mr. Wm. Carpenter was imprisoned six months in King's Bench Prison; Mr. Henry Hetherington was imprisoned three times: twice in Clerkenwell Prison, for six months each time, and in King's Bench for twelve months. Mr. James Watson was imprisoned twice in Clerkenwell Prison, for six months each time; Mr. John Cleave, for two months in Tothill Fields Prison; and in the City Prison till a fine inflicted on him was paid; together with the seizure of his printing press and printing materials. Mr. Abel Heywood, of Manchester, was imprisoned three months; Mrs. Mann, of Leeds, three months, and several others. None of the victims being allowed trial by jury, but merely condemned in a summary manner by the magistrates; the police being mostly the witnesses, and Mr. Timms, from the Stamp Office, the prosecutor. And what adds to the monstrous injustice of this government persecution is the fact that, after so many hundred persons had been fined and imprisoned for selling the *Poor Man's Guardian*, it was finally declared before Lord Lyndhurst and a special jury, to be *a strictly legal publication*. This warfare, however, eventually created a public opinion sufficiently powerful to cause the government to give up the *fourpenny stamp* upon newspapers, and to substitute a *penny stamp* instead.* But this triumphant change was by no means so important as the amount of good that otherwise resulted from the contest. For the unstamped publications may be said *to have originated the cheap literature of the present day*—for few publications existed before they commenced—and the beneficial effects of this cheap literature on the minds and morals of our population are beyond all calculation. For many of the cheap

---

* This *penny stamp* necessitated another agitation to be got up, several years after, to get rid of it. In this agitation Mr. Richard Moore, Mr. Cobden, Mr. Villiers, Mr. Wilson, Mr. Bainbridge, and others took the leading part; Mr. Dobson Collett acted as their Secretary. To the same body of gentlemen we also owe the repeal of the Duty on Paper.

literary and scientific publications that were published during that period were started with the avowed object of "diverting the minds of the working classes away from politics," and of giving them "more useful knowledge." In fact a new class of literature sprang up for the first time in England avowedly for the millions, and has gone on increasing and extending its beneficial influence from that period to the present. To this cheap literature, and the subsequent cheap newspapers that resulted from our warfare, may be also traced the great extension of the coffee rooms and reading rooms of our large towns, and the mental and moral improvement resulting from their establishment. And although the radical publications first started were, in many instances, tainted with violence and bitterness, yet some allowance must be made for this, when we consider the rabid persecution waged against those who first strove to unshackle the press, and to bring political knowledge within the reach of the industrious classes. The Stamp Office authorities were rampant in their enmity against the publishers of all cheap political publications. It must not be supposed, however, that the zeal of those gentlemen arose from any patriotic desire to save or add to the revenue, as the following fact tends to prove. For it happened at that time that great complaints were made that stamps of various kinds were missing from the stamping department. To guard against such delinquents a gentleman, of the name of Riley, invented a very ingenious stamping machine, which not only stamped rapidly, but *registered the stamps made ;* so that the superintendent had only to set and lock up the machine before the stamping began, and to require from each workman, after the day's work was over, the number of stamps registered. This ingenious invention was highly approved of by a number of scientific men, Dr. Birkbeck and others. Lord Althorp, I think, was Prime Minister at that time and he was so pleased with the invention that he recommended it to the notice of the Commissioners of Stamps. Mr. Riley took his machine to these gentlemen and explained all about it. They seemed not to relish it, however, for they told him that *should they need such a machine they would communicate with him.* In fact they did not seem to want a machine that would guard the revenue too effectually. Mr. Riley, after waiting and sickening over hope deferred, eventually took himself and his machine to America, where similar official conduct has driven a great number of ingenious inventors. The police too, at this period, were encouraged to hound out the vendors of the unstamped by the reward of a sovereign for every person they could succeed in convicting.* Many persons were also induced, by the offer of places in the police, to volunteer the sale of those publications, so as to be the better able to trace out and betray the poor fellows who were endeavouring to earn their bread by selling them. As for poor Hetherington, he was hunted from place to place by the police like a wild beast, and was obliged to have resource to all kinds of manœuvres in order to see or correspond with his family. I paid him a secret visit on one occasion at the village of Pinner, some little distance from London, where he lived in a retired cottage for upwards of a year under the assumed name of Mr. Williams; the police in the meantime hunting for him in different parts of the kingdom. And here, too, I think it but justice to the memory of John Cleave to declare that, independent of his fines and imprisonment, he made great sacrifices, both in his business and otherwise, during the many years of this contest. For long before he commenced the publishing of his *Police Gazette*—which was very successful for a time—he was indefatigable in going about in all directions advocating the cause of an unshackled press, and in promoting the sale of the unstamped. Owing also to our Victim Committee meeting at his coffee house, and the victims coming there to be paid (many of them poor, ragged and dirty), the best portion of his customers were led to desert him; and few were the radicals who sought to

---

* A person of the name of Thomas Colley, employed by the Solicitor of the Stamp Office, admitted that he had been the means of convicting *seventy persons* for selling unstamped publications; and that he had received *a pound for each* at the Stamp Office.— *Morning Chronicle.*

supply their place. John Cleave (though, like most of us, not without his faults) was also warmhearted and benevolent; and that without much means at his disposal. I have known him, and his kind-hearted wife, to preserve from perishing many of the poor starving boys that were often to be found about the pens of Smithfield; by taking them into his kitchen when cold, hungry, and filthy; by feeding and cleansing them; while he has gone round among his friends to beg some old clothes to cover them. And these poor boys he has generously fed, and otherwise taken care of, till he had finally got them berths at sea, or otherwise provided for them the means of earning their living.

About the period of Mr. Hetherington's first conviction in 1831, I had my little stock of household furniture taken away from me by the Government because I refused to serve in the Militia, or to pay a sum of money as a substitute. At the drawing for the Militia, previous to this legalized robbery of myself, I was forcibly struck with the great injustice of these constantly recurring *drawings for the Militia*, by which a great number of poor men were periodically fleeced of their money, or frightened away from one town to another; and that too in a time of profound peace. An acquaintance of mine, newly married, a Mr. Hilson, who had just commenced business for himself, had the misfortune to be drawn for the Militia. Foreseeing that his business would be ruined if he personally served, he sought about, and engaged a young man in the neighbourhood to become his *substitute*, and with him went to the authorities. His substitute was a fine healthy fellow, better fitted in every respect for a soldier than my short fat friend, but the personages before whom he appeared laughed and scoffed at him for the trouble he had taken. They insolently told him that they wanted not his substitute but *his money*, and then they could choose for themselves. Now, although I had previously seen many of my shopmates placed in a similar manner, I had never been so forcibly struck with the injustice of the system as I was in this instance; probably because my radical convictions had not become sufficiently matured When, therefore, I heard of the next schedules for the Militia being distributed (in January, 1831), I sent a note to " Carpenter's Political Letters " suggesting that the filling up of the Militia papers afforded a good opportunity for the people to record their protest against the system ; at the same time pointing out a mode in which they might fill up their papers.   A number of persons filled up their schedules according to the plan suggested.   It was called at the time " the no-vote no-musket plan."   However, whether fairly or unfairly, I was drawn ; and summoned at the Coliseum Coffee House, New Road, before the Deputy Lieutenant of the County and other authorities to show what grounds of exemption I had to make against serving in the Militia.   I told them that I objected " on the grounds of not being represented in Parliament, and of not having any voice or vote in the election of those persons who made those laws that compelled me to take up arms to protect the rights and property of others, while my *own rights*, and the only property I had, *my labour*, were not protected."   Those grounds of exemption, as might be supposed, did not suit the authorities, one of whom, a magistrate of the name of Chambers, was very much incensed against me.   In a short time, after my refusal to serve, a party of constables accompanied by a broker of the name of Bradshaw, were sent to seize my goods.   Their warrant authorized them to seize to the extent of fifteen pounds, but they took goods away that cost me upwards of thirty, although most of them were made by myself.   I need scarcely say that we highly valued them on that account ; but my dear wife proved herself a heroine on that occasion, and suffered them to be carried off without a murmur.   She had been offered the means of saving them a day or two previously, but she very nobly resisted the temptation.   I was at that time building a large wooden house for an acquaintance of mine ; and he being very anxious for my completion of it (for we knew not whether they would seize my goods or send me to prison) offered her money to go privately to the authorities and pay for a substitute, without letting me know anything about it ; but, as I have said, she very properly refused. So much so was the public feeling excited against this robbery in support of the Militia laws, that several brokers refused to sell the goods after they were seized, and the authorities, after keeping them some time, got them sold at last at Foster's Sale Rooms as *goods seized for taxes,* without giving me any previous notice of the sale, or rendering me any account of what they sold for. I drew up a petition to the House of Commons on the subject, which was presented by Mr. Hunt, and very ably supported by Mr. Hume. Suffice it to say the public excitement on the subject, the belief that many would follow my example in future, and the able manner in which the balloting system was exposed in the House, had a very beneficial effect, as no *drawing* for the Militia has taken place from that time to the present.

CHAPTER IV.

In 1831 I joined a new Association, composed chiefly of working men, entitled "The National Union of the Working Classes and Others," its chief objects being " the Protection of Working Men; the Free Disposal of the Produce of Labour; an Effectual Reform of the Commons' House of Parliament; the Repeal of all Bad Laws; the Enactment of a Wise and Comprehensive Code of Laws; and to collect and organize a peaceful expression of public opinion." This Association was organized somewhat on the plan of the Methodist Connexion. *Class-leaders* were appointed at public meetings of the members in the proportion of one for about every thirty or forty members; the Class-leaders mostly meeting with their classes weekly at their own houses. At those meetings political subjects were discussed, and articles from the newspapers and portions of standard political works read and commented on. Branches of the Union were established in various parts of the Metropolis. Public meetings were held weekly in various districts, and speakers appointed to attend them. A great number of similar associations were also organized in different parts of the country. Those associations were greatly efficient in aiding our agitation in favour of a Cheap and Unrestricted Press; in extending public opinion in favour of the Suffrage of the Millions; and in calling forth the condemnation of the people against various unjust and tyrannical acts of the authorities of the day; and could the violence and folly of the hot-brained few have been restrained a far larger amount of good might have been effected. But, as in almost all associations that I have ever been connected with, our best efforts were more frequently directed to the prevention of evil by persons of this description, than in devising every means, and in seeking every opportunity for the carrying out of our objects. In this Union we had no trifling number of such characters; and night after night was frequently devoted to prevent them, if possible, from running their own unreflecting heads into danger, and others along with them. Among the first projects of these men that we had to contend against was the calling together "*a Secret Convention*" of delegates from the working class Unions of the kingdom on the subject of reform. Now Cleave, Watson, Hetherington, and myself, as well as a number of others who acted with us, were always opposed to *secret* proceedings. We were for always showing an open and determined front to the enemy, knowing that boldness and honesty in a good cause mostly carry with them public sympathy and support; while the attempts to shun danger by secret plotting, and sneaking contrivances, disgust the public, call forth the suspicion of friends, and place weapons in the hands of the enemy to seal your fate and secure his triumph. By appealing therefore to the warm-hearted and right-minded portion of our members, we generally managed to frustrate those secret schemes, and in this instance prevented our Association from joining, though not without a large share of abuse from those who were secretly corresponding with others in the country respecting it. But to show the kind of persons we refrained from joining in this *secret convention* I may mention that Mr. Hetherington being in the country about twelve months after this affair, learnt the following particulars regarding them. That, owing to the unwillingness of many associations to take part in it, but few delegates assembled at the place and time agreed on. Those few, however, having been tolerably well supplied with money, resolved on taking a trip over to Ireland, provided with a lass a-piece. There they stopped till the Whig Reform Bill was published, when they cooked up out of it a report or bill on the subject of reform, which they presented to their constituents as the result of their labours at the "secret convention."

Soon after I became a member of this union I was deputed, with another person, to address a public meeting at Spitalfields.   At the conclusion of the meeting a person got up and asked me my advice under the following circumstances.   He said that a friend of his (an honest sober man) had been out of work for a long time, and being exhausted from the want of food, had a few days ago dropped down in a fainting fit; in which state he was taken to the workhouse, and his wife and family compelled to follow him.   That the workhouse being over-crammed (fifteen hundred persons being in it) eight and ten persons were often placed, head to feet, in one bed; and, from the putrid and noxious atmosphere, they were dying off like rotten sheep.   That his poor friend had been separated from his wife, and the children from their mother; and that two of the children were then dying from the fever they had caught there.   That his friend had been placed in a bed with a fever patient, from which bed a person had but just been taken out dead of the fever, without even the bed-linen being changed.   The result was that his poor friend was in a state bordering on madness.   He also added that at that very time three lying-in women, with their infants, might be seen in one bed.   This appeared to me such a horrible story that I deemed it necessary to write it down in the presence of the person, and of many friends who knew him, and got him to append his signature to it; my object being to give it publicity through the press.   It so happened, however, that there was one of the police present dressed in plain clothes, whose report to his inspector caused that gentleman to inform the master of the workhouse of our proceedings, telling him that if any publicity was made by us, a mere denial of the truth of it from him would be sufficient against a few ignorant radicals.   The next morning, however, the master of the workhouse deemed it necessary to send for the person who had given me the information, and by threats and cajoling induced him to come to us with a note (which he had prepared) modifying some and denying other portions of the statement he had made the previous evening.   But it so happened that in his flurry he gave him the note which the inspector had sent to him instead of the one he had prepared; and thus were we made acquainted with the whole affair. At that period Mr. Wakley (the proprietor of the *Lancet*) was the editor of the Ballot newspaper, and generally took a warm interest in all matters of reform. On making him acquainted with the above story, he requested Mr. Cleave and myself to go with him to investigate to some extent the state of things then existing in Spitalfields. We accordingly went, and we found not only that the horrible state of the workhouse was true as described, but that the state of vast numbers out of it was even worse, for hunger and nakedness in many cases were added to the disease and wretchedness that prevailed. In whole streets that we visited we found nothing worthy of the name of bed, bedding, or furniture ; a little straw, a few shavings, a few rags in a corner formed their beds—a broken chair, stool, or old butter-barrel their seats—and a saucepan or cup or two, their only cooking and drinking utensils. Their unpaved yards, and filthy courts, and the want of drainage and cleansing, rendered their houses hotbeds of disease; so that fever combined with hunger was committing great ravages among them. In the first house we visited we met a little girl on the stairs screaming for help, saying that her father was killing himself. We hurried up and found that the poor fellow was trying to destroy himself by running a fork into his throat, and we were fortunately in time to prevent anything serious from being effected. He seemed to have been reduced to a miserable state of despondency from the want of food; and we finding that his state of health required medical assistance sent for the parish doctor. When he came he was disposed to be rather insolent towards " the radicals " until he discovered that one of them was Mr. Wakley, the editor of the *Lancet,* and the exposer of much professional incapacity, when he became exceedingly civil, and attended to the poor patient's wants very promptly. I may add that our visit to Spitalfields and the stir we made there were the means of great alterations being made in the workhouse ; more room being provided, and the poor inmates better attended to.

The members of our association, having on various occasions maintained the right of the toiling millions to some share in the Government of the country they were enriching by their labours called forth, both from the Whig and Tory press, the bitterest feelings of hostility against them. They were denounced as "destructives, revolutionists, pickpockets, and incendiaries; meditating an attack upon every possessor of property, and the uprooting of all law and order." Gibbon Wakefield and his brother also contributed in no small degree to incense the public against them by the publication of a pamphlet entitled "Householders in danger from the Populace;" in which the Rotunda Radicals and the London thieves were classed together as especial objects of dread to all householders. I cannot help thinking, however, but that my refusal to join Mr. Wakefield and Mr. Gougher in their New Zealand scheme of emigration, and my public opposition to it at Exeter Hall, as a plan calculated to place the labourers of our colonies at the mercy of a few capitalists, were the chief inducements that led to the publication of this very exciting pamphlet. Mr. Wakefield, knowing how anxious many of the co-operators were at that time for establishing communities, was very pressing on me to join him, as, from my office of secretary, I was in correspondence with a great number of them in different parts of the country. We were not, however, deterred by threats or abuse from the advocacy of what we believed to be right and just; and when the Whig project of the Reform Bill was put forth we were among the first out of doors who proclaimed its short-comings. Among other means for making known our opinions on this subject, as well as for ascertaining the opinions of others, we put forth the following declaration of our principles; it was drawn up by Mr. Watson and myself.

DECLARATION OF THE NATIONAL UNION OF THE WORKING CLASSES.

" Labour is the Source of Wealth."

" That Commonwealth is best ordered when the citizens are neither too rich nor too poor."—THALES.

" At this moment of great public excitement, it is alike

the interest of as well as the duty of every working man
to declare publicly his political sentiments, in order that
the country and Government may be generally acquainted
with the wants and grievances of this particular class—in
accordance with which we, the working classes of London,
declare :—

"1.—All property (honestly acquired) to be sacred and
inviolable.

"2.—That all men are born equally free, and have
certain natural and inalienable rights.

"3.—That all governments ought to be founded on those
rights; and all laws instituted for the *common benefit in* the protection and security of *all the people* :
and not for the particular emolument or advantage of any single man, family, or set of men."

"4.—That all hereditary distinctions of birth are unnatural, and opposed to the equal rights of man;
and therefore ought to be abolished."

"5.—That every man of the age of twenty-one years,
of sound mind, and not tainted by crime, has a
right, either by himself or his representative, to
a free voice in determining the nature of the
laws, the necessity for public contributions, the
appropriation of them, their amount, mode of
assessment, and duration.

"6.—That in order to secure the unbiassed choice of
proper persons for representatives, the mode of
voting should be *by ballot,* that intellectual fitness and moral worth, *and not property,* should
be the qualification for representatives, and that
the duration of Parliament should be but for
one year.

"7.—We declare these principles to be essential to our
protection as working men—and the only sure
guarantees for the securing to us the proceeds of
our labour—and that we will never be satisfied
with the enactment of any law or laws which
do not recognise the rights we have enumerated
in this *declaration.*

" In order to ascertain the opinion of the working classes

throughout the kingdom, as well as of all those who think with them, we hereby call a Public Meeting of the useful Classes of London to be held on the space in front of White Conduit House, on Monday, November 7th, 1831, at one o'clock precisely, for the purpose of solemnly ratifying this declaration. And we therefore particularly press upon our fellow labourers, in all parts of the country, to re-echo these principles *on the same day* in public meetings throughout the country."

Mr. Thomas Wakley, afterwards M.P. for Finsbury, having agreed to take the chair on that occasion, the declaration was printed and largely distributed. I may add that the following resolution was agreed to at the same time as our declaration :—" That as our object is just, we wish our proceedings to be peaceably conducted, and therefore, earnestly impress on every working man to conduct himself with order and propriety, and to consider himself a special constable for that day, for the purpose of enforcing peace from others if necessary." This resolution was called forth by the ferocious conduct the new police had exhibited on various occasions, a few days previously they having made an unprovoked attack upon Mr. Savage, and a number of radicals from Marylebone, on their way to the Home Office to present a petition to the King.

In the interim, previous to our public meeting, an announcement was made for the formation of the " National Political Union." The committee of our association having been informed that this new union was not disposed to go for any measure of reform beyond the Whig Reform Bill, and that its chief object was to support the Whigs in the carrying of that measure at all risks, deemed it necessary to attend the public meeting called, with the view of proposing an amendment in favour of *universal suffrage*. But Mr. Cleave and myself had no sooner entered into the Crown and Anchor (the intended place of meeting) than we were requested to go into the Committee-room, as they wanted some conversation with us. When we presented ourselves, the chairman, Mr. Place, stated that they had been informed of our intention to oppose them, and wished to know what the nature of our opposition would be. We said that that would depend on the resolutions they submitted to the meeting. These being shown to us, I made some remarks on their exclusive character, and informed them that as they were about to appeal for the support of the working classes, I should deem it my duty to move an amendment for extending the suffrage to persons of that class. Mr. Roebuck and some others who were present, were very anxious for the committee to make that a part of their resolutions, but in this desire they were in the minority. I may now add that well would it be for the middle and working classes of the present day if this just and reasonable proposition of Mr. Roebuck had been adopted—much of the strife, persecution, and sacrifice, that both have since suffered, might have been avoided, and our country be progressing in peace, prosperity, and happiness, instead of being plunged into ruinous expenses, and disgraceful sacrifices, by aristocratical insolence, ignorance, and official inaptitude.

The room at the tavern not being large enough for the numbers that attended, they adjourned the meeting to Lincoln's Inn Fields. Sir Francis Burdett was the chairman appointed. The Committee and their friends, knowing of our intention to propose an amendment, so arranged themselves that they drowned by their noise and clamour every effort that Mr. Cleave and myself made in proposing our amendment to the meeting. Mr. Wakley, however, was a little more successful, for, after various efforts to make the chairman put his amendment, it was carried that one half of the council should be working men, which was said to be the cause of Sir Francis retiring from the union in disgust : so much for his patriotism at that time.

Our proceedings in this affair, joined to the former prejudices against us, caused a *Proclamation* to be issued against our intended meeting. Special constables were sworn in — the soldiery were marched in great numbers into Islington — and orders were issued to the police to seize on every member of our committee that made his appearance at the meeting. The

Press, also, were not behind in their denunciations of us. They declared that we wanted to re-enact the Bristol riots, and that we had great numbers of pikes and arms of various kinds preparing in Whitechapel and Spitalfields. These false statements caused us to appoint a deputation to wait upon Lord Melbourne, to explain to him our conduct and intention as regarded the meeting. On being introduced to his lordship, he asked whether the parties were present who signed the printed declaration, which the Government considered highly seditious if not treasonable? Mr. Watson, and Osborn the secretary, replied that we were the parties. We were then requested to call again at three o'clock, it being then about twelve. When introduced the second time we found the minister accompanied with his brother, Mr. Lamb, and the chairs so arranged as if to form a barrier between them and us. A posse of the new police were also posted in the next room; for happening to slightly move the chair before me in speaking, the side door suddenly pushed open, enabling us to see a number of them arrayed truncheons in hand. I suppose they thought that prime ministers could not be safely trusted with men who had declared that all hereditary distinctions ought to be abolished. We informed his lordship that we wished to undeceive him as regarded our intentions in calling the public meeting which the Press had so wilfully misrepresented; that so far from entertaining any idea of disturbing the public peace we were readily disposed to aid the authorities in preserving it, having offered to be sworn in as special constables. That we had been charged with a desire to imitate the Bristol proceedings, while the fact was that our declaration was posted on the walls of London before that unfortunate affair was known or even thought of. That as regards the principles set forth in that document (which his lordship said was seditious and treasonable) we had read them in the works of many eminent men, and were not aware that the simple fact of putting them in the form of a declaration would subject us to so serious a charge. That they were, however, our opinions, and we saw no impropriety in ascertaining how far our fellow workmen agreed with us.

Mr. Watson then asked his lordship some questions as regards the intention of the Government, when he read to us the circular issued to the Magistrates, to the effect of the illegality of the meeting, and warning people against it. I replied to him that I thought it a great injustice that the middle classes should be allowed to have their unions and open-air meetings, while the working classes should be prevented from holding their meetings. The minister, however, persisted that our meeting was highly illegal, and that any person attending it would be in the act of committing high treason. Mr. Cleave wished to address him further, but his lordship, it would seem, not wishing to hear more, bade us good morning. At our committee meeting in the evening a very warm debate took place regarding the propriety of holding or postponing our public meeting. One portion of the committee were for holding it at all risks, but the majority, believing that the Government were determined by all the force at their disposal to prevent the meeting from taking place, thought it prejudicial to the cause to provoke the sacrifice that would necessarily ensue. Reason and prudence, however, at last prevailed, and an unanimous vote was ultimately agreed to for the postponement of the meeting. I may here state that while the working classes were thus prevented from giving expression to their opinions, the middle classes were devising all kinds of schemes, treasonable and seditious, for the carrying of the Reform Bill—the Whig Press was teeming with daily attacks against our aristocracy for doing all they could to frustrate the measure, and at the same time threatening them with a force of *a hundred and fifty thousand armed men* who were ready to come up from the country to support the Whigs in carrying it.

Shortly after this affair Mr. Cleave and myself had again to trouble Lord Melbourne on behalf of a number of working men at Manchester, who had been committed for trial at the Lancaster Assizes on a charge of *unlawfully assembling on a Sunday evening*. His lordship having accepted and replied to an address to the King, emanating from a meeting of the same parties on the previous

Sunday, praying that the lives of the Bristol and Nottingham rioters might be spared, it was deemed desirable that he should be summoned on the trial. He being a Cabinet Minister, this could only be done through the Crown Office, and our Union being applied to on the subject by the Radicals of Manchester, Mr. Cleave and myself were deputed to endeavour to subpœna his lordship. We accordingly made the application for the summons at the Crown Office, but it was not until a messenger had been sent off to the Home Office to apprise Lord Melbourne of our intention that we obtained it. When, therefore, we got there, Mr. Phillips, the under-secretary, refused us admission to his lordship. This afforded us an opportunity of reminding him of the bad example this was setting to the people, in not readily complying with the requirements of law and justice; and of the great want of humanity on the part of his lordship in not readily coming forward to tender his evidence when the lives and liberty of a number of poor working men were thus threatened. The result of this altercation with the under-secretary was, that he allowed us to leave the summons, promising to deliver it to the minister. When, however, the trial came on, Lord Melbourne sent a letter to the judge, admitting his having received and replied to the address the parties had sent, but requesting to be excused from personally attending on account of his official duties. Four of the poor Radicals were, however, found guilty, and sentenced to twelve months' imprisonment to Lancaster gaol *for assembling on a Sunday evening.*

In March, 1832, the Government, at the instigation of the would-be saintly Percival, ordained a general fast to be observed throughout the kingdom, for beseeching God to remove the cholera from among us. Now, most of the members of our union had seen enough in Spitalfields and other districts at that period to convince us that the ravages made by that dreadful disease were chiefly to be attributed to the want and wretchedness that prevailed there; and therefore thought that Parliament would have shown more Christian feeling if they had called upon Percival and his bigoted coadjutors to give up a portion of their annual fleecings of the public to enable a portion of those poor wretches to *feast*, instead of hypocritically acceding to a *fast*. We believed also that the causes that matured and extended that disease were greatly within the power of Government to remove; and; therefore, saw in this proposed fast an attempt on the part of rulers to father their own iniquitous neglect upon the Almighty.* We saw also that the bigots who originated and promoted the solemn mockery, were first and foremost among those whose injustice, oppression, and gross neglect had occasioned so much ignorance, poverty, and misery in the country, and consequently their concomitants of filth and disease. We resolved, therefore, from the first, that we would not comply with this piece of hypocrisy, but that we would enter into a subscription to provide the members of our union with *a good dinner on that day*; those who could afford it to provide for those who could not. This we conceived would be a better religious observance of the day than if we had selfishly feasted (as we knew many would) on salt fish with egg sauce, and other delicacies. As we were prevented by law from working on that day, we first thought of holding public meetings in different parts of London; but having consulted a barrister on the subject—now a celebrated magistrate—and finding that we should subject ourselves to the mercies of the ecclesiastical court, we resolved on taking a peaceable and orderly walk before dinner. We understood from our legal adviser that there was no law to prevent us from forming a peaceable procession through the streets at any time, provided we had no flags, nor banners, nor weapons of defence. On the morning of the fast day we accordingly assembled in Finsbury Square; the *Morning Chronicle* estimating the numbers of our union to be upwards of twenty thousand, and at least a hundred thousand persons in connection with the object of the procession. We there formed

---

* Some idea may be formed of the causes that contributed to the cholera and other diseases of that period, when I state on the authority of the medical officers of the Holborn Union, in their report, that the London cesspools, if united, would form a channel ten miles long, fifty feet wide, and six feet deep; and that they supplied to the River Thames daily 7,000 loads of poisonous filth that might have been converted into the most valuable manure.

ourselves in order four abreast, Hetherington, Watson and myself being at the head of the procession; our object being merely to take a walk through the Strand, Piccadilly and Hyde Park, and to return to our respective classes to dine, by way of Oxford Street and Holborn. But this route we were not allowed to take, for after we had walked peacefully and uninterruptedly through the City our progress through the Strand was obstructed by the new police drawn across Temple Bar armed with staves and drawn cutlasses, said by the newspaper to be " admirably adapted for fighting in a crowd." We, however, having no intention to fight (not having a walking-stick among us) turned up Chancery Lane into Holborn. Here again was another body of the police drawn across to prevent us from going up Holborn, and as we wheeled in front of them to go down towards Gray's-Inn Lane we fully expected to feel the weight of their truncheons. Thus we went on, opposed at different points in our progress, towards Hetherington's; Castle Street; and other places of meeting; till in Tottenham Court Road the police, coming down Howland Street, threw themselves across our procession. Benbow and a few others here lost all patience, and forced their way through the ranks of the police, which caused them to exercise their staves rather freely. Fearing further disturbance if we went on with the procession we drew up in the North Crescent, and there we having addressed a few words to the people on the object of the procession, they, by our advice, broke up, and retired to their respective classes to dine. It will be seen by this slight sketch that the police did all they could on that day to provoke a disturbance; they came out fully prepared, with staves and cutlasses, to have their revenge on us, and they could not forbear from openly expressing their disappointment. In the course of a few days Benbow was apprehended for taking part in this procession, and shortly after Mr. Watson and myself. My arrest took place outside the office door in Marlborough Street, having gone there to hear the case of some young men who had been taken up for practising the broad sword exercise *with wooden swords*. Bail for me was at once tendered, but the magistrate required time, he said, to make enquiries. I was accordingly locked up in a dark cell, about nine feet square, the only air admitted into it being through a small grating over the door, and in one corner of it was a pailful of filth left by the last occupants, the smell of which was almost overpowering. There was a bench fixed against the wall on which to sit down, but the walls were literally covered with water, and the place so damp and cold, even at that season of the year, that I was obliged to keep walking round and round, like a horse in an apple-mill, to keep anything like life within me. As it was, I caught a severe cold and hoarseness, from which I did not recover for some weeks. I had taken no food since my breakfast, and that which was brought me by my friends was refused to be admitted, so that I had none till about eight o'clock at night, when my friend Julian Hibbert put me a few crumbs of biscuit through the wire grating over the door. It being near the sessions we succeeded in traversing our case till the next, which took place at Clerkenwell Sessions House on the 16th of May, 1832. The indictment charged us with being "disaffected and ill-disposed persons, who with force and arms had made a great riot, tumult, and disturbance on the day stated, and with having for the space of five hours caused great terror and alarm to all the liege subjects of the King." And to show the animus of the authorities towards us, they mixed up in our indictment the case of two lads (strangers to us) said to have been detected committing some disturbance in Finsbury Square on the evening of the fast-day, while we were meeting in our classes, which the Chairman himself admitted had no reference to our case. The evidence against us was given for the most part by the police who provoked the disturbance. The three of us defended ourselves as we best could, though not without frequent interruptions from the Chairman (a Mr. Rotch, or Roach), ours being his first case after his election as chairman of the sessions. A number of witnesses voluntarily came forward to depose to our peaceful and orderly conduct during the day, among others Mr. Richard Taylor, one of the Common Council of the City of London. One of the witnesses testified to his having heard one of the directors of the police say to his men, in Tottenham Court Road, " Out with your truncheons, and fall on them and show them no quarter." Suffice to say we found an honest jury and were triumphantly acquitted, a verdict which was received with great cheering and rejoicing by a very crowded assembly both within and without the court.

This trial, however, was the cause of Mr. Watson and myself withdrawing our names from the committee of the Union, although we did not resign our membership. This was owing to Benbow's underhanded conduct in matters relating to the trial, and by him and the lawyer he employed uniting together to impose a very unjust bill upon the funds of the Union, in which acts we thought him countenanced by his re-election on the committee.

In May in the following year the unfortunate Calthorpe Street affair took place. This had its origin in a public meeting called by the Union of the Working Classes on the Calthorpe Estate, Cold Bath Fields, for taking preparatory steps respecting the calling of a National Convention. The proceedings, however, had no sooner commenced than the police made a furious onslaught upon the assembled multitude, knocking down, indiscriminately, men, women, and children, great numbers of them being very dangerously wounded. In the affray a policeman, of the name of Robert Cully, lost his life, he being stabbed by a person whom he had struck with his truncheon. On the inquest held on him, the following verdict was returned by the jury: " We find a verdict of Justifiable Homicide on these grounds—That no Riot Act was read, nor any proclamation advising the people to disperse ; that the government did not take proper precautions to prevent the meeting from assembling ; and that the conduct of the police was ferocious, brutal, and unprovoked by the people ; and we, moreover, express our anxious hope that the government will in future take better precautions to prevent the recurrence of such disgraceful transactions in the metropolis." A person of the name of George Fursey was subsequently tried at the Old Bailey, charged with the stabbing of a policeman of the name of Brook at this meeting, with intent of doing him some grievous bodily harm. He was also acquitted by the jury, amid great applause from the people assembled. Not approving of this meeting, I took no part in it, although I was nearly entrapped into it by the representations and the request of a police spy, then thought by me to be one of our warmest friends. This person for some time previously had been known to Mr. Hetherington and other radical friends from his frequent attendance at our meetings; his regular subscriptions to the Victim Fund; his constant visits to Hetherington's shop for the purchase of periodicals; and for the great zeal and interest he seemed to take in all our proceedings. He dressed well, professed himself a Republican in politics, and represented himself to belong to an aristocratic family, who had discarded him for the part he had taken in the war of South American Independence. The day previous to the Calthorpe Street meeting, I met with him at a public meeting at the Crown and Anchor. He requested me to go with him to have something to drink, as he particularly wished to have some conversation with me regarding our Working Class Union. I said that I would prefer going to a coffee house to any other place, on which he took me into the coffee room of a tavern at the bottom of Wych Street, and saying something at the bar in passing, we had two glasses of brandy and water set before us. There was only one man in the coffee room at the time, and he sat in the box behind me so that he could hear all that was said. My supposed friend began talking of the Victim Fund, and of our chances of success with " the unstamped," and finally of the intended meeting. I frankly told him that I thought it a foolish affair, as we could do more in our respective districts in favour of our objects than we could in any such convention ; and that entertaining that opinion (in conjunction with many other members of the Union) I had determined to take no part in the meeting. At this he expressed his very great regret, and said he believed it to be one of the best efforts we had yet made. But, he added, if you and others—whom he named —stand aloof from it, I fear it will be a very sorry affair

He then urged me very warmly to attend the meeting, even if I did not take part in it, and to get as many of my friends as possible to be there to give it some kind of countenance, and prevent it turning out the failure which he otherwise anticipated. He at the same time pressed me very heartily with the drink, but one glass sufficed; whilst he, having taken three or four, began to talk very lively, and to be less guarded. In replying to a question which he put to me regarding the organisation of the Union, I fancied I saw him making signs to the person in the box behind me, and this for the first time excited my suspicion respecting him; I therefore tried to change the subject of conversation, and became exceedingly cautious regarding what I said for the remainder of the evening. The next morning, however, he called at my house, and learning from my wife that I had gone to my work, he set off to find me without even asking for the address. This he seems to have previously obtained in some way, for without any enquiry he came upstairs at once in the shop where I was at work. He began making some kind of apology for having, as he thought, offended me on the previous evening, he being, he said, a little tipsy at the time. He said that his principal object in calling on me was to give me half-a-sovereign for the Victim Fund, which he had forgotten to do on the previous evening. He seemed so hearty and so earnest, and talked about the intended meeting in such a manner as to entirely remove from my mind the slight suspicion I entertained of him from the previous evening; so that I promised him to be at the meeting. On leaving, he expressed a wish that I would be there punctually by two o'clock, as he should be there to meet me. It so happened, however, that I was making a set of dining tables, and had very nearly completed them, when my employer came in to inform me that the gentleman they were for had just called at his house to request that the tables should be sent home that afternoon. He begged, therefore, that I would stop to finish them before I set off to the meeting, which I readily consented to do. My employer, being himself a radical and an earnest good man, would have gone with me to the meeting at the time specified, but for this pressing request about the tables. The finishing of them therefore caused us to be about half an hour behind the time that the meeting was called for. Before, however, we were able to set off, the news came to us of this brutal attack of the police; otherwise, in all probability we should have fared badly. For we afterwards learnt that this very plausible personage, who had tried so hard to get me to attend the meeting, figured very actively on the side of the police on that day. I need scarcely say that he never came near me again; I saw him afterwards on two occasions, but he strived to skulk away from me. In fact, it appeared very clearly that he was for years a spy upon our actions, and when needed, a decoy to induce victims to enter his masters' trap. I may here notice, that about this period *the spy system* was as rife as in the days of Sidmouth and Castlereagh; proofs of which were subsequently brought home to the Melbourne Ministry by the indefatigable William Cobbett, aided by some members of our Union. In a committee which he obtained, while he was the member for Oldham, ample proofs were afforded to prove that Popay and other police spies were employed by the government, and paid out of the secret service money. This Popay had joined different branches of our Union, and worked himself into their confidence by his activity and professions; introducing at the same time his wife into their different families, and making her a confederate in his villany. He was known to have suggested, and in many cases to have drawn up resolutions of the most violent character; and to have urged on individuals the procuring of arms of various kinds. He attended our class meetings and public meetings constantly for the purpose of reporting them to government. The following extract from Mr. Cobbett's report of the evidence that had been laid before the Select Committee, will convey some idea of the rascal. " Your Committee request the House first to cast their eyes over the ten months' deeds of this most indefatigable and unrelenting spy; to survey the circle of his exploits from the Borough Town Hall to Blackheath, and from Copenhagen House to

Finsbury Square. To behold him dancing with the wife of the man whom he had denounced in his reports, and standing on a tombstone writing down, and then reporting the words uttered over the grave of a departed reformer.* To trace him going from meeting to meeting, and from group to group, collecting matter for accusation in the night, and going regularly in the morning bearing the fruits of his perfidy to his immediate employer, to be by him conveyed to the government. To follow him into the houses of John B. Young, and of Mr. Sturges, and then see him and his wife and children relieved and fed and warmed and cherished; and then look at one of his written reports, and see him describe Young's Union Class as armed to a man, and at another, see him describe Mr Sturges as the teacher of a doctrine that 'fitted man for the worst of offences,' and see Lord Melbourne writing on the back of this report that 'it is not unimportant, and ought not to be lost sight of.' To look at him making the hearts of these honest men and kind petitioners ache, and bringing tears into their eyes by his piteous tales of poverty ; to contemplate his profound hypocrisy, his assumed melancholy and distress of mind, his affected inclination to self-destruction ; and his putting his wife forward as an auxiliary in the work of perfidy. Your Committee request the house to cast their eyes over these ten months of the life of this man and then consider whether it be possible for a government to preserve the affections of a frank and confiding people, unless it, at once, and in the most unequivocal manner, give proof of its resolution to put an end, and for ever, to a system which could have created such a monster in human shape."

The great excitement occasioned by the Trades Unions in 1834 was the cause of our National Union of the Working Classes gradually declining in numbers, and eventually of its dissolution. This vast combination of working men in different parts of the country, unitedly known as "The Consolidated National Trades Union," had its origin, I

---

* This was the speech of Thelwall over Hardy's grave, in Bunhill Fields' burying ground.

believe, in 1833. Not that this was the origin of Trades Unions in general, but of this particular one; for Unions of particular trades have existed in this country for hundreds of years, in some form or other. I think the origin of the Consolidated Union may be traced to an attempt on the part of the master manufacturers of Leicester and Derby to break up the particular Trades Unions of these towns; and the resolve on the part of other trades throughout the kingdom to frustrate their efforts. Soon after its formation, a great stimulus to its extension was found in the transportation of six poor Dorchester labourers belonging to a friendly society of agricultural labourers, having for their object the improvement of their miserable wages; their alleged offence being the taking of an oath on their admission as members. One of the most remarkable processions that perhaps ever walked through the streets of London, was got up by the Consolidated Union to present an address to the King (through Lord Melbourne) in favour of those poor labourers. The address was signed by two hundred and fifty thousand persons; the members and friends of the Trades Unions of the metropolis. About a hundred and twenty thousand persons walked in procession from Copenhagen Fields, where the Cattle Market now stands, to the Home Office, to present the address; myself being one of the number. But when the deputation, who had been appointed, took it into the Home Office, it was refused by Lord Melbourne on account of the great numbers accompanying it. Many of us radicals joined this Consolidated Union, as most of us were members of trade societies. We had also in view the inducing them, if possible, to declare in favour of Universal Suffrage, but in this we were unsuccessful; their principal object being to obtain a fair standard of wages by combination and strikes. In addition to which they had copied a great number of the forms, ceremonies, signs and fooleries of freemasonry, and I believe thought more of them, at that time, than of just principles. A number of unsuccessful strikes, however, in different parts of the country subsequently led to the breaking up of this gigantic Union.

Our co-operative store in Greville Street having been broken up in this year, I opened the same premises as a coffee house, one of the rooms being fitted up as *a conversation room*, so as to separate the talkers from the readers. I took in what at that time was considered a large supply of newspapers and periodicals, and had moreover a library attached to it of several hundred volumes. The conversation room was tolerably well attended of an evening, in which debates on various subjects were held, and classes, critical readings, and recitations carried on by the young men who attended. There was also a little society established there for a short time known as the "Social Reformers." The place however being in a back street, and I being somewhat notorious as a radical, operated very much against me ; and after struggling with it for about two years at a loss, I was obliged very reluctantly to give it up. I was told by a coffee-house keeper as soon as I opened it that I should never succeed if I continued to sell my tea and coffee genuine at the prices I adopted, the custom in the trade being to mix them with other ingredients. I persevered however in doing what I believed to be just, although I realized the truth of the prediction. But notwithstanding my want of success, I now look back upon those two years of my life with great pleasure and satisfaction, for during this period I gained a considerable amount of information, and was, I believe, the means of causing much useful knowledge to be diffused among the young men who frequented the place.

Among the number of young men that frequented it was a very clever chronometer maker, of the name of Glashan, from whom I derived a great deal of information, for he had read much and was of a scientific turn of mind. I remember going with him on one occasion to the Webb Street School of Anatomy, soon after the dissection of the celebrated Jeremy Bentham, where we saw his head on one of the shelves of the place. I remember that we were both struck with his very large perceptive faculties, but thought his head not so very large considering the vast amount of intellectual labour that he had performed. It was at my coffee house, too, that I first became acquainted with Mr. Richard Moore, a cabinet carver, and a person of considerable mental attainments. I was connected with him in several associations, and since then he has taken a very active part in getting rid of the penny stamp on newspapers; and also a leading part in most elections for the liberal members for Finsbury. It was during my residence in Greville Street too, that I became acquainted with Mazzini, who about that time opened a school, nearly opposite to us, for the instruction of the poor music boys and image boys.

In this year also (1834), our Victim Fund sustained a great loss by the death of our estimable friend Julian Hibbert, our treasurer. He was a person of extreme liberal views both in politics and religion; indeed, he used frequently to say that he could wish to practise the good found among all religions, but had no faith in any of their creeds. He belonged, I believe, to an aristocratic family; had received an excellent education, and was, I understand, a capital Greek scholar. From my intimate knowledge of him I know that he possessed a kind and generous disposition, and that he was ever foremost in helping the down trodden and oppressed without show or ostentation. Acting as treasurer, he was the chief prop of our Victim Fund for nearly four years, and during that period I was a witness of the invaluable aid he rendered in many ways to the cause of the oppressed. I have also cause for believing that for a number of years before he came among us he was the chief pecuniary supporter of the men whose labours, battles, and sufferings eventually established in this country *the right of free discussion in politics and religion*. And however persons may differ from the religious or political views of Richard Carlisle, Robert Taylor, James Watson, and the number of others who laboured and suffered with them, as far as they helped to establish the right *of all men* to honestly declare and publish their opinions regarding what they believe to be right and true on those important questions, they will merit the thanks of posterity.

CHAPTER V.

In 1836 I was appointed, at a public meeting held at the Mechanics' Institute, one of the committee for the drawing up of an Act of Parliament for the regulation of benefit societies—an act that became law in the same year, and by which a person was appointed to certify that the rules of such societies are in accordance with the Act; Tidd Pratt being the first official appointed.

About this period too, I drew up a petition to Parliament, praying that the landowners may be compelled to fulfil the conditions upon which they hold their lands; namely, by defraying the expenses of the state. The petition set forth the monstrous injustice of the land of the country—which a bountiful Creator bestowed upon all his children—being engrossed and held in possession by comparatively a few persons; and who, by virtue of an almost exclusive power of legislation, have enacted the most oppressive laws to protect what they call their property. That no agreement, however, which gives an *absolute right* in land or in things which are common to all, to any man or body of men, can be binding on those who may subsequently come into existence. The people of a country may delegate power to an individual or a body of men to use or convert certain natural productions to their purposes *conditionally* and for the benefit of all, *but the land itself cannot be given exclusively to any.* That we had found on enquiry that all the lands of this kingdom are in fact held *conditionally* of the king, as the executive of the people; for Mr. Justice Blackstone has declared in his Commentaries, book 2, cap. 7, " that no subject in England has *allodial property*, it being a received and now undeniable principle in the law that *all the lands in England are holden mediately or immediately of the king.*" We have also learnt that the conditions upon which the lands of this country are held are—that the holders do defray all the expenses of the army and navy, of the household of the king, and other expenses attendant upon the carrying on of the government and defending the country.

This petition was signed by a great number of persons, and was presented to the House of Lords by Lord King, and to the House of Commons by Mr. Cobbett.

Towards the conclusion of the unstamped warfare public opinion had so far progressed in our favour that we were enabled to get together a large and influential committee for raising subscriptions to pay off the last fines which government had imposed on Messrs. Cleave and Hetherington. Dr. Birkbeck and Francis Place were the joint treasurers of that committee, and Mr. J. Roberts and myself the secretaries. The money for paying those fines was raised in a comparatively short time, and our affairs very appropriately wound up by a public dinner given to Messrs. Cleave and Hetherington, the twin champions of the unstamped. A short time however before this an attempt was made towards the formation of " A Society for Promoting a Cheap and Honest Press," but little was done beyond the publication of an excellent address on the subject, written by Dr. J. R. Black, an American, who had previously taken an active part in the collection of Cleave's and Hetherington's fines. We found, however, that we had collected together a goodly number of active and influential working men, persons who had principally done the work of our late committee; and the question arose among us, whether we could form and maintain a union formed exclusively of this class and of such men. We were the more induced to try the experiment as the working classes had not hitherto evinced that discrimination and independent spirit in the management of their political affairs which we were desirous to see. A lord, a M.P., or an esquire was a leading requisite to secure a full attendance and attention from them on all public occasions, as well as among those who called themselves their betters. They were always looking up *to*

leadership of one description or another ; were being swayed
to and fro in opinion and action by the *idol* of their choice,
and were rent and divided when some popular breath had
blown that *idol* from its pedestal. In fact the masses, in
their political organisations, were taught to look up to
"*great men*" (or to men *professing greatness*) rather than
to great principles. We wished therefore to establish a
political school of self-instruction among them, in which
they should accustom themselves to examine great *social
and political principles*, and by their publicity and free
discussion help to form a sound and healthful public
opinion throughout the country. We had seen enough of
the contentions of leaders and battles of factions to convince
us that no sound public opinion, and consequently no just
government, could be formed in this country as long as
men's attention was constantly directed to the useless warfare of pulling down and setting up one idol of party after
another. We felt further convinced that no healthful
tone of political morality could be formed among us sufficiently powerful to resist the bribing and treating influences
of unprincipled candidates for power, so long as our fellow-
workmen continued to croak over their grievances with
maudlin brains, and to form and strengthen their appetites
for drink amid the fumes of the tap-room. The result of
our deliberations on those questions was the formation of
"The London Working Men's Association." It was first
formed at No. 14, Tavistock Street, Covent Garden, and
shortly after we took premises at No. 6, Upper North
Place, Gray's Inn Road. The objects of the Association
were the following :

"1. To draw into one bond of *unity* the *intelligent* and
influential portion of the working classes in town and
country.

"2. To seek by every legal means to place all classes of
society in possession of their equal political and social
rights.

"3. To devise every possible means, and to use every
exertion, to remove those cruel laws that prevent the free
circulation of thought through the medium of a *cheap and
honest press.*

" 4. To promote, by all available means, the education of the rising generation, and the extirpation of those systems which tend to future slavery.

" 5. To collect every kind of information appertaining to the interests of the working classes in particular and society in general, especially statistics regarding the wages of labour, the habits and condition of the labourer, and all those causes that mainly contribute to the present state of things.

" 6. To meet and communicate with each other for the purpose of digesting the information required, and to mature such plans as they believe will conduce in practice to the wellbeing of the working classes.

" 7. To publish their views and sentiments in such form and manner as shall best serve to create a moral, reflecting, yet energetic public opinion ; so as eventually to lead to a gradual improvement in the condition of the working classes, without violence or commotion.

" 8. To form a library of reference and useful information ; to maintain a place where they can associate for mental improvement, and where their brethren from the country can meet with kindred minds actuated by one great motive—that of benefiting politically, socially, and morally, the useful classes. Though the persons forming this Association will be at all times disposed to co-operate with all those who seek to promote the happiness of the multitude, yet being convinced from experience that the division of interests in the various classes, in the present state of things, is too often destructive of that union of sentiment which is essential to the prosecution of any great object, they have resolved to confine their members as far as practicable to the working classes. But as there are great differences of opinion as to where the line should be drawn which separates the working classes from the other portions of society, they leave to the Members themselves to determine whether the candidate proposed is eligible to become a Member.''*

---

* The persons who took more or less an active part in the London Working Men's Association were Messrs. Henry Hetherington, John

The spirit that actuated the members of this Association when formed, may be judged of from the following extract from their Address to Working Men's Associations :—

"It is a pleasing evidence of the progressive knowledge of those great principles of democracy which we are contending for, to find kindred minds prepared to appreciate, and noble hearts seeking their practical development in the remotest parts of the kingdom.

"But we would respectfully caution our brethren in other societies strictly to adhere to a judicious selection of their members—on this more than on any other of their exertions harmony and success will depend. Let us, friends, seek to make the principles of democracy as respectable in practice as they are just in theory, by excluding the drunken and immoral from our ranks, and in uniting in close compact with the honest, sober, moral, and thinking portion of our brethren.

"Doubtless, by such selections our numbers in many instances will be few compared with the vicious many, but these few will be more efficient for the political and social emancipation of mankind than an indiscriminate union of thousands, where the veteran drunkard contaminates by his example, and the profligate railer at abuses saps by his private conduct the cause he has espoused.

"In forming Working Men's Associations, we seek not a mere exhibition of numbers unless, indeed, they possess the attributes and character of *men!* and little worthy of the name are those who have no aspirations beyond mere sensual enjoyments ; who, forgetful of their duties as

---

Cleave, Richard Moore, James Watson, W. Lovett, Henry Vincent, Robert Hartwell, Henry Mitchell, William Hoare, George Tomey, John Rogers, John Gast, William Savage, Richard Cameron, Charles H. Neesom, Julian Harney, John Lawrence, James Lawrence, George Glashan, Wm. Cumming, John Danson, Arthur Dyson, Thomas Ireland, Thomas White, S. Calderara, Wm. Pearse, Wm. Isaacs, Wm. Dixon, James Jenkinson, Edward Thomas, John Jaffray, John Skelton, Wm. Moore, Daniel Binyon, Thomas Engall, Arthur Milner, Thomas Slater, Henry Lemon, R. Jameson, Thomas Thorne, Cowper Lacey, and others.

fathers, husbands, and brothers, muddle their understandings and drown their intellect amid the drunken revelry of the pot-house—whose profligacy makes them the ready tools and victims of corruption or slaves of unprincipled governors, who connive at their folly and smile while they forge for themselves the fetters of liberty by their love of drink.

"We doubt not that the excessive toil and misery to which the sons of labour are subject, in the absence of that knowledge and mental recreation which all just governments should seek to diffuse, are mainly instrumental in generating that intemperance, the debasing influence of which we perceive and deplore. But, friends, though we possess not the political power to begin our reformation at the source of the evil, we cannot doubt the efficacy of our exertions to check by precept and example this politically-debasing, soul-subduing vice.

"Fellow-countrymen, *when we contend for an equality of political rights*, it is not in order to lop off an unjust tax or useless pension, or to get a transfer of wealth, power, or influence, for a party; *but to be able to probe our social evils to their source, and to apply effective remedies to prevent, instead of unjust laws to punish.* We shall meet with obstacles, disappointments, and it may be with persecutions, in our pursuit; but with our united exertions and perseverance, we must and will succeed.

"And if the teachers of temperance and preachers of morality would unite like us, and direct their attention to *the source* of the evil, instead of nibbling at the effects, and seldom speaking of the cause; then, indeed, instead of splendid palaces of intemperance daily erected, as if in mockery of their exertions—built on the ruins of happy home, despairing minds, and sickened hearts—we should soon have a sober, honest, and reflecting people.

"In the pursuit, therefore, of our righteous object, it will be necessary to be prudent in our choice of members; we should also avoid by every possible means, holding our meetings at public houses; habits and associations are too often formed at those places which mar the domestic happiness, and destroy the political usefulness of the millions.

Let us, then, in the absence of means to hire a better place of meeting—meet at each others houses. Let us be punctual in our attendance, as best contributing to our union and improvement; and, as an essential requisite, seek to obtain a select library of books, choosing those at first which will best inform of our political and social rights. Let us blend, as far as our means will enable us, study with recreation, and share in any rational amusement (unassociated with the means of intoxication) calculated to soothe our anxieties and alleviate our toils.

"And, as our object is universal, so (consistent with justice) ought to be our means to compass it; and we know not of any means more efficient, than to enlist the sympathies and quicken the intellects of our wives and children to a knowledge of their rights and duties; for, as in the absence of knowledge, they are the most formidable obstacles to a man's patriotic exertions, so when imbued with it will they prove his greatest auxiliaries. Read, therefore, talk, and politically and morally instruct your wives and children; let them, as far as possible, share in your pleasures, as they must in your cares; and they will soon learn to appreciate your exertions, and be inspired with your own feelings against the enemies of their country. Thus instructed your wives will spurn, instead of prompting you to accept, the base election bribe—your sons will scorn to wear the livery of tyrants—and your daughters be doubly fortified against the thousand ills to which the children of poverty are exposed.

"Who can foretell the great political and social advantages that must accrue from the wide extension of societies of this description acting up to their principles? Imagine the honest, sober and reflecting portion of every town and village in the kingdom linked together as a band of brothers, honestly resolved to investigate all subjects connected with their interests, and to prepare their minds to combat with the errors and enemies of society—setting an example of propriety to their neighbours, and enjoying even in poverty a happy home. And in proportion as

home is made pleasant, by a cheerful and intelligent partner, by dutiful children, and by means of comfort, which
their knowledge has enabled them to snatch from the
ale-house, so are the bitters of life sweetened with
happiness.

"Think you a corrupt Government could perpetuate its
exclusive and demoralizing influence amid a people thus
united and instructed? Could a vicious aristocracy find its
servile slaves to render homage to idleness and idolatry to
the wealth too often fraudulently exacted from industry?
Could the present gambling influences of money perpetuate
the slavery of the millions, for the gains or dissipation of
the few? Could corruption sit in the judgment seat—
empty-headed importance in the senate-house—money-getting hypocrisy in the pulpit—and debauchery, fanaticism,
poverty, and crime stalk triumphantly through the land—
if the millions were educated in a knowledge of their
rights? No, no, friends; and hence the efforts of the exclusive few to keep the people ignorant and divided. Be
ours the task, then, to unite and instruct them; for be
assured the good that is to be must be begun by ourselves."

The Working Men's Association was formed on the 16th
of June, 1836. Shortly after its formation we were induced
by a gentleman of the name of J. B. Bernard to have an
interview and discussion with a deputation from the
farmers of Cambridgeshire regarding the general distress
of the country, which they attributed to the operation of
"Peel's Bill." The remedy they sought to apply being
an adjustment of the currency, so as to raise prices to
enable them to meet their engagements, or a reduction of
burthens proportionate to their means. To this raising of
prices we objected as being inimical to the interests of
working men; but quite agreed with them on the reduction of burthens. As, however, political power was
necessary to this end we urged on them the necessity of
co-operating with us for the attainment of the suffrage.
With this proposal they seemed, at the time, to concur;
but subsequently finding that we differed materially from
them in our definition of universal suffrage a split took
place between us.

To the Working Men's Association belongs the honour, I believe, of first introducing the mode of *international addresses* between the *working men* of different countries that has since been practised by other bodies so beneficially on several important occasions. Our first address of this description was issued to the Working Classes of Belgium in November, 1836. It was called forth by the persecution of a working man of Brussels, of the name of Jacob Katz; who was fined and imprisoned by the authorities for calling together a public meeting of his fellow labourers to talk over their grievances. The feeling of our address to them may be judged of by the following portion of it.

"Brothers, our enquiry has taught us that the cause of those foolish dissensions between nations lies in *the ignorance of our position in society*. Ignorance has caused us to believe that *we* were 'born to toil,' and *others* to enjoy—that we were naturally *inferior*, and should silently bow to the government of those who were pleased to call themselves *superior*; and consequently those who have governed us have done so for their own advantage, and not ours. The existence of their power depending on the ignorance, the instilled prejudice, and cupidity of the multitude, they have formed their institutions for hoodwinking and keeping them in subjection—their laws have been enacted to perpetuate their power, and administered to generate fear and submission towards self-constituted greatness, hereditary ignorance, or wealth, however unjustly acquired.

"Happily, however, for mankind, the floodgates of knowledge, which the tyrants of the world have raised to stem its torrent, are being broken down. We have tasted its refreshing stream; the mist of ignorance and delusion is past; we *perceive* the injustice practised on us, and *feel* the slavery from which we have *not yet power to free ourselves*. Our emancipation, however, will depend on the extent of this knowledge among the working-classes of all countries, on its salutary effects in causing us to perceive *our real position in society*—in causing us to feel that we, being *the producers of wealth*, have *the first claim* to its enjoyment—that as education developes the intellect and better prepares men to fulfil their respective duties in society, those who produce *the means of education* have an *equal* and *a national right to its benefits*—that as government is for the benefit of all, all have *equal rights*, according to their abilities, to fill any of its offices ; and, as the laws are said to be for the benefit of all, *all* should have a voice in their enactment. When these principles are well understood by the working-classes, the *power* which knowledge generates will soon lead to their general adoption ; and then, fellow workmen, the tyrants of the world will lose their power, hypocrisy her mask, and the deceivers of mankind their credulous disciples. We are aware that even the promulgation of these principles is fraught with difficulties and danger, opposed as they are to all existing corruptions. Many of those who compose this association have suffered imprisonment and persecution in various ways for seeking to enlighten and instruct their fellow men, but they have been rewarded in seeing the extension of their principles, and, still more, in feeling the justice of their cause.

"We hear, too, and deeply lament, that many of your countrymen have suffered incarceration for expressing sentiments repugnant to the aristocracy of Belgium. That power, friends, which is founded on injustice, fears even the whispers of truth, and *force*, the weapon of conscious weakness, has been the only reasoning of kings. We hope, however, that Jacob Katz and his brave associates are now doubly assured *of the justice of their cause* from the treatment they have experienced, and that the attempt to put down the right of free discussion will stimulate thousands in its support, and raise up a power in Belgium to frown down those enemies to truth and justice."

This was replied to by an able and eloquent "Address from the Working Men of Belgium," signed on their behalf by committees of working men at Brussels, Ghent, and Liége."* Our address, and the reply to it,

* " The Address from the London Working Men's Association to their brothers in Belguim, has produced magnificent results. In

were printed in many of the continental papers, among others by the *Journal du Peuple*, which was prosecuted by Louis Philippe's Government for having copied them, but was fortunately acquitted.

Following this address was the publication of a pamphlet by the Working Men's Association, entitled, "The Rotten House of Commons," being an Exposition of the State of the Franchise, and an Appeal to the Nation on the course to be pursued at that period. The Analysis was the work of a committee, the Appeal was drawn up by myself. A few extracts from it will serve to show its spirit:—

"Fellow Countrymen,—Have you ever enquired how far a just and economical system of government, a code of wise and just laws, and the abolition of the useless persons and appendages of State, would affect the interests of the present 658 members of the House of Commons? If you have not, begin now to enquire, and you will soon lose any hopes you may have entertained from that house as at present constituted. Nay! if you pursue your enquiries in like manner respecting the present constituents of that house, to see how far their interests are identified with yours, and how just legislation and efficient reform would deprive them of the power they have used to grind and oppress you, you would be equally hopeless of benefits from that quarter. To satisfy yourselves in this respect propose for your own judgment and reflection the following questions:—

"Is the *Landholder*, whose interests lead him to keep up his rents by unjust and exclusive laws, a fit representative for working men?

Brussels, Liége, and various other parts of Belgium, Working Men's Associations are established; they have founded two journals for the propagation of democracy, the one in French, called *Le Radical*, and the other in Flemish, entitled the *Volk Frend*, or *Folk's Friend*. In France the publication of these mutual addresses, from the Working Men of Belgium and Britain, caused a great sensation. They were republished there by the newspapers, both democratic and monarchical, the former propounding their principles as worthy of imitation, and the latter denouncing them as anarchical and damnable."—*The London Dispatch.*

"Are the whole host of *Moneymakers, Speculators,* and *Usurers,* who live on the corruptions of the system, fit representatives for the sons of labour?

"Are the immense numbers of *Lords, Earls, Marquises, Knights, Baronets, Honourables,* and *Right Honourables,* who have seats in that house, fit to represent our interests? many of whom have the certainty before them of being the *hereditary legislators* of the other house, or are the craving expectants of place or emolument; persons who cringe in the gilded circle of a court, flutter among the gaieties of the ball-room, to court the passing smile of Royalty, or whine at the Ministers of the day; and when the interests of the people are at stake in the Commons are often found the revelling debauchees of fashion, or the duelling wranglers of a gambling-house.

"Are the multitude of *Military* and *Naval Officers* in the present House of Commons, whose interest it is to support that system which secures them their pay and promotion, and whose only utility, at any time, is to direct one portion of our brethren to keep the other in subjection, fit to represent our grievances?

"Have we fit representatives in the multitude of *Barristers, Attorneys,* and *Solicitors,* most of them seeking places, and all of them having interests depending on the dissensions and corruptions of the people?—persons whose prosperity depends on the obscurity and intricacy of the laws, and who seek to perpetuate the interests of '*their order*' by rendering them so abstruse and voluminous that none but *law conjurers* like themselves shall understand them—persons whose *legal* knowledge (that is, of fraud and deception) often procures them seats in the Government, and the highest offices corruption can confer.

"Is the *Manufacturer* and *Capitalist,* whose exclusive monopoly of the combined powers of wood, iron, and steam, enables them to cause the destitution of thousands, and who have an interest in forcing labour down to the *minimum* reward, fit to represent the interests of working men?

"Is the *Master,* whose interest it is to purchase labour at the cheapest rate, a fit representative for the *Workman,* whose interest it is to get the most he can for his labour?

" Yet such is the only description of persons composing that house, and such the interests represented, to whom we, session after session, address *our humble petitions*, and whom we in our ignorant simplicity imagine will generously sacrifice their hopes and interests by beginning the great work of political and social reformation.

" Working men, inquire if this be not true, and then if you feel with us, stand apart from all projects, and refuse to be the tools of any party, who will not, as *a first and essential measure*, give to the working classes *equal political and social rights*, so that they may send their own representatives from the ranks of those who live by labour into that house, to deliberate and determine along with *all other interests*, that the interests of the labouring classes—of those who are the foundation of the social edifice—shall not be daily sacrificed to glut the extravagance of the pampered few. If you feel with us, then you will proclaim it in the workshop, preach it in your societies, publish it from town to village, from county to county, and from nation to nation, that there is no hope for the sons of toil, till those who feel with them, who sympathise with them, and whose interests are identified with theirs, have *an equal right to determine what laws shall be enacted or plans adopted for justly governing this country.*"

In February, 1837, our Association convened a public meeting at the Crown and Anchor in the Strand, for the purpose of petitioning Parliament for Universal Suffrage, no Property Qualification, Annual Parliaments, Equal Representation, the Payment of Members, and Vote by Ballot. The petition submitted for the approval of the meeting embraced most of the facts contained in the pamphlet alluded to, its prayer being a brief outline of a Bill embodying " the six points." In fact, the prayer of that petition formed the nucleus of the far-famed *People's Charter*, which may be said to have had its origin at this meeting. The public meeting was the most crowded and at the same time the most orderly one I ever attended. All our resolutions were unanimously agreed to, and our petition signed by about three thousand persons. Some further account regarding our proceedings in connection with this meeting will be given hereafter.

When Lord John Russell proposed to Parliament his infamous resolutions for the coercion of the Canadians (in 1837), proposing to destroy their right of suffrage, and to compel them to be plundered and enslaved by a few officials in the interests of England, our Association, in common with all right-thinking men, felt indignant on the subject. We accordingly called a public meeting to petition Parliament in their favour, which, in common with our own members, was addressed by Sir Wm. Molesworth, Col. Thompson, D. W. Harvey, J. T. Leader, O'Connor and others. As the petition agreed to set forth their most prominent grievances, as well as our own views, I deem it necessary to insert the whole of it, as it was drawn up by myself.

"That your petitioners are deeply impressed with the conviction that the colonial policy of England has for many centuries past been fraught with tyranny and injustice towards the mass of the people.

"That by far the greater number of our colonies have been originated by means no-ways justifiable on principles of morality; and to establish and secure which have millions of money been wasted, and millions of our brethren been doomed to an untimely end.

"That when by their sacrifices they have been secured, instead of regarding them as auxiliaries to the progress of civilization, and teaching them the most efficient means of developing their natural resources so as to promote the general welfare of humanity, we seem to have considered them as legitimate objects of our prey, or as places where the shoots and underlings of despotism might practise their oppression, shameless and regardless of consequences.

"That the history of our colonial government in the Canadas is pregnant with evils springing from such a source; and now, after years of complaints and petitioning for justice, we find your Honourable House about to stifle their supplications by as wanton and flagrant an act of despotism as that which, when imposed on the American people, aroused them to proclaim their celebrated Declaration of Independence.

"That, regarding the people of Canada as brothers in interest, we have carefully investigated into their grievances, a brief outline of which we respectfully submit to your Honourable House, in order that the working classes of England may determine how far they will sanction the outrage about to be inflicted on their Canadian brethren by your House as at present constituted, how far they will suffer a brave and oppressed people to be effectually enslaved to glut the appetites of hungry officials or the peculating delinquents of an insignificant party.

"The Canadians inform us that, though they possess an extension of the suffrage almost universal, and have representatives in the House of Assembly honestly seeking to promote the welfare and happiness of the whole people, but that these inestimable blessings are rendered nearly useless by the intolerable despotism of the Legislative and Executive Councils, whose selfish powers are continually exercised in thwarting the wants and wishes of the people

"That the Legislative Council is chosen for life by the King of England! that it is for the most part composed of Government officers, their clerks, their dependents, the clergy of the Established Church, and a few successful merchants; and that this Assembly is responsible to none but the King of England, *acting through the officials of the Colonial Office.* They complain that this is a body factiously opposed to the feelings and wants of the people; that it is the stronghold of oppression and abuses; and that all the beneficial measures of the House of Assembly are rendered useless by this irresponsible body.

"They complain also that the Executive Council, or privy-council of the Governor, being composed of the judges and Government officers, responsible only to the King (or rather the Colonial Office) have taken all the waste lands of the Colony, as well as the saleable timber found thereon, which they dispose of for the personal advantage of their members, their friends and underlings, as well as for corrupting the representation of the people, and with the unjust plea of their being the hereditary possessions of the King, deprive the Canadians of the means of improving their country or educating their children.

" They complain that their judges are not made responsible to the people, nor can they be impeached for misconduct by the House of Assembly, as English judges can by the Commons' House of Parliament; that they are only responsible to the Executive Council, *of which they themselves form a part,* and that by this irresponsibility the source of justice is poisoned, and the cases of the grossest peculation and delinquency have received the countenance and support of this body.

" They complain that notwithstanding *four-fifths* of the inhabitants are Catholics in religion, and that men of all creeds and religious opinions live harmoniously amongst them, that a Dominant Church is set up, and religious prejudices are sought to be engendered by the application of *one-seventh* of the whole land of the colony to support the clergy of the Established Church of England.

" They complain that the official party seek to foment the absurd prejudices of country and religion amongst them ; that the whole administration of Government is one of favouritism and injustice ; that the revenues of their country are employed and squandered away by persons not responsible to the people ; that they are unable to get accurate accounts of receipts or expenditure, and when delinquency is detected, are refused the power to punish, or to prevent it in future.

" And now, after bearing with these insults and oppressions for nearly half a century; after every effort to improve their country by wise and salutary laws has been frustrated by these united aristocratic powers; and after repeated applications and petitions for justice, they have almost unanimously declared that there is no hope for the adoption of wise laws and just Government, *until the Legislative Council be elected by the people—-the whole revenue placed under the control of the people—and their judges made responsible to their own Legislature, instead of to the King of England.*

" These reasonable requests having been scorned and scouted by those in power, the people of Canada have, for the last three years, refused to sanction, by the vote of their Assembly, the application of the public revenues towards paying the salaries of those official persons who continue to mar all their benevolent exertions for the public weal.

"Instead, however, of your Honourable House honestly investigating into these grievances, or conceding to those just and reasonable demands, we find you sanctioning His Majesty's ministers *in setting aside the people and their representatives altogether;* dispensing with the necessary vote, as guaranteed by their charter, and paying the salaries of those official persons in spite of the Canadian people.

"This conduct appearing to your petitioners to be highly tyrannical—involving the question of liberty for the many, or despotic rule for the few—and which injustice we feel satisfied will never be tamely submitted to by the Canadian people, especially when they have the history of the past, and the bright example of the present democracy of America to refer to, of what can be effected by a united people, when free from the mercenary grasp of aristocratic or kingly dominion. Your petitioners therefore pray your Honourable House that you will yield to the wishes of the Canadians, and allow them to elect the Legislative Council, place the revenue of their country at their disposal, and allow their judges to be made responsible to their own legislature, instead of to the King of England."

Our petition was followed up by others from different parts of the country, but the Whigs, ever too proud to listen to the supplications of the humbler classes, and seconded in all their coercive plans and base proposals by "a Reformed Parliament," carried all the measures with a high hand for the subjugation of the Canadian people. But Canada was too near America for them to bow their heads silently to such injustice; they met, and denounced the atrocious resolutions of the Whigs, from one extremity of the colony to the other. They passed resolutions declaring that as their public revenue was imposed without their control, and was about to be made a further means of oppression in the hands of their enemies, that they would diminish it as much as possible, by abstaining from the consumption of tea, tobacco, sugar, and rum, and as far as possible from all the manufactures of England. The excitement of the people was further stimulated by Governor Gosford, a pompous aristocrat, commencing a system of dismissing from the magistracy, and other offices, all persons who presumed to attend these patriotic meetings of the people. It was at this period that our Working Men's Association sent the following "Address to the Canadian people."

"Friends in the cause of freedom, brothers under oppression, and fellow-citizens living in hope—

"We have witnessed with delight the noble spirit you have evinced against the despotic ordinances and tyrant mandates of your oppressors. Inspired by the justice of your cause, you have nobly begun the glorious work of resistance; may the spirit of perseverance inspire you onwards, till the basely-concocted resolutions are withdrawn, your constitutional rights and wishes respected, or your independence secured by a charter won by your bravery!

"While freemen stand erect in the conscious pride of thinking right and acting well their honest front will ofttimes scare the tyrant from his purpose, or check his mad career; for experience has taught them that *liberty in a smock-frock is more than a match for tyranny in armour;* but if they chance to crouch submission, or yield but a hair's-breadth to his wish, their doom is fixed; for tyrants delight to crush the yielding suppliant slave.

"Onward, therefore, brothers in your struggle—you have justice on your side, and good men's aspirations that you win. Nay, we trust that the wide-spreading information of the present age has so far enlightened the minds, and expanded the sympathies of most classes of men, that even the British soldier (cut off and secluded as he is from society), on turning to the annals of atrocious deeds which mark the track of kingly despotism, and more especially those which characterised its career of cruelty against American liberty, when the savage yell, the tomahawk, and the scalping-knife were the frightful accompaniments of the bayonet, must blush for his country and his profession.

"Yes, friends, the cause of DEMOCRACY has truth and

reason on its side, and knavery and corruption are alone its enemies. To justly distribute the blessings of plenty which the sons of industry have gathered, so as to bless without satiety all mankind—to expand by the blessings of education, the divinely-mental powers of man, which tyrants seek to mar and stultify—to make straight the crooked paths of justice, and to humanize the laws—to purify the world of all the crimes which want and lust of power have nurtured—is the end and aim of the democrat; to act the reverse of this is the creed and spirit of aristocracy. Yet of this latter class are those who govern nations—men whose long career of vice too often forms a pathway to their power—who, when despotic deeds have stirred their subjects up to check their villany, declaim against ' sedition,' talk of ' designing men,' and impiously invoke the attributes of the Deity to scare them from their sacred purpose.

"It gives us great pleasure to learn, friends, that you are not so easily scared *by proclamation law*—by the decree of a junta against a whole nation. Surely you know and feel, though Governor Gosford may not, that ' A NATION NEVER CAN REBEL.' For when the liberties of a million of people are prostrated to the dust at the will of a grasping, despicable minority—when an attempt is made to destroy their representative rights, the only existing bond of allegiance, the only power through which laws can be justly enforced, is broken. Then has the time arrived when society is dissolved into its original elements, placing each man in a position freely to choose for himself those institutions which are the most consonant to his feelings, or which will best secure to him his life, labour, and possessions. If the mother country will not render *justice* to her colonies in return for their allegiance—if she will not be content with *mutual* obligations, but seek to make them the prey of military nabobs and hungry lordlings, executing their decrees with force, she must not be disappointed to find her offspring deserting her for her unnatural absurdities and monstrous cruelty.

"Your Legislative and Executive Councils, feeling the great inconvenience of submitting to your constitutional rights, have endeavoured to frown you into compliance by *British* Legislation.

" You have wisely questioned such authority, and justly branded their decrees with the infamy they deserve. They now loudly threaten you with Gosford-law of their own enactment. Should you be firm to your purpose (as we think you will), they will have recourse to diplomacy and cunning. They will amuse you with the name of Royalty, talk of your youthful Queen's affection for you, and resort to every specious art their craft can dictate—but they will carefully keep back from royal ears the wrongs they have generated—the crimes of open plunder and private peculation which have made the breach between you; they'll tell their garbled tale of 'treason and sedition,' poisoning the youthful mind to suit their purpose.

"Canadian brethren! hear us, though we be only working men;—trust not too much to princely promises when your own ears are the witnesses; less so, when oceans roll between, and interested chieftains tell the tale. Trust to your righteous cause, and honest deeds to make that cause secure.

" We have received, with considerable satisfaction, your resolutions approving of our humble exertions in your behalf—though we did but our duty in endeavouring to arouse the feelings of our fellow-men against the injustice we saw was about to be perpetrated on a distant portion of our brethren; and in this we have been successful to a degree we did not anticipate, for we have received letters of approval from considerable bodies of working men joining their feelings and sympathies with ours towards you. Do not, therefore, believe that the working millions of England have any feelings in common with your oppressors; for if they have not unitedly condemned their infamy, it is that the severity of their own misfortunes and oppressions diverts their attention from those of their neighbours. When the voice of the millions shall be heard in the senate house, when *they* shall possess power to decree justice, our colonies will cease to be regarded as nurseries for despots, where industry is robbed to pamper vice.

" We beg to congratulate you on the number of choice spirits which the injustice inflicted on your country has called into action. With such leaders to keep alive the sacred flame of freedom, and such devotedness and self-denial as you have evinced from the onset, we augur to you success.

" Hoping that you will continue to stir up the timid and cheer on the brave—to teach your children to lisp the song of freedom, and your maidens to spurn the hand of a slave—and that you may yet witness the sun of independence smiling on your rising cities, your cheerful homes, tangled forests, and frozen lakes, is the ardent wish of the members of the Working Men's Association."

This Address was widely circulated in Canada and called forth an admirable spirit-stirring reply, drawn up by the Permanent and Central Committee of the County of Montreal, and signed on their behalf by twenty persons; among them Louis Joseph Papineau, Raymond Plessis, and most of the leading members of the House of Assembly. The engrossed *parchment copy* of the reply, however, never reached us; we heard that it was destroyed when the office of the *Vindicator* newspaper was burnt down by a Tory mob.

Vain, however, were all petitions, were all efforts to check the despotic proceedings of our government towards the Canadians; and it was not till after they had been goaded into madness and revolt, that Lord Durham was sent over to do something towards healing the wounds that despotism had inflicted. What, however, the Whigs would not yield to peaceful prayers and petitions, they were subsequently obliged to concede, in order to quench the embers of rebellion, which their merciless soldiers and officials could not achieve. And now, when justice has triumphed and the people are supreme, no colony so loyal, no people so true to the mother country, as the French and English Canadians.

By this time our example in London had caused a great number of Working Men's Associations to be organised in different parts of the country; and we, being solicited from many towns for some personal aid towards the formation of others, deputed Messrs. Hetherington, Cleave, Vincent, and Hartwell, to go out at different times as missionaries for that purpose. They were eminently successful in promoting the formation of many of those societies; and did great service by their able and stirring appeals to the people in favour of our principles. It was to thank a great number of those associations for their kindness towards our missionaries that we issued our "Address to Working Men's Associations;" which has been already noticed in the early part of this chapter.

Our petition in favour of the suffrage agreed to at the Crown and Anchor, was entrusted to Mr. Roebuck for presentation to Parliament; we believing him to be one of the most staunch and resolute advocates of democratic principles in the House of Commons. He, having resolved to found a motion on it in favour of Universal Suffrage, was desirous of having the support of all those members of the House who were considered Radicals. This induced us to issue out a circular to all those we believed to be such, inviting them to meet us on the subject at the British Coffee House, in Cockspur-street, on the 31st of May, 1837. This meeting was attended by a number of our own members, and by the following members of the House of Commons:—Joseph Hume, D. O'Connell, Dr. Bowring, J. T. Leader, Col. Thompson, Benjamin Hawes, Wm. S. Crawford, and Charles Hindley. Having been appointed by our association to introduce the business, I informed them that our object in inviting them was to ascertain how far Members of Parliament were prepared to make exertions for carrying those principles into practice, which from their speeches and writings we believed most of them to entertain. I concluded some further remarks by putting to them the following questions:—In the first place, would they support the petition for Universal Suffrage, &c., which Mr. Roebuck had to present from the association? And in the second place, would they bring in and vote for a Bill embracing the principles contained in the prayer of that petition? *Mr. Hume* replied by saying that he agreed with most of the principles contained in the petition; but differed on some of the details such as annual parliaments, thinking triennial preferable; and he thought the country not prepared to carry them into practice. *Mr. O'Connell* also agreed with the principles, though not with all the details; but he doubted the policy of pressing them with the present constituencies. *Mr. B. Hawes* did not agree with all the principles of the petition, neither with annual parliaments nor Universal Suffrage; he would have to surrender up his seat if he did. *Mr. C. Hindley* agreed with all our principles, but feared the people were not sufficiently enlightened. *Dr. Bowring* also agreed with the principles of our petition, but thought we should progressively seek to carry them into practice; he thought we should begin with household suffrage. *Col. Thompson* agreed with our principles, but doubted the policy of forcing them at present. *Sharman Crawford* agreed most fully with the principles of our petition, and differed from the other hon. members as regards their fears of impracticability; he thought the way to make these principles practicable was by agitation and enquiry. *Mr. Leader* agreed with the petition, and thought some steps should be taken towards carrying the principles it contained into practice. After hearing the different speeches of which the above is a mere abstract, taken from our minutes, I replied, that it was evident enough that gentlemen thought more of their *seats* in Parliament than they did of their *principles*; for if they entertained a sincere attachment for them they would continue to advocate them at all times and in all places, with the view of creating a public opinion in their favour; and whether *in* or *out* of Parliament they would care little, provided those principles they believed essential to their country's welfare were rapidly extended. But instead of doing this we found them professing our principles on the hustings, and on other occasions out of doors, with the mere object it would seem of pleasing the multitude, but never taking any steps in Parliament to cause the principles they professed to become a practical reality. These observations, spoken rather warmly, called up Mr. O'Connell, who began a very warm and eloquent philippic against me, commencing by saying that the gentleman who has just addressed you has spoken with all the impassioned eloquence of *impracticability*, not very likely to be attended with any beneficial results. And then he continued in a strain calculated to crush me, by the mere power of words, had he been addressing an Irish audience. But he had no sooner done than he was replied to by Messrs. Cleave, Hetherington, and others, who very soon showed him how hollow all mere professions and pretensions were regarding our political rights, unaccompanied by earnest efforts for their realization. This meeting having been adjourned, on a motion by Mr. O'Connell, on the following week he brought forward a written " Plan of an Association to procure Justice for the Working Classes, by an effectual reform of the Legislature,"* which he introduced by a speech in its favour. To this I replied that the formation of a new society for this object was not necessary in England, as our own Association, as well as the various Working Men's Associations throughout the country had the same or similar objects in view as the one suggested. What was wanted was, that some steps should be taken by Members of Parliament towards the carrying of those objects into practice. With that view our Association had prepared four resolutions which I had been requested to submit for their approval or rejection, handing them at the same time to Mr. O'Connell. He having perused them for a few moments got up and proposed the first of them, which, having been seconded by Mr. Hindley, was unanimously adopted. The three others were agreed to in the same unanimous manner. The following are the resolutions :—

" 1st. That we agree to support any proposition for universal suffrage, made on the Petition emanating from the Working Men's Association, when presented to the House of Commons by Mr. Roebuck.

Proposed by Mr. D. O'Connell,
Seconded by Mr. C. Hindley.

---

* I have the original of the Plan by me.

"2nd. That we agree to support and vote for a Bill or Bills to be brought into the House of Commons, embodying the principles of universal suffrage, equal representation, free selection of representatives without reference to property, the ballot, and short parliaments of fixed duration, the limit not to exceed three years.

Moved by Mr. D. O'Connell,
Seconded by Mr. C. Hindley.

"3rd. That we agree to support and vote for a Bill or Bills to be brought into the House of Commons for such a reform in the House of Lords as shall render it responsible to the people.

Moved by Mr. D. O'Connell,
Seconded by Mr. W. Sharman Crawford.

"4th. That a Committee of twelve persons be appointed to draw up a Bill or Bills in a legal form embodying the principles agreed to, and that they be submitted to another meeting of the liberal members of parliament, and the Working Men's Association.

Moved by Mr. J. T. Leader,
Seconded by Mr. Hartwell."

The following were the persons appointed.

Messrs. D. O'Connell,
J. A. Roebuck,
J. T. Leader,
C. Hindley,
Col. Thompson,
W. S. Crawford,

Messrs. H. Hetherington,
J. Cleave,
J. Watson,
R. Moore,
W. Lovett,
H. Vincent.

After these four resolutions were agreed to we told the members present that we intended to write them out fairly on a large sheet of paper, and to go round to their and other members' houses to obtain the signatures of as many as we could get; an arrangement to which they all assented. Accordingly the next morning, Mr. Cleave and myself waited first on Mr. O'Connell, who readily signed them, and at the same time gave us a list of such of the Irish Members as he thought would also. He expressed himself highly gratified at the result of our two meetings, and said that he believed great good would result from them. Observing very jocosely to me, " By the powers, Lovett, you are right after all, for the Working Classes cannot be expected to strive for any extension of the franchise, unless they are made participators of the benefit." So far did he then seem to be in earnest, of which, I am sorry to say, I have since had occasion to express doubts.*

We then took our document round to other members, and had only got nine signatures appended to it when the King, William the Fourth, died, which put a stop to our progress, for the Parliament being dissolved in consequence, the members soon posted off to their several constituencies. We were, therefore, obliged to wait till the new Parliament was chosen, and had again assembled in town, before we could call the committee together who had been appointed to draw up the bill for the suffrage. In the interim, however, we put forth the following " Address to Reformers on the forthcoming Elections," informing them of what had been done, and what were our intentions :—

" Fellow Countrymen,—It is now nearly six years since the Reform Bill became a part of the laws of our country. To carry that measure, despite the daring advocates of corruption, the co-operation of the millions was sought for, and cheerfully and honestly given. They threw their hearts into the contest, and would have risked their lives

---

* My doubts in his sincerity, in this particular, have since been fully confirmed. On Wednesday, June 11th, 1856, I met Mr. Swain —a well known friend of Wm. Cobbett, who, in the course of conversation, informed me, that, shortly after our interview with O'Connell, Mr. Williams, the Member for Coventry, came into his shop in Fleet Street, and requested him, *in a confidential manner,* to warn the members of the Working Men's Association against O'Connell; as he had informed him, that he had signed our resolutions, and would get as many members as he could to sign them, *for the purpose of frustrating the intentions of the Working Men's Association.* I may add that we had previously heard of this conversation through Mr. Swain's foreman, who had overheard the warning given, but now the whole particulars were given me, and confirmed by the principal. Mr. Swain further said that this was the chief cause of O'Connell losing his seat for Dublin, the liberal electors being informed of this treachery.

to obtain that which they were led to believe would give *to all* the blessings of LIBERTY. Alas! their hopes were excited by promises which have not been kept, and their expectations of freedom have been bitterly disappointed in seeing the men, whom they had assisted to power, spurning their petition with contempt, and binding them down by still more slavish enactments:—at seeing the new constituency they had raised forgetting their protestations, and selfishly leaguing themselves with their oppressors. But *Liberty* has a power which watches over her destiny—the selfishness of those men who sought only their own exclusive interests has been frustrated for the want of that very enthusiasm which their ingratitude has subdued into apathy. The public voice which raised them up, by its silence alone permits their enemies to triumph over them.

"The result of this ungrateful conduct must now be apparent to every reflecting enquirer; the people, seeing both parties intent on keeping them in subjection, and equally the object of their prey, have looked with apathy on their contentions for power and plunder, waiting the events of time; and thus while *one* faction is hypocritically talking of liberty, the *other* is sparing no pains to destroy the spirit of freedom that has gone forth, and to re-establish Tory ascendancy and misrule.

"What, at this important crisis, then, is the duty of every honest reformer? Is it to allow despotism to triumph? as it inevitably will unless the slumbering energies of the millions be aroused to prevent it.

"But the people have learnt a profitable lesson from experience, and will not again be stimulated to contend for any measure which excludes them from its advantages. They now perceive that most of our oppressive laws and institutions, and the consequent ignorance and wretchedness to which they are exposed, *can be traced to one common source*—EXCLUSIVE LEGISLATION; and they therefore have their minds intently fixed *on the destruction of this great and pernicious monopoly*; being satisfied that, while the power of law-making is confined *to the few*, the exclusive interests *of the few* will be secured at the expense of the many.

"Seeing this, it will be well for their cause if honest Reformers throw their fears and scruples aside, and generously repose confidence in those who have no exclusive interests to protect, unjust privileges to secure, or monopolies to retain; but whose interest is in the peace and harmony of society, and in having a parliament selected from *the wise and good of every class*, devising the most efficient means for advancing the happiness of all.

"But it has been urged, as a plea to keep up exclusive legislation, that the people are *too ignorant* to be trusted with the elective franchise. Are Englishmen less enlightened than Americans?—and has the exercise of their political liberty proved them not to have deserved it?— Nay, in our own country, are the unrepresented *as a body* more ignorant than the present possessors of the franchise? —Can they possibly return more enemies to liberty, more self-interested legislators than are returned by the present constituency to Parliament? The ignorance of which they complain is the offspring of exclusive legislation, for the exclusive few from time immemorial have ever been intent in blocking up every avenue to knowledge. POLITICAL RIGHTS necessarily stimulate men to enquiry—give self-respect—lead them to know their duties as citizens— and, under a wise government, would be made the best corrective of vicious and intemperate habits.

"Fellow countrymen,—With these facts and convictions strongly impressed upon us, we have from the commencement of our Association diligently sought to impress on our fellow-men the necessity of contending for political power as the most certain means of redressing all their wrongs. We have shown in the addresses and publications we have put forth the utter hopelessness of their ever obtaining justice from the House of Commons as it is now constituted; and have repeatedly endeavoured to convince them that the great work of political regeneration *must begin with themselves*. We have assured them that when they shall evince such a disposition, assistance would be afforded them by all those who have their emancipation at heart. How far we were right in this latter conclusion we are about to inform you.

" It is now generally known to Reformers (because great publicity has been given to it), that a large public meeting was held at the Crown and Anchor, on the 28th of February last. At that meeting a petition was agreed to, embodying the principles of Universal Suffrage, Equal Representation, Annual Parliaments, No Property Qualification, Vote by Ballot, and Payment of Members ; and at the same time most of the Liberal members of Parliament were called upon to give it their support. We have accordingly held two meetings at the British Coffee House, Cockspur Street, with several of these gentlemen —have amicably discussed the important principles contained in that petition—and nine members of Parliament have voluntarily attached their signatures, and are pledged to the following important resolutions :—

(Here follow the Resolutions already mentioned at page 113.)

" In the course of a few weeks this Bill will be prepared and printed for circulation, under the title of ' THE PEOPLE'S CHARTER,' and will form a rallying-point for Radical Reformers ; *a standard by which to test all those who call themselves friends of the People.*

" In the recent exertions we have made, among those called the *Liberal Members of Parliament*, we regret to find that a considerable number of them (who even admit the justice of these great principles, and consider them essential to the well-being of society), timidly shrink from the performance of a most sacred duty, apprehensive of the ignorance, prejudice, or selfishness of their constituents, and are, indeed, fearful of losing their seats in Parliament. Now, to break down those narrow prejudices and lead onward the public mind, great moral courage and intellectual powers are necessary ; and if these qualities are not found among the reflecting few, *whose minds are convinced of the justice of their principles,* where can we hope to find them ? Nay ; if, on the contrary, we find them disposed to administer to the selfishness or ignorance of their constituents—to doubt publicly what they believe privately—to retard by petty measures important principles, and place greater importance on a seat in Parliament than on the enlightenment of the people, and the progress of liberty, what hopes can we have of happiness for ourselves or posterity?

"In the course of a few weeks a general election will take place, and the contest will be, whether the People or the Aristocracy shall prevail; whether such timely reforms in Church and State shall be effected as the social welfare demands, or a monopolizing faction retain their power, and perpetuate their corruptions. The time has gone by *for any go-between class* to possess efficient power to stem the evils of aristocratic sway without the aid of the millions. To obtain that aid their political rights must be conceded to them; they have recently learnt to appreciate just principles and not, as formerly, to be amused in the setting up of Whigs, Tories, or Radicals, as idols of their political salvation.

"Let those great principles, therefore, form the pledge of every candidate who presents himself on the hustings. Fellow-men! do not be led away by promises of repealing the detested Poor Law, or any of the other infamous laws which Whig and Tory have united to enact, and to laud their excellence, *unless the promise be accompanied by the pledge of Universal Suffrage, and all the other great essentials of self-government.*

"Honest electors, do not therefore shrink from the task of examining and exposing every shuffling candidate, who, from whatever pretext, seeks to perpetuate exclusive legislation. And do you, *the unrepresented,* exert your utmost powers at this momentous crisis; unitedly wait upon each candidate (for as the producers of wealth you have the first claim to his attention), tell him your own tale, convince him that you are not the ignorant destructives which knaves and sycophants would fain make him believe, 'too ignorant for freedom, seeking to mar your own happiness by destroying the means and prospects of others.'

"Fellow countrymen! we are now at the commencement of a new reign, and from the promises of youthful, unbiassed feelings, as well as from the education given to our Queen, great expectations have been generated. But 'put not your trust in princes' was said by a wise man; and, when we find those in her council whose long catalogue of bitter deeds can scarcely be paralleled in the worst days of misrule, without mistrusting *her good intentions*, we had better repose confidence in the justice of our own claims, and our united efforts to advance them, than in the hopes or promises of royalty.

"Among those appointed to prepare the bills we have alluded to, are persons of different views and various opinions on many important subjects. But when they are thus cordially prepared to co-operate with the millions, to contend for their equal rights, and to strive to place them in a situation to manage their own affairs politically and socially, the confidence and cordial support of the millions should be afforded them to carry those measures into effect. We therefore earnestly call upon you to organise and pre-pare yourselves to render them every possible assistance. *On yourselves success must depend.* You formed yourselves into societies, you met and petitioned by thousands to force a measure in which you were not included; show there-fore by similar demonstrations, that you are not unmindful of your own interests. Arouse, therefore, you the unrepre-sented millions—and you honest and true-hearted electors —and call upon your representatives to join the ranks of those who resolve to contend for a just and essential measure of reform for the whole people. Working Men's associations should be established in every town and village throughout the country, and the wise and good of every class who seek justice for the many should be en-rolled among them. The associations and unions already formed should be up and doing; they should meet legally, petition firmly, and never cease their laudable exertions till their end is accomplished. An opinion has gone forth that it is a folly to petition. Working men, do not give your enemies an argument that 'the people seek not to obtain those measures, as they fail to petition for them.' True it is that your petitions are but little regarded in the Houses of Parliament, but still we know that it is the most efficient means of creating, guiding, and ascertaining public opinion.

"We caution you not to form *branch associations*, because the Corresponding Act is still in force ; nor to correspond *privately*, but publicly through the press. We invite one or more intelligent radical reformers in every town to become *honorary* members of our association in London, which they can do, *without payment*, if recommended by some known radical, and thus they can be made acquainted with all our proceedings in a *legal* manner. We intend in a few days to give increased publicity to our rules and objects, and will shortly give you further information through the columns of those newspapers which are disposed to assist us.

"In conclusion, we urge you to organise yourselves and resolve on victory! *With Union* everything will be accomplished; *without Union* nothing!"

Copies of this Address were forwarded to all the working men's associations, radical associations, and political unions we were connected with; among others to the Birmingham Union, which, from its former prestige, we were very anxious should declare in favour of universal suffrage. We had previously sent letters and messages to this important body, and finally sent down Mr. Hetherington as a missionary to urge on them the importance of the subject; but they, considering themselves pledged to the principles of the reform bill, remained for a long time staunch to that measure. A few weeks, however, previous to our issuing the above address, Mr. Atwood had begun to talk of the reform bill being "nothing better than a witch's bantling," and of "the new set of borough-mongers being little better than the old"; and in the course of three months later, on a motion of Mr. P. H. Muntz and Mr. Douglas, they came out nobly in favour of the suffrage.

CHAPTER VI.

WHEN Queen Victoria ascended the throne our association, in common with other bodies, prepared what we believed to be a loyal and outspoken address to her. Having appointed a deputation for the purpose of presenting it, I sent the following letter to the Secretary of the Home Department :—

"Working Mens' Association,
"6, Upper North Place, Grays Inn Road.
"Sept. 1st, 1837.

"My Lord,—The Working Mens' Association of London having prepared an address to her Majesty, they are desirous of having it presented to her personally by a deputation of six persons, whom they have selected for that purpose. They have therefore requested me to ascertain from your Lordship when it will please her Majesty that they shall wait on her with the address ?

"I remain,
"Your most obedient servant,
"WM. LOVETT,
"*Secretary.*

"To the Right Hon. Lord John Russell,
"Sec. of State for the Home Department."

The answer received to this was the following :—

"Whitehall,
"Sept. 6th, 1837.

"Sir,—I am directed by Lord John Russell to inform you, in reply to your letter of the 1st inst., that the address of the Working Men's Association cannot be

resented till her Majesty holds *a levée*, when the deputa-
on must attend *in court dress*. No time for a levée is
et fixed; but it will be publicly announced in the
Gazette.

"I am, sir,
"Your obedient servant,
"F. MAULE."

To this we sent the following reply, accompanied with
the address :—

"Working Men's Association,
"6, Upper North Place,
"Grays Inn Road,
"Sept. 13th, 1837.

"My Lord,—According to your answer of the 6th inst.,
we find that we are precluded by those forms which Gothic
ignorance has imposed, and custom sanctified, from personally presenting our address; for with every respect for
those forms which make personal cleanliness and respectful
behaviour necessary qualifications to approach her Majesty,
we have neither the means nor the inclination to indulge
in such absurdities as dress-swords, coats and wigs. We
beg, therefore, to request that your lordship, in your
official capacity, will at the earliest opportunity present
our address to her Majesty, in hopes she may chance to
read the sentiments of a portion of her *working-class population*, which the necessity of appearing in court dress
excludes from her presence. We hope, my lord, that the
day is not distant when some better means will be devised
for letting the sovereign hear of the addresses and petitions of the people.

"We remain,
"Your lordship's obedient servants,
"The members of the Working Men's Association.
"(Signed) WM. LOVETT,
Secretary.

To the Right Hon. Lord John Russell,
"Secretary of State for the Home Department.

" To the Queen of the United Kingdom of Great Britain and Ireland, and its Dependencies.

" The Address of the undersigned Members of the Working Men's Association.

" Madam,—While we approach your Majesty in the spirit of plain men seeking their political and social rights, apart from mere names, forms, or useless ceremonies, we yield to none in the just fulfilment of our duties, or in the ardent wish that our country may be made to advance to the highest point of prosperity and happiness.

" The feelings which spring from this desire prompt us to call the attention of your Majesty to the present condition of the people, and to point out a course which we are fully persuaded is calculated to promote our wishes, and to produce that result which every sincere friend to mankind must earnestly anticipate.

" The country over which your Majesty has been called on to preside, has by the powers and industry of its inhabitants been made to teem with abundance, and were all its resources *wisely developed and justly distributed*, would impart ample means of happiness to *all its inhabitants*.

" But, by many monstrous anomalies springing out of the constitution of society, *the corruptions* of government, and *the defective education of mankind*, we find the bulk of the nation toiling slaves from birth till death—thousands wanting food, or subsisting on the scantiest pittance, having neither time nor means to obtain instruction, much less of cultivating the higher faculties and brightest affections, but forced by their situation to engender enmity, jealousy, and contention, and too often to become the victims of intemperance and crime.

" We find the majority of the middling classes equally the toiling, and by far too many of them the avaricious pursuers of wealth ;—often following that which eludes their grasp, or if attained, fails of imparting happiness ;—racked with the cares of business, distrust and suspicion, and often filled with apprehensions of bankruptcy and insolvency which few in the present state of things are secure from.

" And even among the exclusive few who possess the chief fruits of all this toil and anxiety; to nurture whom in idleness and pamper in luxury, all this sacrifice is made by the other classes of society, but a trifling portion can be found free from the diseases of sloth, the cares of idleness and debauchery, and of apprehensions and alarms lest the indignation of the multitude summon them to justice, despite of their wealth, powers, and possessions.

" Hence the exclusive few have ever been intent in keeping the people ignorant and deluded, and have sedulously administered to their vices, and fomented their prejudices. Hence the use of their privileges and distinctions to allure the wealthy and corrupt the innocent; hence their desire to retain within their own circle all the powers of the Legislative and Executive, all the riches of Church and State, and of place and emolument, by which they may bribe, coerce and overawe, and thus perpetuate their own despotic sway.

" To this baneful source of exclusive political power may be traced the persecutions of fanaticism, the feuds of superstition, and most of the wars and carnage which disgrace our history. To this pernicious origin may justly be attributed the unremitted toil and wretchedness of your Majesty's industrious people, together with most of the vices and crimes springing from poverty and ignorance, which, in a country blessed by nature, enriched by art, and boasting of her progress and knowledge, mock her humanity and degrade her character.

" Your Majesty must be aware that the conscientious and reflecting few have for ages past directed their energies to the removal or reformation of those social and political evils, which have produced the present distressed condition of the people, and that persecution and death have too often been the reward of their benevolent exertions to serve mankind; yet, through their labours and exertions, have the fires of intolerance been quenched and the sword of war and persecution blunted; the moral, social, and political truths they unfolded have not altogether been silenced by the axe nor stifled by the halter.

" The conscientious Reformer of the present day, equally

intent on removing all those obstacles which oppose the progress of humanity and mar the happiness man would otherwise enjoy, is met by the same *opposing interests* which characterised the former times of persecution and death ; and if they do not execute their desires as formerly, they refrain for want of power, and not for want of inclination.

" These exclusive interests, under the names of Whig and Tory, have for many years past succeeded in making Royalty a mere puppet of their will. In that name they have plundered at home and desolated abroad, and have executed their atrocious deeds, foreign and domestic. Royalty has been schooled and moulded to their purpose, and has been imbued with the spirit and tactics of both, as either party has obtained the ascendancy ; it has been the impelled or willing instrument to hide their corruptions and plead their excuses, and too often has conspired with them in defrauding and fleecing the nation.

" These factions will still endeavour to surround your Majesty, and will have recourse to every stratagem to divide you from the people ; and it will require great strength of mind and prudence to resist their influences. They will seek to inspire you with false notions of your own importance ; they will endeavour to persuade you that to be powerful you must be terrible ; they will strive to dazzle and mislead your understanding with the pomp and gaiety and false glitter of a court ; they will plead the antiquity of abuses for their continuance, and praise the veneration of absurdities, because by them they live in pride, sloth and abundance.

" But *the superstitious days of arbitrary dominion and holy errors are fast falling away* ; the chief magistrate of an enlightened people must learn to know and respect its delegated authority—and must look for power and fame to the welfare of the people, and the exertions it makes to diffuse happiness throughout the land.

" We trust that your Majesty will not permit either of the factions who live on abuses, and profit at the expense of the millions, to persuade you to any course of policy other than that of *right* and *justice*. And we respectfully submit to your Majesty, that *it is not just*, that out of a population of *twenty-five millions of people*, only *eight hundred thousand* should have the power of electing what is called the Commons' House of Parliament; since so small a number, divided as it is, subjects by far the greater portion to be *bribed* or *intimidated* by the wealthy and the powerful; but, that in accordance with justice, those who by their industry support and defend their country have *the first claim* to political rights.

"That it is a flagrant act of injustice that the affairs of a great nation should be made dependent *on two factions*; each seeking its own exclusive interest, and both opposed to the progress of knowledge and the happiness of the people.

"That it is cruel as well as unjust that our Dissenting and Catholic brethren should be compelled to support a Church from whose doctrines they dissent, and whose profligate expenditure they hold in abhorrence.

"That the injustice which the Whig and Tory factions have for a long time past inflicted on our Irish brethren has generated and perpetuated the extremes of want and wretchedness amongst them, and calls for an immediate and radical remedy.

"That the poverty and ignorance which pervade numerous districts of the kingdom justly call for investigation and immediate redress; which can only be effected by a Parliament selected from the wise and good of every class, to consult all interests, and to protect all just rights.

"To effect, however, these essential reforms your Majesty must not be persuaded to believe that a Whig or Tory administration is necessary to secure the peace and safety of your government; but you must call to your cabinet those who are disposed to render *an equality of political rights to the millions;* who earnestly desire *the progress of knowledge,* and *a just diffusion of the bounties of heaven.*

"But we entreat your Majesty that, whoever may be in your councils, you will instruct them, as a first and essential measure of reform, to prepare a Bill for extending the Right of Suffrage *to all the adult population of the kingdom;* excepting such as may be justly incapacitated by crime or defective of the light of reason; together with such other essential details as shall enable all men to exercise their political rights unmolested.

"Then will the voice of the millions be raised to bless you, their arms to defend you from factions at home or despots abroad, and then will they transmit your name to posterity, as the first to break through the trammels of courtly prejudice to render them justice."

In about a week's time from the sending of this Address to Lord John Russell we received the following letter.

"Whitehall, *Sept.* 22, 1837.

"Sir,—I am directed by Lord John Russell to inform you that he has not failed to lay before the Queen the Address of certain of ' the Working Men's Association of London ' which you transmitted to his Lordship for presentation.

"I am your obedient servant,

F. MAULE.

" Mr. William Lovett, &c."

This Address and correspondence were circulated very widely by the newspaper press of that period, and called forth praise or censure according to the politics they espoused. The policy, however, of the Secretary of State in refusing its personal presentation to the youthful Queen by a portion of her working class subjects, *unless in court dress,* was very generally condemned, even by many of those who differed from us in principle. And by many of them the free mode of presenting addresses and petitions to the chief magistrate of Republican America and Despotic Turkey was strongly contrasted with our court's pompous folly, and that with all our boasted freedom.

About this period, also, the Whig and Tory press neglected no possible opportunity of putting forth their embittered attacks, or vending their sneers against the Republican Institutions of America. The deeds of individuals, the clamours of party, or the bickerings of rival states, always afforded in their eyes conclusive proofs of the evils of Republican Government; they never once presuming to entertain the notion, that similar follies and contentions at home, told equally powerful against the evils of our own blessed Monarchial Institutions. Our Association—conceiving that they might do something to neutralize the prejudice thus sought to be engendered between the people of two countries; at least show to the Working Classes of America, that we *their working class brethren* in England entertained far different views respecting them, although not insensible to their defects—sent them the following Address.

"Citizens of the American Republic,—We address you in that spirit of fraternity which becomes working men in all the countries of the world; for, as the subjugation and misery of our class can be traced *to our ignorance and dissensions*—as the knaves and hypocrites of the world live by our follies, and the tyrants of the world are strong because we the working millions are divided—so assuredly will *the mutual instruction and united exertions* of our class in all countries rapidly advance the world's emancipation.

"In addressing you, our fellow-workmen, we are influenced by no other desires than those of mutual enquiry and brotherly friendship; and we therefore hope you will not allow our mutual enemies to influence your opinions by impugning our motives, should our sentiments not altogether accord with your own.

"We are not of that number who seek to stigmatize your institutions because there may be defects in your general or local legislation; but of those who would urge you to purify them of every blemish which mars their excellence, and keeps you from the full enjoyment of their fruits; so that the king and priest-ridden nations of the earth might witness the results of a true democracy, producing abundance to the labourer, and indigence only to the idle.

"We are anxious to express our admiration of those republican institutions which were won by the valour, and secured by the wisdom of your forefathers—men who justly proclaimed the rights of humanity without privilege, and made liberty and equality the basis of social happiness. Little did the fanatics of 'the altar and the throne' imagine when they shook their bloody crests in defiance of human rights, and by their envenomed decrees caused the sons of freedom to go forth to combat with the savage and the brute, that among the tangled recesses of your forests a secure resting-place for liberty would be found; and that among her sons a Jefferson would arise to proclaim those principles which will be revered and honoured when kingly and priestly follies are despised or forgotten.

"You have practically exhibited to the world that a throne is not a necessary appendage to a nation's greatness; that wars are not necessary, either to maintain dignity or to balance power; that liberty and property may be secure without police spies, or hirelings in armour; that the arts and sciences may flourish without the fostering of either title or privilege; that morality may survive the downfall of a state religion; and that presidents perform their duty for £4,000 a year, much better than kings or queens ever did, or ever will do, for £400,000.

"You have surmounted difficulties yet to be overcome, and climbed heights of political liberty yet to be attained by all the nations of Europe; and if you have not realized all the social and political advantages of your commanding position—nay, if you possess not the power to assist in the emancipation of others, it is high time to ask yourselves the reason, and to investigate the cause.

"Why, when your institutions are so excellently founded, when your noble race of philosophic statesmen legislated, fought, and bled, to invest you with political power, and left you as their choicest legacy the best advice to use it— why, after sixty years of freedom, have you not progressed further?

"Why are you, to so great an extent, ruled by men who speculate on your credulity and thrive by your prejudices? Why have lawyers a preponderating influence in your country?—men whose interests lie in your corruptions and dissensions, and in making intricate the plainest questions affecting your welfare? Why has so much of your fertile country been parcelled out between swindling bankers and grinding capitalists; who seek to establish (as in our own country) a monopoly in that land which nature bestowed in common to all her children? Why have so many of your cities, towns, railroads, canals, and manufactories, become the monopolized property of those 'who toil not, neither do they spin'?—while you, who raised them by your labours, are still in the position of begging leave to erect others, and to establish for them similar monopolies? Tell us also, we pray you—for you have the privilege of investigating the whole machinery of government—why the industrious pursuits of the millions are subject to be suspended, and the homes of happiness of to-day converted into those of misery on the morrow, through the instrumentality of numerous bits of paper, which the cunning few have dignified with the name of money?

" Whence also the opinionative distinctions which prevail in your schools or colleges? or why has sectarianism its undue influence among a people whose institutions are established on an equality of political and social rights? Why has education partaken more of party views and class-contracted interests, than in the desire of training up a great nation, physically, morally, and intellectually, to progress onwards in holy brotherhood, to the attainment of all the physical and mental enjoyments destined for humanity?

" With no disposition either to question your political sincerity, impugn your morality, or to upbraid you for vices you did not originate, it is with feelings of regret, brethren, that we deem it is even needed to enquire of men who for more than half a century have had the power of government in their hands, why the last and blackest remnant of kingly dominion has not been uprooted from republican America?

" Why, when she has afforded a home and an asylum for the destitute and oppressed among all nations, should oppression in her own land be legalized, and bondage tolerated? Did nature, when she cast her sunshine o'er the earth, and adapted her children to its influence, intend that her varied tints of skin should be the criterion of liberty? And shall men, whose illustrious ancestors proclaimed mankind to be brothers by nature, make an exception to degrade to the condition of slaves, human beings a shade darker than themselves?

"Surely it cannot be for the interests of the Working Classes that these prejudices should be fostered—this degrading traffic be maintained. No! no! it must be for those who shrink from honest industry, and who would equally sacrifice, to their love of gain and mischievous ambition, the happiness of either *black* or *white*. We entertain the opinion, friends, that those who seek to consign you to unremitting toil, to fraudulently monopolize your lands, to cheat you in the legislature, to swell your territory by injustice, and to keep you ignorant and divided, are the same persons who are the perpetuators and advocates of slavery.

"That they are rich and powerful, we judge from their corrupting influence; for, with few honest exceptions, that surest guarantee of liberty, *the Press*, is diverted to their purpose and subject to their power, instead of performing its sacred office in developing truth, and in extirpating the errors of mankind—and shame to their sacred calling, there are *preachers* and *teachers*, and *learned men* among you, who plead eloquently against the foibles of the poor, but shrink from exposing vice in high stations—nay, *who are even the owners of slaves, and the abettors and advocates of slavery!*

That wealth and title should command a preponderating influence where the power of government is alone vested in men of wealth (as in our own country), we can readily imagine; but that such baneful power and influence should exist for so long a period *where the franchise is vested in the millions* would be hard to be believed, if we had not been taught that *knowledge is the best auxiliary of political power.*

"We doubt not your general knowledge in the arts, sciences, and literature, commonly taught in your schools—nay, that your country has an advantage over ours, as far as the rudiments of knowledge are taught; but with all this we greatly doubt your knowledge of the *very principles on which your government is founded.* We judge from your present position and the facts before us, that, with all your general knowledge, you do not understand *the democratic principles* contained in your Charter of Independence to the extent which it becomes you to understand them.

"We have been thus candid in pointing out what we conceive to be the cause of such evils as we find you complaining of, and of others which we think it should be your duty to attend to; and, in saying this, we are not unmindful of our own degraded condition.

"But, fellow-workmen, we are now desirous of informing you of the steps we have taken to correct our own evils, which may not be altogether unprofitable or unworthy of your notice. And it will at all times afford us the highest gratification to hear of each progressive step you are making towards that consequence and happiness the producing classes ought always in justice to enjoy.

"Seeing the result of our ignorance and divisions, subjecting us to be the tools of party, the slaves of power, and the victims of our own dissipations and vices, we have resolved *to unite and mutually instruct ourselves;* and, as a means to that end we have formed ourselves into Working Men's Associations.

"We seek to generate *a moral stamina in the ranks of the millions,* and accordingly make moral conduct the test of membership; convinced, as we are, that a drunken, a dissipated, and an immoral people, will never attain to political or social greatness; that whatever may be the form of their government, they will be the slaves of their own vices, and, consequently, the fitting slaves of others.

"Feeling satisfied that true liberty, its obligations and duties, are never appreciated by the ignorant, we seek to instruct ourselves and fellows in all that regards our political and social rights. To that end we seek to establish *libraries* of the best and choicest works appertaining to man and to society. We seek to promote conversations, discussions, and public meetings among us, and thus not only make the sons of labour acquainted with their rights, but qualify them also to carry their knowledge into practice.

"We seek to make the mothers of our children fit instructors to promote our social and political advancement, by reading to and conversing with them on all subjects we may be acquainted with; and thus, by kindness and affection, to make them our equal companions in knowledge and happiness, and not, as at present, the mere domestic drudges, and ignorant slaves of our passions.

"Such are the means we are pursuing to correct our vices and attain our rights; and we would respectfully urge you to enquire whether similar means might not be more advantageously and extensively employed in your country, and whether they might not tend to place you in a position the better to enjoy the fruits of your democratic institutions. We remain, yours in the cause of human liberty,
"THE MEMBERS OF THE WORKING MEN'S ASSOCIATION."

As also one of the objects of our Association was "to promote, by all available means, the education of the rising generation, and the extirpation of those symptoms which tend to future slavery," it was to some extent incumbent upon us to put forth our views on this important subject. For, while a large portion of the hawks and owls of society were seeking to perpetuate that state of mental darkness most favourable to the securing of their prey, another portion, with more cunning, were for admitting a sufficient amount of mental glimmer to cause the multitude to walk quietly and contentedly in the paths they in their wisdom had prescribed for them. A few, indeed, had talked of education as a means of light, life, liberty, and enjoyment for the whole human family; but these were, of course, *the Utopians of the world;* men who failed to perceive that God had made one portion of mankind to rule and enjoy. and the other to toil for them, and reverentially obey them. When, however, the wide-spread poverty, the drunkenness, vices, and crimes of society were clearly traced to the absence of mental and moral light, and the necessity was shown for some comprehensive means for imparting these blessings to all men, bigotry at once commenced its ravings from every church and conventicle in the kingdom, declaring all light to be impious and godless, unless it were kindled at their particular altars. Thus, from that period to the present, have those so-called "Christians" been able to selfishly thwart, or retard every effort in favour of a wise and general system of education; and, better far, that they should continue to do so, and education depend on individual effort, than that *bigotry* under the name of *religion,* should be allowed to mar and stultify the great effort of making education the instrument of *mental freedom* and *national progress.*

The following is the Address which was issued to the working classes on the subject of education in 1837 :—

"Brethren,—At this important era of intellectual enquiry, when the moralist begins to doubt the efficacy of his precepts to counteract the torrent of pernicious example—when the *rigid* deviser of punishments has become sceptical of the efficiency of *his enactments*—and when the speculative philanthropist is urging an enquiry into the merits of *national education,* as the most efficient cure for our national evils ; we trust it will not be thought presumptuous if we—a portion of that class most in need of education—should state our ideas on the subject in common with others.

"We are the more induced to do this, as we fear that *class interests in some,* and *unfounded jealousies in others,* have their pernicious influences to prevent, or mar the unbounded good that the working millions must derive from a wise and just system of education.

"As, however, various honest opinions seem to be about equally divided between *a national* and *an individual system* of instruction, we are desirous of testing both these views by what we conceive to be *first principles,* the best criterion by which to judge all national and important questions.

"We assume then, *as a principle,* that all just governments should seek to prevent the greatest possible evil, and to promote the greatest amount of good. Now, if ignorance can be shown to be the most prolific source of evil, and knowledge the most efficient means of happiness, it is evidently the duty of Government to establish *for all classes* the best possible system of education.

"We further assume, that poverty, inequality, and political injustice, are involved in giving to one portion of society the blessings of education, and leaving the other in ignorance; and, therefore, the working classes, who are in general the victims of this system of oppression and ignorance, have just cause of complaint against *all partial* systems of education."

"Now, the annual catalogues of crimes in this country afford lamentable proofs of the great neglect of public duties. They will stand in the records of the past as black memorials against the boasted civilization and enlightened philanthropy of England, whose Legislators are famed for devising modes of punishing, and in numerous instances for fostering crime, but exhibit, year after year, presumptuous proofs of their great omission *to prevent it.* It will be said of them that they allowed the children of misery to be instructed in vice, and for minor delinquencies subjected them to severity of punishment, which matured and hardened them in crime; that, when callous to consequences, they had gone through all the gradations of wretchedness, from the common prison to the murderer's cell, that their judges gravely doomed them to die, gave them wholesome advice and the hopes of repentance; that eventually, when the fruits of their neglect and folly were exhibited on the gallows, they gave the public an opportunity of feasting their brutal appetites with the quivering pangs of maddened and injured humanity.

"Apart, then, from those benevolent feelings of our nature, which should urge us to save a human being from destruction under all circumstances—should it not stimulate us, fellow citizens, to prevent those beings from becoming the ignorant and degrading disturbers of our peace, against whom our lives and property are not secure, with all our vigilance and precaution? As parents, too, is it not our especial duty to prevent the evils of vice by the regenerating influence of knowledge, when our children may hourly suffer from pernicious example, and whose eyes and ears, with all our anxiety, we cannot shut against the brutal behaviour and foul language which ignorance engenders? Nay, how many fond parents, who have carefully trained up their offspring free from such contamination, and have sought, by the most judicious education in their power, to fortify them against the evils to which they might hereafter be exposed, have yet been compelled to witness the powerful and seductive vices which the want of intellectual and *moral training* has encouraged and made fashionable in society, blighting all their hopes and desires. There is indeed, scarcely a situation in life, as citizens, fathers, or brothers, where the pressing demands of duty should not awaken us to the dangers and consequences of ignorance, and the necessity of a more useful and extended system of education.

" But, unhappily, though the time has gone by for the selfish and bigoted possessors of wealth to confine the blessings of knowledge wholly within their own narrow circle, and by every despotic artifice to block up each cranny through which intellectual light might break out upon the multitude, yet still, so much of the selfishness of *caste* is exhibited in their fetters on the Press, in their Colleges of restriction and privilege, and in their dress and badge-proclaiming charity schools, as to convince us that they still consider education as their own prerogative, or *a boon to be sparingly conferred upon the multitude*, instead of a universal instrument for advancing the dignity of man, and for gladdening his existence. Yet the selfishness of those exclusives fails not to react upon themselves; the joint influences of the poverty and ignorance their own folly has produced, fill them with the cares of the present, and dark forebodings of the future. The modicum of mental light they have permitted, or *failed to restrain*, has been sufficient to expose their gross selfishness, but not to generate the spirit of enlightened benevolence and justice.

" Thanks, however, to those latent energies which have stimulated the few to investigation and enquiry, *that light is now diffusing itself* in spite of all the barriers of pride and power, and, we hope, is teaching all classes to perceive the importance, not merely of cultivating the arts of reading and writing, but of all those higher faculties which bountiful Nature has so universally bestowed—not to sleep in ignorance, or be diverted to vice, but, doubtless, to reciprocate and swell the amount of human enjoyment.

" Is it consistent with justice that the knowledge requisite to make a man acquainted with his rights and duties should be purposely withheld from him, and then that he should be upbraided and deprived of his rights *on the plea of his ignorance?* And is it not equally cruel and unjust to suffer human beings to be matured in ignorance and crime, *and then to blame and punish them?*

" Let our rulers ask themselves, when they see our prisons filled with victims, our land covered with paupers, and our streets infested with intemperance and prostitution, how much of those terrible evils are occasioned by ignorance, the consequence of their own neglect?—and how many of their sanguinary laws might have been spared, how many of their Prisons, Bridewells, and Hospitals dispensed with, and how many millions of public and private wealth, arrogantly given and ungraciously received, might not have been better appropriated in diffusing the blessing of education?

" We are certain that enquiry will convince them of the fact ; and will lead them to perceive, that *knowledge,* like the balmy breeze, cheers and refreshes in its progress, but *ignorance,* like the tainted air, scourges with disease as it sweeps onwards in its desolation.

" We trust we have, in some degree, succeeded in showing the great importance of education, and the necessity *of publicly extending it;* not as a charity, BUT AS A RIGHT, a right derivable from society itself. As society implies a union for *mutual benefit,* and consequently to *publicly* provide for the security and proper training of all its members, which if it fails to effect, the bond of social obligation is dissolved, and it degenerates into an unholy compact, selfishly seeking its own advantage, to the prejudice of the excluded.

" Independent of which, *charity,* by diminishing the

energies of self-dependence, creates a spirit of hypocrisy and servility all just governments should seek to prevent. We contend, therefore, that it is the duty of the Government to provide the means of educating the whole nation; for as the whole people are benefited by each individual's laudable exertions, so *all* ought to be united in affording the best means of developing the useful powers of *each.**

"But how, it may be asked, are the means to be provided? We may reply, by asking how were the means provided for less worthy purposes? We remember that twenty millions were paid to compensate the owners of slaves for relinquishing their unjust traffic. That the means were provided for paying extravagant pensions, and for erecting useless palaces for royalty; and are still found to support an almost interminable list of idlers from year to year. Whence, too, we may enquire, came our means to war against freedom wherever it raised its head, and to assist all the despots in Europe to keep their people in ignorance and slavery? Were but half the anxiety evinced to train the human race in peace and happiness, as has hitherto been exerted to keep them in subjection to a few despots, abundant means would be afforded for the purpose.

"But though we hold it to be the duty of Government to

---

* If additional reasons are needed to prove that education ought to be *free to all our people*, and *free also from religious squabbles*, they are afforded by the contests continually taking place over the miserable abortion of Mr. Forster and his clerical allies. A measure which has intensified religious feuds, and created religious antagonism in almost every village in the kingdom; the ruling sects in each, either trying to prevent the establishing of School Boards, or if established to obtain the mastery in them. It has been a subject of constant dispute, because of *religious teaching*, and has engendered great bitterness among the poorest of our population who, with large families and scanty means, *cannot afford the school fees,* low as they may be. Why, then, should we not have *free schools* for our people, and free also from religious teaching, so that all may labour harmoniously in the great work. The advantages of free, or very cheap education, is seen in America, in Scotland, and other places. This, given to the people of Scotland, has opened up to the poorest of them means of living and thriving in various parts of the world, which the uneducated of Ireland and England do not possess; and this defective state of education we owe to religious conflict, to selfish cliques, and to the want of a wise and just code.

raise the means of education, by taxation or otherwise; to see it properly apportioned in the erecting of suitable and sufficient schools, and for superintending them so far as to see the original intention of the people carried into effect, we are decidedly opposed to the placing such immense power and influence in the hands of Government as that of selecting the teachers and superintendents, the books and kinds of instruction, and the whole management of schools in each locality. While we want a uniform and just system of education, we must guard against the influence of irresponsible power and public corruption. We are opposed, therefore, to all concentration of power beyond that which is absolutely necessary to make and execute the laws; for, independent of its liability to be corrupt, it destroys those local energies, experiments, and improvements so desirable to be fostered for the advancement of knowledge, and prostrates the whole nation before one uniform, and, it may be, a power of, despotism. We perceive the results of this concentration of power and uniformity of system lamentably exemplified in Prussia and other parts of the continent, where the lynx-eyed satellites of power carefully watch over the first indications of intelligence, to turn it to their advantage, and to crush in embryo the buddings of freedom.

"We think, therefore, that the selection of teachers, the choice of books, and the whole management and superintendence of schools in each locality should be confined to a SCHOOL COMMITTEE of twenty or more persons, elected by *universal suffrage* of all the adult population, male and female. And to prevent local prejudices or party feuds from being prejudicial in the choice, the district for selecting the committee should be extended beyond the locality they should be called on to superintend. They should wholly, or in part, be elected annually; should give a public report of their proceedings, and an account of the money received and expended every six months, and be responsible at all times to the majority of their constituents.

"We conceive that the *erection of Schools and Colleges should be at the expense of the nation,* and that the numerous endowments and charitable bequests given for the purposes of education would be justly devoted towards that object, as well as other lucrative branches of public revenue. That the whole application and management of them should be confined to a COMMITTEE OF PUBLIC INSTRUCTION, of twelve persons, selected by Parliament every three years. They should report annually, they should be responsible for all monies received and expended, and for the due fulfilment of all their duties, which duties should be publicly defined to them from time to time by Acts of Parliament.

" We think also that *the whole expenses of conducting and keeping those schools in proper condition* should be provided for by *an annual rate*, to be levied by the School Committees in local districts ; these districts to be divided, so as to embrace as nearly as possible an equal number of inhabitants, in order that all localities may share as equally as possible in the expenses and the advantages.

" In order to provide competent and efficient teachers for those schools, NORMAL OR TEACHERS' SCHOOLS should be established in different districts throughout the country, in which gratuitous instruction should be afforded to a competent number of persons, who by their dispositions and abilities were fitting, and might wish, to become teachers. Those schools should be managed and conducted by competent professors of every useful branch of art and science, who should be responsible to the local committees, and to the Committee of Public Instruction for the time being. No teacher should be permitted to teach in any school who had not properly qualified himself in a Normal School, and could produce a certificate to that effect. We think that one of the most essential things to be observed in the education of those teachers, is to qualify them *in the art of simplifying knowledge*, of imparting it with effect, and kindness of disposition. Beyond these, we think there should be four different descriptions of schools :—

" 1st. INFANT SCHOOLS, for children from three to six years old.

" 2nd. PREPARATORY SCHOOLS, for children from six to nine.

" 3rd. HIGH SCHOOLS, for children from nine to twelve.

" 4th. FINISHING SCHOOLS, or COLLEGES, for all above

twelve, who might choose to devote their time to acquire all the higher branches of knowledge.

"A sufficient number of all those schools, for both sexes, ought to be judiciously erected, to suit the convenience of each locality. *The general training in all* ought to embrace the harmonions development of the physical, moral, and intellectual powers of each child; to best preserve him in strength, morality, and intellect, so as to enable him to enjoy his own existence, and to render the greatest amount of benefit to others.

"THE INFANT SCHOOLS should be open *to all* children between the ages of three and six; *cleanliness and punctual attendance* should be scrupulously insisted upon, as the best means of amalgamating of class distinctions, and preserving the children from corrupting influences. We think the first object of the teachers should be, to place the children in accordance with the laws of their organization. And it is, doubtless, in opposition to those laws, to confine them in close atmospheres, drilled to sit in one posture for hours, and to have their little feelings operated upon by the fears of the rod, of confinement, and of all the numerous follies at present practised to compel submission. The air and exercise of the playground and garden are the first essentials at this early stage, where their teachers should as carefully watch over them as in the schoolroom, and, when all their faculties are in full activity, infuse those principles of action, justice, and kindness necessary to form their character, which at that age will be more impressive than book instruction. They should be taught a knowledge of *things* as well as of *words*, and have their properties and uses impressed on their senses by the exhibition and explanation of objects. Principles *of morality* should not be merely repeated by rote, but *the why and wherefore* familiarly explained to them. Without dwelling on minute details, such we conceive should be the general outline of Infant Education.

"The next step should be THE PREPARATORY SCHOOLS for children between the ages of six and nine. In these, as in the infant schools, habits of regularity and cleanliness should be enforced. They should, as best fitting to their physical development, have sufficient time for healthful exercise and recreation. They should be carefully taught the *laws of their organization*, and the evils of infringing them—as forming the most important lessons to inculcate temperance in eating and drinking, and in all their physical enjoyments. They should be equally taught the evils that are certain to arise to themselves and society from the infringement of *the moral laws of their nature*. It should be the duty of their teachers familiarly to acquaint them with the *social* and *political* relations that exist between them and their fellow-beings. They should be taught by the most simple explanations and experiments to perceive and discover the use, property, and relationship of every object within their own locality, and learn to express in writing, and in correct language, the ideas they have received. The use and principles of arithmetic should be taught them by the most simple methods. They should be taught to understand the principles and practice of music, a gratification and a solace even in the hut of poverty. Their imagination should be sedulously cultivated by directing their attention to everything lovely, grand, or stupendous around them; as affording a wholesome stimulus to greatness of mind, and as powerful antidotes against the grovelling vices so prevalent in society. In fact, the end and object of their teachers should be the equal and judicious development of all their faculties, and not the mere cultivation of the intellect.

"The High Schools, as the name implies, should be for the still higher development of all those principles taught in the preparatory schools. In addition to which, the children should be taught a more extensive acquaintance with the topography, resources, pursuits, and habits of the country they live in, and with the physical and natural phenomena of the globe they inhabit. They should be instructed in the principles of Chemistry, and its general application to the arts, trades, and pursuits they might hereafter be engaged in; also the principles of design, and its general utility in all their avocations. They should possess a general knowledge of Geology and Mineralogy, and their most useful application; also of Social Science, of

Physiology, and the laws of health, and the outlines of such other sciences as may be found useful. With the variation required for male and female, they should be taught the first principles of the most useful trades and occupations, by having workshops, tools, &c., attached to every such school. In addition to which a portion of land, where practicable, should be also attached, on which they should practically be taught a general knowledge of Agriculture and Gardening. In fact, they should here be fully educated to love knowledge and morality for their own sakes, and prepared to go out into active life with sound practical information to direct them, and a moral stamina to withstand its numerous temptations.

" THE COLLEGES, in our opinion, should be gratuitously opened for all those who choose to cultivate the highest branches of knowledge. We think that an intimate acquaintance with all known facts would be a valuable addition to antiquated lore, and greatly superior to the mystical absurdities at present cultivated more from vanity than for utility. That the acquisition of the living languages should also be preferred to the dead; not that we advocate the neglect of the latter, but in order to promote a more intimate acquaintance with the inhabitants and literature of other countries, and thus help to break down those national prejudices which the tyrants of the world are too prone to take the advantage of in fomenting the evils of war and all its terrific consequences. We think further, that the education at these colleges should comprise a knowledge of all the higher branches of the Mathematics, Chemistry, Geology, Mineralogy, Agriculture, Botany, Architecture (Civil and Naval), Natural Philosophy, the Science of Government, Political Economy, and every other science fitted to the capacity of the scholars.

" In furtherance also of the great object of education, we think those schools, should be open every evening, to enable all *the adult population* who choose to avail themselves of the benefits of mutual instruction societies, singing, lectures, or any other rational pursuits or amusements, unassociated with the means of intoxication and vice, that they wish to indulge in.

" Such we conceive to be the outline of a system of education necessary to be established for extirpating the ignorance and immorality that prevail, and for training up our people to be politically free, morally honest, and intellectually great.

" On the subject of corporal punishments, it may be necessary for us to express our opinion. We think them highly mischievous at all times, and in every form. They call forth and strengthen the most revengeful propensities in some, and cow the timid minds of others into slavish subjection. Reason may direct the intellect to see impropriety of conduct, and kindness subdue the feelings of anger, but harsh blows and injudicious privations only strengthen a harsh disposition.

" Taking also into account the numerous religious sects and political parties that exist in our country, to many of whom we are highly indebted for our present mental and moral improvement, we think no particular forms of religion should be taught in the schools. We conceive that no particular doctrine can be safely determined on without just cause of complaint to some who might, notwithstanding, insist upon and urge its great importance when otherwise taught. No particular creed or form of religion can be *justly* adopted* ; those who would impose them in the

---

* Mr. Spurgeon—the popular preacher—in once addressing an audience on the subject of Education, spoke of a wonderful bottle belonging to his grandmother, which had a large apple within it, and which had often excited his childish wonder as to how so large an apple could enter the small neck of the bottle. As he grew older, however, he found out that his grandmother must have put the bottle over the apple when it was very small, so that it grew to its large size within the bottle. Hence he urged the necessity of putting children within the religious bottle when very young, and for rearing them up in the bottle, a course which his audience very generally approved of. But when we have so many kinds of religious bottles in society, into which the proprietors of each all want to cram as many of the young and unreflecting as they can, and to rear them up in their own creed, and their own notions of religion, it would be well to ask Mr. Spurgeon and his disciples how they would like their own children to be crammed into the Catholic bottle, the Church bottle, or any other of their opponents' bottles ? As they would doubtlessly object to this, how much better would it be to defer all those kinds of religious notions till the child had acquired strength of mind to judge for itself.

public schools *upon the children of parents of all denominations*, have profited little, we think, from the advice of Him who associated with publicans and sinners, who said he was 'no respecter of persons,' who cautioned his disciples to 'love one another,' and to 'do unto all men as they would that others should do unto them.' Surely when abundant time can be found for imparting religious instruction beyond that dedicated to the purposes of the school, and when so many religious instructors of all denominations can be found most willing to impart their peculiar opinions, it would seem to be more in accordance with those precepts of Christ, mutually to unite in morally educating our children, *to dwell in peace and union*, which are the great essentials of religion, than by our selfish desires and sectarian jealousies, suffer ignorance, vice and disunion to prevail.

" We submit these views and opinions in the spirit of brotherhood, hoping you will investigate the subject and judge for yourselves."

CHAPTER VII.

In the general election, consequent on the death of the King, the Liberal cause sustained a loss, for a season, in the defeat of Messrs. Roebuck, Colonel Thompson, Ewart, and Sharman Crawford. The defeat of the two first was, I believe, occasioned by their freedom of opinion in opposition to some of their sabbatarian constituents; and of the others by the Whigs and Tories uniting their influence against them. In furtherance of the cause of Radicalism, we deemed it necessary to entertain those friends of the people, by giving them a public dinner at White Conduit House; at which all the other Radical Members of the House of Commons were invited, and most of them attended; among others Mr. D. O'Connell, whose invitation, it would seem, gave great offence to Mr. Fergus O'Connor, a gentleman whose subsequent career proved so injurious to the Radical cause. The first time we heard of Mr. Fergus O'Connor in London was, I believe, at a meeting at Cockspur Street Tavern, where he avowed himself a follower and supporter of the great agitator of Ireland; in fact, he then regarded himself as one of O'Connell's tail. Shortly after this, I have been given to understand, some electioneering matters gave rise to a quarrel between them; when O'Connor came over to reside in London, and began to attend our radical meetings. Soon after his quarrel Mr. Hetherington, myself, and some other radical friends, believing him, at first, to have been unjustly treated by Mr. O'Connell, called a public meeting at Theobald's Road, to express an opinion on the subject. A great number of Mr. O'Connell's friends attended on that occasion, and gave their version of the subject, so that we were all but outvoted on the resolution proposed; and, although Mr. O'Connor was in the gallery at the time, he left us to fight his battle as we best could.

In December of this year, the Birmingham Political Union having put forth an admirable address to the Reformers of Great Britain and Ireland in favour of the suffrage, our Association replied to it as follows :—

"Fellow-countrymen,—We have read with delight the noble declaration of principles you have put forth in your address to the reformers. Your determination to firmly contend for those great principles of liberty, Universal Suffrage, the Ballot, and short and certain parliaments, entitle you not only to our cordial approbation and generous confidence, but also of all other similar Associations of Working Men.

"We would merely direct your attention to what we feel satisfied was not an intentional omission in your address, we mean the abolition of Property Qualifications for Members of Parliament; without which men of wealth must be universally selected, instead of men of honesty and talent.

"On reading your excellent introductory observations, we felt that if there were any just cause for regret, it was that you, the men of Birmingham, who in 1832 stood among the foremost ranks of reformers, who by your daring front drove the Tory minions from power, have so long and patiently been silent with the hypocritical, conniving, and liberty-undermining Whigs—have silently suffered them to pursue their treacheries and persecutions, foreign and domestic; to equally undermine the freedom of labour, the rights of man, and the liberty of nations.

"We accept however, with confidence, your honest explanation. You gave them credit for virtues and intentions as remote from Whiggery as honesty of purpose is from Toryism. We cordially join therefore with you, in calling upon our brethren in all parts of the kingdom to make *another enthusiastic effort for freedom;* to re-organise their Political Unions, and form themselves into Working Men's Associations, in every district, town, and parish in the country; and never to cease their agitation, nor rest satis-

fied till they have established our representative system
upon a just and equitable basis.

"Uniting upon the broad principle of universal right, we
shall have the confidence and support of all good men
with us. The exclusive few alone, who seek for selfish
power and benefits, will stand apart till the diffusion of
knowledge shall have taught them correct principles of
truth and justice.

"We all think with you, that the cause of England and
Ireland is one; and that our representatives are wanting,
either in judgment or honesty, who under the plea of
'*justice*' to our country, will maintain by their influence
persons in office who have declared against the further
progress of reform, and consequently of liberty in both.

"*Justice*, therefore, we say equally for Whig and Tory
They are equally opposed to the rights of the people
(they differ only in their policy), and every man who is the
advocate of those rights ought never to hesitate in driving
and keeping both factions from office. Let not the Tories
therefore believe that the old game of *ins* and *outs* is continually to be played for their especial advantage. The
time has arrived when no set of men can long retain office
who refuse to progress with the intelligence of the age,
and to accord justice to the millions.

"The absurd notion entertained by the *Court* must yield
to the dictates of reason found without its precincts—that
there is no necessity for the the Tories coming into office,
for the want of more efficient persons to fill it than the
Whigs.

"With every respect for the judgment of Her Majesty,
we think a cabinet could be selected of neither Whig nor
Tory principles, yet possessing greater talent than have
hitherto been found in the councils of Royalty—men disposed to the carrying forward of such measures of Reform
as will give equal political rights and equal means of instruction to all the people, and consequently to afford the
only efficient means by which our country shall progress
in liberty, knowledge and happiness.

"But in order to enable any set of men to progress in
favour of liberty, against the corrupting influences that

exist to oppose it, the people must be united to support them; and as power has a corrupting influence, the people must carefully watch over and remind them of their duty. If the people will do this, their cause will succeed to the extent of their desires; but if they are indifferent to their rights, their enemies will enslave and eventually triumph over them. Strong in the hopes that our brethren will respond to your call for union, we remain &c., &c."

In the commencement of the following year (1838) our Association having heard of still further excesses committed by the officials of Canada, under the sanction and authority of our Whig Government, presented another petition to the House of Commons, praying them to impeach the ministers for high crimes and misdemeanours. This petition was drawn up by Mr. Hetherington, and contained a reiteration of the grievances to which the Canadians were subjected. But as the House of Commons had previously sanctioned the Whigs in their wrongdoings against Canada, our prayer for impeachment was very much like appealing to culprits for a judgment against themselves.

Our Association, about this period, having received a great number of addresses and communications from different bodies, among others from the Polish emigrants, thought it a suitable opportunity for putting forth their views on European politics. These were embodied in the following "Address to the Working Classes of Europe, and especially to the Polish people:"—

"Brethren,—In reply to the Polish Democrats who have recently addressed us, we beg it might be understood, not only by them, but by the working classes of Europe, that while we are zealously labouring to diffuse a knowledge of true principles among our own brethren, we are not unmindful of that great principle of democracy that 'all mankind are brothers.' And though the perversion of truth and justice has called forth the exclusive feelings of the few, to conspire and rebel against the happiness of the many; yet, when knowledge shall have expanded the intellect of mankind, they will assuredly perceive that all the nations of the earth have in reality *but one brotherly interest.*

" Possessing this conviction, we feel persuaded that every effort that can be made towards eradicating those national prejudices and bigoted feelings which the selfish and despotic rulers of mankind have implanted and perpetuated for their own advantage, will tend towards that great consummation of national and universal happiness, when equality of rights shall be established, and when '*men shall love one another.*'

" And we know no better means of effecting this righteous object, than by availing ourselves of those great rights and privileges of humanity our countrymen have achieved through persecution and death, and which your oppressors have unjustly deprived you of, or prevented you from obtaining—we mean the right of investigating and enquiring, through the means of *public meetings, open discussions,* and *the press* (stamped and trammelled as it is), which is the most desirable form of government—the best mode of instructing the people—the most economical mode of producing wealth, and the best means of its just distribution—and of causing all the corruptions and anomalies of church, state, and individuals to pass in review before the great tribunal of public opinion, from which all power should emanate, and to which alone it should be responsible.

" True it is that the friends of freedom throughout the continent have just cause to remember with feelings of execration the base conduct of the Government of England, in secretly undermining, or openly opposing every attempt they have made to check the inroads of despotism, or to advance the cause of democracy. But it should be remembered that the same rampant spirit of aristocracy, which, by a corrupt legislative assembly, a hypocritical money-loving priesthood, and a standing army of soldiers, placemen, pensioners, and expectants, keep the working millions in ignorance and subjection, have been, and still continue to be, *the persecutors of liberty throughout the world,* and not the reflecting portion of the people of England.

" But, brethren, we think we have discovered the great

secret of their power : it is *our own ignorance of society and of government—our prejudices, our disunion, and distrust—* and we feel that our enlightenment, union, and confidence will best dissolve this unholy compact of despotism.

" Fellow-workmen, have you ever asked yourselves by what powerful spell the productive millions of Europe are held in subjection to a puny insignificant number of human beings ?   If you have not, begin now to enquire ; and we think that reflection will convince you, that *the people themselves have raised up and continue to support those few idols of wealth and power, which constitute at once their fear and adoration.*   The foolish aspirations after power, the lust of riches, and *the servile fear* diffused throughout society, prepare mankind for *the concentration of their own feelings,* in the power, pomp, and pageantry of a crown.

" Who, instead of questioning the choice, and fitness for office, are the first to bow before the antiquated name of royalty—to admire the splendid show and littleness of folly—to swell the slavish train of flatterers, who by their cringing make and mould the tyrant ?—who but the giddy unreflecting people ?

" By whose labours are the citadels and fortifications of despotism erected, and all the waste and profligacy of courts and camps upheld ?—The people's, who glory in the means which keep them slaves.   Where, but from the ranks of labour, have the despots of Europe raised their fighting slaves to keep their brother slaves in awe ? Who, but the people themselves, form the warlike phalanx round their tyrants' thrones, and glory in the privilege to wear their slavish trappings, and at some minion's bidding drench the land with blood ?

" Who, but the people, toil from birth till death, and thousands pine in misery—to support these idle few in all their oppressions and debaucheries, and think it just to do so ?—nay ! bow before the hireling priest who impiously declares *that God has ordained it !*

" Democrats of Europe—you who aspire to place liberty upon the throne of justice—to establish the laws on the basis of equality—and to awaken the dormant faculties of mind to appreciate the social and political happiness of our race—be assured, that though the power of despotism can check the progress of knowledge, it is *the ignorance of our brethren* which generates and fosters the despot.

"What thousand ineffectual efforts of freedom have been crushed by ignorance! How many millions of generous hearts, panting for liberty, have been sacrificed by the allied despots of Europe, backed up as they have ever been by the ignorance and fanaticism of the millions? When young freedom first broke her bonds of servility in France, and proclaimed the eternal rights of humanity, how few of her enthusiastic sons could appreciate the blessing! When, in noble daring, she stretched forth her hand to emancipate Italy, to enfranchise Germany, and to raise up Switzerland from her political lethargy, what were the powers that paralysed her generosity? The ignorance and prejudices of the masses, subjecting them to be the slaves of priests and nobles, and blind instruments of the wealth and title-hunting minions of despotism. The 'altar and the throne' formed the magic spell by which European despots kindled the flame of loyal fanaticism, and the blind confidence reposed in an ambitious chieftain, rivetted anew the chains of kingcraft and priestcraft. The subsequent struggles for freedom have again been fruitless of benefits to those who bled to effect it; the courageous few who broke the dominion of legitimacy in France, and who sought to establish *equal rights for all,* were constrained by the prejudices of the many in favour of royalty to set up the idol of wealth on the ruins of privilege.

"The strange infatuation and foolish fears which cause the present electors of France to support a soulless tyrant in power, who, despite of oaths and protestations, has sacrificed one by one the liberties of their country, and now mocks them with his boasted alliances with despots, afford another presumptuous proof that principles are sacrificed by ignorance, or that conviction of mind has not yet engendered determination of purpose to expel such a perfidious tyrant from their soil.

"The brave Belgians, touched by the electric spark

excited by the heroes of July, united in subduing one species of despotism to fall the disunited victims of another. Their foreign king, by exciting national prejudices against Dutchmen, by a corrupt press, and a system of German espionage, has succeeded in nullifying their revolution, and in keeping back the tide of political improvement— the work he was set by Whigs and Tories to perform.

"In turning to Poland, the land of Kosciusko, what, let us enquire, was the curse that withered the principles of her ancient liberty, and hastened her downfall? It was the curse of privilege. It was the prejudice of caste, the offspring of ignorance, the source of political and social degradation, that paralysed the enthusiasm of the generous few who sought to free their country. For it should be remembered that the nobility of Poland, by diplomacy, intrigue, and domestic despotism, were the immediate or accelerating cause of her subjugation. Taking advantage of national prejudices, by holding the millions as property inseparable from their soil, they destroyed the only effective energies that could resist the desolating progress of Russian barbarity.

"When the news of her recent struggle called forth the sympathy of every friend to freedom, what was the reason assistance was withheld them? The people of France had foolishly prostrated their liberties before their Citizen King —the prototype of Nicholas himself. The English, charmed with their sailor idol and his " *reforming ministry,*" lauded and admired their *pacific policy!*—like their successors, very pacific when despotism is crushing the liberties of a country, but vigorous and warlike when liberty has the chances in her favour, as their present policy in Canada testifies. The Russian tyrant, thus secure, and openly encouraged by the despots of the Continent, recklessly pursued his victim; not a voice was raised to cheer, nor an arm to defend her; Poland was eventually conquered, her sons have been persecuted and scattered through the earth, and her daughters have become the reward of her ferocious spoilers. Heaven grant that her children may gather such seeds of democracy in their exile as, at no distant period, may be planted in their cherished country to produce fruits of national freedom and enlightened brotherhood.

"Passing onward to the German and other despotic states, what, let us ask, has generated their iron system of injustice? Why are all the powers of each state—the laws, revenues, church, education, and the press—all vested in one man? Evidently because of the ignorance of the multitude! *An enlightened people would never submit to despotism.* Whence came their soldiers, spies, and informers, but from the ranks of the people? and who would consent to be such miscreant tools of despotism but the morally depraved and mentally ignorant?

"It has been the enlightened few in all countries, whose generous efforts to improve their species have been frustrated through the cowardice or servility of the masses; and who have been made to bleed on the scaffold, to pine in the dungeon, or to become wanderers through the world.

"Need we revert to Hanover, where the prejudice in favour of hereditary sway has enabled a Tory chieftain to set aside constitutional rights, and to play the tyrant with impunity. And shame to the servility of that country, the conscientious professors of Gottingen have been banished at his royal mandate, because they would not break their oaths to enslave their country. Think you, if the intelligence and courage found among the professors and students of that city pervaded the multitude, that such infamous tyranny would escape the justice it so highly merits?

"In Italy, where liberty has stamped immortality on her very ruins, where every step recalls the greatness of the past to mock the littleness of the present, the multitude— slaves to priest or prince—are insensible to the lesson. The ardent few who, brooding over their illustrious forefathers, catch the inspirations of freedom, are, by the supineness or treachery of their brethren, made the victims of Austria, or of the petty princes who are the jackals of his power. YOUNG ITALY, like the young in all countries, where knowledge has enlightened the understanding, is virtuously resolved in favour of liberty; but the old sins of ignorance, prejudice, and fanaticism, diffused among the masses, form a drag-chain to their progress, a barrier to their freedom.

"Throughout the Continent the efforts of democracy have ever been checked and blighted by the same retarding curse. The Greeks shook off the yoke of Turkey; the despots of Europe united to give them a child to rule them, and England the means to uphold his despotism. The Spanish democrats rose against the union of priests and nobles, and proclaimed the Constitution of 1812, and abolished that retarding curse of just legislation, a privileged House of Nobles. Our rulers and yours, through the ignorance of the multitude, intrigued and re-established it. Under the plea of fighting against bigotry and absolutism, our rulers sent their bands of ignorant soldiers, to enable another set of plunderers, worse even than the former, to keep back the progress of freedom. And, by their well-organised system of falsehood, too successfully imposed the belief on popular credulity. But the republican insurrections at Cadiz, and all the principal towns, in favour of the Constitution of 1812 (*which was suppressed by English soldiers and sailors*), give the lie to those who contend that they were sent there to fight in favour of freedom.

"Similar demonstrations in favour of liberty have been crushed in Portugal, and that by similar means; proving that, though the despots of the world may quarrel for territory or plunder, they are cordially united to keep the people in subjection.

"Fellow producers of wealth! seeing that our oppressors are thus united, *why should not we, too, have our bond of brotherhood and holy alliance?* Seeing that they are powerful through our ignorance, why should not we unite *to teach our brethren a knowledge of their rights and duties?* Perceiving that their power is derived from our ranks, why should not we unite in holy zeal to show the injustice of war, the cruelty of despotism, and the misery it entails upon our species?

"Be assured, brother Democrats, that the success of our principles, and the consequent happiness of mankind, will best depend *on our union and knowledge.* We must not rely on the mere excitation of the multitude to condemn bad men or measures, or to change one despot for another —we must labour to diffuse such political, social, and

moral information among them, as shall enable them to
found their institutions on principles of equality, truth,
and justice.

"And what man can look around him, and witness the
governments that any ways approximate to those principles of liberty, and contrast the comfort and happiness of
the inhabitants, with those founded on exclusive power and
privilege, without being prepossessed in their favour!

"Those of the cantons of Switzerland, where universal
suffrage is established, where trades, manufactures, and
agriculture are greatly combined—in spite of foreign intrigues and persecutions—are blessed with intelligence
and happiness in proportion as they are free. The Republic
of America, cursed as it is with slavery and the remnants
of royal dominion, is a beacon to freedom: and even the
inhospitable shores of Norway bear witness in favour of
democracy.

"Let us, therefore, brethren, cultivate feelings of *fraternity among nations, and brotherly union in our respective
countries.* Let us not be so ignorant as to allow ourselves
to be converted into soldiers, police, or any other of the
infamous tools by which despotism is upheld, and our
brethren enslaved. Let us be prepared to make any
sacrifice in the dissemination of truth, and to cultivate
feelings of toleration between Jew, Catholic, Protestant, or
Dissenter. Let us respect the conscientious belief and
opinions of each other; knowing how much depends on
the education we receive, the books we read, the conversations we hear, and the government we live under. Let us
leave persecution for opinions to despots, and resolve that
henceforth it shall not be found in the ranks of labour.

"The organs of government, at this moment, are
endeavouring to weaken our sympathies, by exciting our
prejudice against the French Canadians. The party who
seek to keep Ireland in subjection, seek to excite our
feelings against Catholicism from the same motives;
therefore let us be assured, friends, that all those *are the
enemies of the people* who seek to oppose the great
Christian precept of 'love and charity.'

"With the view of generating enquiry among the

masses, and stimulating the few to renewed exertions, we have stated what we conscientiously believe are the great obstacles to human liberty. But let not our enemies believe that we think our brethren less competent to exercise their political rights than those who now possess them. No! *we regard the franchise as the best of school-masters*, and we point to the intelligence of America and Switzerland as proofs of the correctness of our opinions."

In 1837 a furious attack was made upon the trade unions of the kingdom by Mr. O'Connell and a large portion of the master manufacturers, aided by a portion of the press devoted to their interests. It had its origin in a *strike* made by the journeymen cotton-spinners of Glasgow against a reduction of wages proposed by their employers. During this strike a person of the name of Smith was shot in the public street, which was at once charged upon the cotton-spinners, and a number of them were arrested and put upon their trial. The indictment and evidence against them (forming two folio volumes) embraced charges of conspiracy, fire-raising, and murder, extending backwards over a period of twenty-five years. The principal charges against them, however, could not be proved; but on one charge, that of conspiring together *to intimidate a person from working*, they were sentenced to transportation for seven years. The horrible charges trumped up against these men were re-echoed through the press, as the acts and deeds of *trade unions in general*, and no language was thought too severe to be used against them. This attack induced the trade associations of Glasgow to appoint a deputation to come up to London to lay the case of the cotton-spinners before the public, as well as for petitioning Parliament to institute a fair enquiry regarding the charges made against them. Mr. Daniel O'Connell, however, having previously joined in the attack made upon trade unions, opposed the enquiry, unless the investigation extended also to the Dublin trades. This the Government agreed to, and the enquiry was made general; a Select Parliamentary Committee having been appointed in February, 1838, to enquire into the operation of the Combination Act, and the Constitution and Proceedings of Trade Unions in general. The trade-unions of the kingdom, while they were fully prepared for any investigation into their proceedings, could not but feel indignant in being charged with the acts of individuals committed before many of them were born; as was the case on the cotton-spinners' trial. They, therefore, viewed the parliamentary enquiry as an attempt to establish some plea for repealing the Combination Act, and for thus crushing, if possible, all union among working men. This feeling caused the majority of trades in town and country to make every arrangement for securing, if possible, a fair investigation by the Parliamentary Committee. A General Committee was accordingly appointed by the trades of London; local committees were appointed in other towns; a Parliamentary Agent was engaged; and I was so far honoured by their confidence as to be chosen their Secretary.

It was on the eve of this enquiry that Fergus O'Connor sought to prejudice public opinion against our Working Men's Association, in attributing the enquiry to us. The charge was made in a letter to John Fraser, of Edinburgh, the Secretary of the Edinburgh Radical Association; in which he said " the first step in this deadly course was taken by the Working Men's Association of London." The following letter in reply to him will best convey what part we took in the affair, as well as our opinion of that gentleman at this early period of his history :—

" Sir,—In the *Northern Star* of last week, you were pleased to make an unprovoked attack upon our Association. Alluding to the appeals that had been made to the House of Commons on behalf of the unfortunate cotton spinners, you said that ' that the first step in this deadly course was taken by the Working Men's Association.' And then you proceed to say that you attended our meeting to point out the fallacy of our proceeding—and it would seem, because we did not yield to your dictation, we have grievously offended. Sir, we are exceedingly obliged for your unusual bit of candour in thus speaking out the venom of your spleen; your language has hitherto been cautiously enigmatical, abounding in inuendoes, wishing by the hackneyed terms of 'Whig Malthusian,' 'Working Class Coadjutors,' and such like epithets to convey a slanderous meaning, your courage never till now embodied in plainer language. Now it so happens that *you do not speak truth* when you say that the first step in this 'deadly course' (which you are pleased to call it) was taken by us, for the Committee of Trade Delegates were the first to petition Parliament on the subject, and their motives in that step were doubtless as pure as our own— that of endeavouring to remit the sentence of the unfortunate men. Indeed, the odious colours in which the press depicted the proceedings of Glasgow ; the horrid recital of oaths, secresy, murdering and fire-raising—said to have been committed by the Cotton Spinners' Association—had created in many of our minds (as we have no doubt it had in those of thousands) a strong impression of their guilt, until the trade delegates from Glasgow had fully explained to us the whole of those horrid charges which were gleaned together over a period of twenty years and upwards, to suit the purposes of the prosecutors. And we appeal to Messrs. McNish, Cuthburtson and Campbell, whether they were not urgent in their desire that the whole affair should be fully investigated in order to prove the innocence of the men, and to remove the foul calumnies which a corrupt press had fastened on the Cotton Spinners' Association ; and through them to a great extent on trades' unions in general. The feelings, which conscious innocence inspires, caused them to court the fullest enquiry into their affair, and we appeal to every reflecting mind whether we were wrong in seconding their praiseworthy exertions. But, sir, it is your evident intention to impress the working classes with the belief that the enquiry into trades' unions in general originated with us. So far from this, we appointed a deputation on the 9th of January last to wait on Mr. O'Connell whenever he came to town, to know his reasons and intentions regarding the enquiry he had threatened to make several weeks previous, so that we might be prepared to meet any evil arising from a partial enquiry in a House of Commons constituted like the present. Indeed, as most of us are members of trades' unions, we have the motives of self-preservation to be tremulously alive to every circumstance that may in any way injure or impair the usefulness of trade societies. But when the black charges of conspiracy and murder are made against a trade society, and when the lives of five men are jeopardised by prejudiced public feelings, we think it little serves the purposes of justice or humanity to shrink, or advise shrinking, from that investigation which would serve to dispel the one, and save the other from destruction. Sir, you might have beaten the big drum of your own vanity till you grew sick of its music, and revelled in your own selfish idolatry till common sense taught your audience that the sacrifice was greater than the benefit, had you been pleased to excuse us from worshipping at your altar. But no, your own vain self must be supreme—you must be ' the leader of the people '—and from the first moment that we resolved to form an association of working men, and called upon them to manage their own affairs, *and dispense with leadership of every description:* we have had *you* and *patriots of your feelings* continually in arms against us. You have made three or four attempts to get up associations in London where you might be ' the leader '—not brooking that working men should dare presume *to think of principles* instead of public idols. You have failed in all your attempts. You have christened public meetings ' great associations ' to suit your purposes —you have dubbed yourself ' the missionary of all the Radicals of London,' your constituents being your own presumptuous boastings. You ' are the founder of Radical Associations ! ' Heaven save our ignorance ! or blot out the memory of Cartwright, Hunt and Cobbett. You tell the country that you alone ' have organised the Radicals of London '—and tell the Londoners the wonders your genius has performed in the country. You carry your fame about with you on all occasions to sink all other topics in the shade—you are the great ' I AM ' of politics, the great personification of Radicalism—Fergus O'Connor. Could self-idolatry do more, without blushing, than you did in your paper last week ? The mechanics of London, met to hear the statements of the Glasgow delegates— their eloquent and pathetic tale at once annihilated the prejudices formed by a corrupt press. You intruded yourself on that meeting in opposition to a resolution that none but members of trade societies should speak. In your *expressly made report*, your sympathy to the cotton spinners gave about a dozen lines of what all others had said, and about three columns of your own speech, whole sentences in which, by-the-bye, you had not the courage to speak, though you had the vanity to insert them in your paper. We beg to remind you that these sentiments have been called forth by your slanderous attack on us ; you would have it believed, to our prejudice, that we have been neglectful of the interests of working men, because we choose another path from yours. But time will show, and circumstances soon determine, who are their real friends ; whether they are 'the leaders of the people' who make furious appeals to their passions, threatening with fire and sword, or those who seek to unite them upon principles of knowledge and temperance, and the management of their own affairs."

O'Connor published a shuffling reply to this in the *Northern Star*, which concluded with a threat, that " we must either crush him, or he would annihilate our association ;" a threat which evinced the spirit of the man, who, after he had made a false charge, threatened us with annihilation for complaining.

To detail our labours in the " Trade Combination Committee " would form a lengthened story ; suffice it to say that we commenced our proceedings with an " Address to the Working Classes, in reply to the attacks made upon Trade Unions ;" that we opened up a correspondence with most of the trade associations in the three kingdoms, and got them to send up competent persons to be examined before " The Select Committee," to rebut the charges made against them. Unfortunately, Mr. Wakley and Mr. Hindley, the persons on the committee on whom we chiefly relied to examine our witnesses, were taken ill soon after the examination commenced, which gave our opponents a great advantage over us, for Mr. O'Connell was the masters' exclusive advocate, and our bitter opponent, supplying them *secretly* with the evidence given. Several witnesses were examined regarding the cotton trade and some of the Dublin trades, and, although both masters and men were proved to have been guilty of many foolish and unjustifiable acts, the horrible charges previously made against trade associations were not substantiated. The evidence was printed, but no report made; a Commentary on and an analysis of which was drawn up by myself and subsequently published by our committee, entitled " Combinations Defended."

CHAPTER VIII.

IT has been stated, in a previous chapter, that no sooner was the committee appointed for the drawing up of the Bill (since designated the People's Charter), than a dissolution of Parliament took place, and they could not be called together again until the new Parliament was elected, and the members came again to town. On their being again assembled at the British Coffee House, they resolved on making the prayer of the petition, agreed to at the " Crown and Anchor," the basis of the bill, and appointed Mr. Roebuck and myself to draw it up. We agreed to divide the work into two parts, but unfortunately the Canadian Revolution taking place, and Mr. Roebuck being interested so much in that event, he being their advocate, had no time to attend to the drawing up of the bill. I was therefore urged, both by him and our own members, to do what I could myself towards the completion of the whole. Having my bread to earn, and but little time at my disposal, it necessarily took me some time. In the mean time, the Radicals in different parts of the country began to be impatient respecting it, they having read of the appointment of the committee in our " Address to the Electors." When I had finished my work, I took it to Mr. Roebuck, who, when he had read it, suggested that I should show it to Mr. Francis Place, of Brompton, for his opinion, he having taken a great interest in our association from its commencement. I may here observe that my intimate acquaintance with this clear-headed and warm-hearted old gentleman arose out of a public controversy between us regarding the state and condition of the working classes ; several of our letters on the subject may be found in Mr. Hetherington's Twopenny *Dispatch*. The copy of the bill I had prepared, together with that of the petition, I accordingly took down to Mr. Place for his perusal. In a day or two he sent them back again, accompanied with suggestions for arranging the provisions of the bill under different heads, instead of running on in the usual form of acts of parliament, together with other valuable hints. This idea being approved by Mr. Roebuck, necessitated my re-writing the whole over again, in order to arrange the different provisions under their respective heads, as "Arrangement for Registration," "Electoral Districts," &c. When the bill was so prepared, a meeting of the committee of twelve was called at the office of the Combination Committee, Bridge Street, Westminster, to submit it for their opinion. The bill having been read, Mr. O'Connell suggested a new preamble to it, the one prepared having set forth several reasons for the enactment of the measure. He dictated one which he thought would suit the purpose, but that not being approved of by the committee they requested Mr. Roebuck to prepare one against the next meeting. He did so, and that which he wrote now forms the preamble or first three paragraphs of the bill. They then went through the various clauses, and after some trifling amendments it was ordered to be submitted to the Working Men's Association previous to its being printed. The bill was then discussed, clause by clause, by the members of that association, and after some slight alterations was ordered to be printed and sent to all the Working Men's Associations and Radical Associations of the kingdom for their opinions respecting it. Among the few suggestions thus made for its improvement was one by Mr. Hume, at the Radical Club, respecting the mode of placing names on the register, which was adopted. Another suggestion adopted was made by a Scotch Association (the name I have forgotten), for substituting the registration clerk for the parish clerk, they having no such parochial officer as the latter in many parts of Scotland. These alterations rendered it necessary that I should re-write the whole again previous to its being submitted to the general public. By the request of the committee, I also drew up the following address to be appended to it :—

" Fellow-countrymen,—Having frequently stated our reasons for zealously espousing the great principles of reform, we have now endeavoured to set them forth practically. We need not reiterate the facts and unrefuted arguments which have so often been stated and urged in their support. Suffice it to say, that we hold it to be an axiom in politics, that *self-government, by representation, is the only just foundation of political power*—the only true basis of Constitutional Rights—the only legitimate parent of good laws ;—and we hold it as an indubitable truth that all government which is based on any other foundation, has a perpetual tendency to degenerate into anarchy or despotism ; or to beget class and wealth idolatry on the one hand, or poverty and misery on the other.

" While, however, we contend for the principle of self-government, we admit that laws will only be just in proportion as the people are enlightened ; on this, socially and politically, the happiness of all must depend ; but, as self-interest, unaccompanied by virtue, ever seeks its own exclusive benefit, so will the exclusive and privileged classes of society ever seek to perpetuate their power and to proscribe the enlightenment of the people. Hence we are induced to believe that the enlightenment of all will sooner emanate from the exercise of political power by all the people, than by their continuing to trust to the selfish government of the few.

" A strong conviction of these truths, coupled as that conviction is with the belief that most of our political and social evils can be traced to *corrupt* and *exclusive legislation,* and that the remedy will be found in extending to the people at large the exercise of those rights now monopolised by a few, has induced us to make some exertions towards embodying our principles in the following Charter.

" We are the more inclined to take some practicable step in favour of Reform, from the frequent disappointments the cause has experienced. We have heard eloquent effusions in favour of political equality from the hustings, and the senate-house, suddenly change into prudent reasonings on property and privileges, at the winning smile of the minister. We have seen depicted in glowing language bright patriotic promises of the future, which have left impressions on us more lasting than the perfidy or apostasy of the writers. We have seen one zealous Reformer after another desert us, as his party was triumphant or his interests served. We have perceived the tone of those whom we have held as champions of our cause lowered to the accommodation of selfish electors, or restrained by the slavish fear of losing their seats. We have therefore resolved to test the sincerity of the remainder by proposing that something shall be done in favour of the principles they profess to admire.

" In June last we called a general meeting of our members, and invited to attend that meeting all those Members of Parliament who by their speeches and writings we were induced to believe were advocates of Universal Suffrage. Several did attend, and after some discussion another meeting was proposed, at which several Members of Parliament pledged themselves by resolutions, signed by their own hands, '*that they would bring in and support a Bill for Universal Suffrage, Equal Representation, Short Parliaments, the Ballot, &c.*' They also passed another resolution at that meeting, *appointing persons to draw up such Bill.*

" Many circumstances have transpired to cause the great delay that has taken place in the doing of this, but the following outline of an Act of Parliament is the result of our deliberations. It has often been urged that Universal Suffrage, as well as all the other essentials to the free exercise of that right, '*could not be reduced to practice.*' This is therefore an attempt to show to the contrary ; and we think it would be practically found to be a simpler, cheaper, and better mode of securing to the whole people their elective rights, than the present expensive machinery by which the rich and ambitious few are enabled to pauperise and enslave the industrious many.

" Although this may be a new form of putting forward our claims, they are in themselves by no means new. In former times Parliaments were only *sessional*, and the Members received *pay* for their attendance. In 1780 the

Duke of Richmond introduced a Bill into the House of Lords for the purpose of establishing *Annual Parliaments*, and for giving the right of voting *to every man not contaminated by crime, nor incapacitated for want of reason.* Three years after this, in his celebrated letter to Colonel Sharman, he says 'The subject of Parliamentary Reform is that which of all others most deserves the attention of the public, as I conceive it would include every other advantage which a nation can wish; and I have no hesitation in saying, that from every consideration which I have been able to give this great question, that for many years has occupied my mind, and from every day's experience to the present hour, I am more and more convinced that the *restoring* the right of voting to every man universally who is not incapacitated by nature for want of reason, or by law for the commission of crimes, together with annual elections, is the only Reform that can be effectual and permanent.' In 1780, the electors of Westminster in public meeting appointed a committee, out of which a sub-committee was appointed to take into consideration the election of Members of Parliament. Charles James Fox, the leader of the Whigs, and Thomas Brand Hollis, Esq., were the chairmen of these committees. In their report to the electors they recommended Annual Parliaments, Universal Suffrage, equal Voting Districts, no Property Qualification. Voting by Ballot, and Payment of Members.

" The *Society of Friends of the People* was established in 1792, by Charles Grey, Esq. (now Earl Grey), the Hon. Thomas Erskine, Mr. (afterwards Sir James) Mackintosh, several noblemen and Members of the House of Commons. In 1795 they resolved to publish a Declaration in which the right of voting should be so moderate that there should be no condition in life in which it might not be acquired by labour, by industry, or talents.

" These are the doings of the Whigs of former times, persons whose speeches *on every other subject* our modern Whigs quote with ancestral reverence as texts from holy writ. Like every other irresponsible body, they have, however, degenerated. The only remedy for the evil is to render Whig, Tory, and Radical legislators alike *responsible to the people,* and to instruct the people in a knowledge of their rights and duties.

"And we could wish it to be engraven on the memory of every Reformer, 'that the people must be free, in proportion as they will it,' not by foolishly lending themselves to bigotry or party, to become the instruments of the conceited or selfishly ambitious, as they have too often done, nor by *violently* overthrowing the empire of title, the folly of privilege, or the domination of wealth; for the experience of the past has clearly written for our guidance that a change of men is not always a reformation in principle, and when a knowledge of their rights and duties shall have taught the people *that their own vices and ignorance are the chief instruments by which they are bowed to the dust,* titles, privileges, and wealth will lose their potency to enslave them.

"Fellow-countrymen,—The object we contemplate in the drawing up of this Bill is to cause the Radicals of the kingdom to form, if possible, a concentration of their principles in a practical form, upon which they could be brought to unite, and to which they might point, *as a Charter they are determined to obtain.*

"We intend that copies of it shall be forwarded to all the Working Men's Associations and to all Reform Associations in the kingdom to which we can have access, and we hereby call upon them, in the spirit of brotherhood, to examine, suggest, and improve upon it, until it is so perfected as to meet, as far as possible, with general approbation. When it is so far improved, and has received their sanction, we intend that it shall be presented to Parliament, and we trust that petitions will not be wanting to show how far we are united in demanding its enactment. We hope, also, that electors and non-electors will continue to make it the pledge of their candidates; will seek to extend its circulation; talk over its principles; and resolve that, as public opinion forced the Whig Reform Bill, so in like manner shall this Bill eventually become the law of England.

"In drawing it up we have found some difficulty in fixing the requisite qualification of electors, because of many of the barbarous and unjust laws which corrupt and selfish legislators have enacted. While, for instance, we agree with most reformers that felony should lead to the deprivation of political rights, we think the law which makes it felony for a boy to steal an apple, or to kill a wild animal which crosses his path, is as cruel as it is unjust.*

"We think, also, that the present alien laws, which had their origin in the bigoted and prejudiced feelings of other days, should be so modified as to permit the right of citizenship to those who, for some definite period, have taken up their abode among us, and are willing to declare their allegiance as citizens, and thus break down those barriers which kingcraft and priestcraft have erected to divide man from his brother man. But we deemed it far better to lay down just principles, and look forward to the rational improvement of those laws, than to make exceptions to injure the character of the measure we wish to make as perfect as possible.

"In conclusion, we think that no unprejudiced man can reflect on the present unjust and exclusive state of the franchise, where property (however unjustly acquired) is possessed of rights that knowledge the most extensive, and conduct the most exemplary, fail to attain ; can witness the demoralizing influence of wealth in the Legislature; and the bribery, perjury, tumults, and disorders attendant on the present mode of elections, but must admit that the object contemplated is worthy of the task we have imposed upon ourselves, however we may have fallen short in providing an efficient remedy."

I have deemed it necessary to give this brief history of the origin of the People's Charter,† a document that has excited, among the industrious classes, a more extended and united public opinion in its favour, than perhaps any other political document that has issued from the press. Among the good resulting from its publication is the

---

* I may here state that the first draft of the Bill, afterwards called the People's Charter, made provision for the suffrage of women, but as several members thought its adoption in the Bill might retard the suffrage of men, it was unfortunately left out.

† See a copy of it in the Appendix B.

extensive public opinion it has served to create among the millions in favour of an equal, just, and efficient measure of representative reform.

Previous to its publication the principle of *universal suffrage* was sneered at by the enemies of reform, as an Utopian and impracticable theory. Among reformers of our representative system we had the greatest diversity of opinions regarding what was just and necessary to prevent the House of Commons from being the ready tool and lackey of the Lords, and every variety of organization was found among them according to the conflicting notions they entertained. Some of them were organized and contending for the ballot, some for short parliaments, some for extended suffrage—some for household and some for universal—and the enemies of all reform laughed at their numerous diversified theories, and their opposing and wasted efforts. But the details of the Charter brought home to the minds of the many the justice, the practicability, and the efficiency of the measure. They at once saw in it a plan calculated to give *all classes their legitimate share in the government of their country*, instead of the corrupt and privileged few, who for so many years have bowed down the energies of our country and almost withered its hopes. In less than twelve months from the date of its publication upwards of a million of people had declared in its favour, and it was going on rapidly enlisting new converts and earnest supporters, when a few mad advisers, by furious appeals to the passions of the multitude, stirred up the demons of hate, prejudice, and discord, to obstruct its onward progress. The result is too well known; their violence and folly scared back our friends, and placed the desired weapons in the hands of our enemies. They brought persecution, suffering, and death into our ranks, severed our links of union, cast a gloom across our hopes, and gave the exclusive and privileged classes hopes for believing that Chartism was dead and securely entombed. But, great as are their rejoicings and their triumphs, those persons may yet live to perceive that so much vitality was buried with it, as to enable it to burst its cerements, and that though its body now sleeps its spirit is abroad watching the men and awaiting the hour—that it is yet destined to have a glorious resurrection, unmarked by violence and untarnished by folly—an uprising that shall inspire all classes who love justice to hail it as the hopeful regenerator of their country.

The People's Charter was published on the 8th of May, 1838. The first public meeting it was submitted to was one held at Glasgow on the 21st of May, when Mr. Thomas Attwood and the Council of the Birmingham Union visited Scotland; the persons we appoined to submit it to the men of Glasgow being Mr. Thomas Murphy and Dr. Wade. It very rapidly received the approval of numerous Associations in different parts of the country, and on the 6th of August, by the men of Birmingham at one of the largest public meetings ever held in that town, our Association having previously agreed to make their National Petition *the first petition for the Charter.* It was our waiting for this large meeting to take place that delayed our submitting it to a public meeting in London till the 17th of September following its publication. And here I may state that so favourable were the opinions entertained of our Working Men's Association by a large portion of the Middle Classes, that we were enabled to make a requisition to the High Bailiff, signed by a number of the most influential men of Westminster, for calling our first public meeting for the People's Charter in Palace Yard. Our missionaries also were well received by a large number of the Middle Classes in the different towns they visited; and no inconsiderable portion of the Press republished our Addresses, and advocated our views. In fact, we were fast gathering up the favourable opinion of the Middle, as well as of the Working Classes, when the violent ravings about physical force, by O'Connor, Stephens, and Oastler, scared them from our ranks; they, doubtlessly conceiving that they had better put up with known evils, than trust to an unknown remedy purposed to be effected by such desperate means. It was not, however, till near the time of our Meeting in Palace Yard, that our Working Men's Association began to be mixed up with this violence; it having been for the most part confined to the demonstrations in the North *against* *the new Poor Law,* in which Stephens, Oastler, and O'Connor were the principal speakers. In fact, the People's Charter was published and circulated throughout the country some time before it was even noticed in O'Connor's paper ; * nor was it till after its adoption by the Birmingham Council that he followed public opinion in its favour.

Another circumstance tending to create bad feelings, disunion, and distrust between the Middle and Working Classes on the eve of this Meeting, was the proposed re-agitation against the Corn Laws. The proposal being made at this particular juncture, coupled as it was with the following advice, given in a popular Middle Class newspaper, † naturally excited the belief of the Working Classes that the object aimed at was not so much the repeal of those unjust laws, as it was *to frustrate their agitation in favour of political reform.* " All those who want to stave off as long as possible the trial of strength between the proprietary and the working classes ought to direct the meeting that is to be held in Palace Yard, to

---

* This was the *Northern Star.*—The following account of its origin is taken from a series of articles written by Mr. Robert Lowery, one of our convention, and published in the *Temperance Weekly Record.* " Fergus, having lost his seat for Cork, and quarrelled with Daniel O'Connell, left the Irish agitation, and appeared at the Meetings of the English Radicals. He went down into the factory districts, and, speaking to please, soon became popular. J. Hobson, Mr. Hill, and others in Yorkshire, seeing the want of a newspaper, as an organ for the rising movement, had succeeded in raising some few hundreds of pounds, by shares, to establish one. O'Connor persuaded them that they would not be able to get the necessary amount, and that the mixed authority of a committee would hamper the Editor, and render the paper inefficient. He proposed that the shareholders should lend him the money raised, for which he would guarantee interest, and that he would find the rest of the capital, and commence the paper at once ; and that Hobson should be the publisher and Hill the editor. This was done, and the paper entitled the *Northern Star.* But there is every reason to believe that at that time he had no capital, and that the money of the shareholders was the only money ever invested in the paper. Fortunately for him it soon rose to a very large circulation, reaching at last to some 60,000 a-week."

† It was *The Sun* newspaper.

pass resolutions for the repeal of the Corn Laws, and to move an amendment to the People's Charter." The keynote having been thus struck other journals took it up, and at once Chartism became with them the especial object of denunciation, and the Corn Law agitation the measure to be exalted It was these attacks that caused us to put forth the following address to the people of England, in reply to the objections of the Press :—

" Fellow-Countrymen,—Having great faith in the inherent excellence of humanity, and believing that more of the mental and moral incongruities of men are to be attributed to erroneous convictions than to interested perversions of truth and justice, we should belie our opinions were we to make any foolish attack on the press or its conductors.

" We rather lament that such a powerful instrument towards man's political and social redemption should be constrained by interest or party, to shut out truth from its pages and make error a marketable speculation ; or that men, so competent to direct aright the public mind, should be employed to mystify and mislead it.

" But we think that the many notorious changes and conversions recently witnessed, the skilful balancing of opinions, the fear-to-offend and desire-to-please disposition which have characterized so great a portion of those papers who call themselves " *liberal*," should open the eyes of all those who desire to see the Press as consistent in practice, as it ought to be honest in principle.

" Such eccentric courses, and such conduct, in men professing liberality of sentiment and honesty of intention, can only be countenanced by the public's disregard of all principle, or the private encouragement of those who maintain their fraudulent position by unworthy means.

" We would be the last to restrict the freedom of thought, or the most unbounded expressions that could be given in opposition to our own opinions, as we consider that truth can only be elicited through the severest test of mental conflict ; but when, in the same paper, we see the most ultra-political principles set forth in the strongest language to-day, pertinaciously defended by the most cogent arguments to-morrow, and the most sweeping condemnation and invective bestowed on them the day following, we confess we do not think it free discussion, but direct apostasy.

"We are induced to put forth these observations from the conduct of a great portion of the press, ever since the recent agitation that has commenced in favour of the 'People's Charter and the National Petition,' embracing, as they do, the principles of Universal Suffrage, as well as the other essentials which we believe necessary to a just representative system. Without, however, *individualizing* any paper, or noticing their scurrility or abuse, we will proceed to answer some of the objections they have urged against us, or our principles.

"They say that we are ' adopting and imitating the mischievous conduct of our oppressors, in seeking to make men free and happy by means of legislation !' What, we would ask, but legislation has made the difference between democratic America, despotic Russia, and pauperised and oppressed England ? If the will of the American people, expressed through their legislature, has raised them from such a poor and heterogeneous origin, to become a nation ' better educated than any other under the sun— where two-thirds of the adults are proprietors, and while most of the others have the prospect of becoming so '— what, we would ask the gentlemen who make those admissions, is there in the character of Englishmen to prevent them from realizing similar advantages, were the same political rights conferred on them as on their American brethren ?

"They say that our *ignorance and poverty* should preclude us from the franchise.' We beg to refer them back to the ' beautiful democracy' and all its results, which they admit to exist in America, and ask them whether the intelligence and prosperity of that country *preceded* their political rights, or whether they are not the consequence of their having obtained them ?

"Granting that a number of our countrymen are in poverty, can these gentlemen show, by any valid reasoning, the absolute necessity of their being so, especially in a country blessed by nature with such abundant resources? Nay, can they trace the existence of that poverty to any other source than corrupt and exclusive legislation? Granting too, that ignorance to a great extent prevails, to what other cause can it be attributed than to those who have legislated to keep knowledge from the people? And, therefore, is it not as immoral as it is unjust to make the *effects* of corruption a pretence for upholding the *cause* of it? We would call upon any reflecting individual to take up the history of his country, and to investigate the true cause of all the wars, the superstitions, the oppressions, and the persecutions, which leave so many stains upon our national character, and he will find it to be an exclusive and corrupt government; and he will find that in proportion as the spirit of democracy has forced its influence on the legislature, so have the venomous influences of later times abated.

" Warned, therefore, by the experience of the past, and cheered by the example of modern democracy, whether in Switzerland, Norway, or America, we think that every lover of his species ought to exert his influence to remove that prolific source of evil—*corrupt legislation.* It is not so much by *forms* of government that evils are generated or removed, as by the principles of exclusive or responsible representation; the former acts for itself, the latter for the people. Therefore, according to our humble abilities, in seeking to remedy the evils we complain of, we believe the most effective means will be those we have embodied in the People's Charter.

" We are told that ' Universal Suffrage would produce universal confusion '; that ' the people would only substitute noisy demagogues for an idle aristocracy,' and that therefore ' we had better suffer the ills we know, than fly to others that we know not of.' Those who talk of present ills, we presume, are not among the suffering classes, and they only expose their own selfishness and heartlessness in showing such a disregard to the misery of others. As to the kind of men we should choose, if Universal Suffrage prevailed, that will need experience to test it; but where it has been tested by the descendants of Englishmen, such 'demagogues' as Washington, Jefferson, Franklin, and others equally efficient, seem to cast a doubt upon the prophecy. The 'confusion,' too, likely to flow from removing corruption would, by the same test, be proved more imaginative than real. America had an adventurous and speculative race to begin with, intermingled with fanatics and convicts from Britain, and for the last half century the poor and oppressed of all the countries of Europe have sought and found an asylum on her hospitable shores. The greedy speculator, the ruined bankrupt, the broken down insolvent, and the felon pursued by justice, have also transferred their vices to her soil, but her salutary laws and institutions, *springing from Universal Suffrage*, have enabled her to reform, instruct, and purify the mass, and in despite of that black *remnant of kingly dominion*—'SLAVERY,' she is the most prosperous and free of all the nations of the earth.

"We have been gravely assured that 'the best test of intelligence is property'—that 'the outward mark of ascertaining the existence of property is house-rent'—that 'a still surer indication of property is direct taxation,' and 'that therefore the present electoral body is a guarantee for fair legislation.' While we, in part, admit the truth of some of these propositions, to the extent that wealth will *give the means* of knowledge, we deny that property is any fair criterion for intelligence. We know of hundreds of rich fools, and thousands of housekeepers whose knowledge does not extend beyond their counters, and who are no more qualified to judge of any man's political capabilities than the most ignorant ploughman, whose common sense would not at least be subject to such influence as the fear of losing a wealthy customer. If *wealth alone* formed 'a sufficient guarantee for just government,' the benevolent portion of mankind would not for so many years have been striving to rescue the enslaved negro from the mercenary grasp of the wealthy planter of India, and the Southern slaveowner of America; nay, further, if *intelligence alone* were sufficient, we should not have such a catalogue of bad laws to complain of.

The great boast of England is 'Trial by Jury'—but why do we prefer the less intelligent jury to the more intelligent judge, who fully knows the law, and is a more competent judge of evidence? Simply, *because honesty is not always united with intelligence.* We have found out that wealthy and iutelligent judges cannot even be trusted in a court of law, and we are therefore pleased to submit to the occasional blunders of an unbiassed jury, rather than trust our lives to a designing judge. If men without responsibility were strictly virtuous, a few intelligent individuals would be found sufficient to make and execute the laws; but as they are not so, we must endeavour to make them honest by making them accountable and responsible for their actions.

" But we are told that 'we are virtually represented '—that ' our interests are identified with those who represent us. This is very false philosophy. Man does not always pursue *his own* real interests; if he did, he would never commit so many crimes and blunders as he does; on the contrary, he pursues an imaginary interest, as passion or circumstances determine; and hence the necessity for laws to regulate his conduct. So with men collectively, so with classes—they uphold the interest of their class according to their power or inclinations; and it is only by a mutual reliance on, and *responsibility to each other*, that oppression can be guarded against.

" Land, labour, and capital are the great sources of wealth; without land and labour capital would be unproductive; without capital and land labour could not be employed; and, without labour, both land and capital would be useless. Here, then, is a mutual necessity for mutual interests; and, being so dependent, each upon the other, justice demands that in all the arrangements necessary for production and distribution, equality in legislation should prevail. But, no; we are told that ' the capitalists dread the labourers, and therefore will oppose giving them their rights.' We would here stop to ask these very consistent gentlemen, who talk of 'virtual representation,' what just cause have English capitalists to dread, or to oppose the English labourer, more than American capitalists have to fear the power of Universal Suffrage in that country. The people there find it to their interest to protect and encourage capital as *the best seed for future production,*—they find it equally beneficial to remove monopolies and develop their own resources, taking care that, as the public cause is promoted, individual interests shall not suffer. They know that *knowledge* is the surest promoter of peace and order, and therefore seek to extend it,—they find that poverty is the most fruitful source of crime, and therefore seek to remove it. Do the opponents of Universal Suffrage imagine that Englishmen would be less wise in pursuing their own interests than Americans are ?

" But there are a class of reasoners who, when foiled by truth and compelled to admit the justice of principles, will fall back upon that old subterfuge of error, *expediency.* We are told that, admitting Universal Suffrage to be just, 'we must demonstrate its expediency.' In answer to which we would say, if the evils of which most classes complain, can be traced to any one cause, it is as *expedient* as it is just to remove that cause. And if we can show that the removal of a similar cause has produced beneficial results in another country, it is ' expedient' to make the trial in our own. We are next informed that ' Household Suffrage would be a more respectable suffrage ' than that which we propose; in reply to which, we think honesty preferable to respectability, and believe that all the ignorance which they say they fear would be embodied in Household Suffrage, *to the exclusion of the intelligence of the towns,* would be embodied in Universal Suffrage.

" But, as a last resource, the opponents to our rights think it necessary to mislead and misdirect us from our object. They tell us that ' the repeal of the Corn Laws is of much more importance than the Suffrage,' as ' it would even give cheap bread, more trade, promote morality, upset the priesthood, and destroy cant.' That the Corn Laws are highly mischievous we admit, but they are only *one of the effects* of the great cause we are seeking to remove ; and in justice we think the question of their repeal ought to be argued *by the representatives of all the people,* and not by a faction. If they had existed so long that people had forgotten the state of things previous to their enactment, we might be induced to have faith in all the blessed promises now made us; but the year 1815 is not of very great antiquity. And when we find the following bit of advice given by these 'kindly disposed persons,' we think it exhibits their hollowness and hypocrisy. 'All those who want *to stave off* as long as possible the trial of strength between the proprietary and the working classes, ought to direct the meeting, that is to be held in Palace Yard, to pass resolutions for the repeal of the Corn Laws and to move an amendment to the People's Charter.' This is evidently an attempt to sow divisions and dissensions, in no ways warranted by the disposition of a patient, long-suffering, industrious people; nor by any supposed interest in opposition to persons or to property. But we would caution such advisers against making such 'trials of strength,' and warn them also against exciting prejudices it should be their duty to dispel. In arousing the passions they silence reason, and the weapon they would enlist in their service might be fatal to themselves."

CHAPTER IX.

THE Great Birmingham Meeting on the 6th of August
might be said to be the first *Chartist meeting* at which
O'Connor introduced his physical force notions, or rather
his Irish braggadocio about arming and fighting, for to
fight himself formed no part of his patriotism; for when
his mad folly subsequently incited violent commotion
among " his dear children," he shrank from personal
consequences and slunk over to Ireland. His speech, at
the meeting referred to, about "fleshing swords to the
hilt," having furnished our opponents with a daily text,
and a keen weapon with which to assail us, made us
anxious to prevent if possible a like exhibition at our
Palace Yard meeting. Therefore in our instructions to
the speakers appointed by our Association we requested
them " to keep as closely as possible to the two great questions of the meeting—*the Charter* and *the Petition*,—and as
far as possible to avoid all extraneous matter or party
politics, as well as every abusive or violent expression
which may tend to injure our glorious cause." But though
our own members and most of the country delegates
avoided everything likely to give a handle to the enemy,
O'Connor and Richardson (one of his disciples) marred
the moral effect of our meeting by their physical force
swagger. At this meeting the People's Charter and the
National Petition were adopted, and eight persons
appointed to form part of the *convention* that were to meet
in London in February following, " to watch over the
presentation of the petition, and to obtain, by all legal and
constitutional means, the enactment of the People's

Charter." The numbers attending our meeting were variously estimated ; suffice to say, that we obtained at and during the meeting 16,000 signatures to the National Petition, and that eighty-nine towns sent delegates to attend it.

In the evening after our meeting the delegates assembled at the rooms of our Working Men's Association in Gray's Inn Road, and agreed to resolutions empowering us to prepare an address to the Irish people, the same to be sent round to all the working men's and radical associations of the kingdom to obtain their concurrence and a signature on behalf of each. This measure was the more necessary at this juncture as Mr. O'Connell was endeavouring to persuade the Irish people that the English radicals were their especial enemies ; and although he had been a party to the drawing up of the People's Charter, and had otherwise given us his signature pledging himself to support it, he had become so suddenly influenced by a little whig patronage as to turn round and denounce English radicalism, and the Chartists in particular, with the most virulent abuse, threats and bitterness. Our address when drawn up was sent round and signed on behalf of *one hundred and thirty-six working men's and radical associations*, and was then forwarded to all the associations in Ireland we could get access to, and among them to the Precursor Society, recently established by Mr. O'Connell. The following is the Address :—

" Brothers in Political Bondage,—The deep waters which divide our shores, and the still deeper intrigues of self interest and bigotry which in ten thousand channels have laboured to divide our hearts, have led to the formation of prejudices opposed to our mutual interests. Those mischievous feelings have been carefully fostered by the interested exclusives of both countries. They have employed you to silence our demands for freedom, and we have been engaged to keep your country in poverty and subjection. Prejudice and ignorance have ever been the great allies of despotism, and well do our rulers know it ; union and knowledge are the twin brothers which shall destroy its dominion, and it is for us to let our brethren know it; on that knowledge will our liberty depend, and on the establishment of that liberty our happiness.

"In addressing you, fellow countrymen, our object is union; for though the channel divides, the ocean surrounds us—though bigotry would dissever, charity should unite us—and as the blood of both countries commingle in our veins, and the people of both blend their occupation in the workshop and the field, so, assuredly, under the benign influence of free and equal institutions would our liberties and interests be blended and identified as one united and happy people.

"We can readily imagine that the oppression and injustice you have received through the legislature of Britain have aroused your feelings and deeply rooted your suspicions against our country. But we would urge you to remember that we, too, have shared in the injustice; we have been reciprocally taxed to oppress and drilled to enslave each other; and we are still united victims of the same curse which plunders, oppresses, and blights the happiness of both countries—*the curse of exclusive legislation.* This we feel convinced is the great source of our oppression; ignorance, immorality, poverty and crime have their origin directly or indirectly in exclusive legislation; for as long as exclusive interests are made the basis of law and government, so long will exclusive measures be supported at the sacrifice of peace, happiness, and virtue.

"Therefore it is to this one point especially we would direct your attention; nay, we would urge you to enquire whether you cannot trace the numerous evils you complain of to this baneful origin. Who but your own *exclusive legislators* sold your country? And who but the *exclusive legislators* of England profited by the blood-cemented bargain? Your own legislators, corrupted by the gold, and cankered by the patronage of Britain, rendered your domestic legislature a mere puppet of its will;—there it was where landed supremacy predominated, and English interests swayed, till eventually, perfidy concluded the bargain your own corrupt legislature had begun.

"Since the Union—who have been greater instruments, in the hands of Britain, for binding you to the dust than your own exclusive legislators? With few exceptions, the interest of their own order has been paramount to the welfare of the nation. Grattan, your greatest orator, who in civil war opposed coercive measures, when in the United Parliament supported the very measures he condemned; and his specious example seems not to have been forgotten by the legislators of modern times. The ruling few of Britain have not been deficient in that selfish sagacity which ever seeks to strengthen injustice by corruption; hence they have united in their unholy compact your most talented orators, profound writers, gallant warriors, and able statesmen—they have inspired your vanity with songs and boastings, and have thrown a halo of glory over the sepulchre of your decay.

" Captivated by power and riches, at the expense of justice, your gentry have been rendered greedy by patronage; your yeomen corrupted by preferment; and the choicest of your peasantry moulded into instruments of oppression, to exact by steel and bludgeon, the scanty necessities of the poor, to support the extravagancies of the rich.

" We will not harrow up your feelings in depicting the horrible results of this system, by dwelling on the extremes of wretchedness with which you are familiar, but we would urge you to trust to your own judgment, apart from the captivating tone of eloquence which has so often been your guide—and to ask yourselves whether these evils are wholly attributable to your union with England; and whether they are to be remedied merely by a separation? We are far from denying your right to a domestic parliament, or the justice of self government; but depend upon it friends, *while an exclusive class have the election of the House of Commons, the interest of that class will be supported to your prejudice and ours, whether Parliament meet in London or in Dublin.* The separation of that house would only be a division of evils; your own aristocracy would be strengthened, and one faction would supply the place of another. English influence and intrigue would again predominate, and the evil so far from being remedied would be increased in magnitude and power. Yet this is the chief blessing that is *threatened* to be conferred upon you, if you will not be content with the less measure of happiness our most gracious ministers are disposed to bestow if they were 'free from Tory influences' to dispense their liberal favours!!! The question of extending the suffrage to the millions we never hear of among the blessings to be derived from a separation. You have been assured that your commerce would flourish, and your people be prosperous if you had a Parliament of your own. We believe not, till you have some choice in the electing of it; then indeed when you have legislators whose interests shall be identified with your happiness, will they legislate to effect it, but be assured, not till then.

" The happiness of a country does not depend on her commerce, so much as on the quantity of comforts she can retain for her population. Your commerce has been increasing ever since the Union, and your poverty in a like proportion; to what causes is this anomaly to be attributed? We will presume to express our conviction of the causes for your consideration.

"In the *first* place, exclusive legislators, having their own interests to secure, rather than the general happiness of society, have, by their corrupt enactments, ruinous wars, extravagant expenditure, taxation and monopoly, generated great poverty amongst the people.

" *Secondly*, where poverty exists, there will ignorance and violence exist also; and hence those funds, which ought to be employed in production, have been diverted to the supporting of soldiers, police, prisons, and all those instruments for punishing, what ought in wisdom to have been prevented.

" *Thirdly*, when violence and insecurity exist in a country, coupled with the exactions of fraud, monopoly, and injustice, *capital* will not be secure, and will not be employed there.

" *Fourthly*, for want of those employments capital and wealth would create, nearly the whole population are compelled to have recourse to agriculture; thus the consequent competition for land has forced up nominal rents beyond the power of payment; joined to which, the rapacity of tithe-proctors, collectors, and bailiffs, have further paralysed the hand of industry, and prevented those improvements the owner and cultivator might otherwise enjoy.

"*Fifthly*, the people thus reduced to live on the lowest description of food, their standard of comforts being almost confined to a sufficiency of it being the worst housed, fed, and clothed of any people in Europe—there is no demand for these trades and manufactures which generate and support a respectable middle-class population; excepting perhaps in some few exporting towns.

"*Sixthly*, the long series of injustice, insults, and neglect to which your peasantry in particular have been exposed, have generated that state of poverty and wretchedness among them, which is gradually undermining the comforts of the class above them, and bids fair to involve all in the samec ommon ruin; for as their numbers increase they force themselves upon the towns, and by their low standard of comforts, are the main instruments for bringing down all others to their own miserable condition.

"*Seventhly*, faction has been arrayed against faction, creed against creed, and man against his brother man, not so much from their own conscientious opinions, as from the pernicious counsel and malignant influences of corrupt legislators, who find their own selfish supremacy strengthened by the divisions and dissensions of the multitude.

"If you agree with us, brethren, as to the origin of these evils, we trust you will co-operate with us to effect a remedy, and the only effectual one, we believe, will be that which Mr. O'Connell has sworn to and pledged himself to support, 'Universal Suffrage,' as well as other essentials to the free exercise of that right. In all countries where the people are exercising the right of freemen, they are progressing in knowledge and happiness; wherever class legislation prevails, the interests of the millions are despised and neglected. True liberty cannot exist where man does not exercise the rights of man; for men whose lives and liberties are dependent on others—who are taxed at others' wills—must fight at others' biddings—must pay others before they can write, talk, buy or sell—must toil or starve at the will of others—though they may sing of freedom, are still but the slaves of others.

" But you have been told that you must first and foremost be placed on ' an equality with England,' you must have 'municipal reform,' and ' the franchise equal to that of England.' We fear these counter projects are only intended to baffle the Radicals of England, and create a diversion in favour of the present *patronizing ministry*. We can give you the benefit of our experience as regards these enviable measures of reform. We have men in our municipal corporations who at one time were the greatest advocates of reform ; they have now realized all the reform they wished for, and therefore are the greatest opponents of further progress. Those, too, whose energies were united with the millions to obtain the Reform Bill, are now as energetically opposed to the rights of their former allies. Do you think the same class in Ireland will be more grateful in extending, or less powerful in opposing, any further reform or extension of right than those of England ? If so, you may, like us, find another agitation to be necessary, and need more efficient co-operators to render it productive of benefit, than those who now call upon you for your aid.

" We readily admit the great injustice of compelling the Catholics of Ireland to support a Protestant Church Establishment, and cannot but lament the crooked policy which has prevented the settlement of that question. But lest you may think this a singular injustice, we would take this opportunity of informing you that there are a greater number of persons in England compelled to support a Church from whose doctrines they dissent, than in your own country—nay, there are thousands of conscientious Protestants themselves, who believe that the sanctity of their Church is tainted by its corrupt alliance with the State.

" But you are called upon to get up an exclusive agitation founded on the measures we have referred to ; measures as fruitless and as profitless to the bulk of the people, as they are meant to be mere barriers to secure Whiggery, and stumbling-blocks in the way of Radicalism.

We shall doubtless be condemned as 'Tory Radicals,' in cautioning you against this maudlin delusive scheme; but be assured, you have swallowed more bitterness to retain the present ministry in power, than the united despotism of Whig and Tory could administer, if the friends of the people were justly allied. You are cautioned against us, because we 'are neither combined nor concentrated,' 'nor have skilful or well-tried leaders,' and 'talk of using physical force and the shedding of human blood.'

"Regarding the extent of our combination we will not boast, but are desirous that you should judge of it from the hundreds of thousands who, for the first time, have given up their own projects of reform, and are now pledged and united in favour of the People's Charter and the National Petition.

"We have not, neither do we desire, *leaders*, as we believe that the principles we advocate have been retarded, injured, or betrayed *by leadership*, more than by the open hostility of opponents. Leadership too often generates confiding bigotry or political indifference on the one hand, and selfish ambition on the other. The principles we advocate are those of the people's happiness, and to be justly established each man must know and feel his rights and duties; he must be prepared to guard the one, and perform with cheerfulness the other; and if nature has given to one man superior faculties to express or execute the general wish, he only performs his duty at the mandate of his brethren; he is 'the leader' of none, but the equal of all.

"Regarding the other assertion, that we 'have talked of physical force,' which comes with a mock reproach from him who has so often boasted of physical force. We are not going to affirm that we have been altogether guiltless of impropriety of language, for when the eye dwells on extremest poverty trampled on by severe oppression, the heart often forces a language from the tongue which sober reflection would redeem, and sound judgment condemn. But we deny that we are influenced by any other feelings than a desire to see our institutions peaceably and orderly based upon principles of justice. We believe that a Parliament composed of the wise and good of all classes, would devise means of improving the condition of the millions, without injury to the just interests of the few. We feel that unjust interests have been fostered under an unjust system, that it would be equally unjust to remove without due precaution ; and, when due, individual indemnification. We are as desirous as the most scrupulous Conservative of protecting all that is good, wise, and just in our institutions, and to hold as sacred and secure the domain of the rich equally with the cottage of the poor.

" But we repeat that we seek to effect our object in peace, with no other force than that of argument or persuasion ; and we call upon you, as we do upon the wise and good of every class, to unite with us in our most holy compact, the ultimate object of which is the freedom and happiness of Britain, and, through her example, that of the world.

" We call upon you to unite with us to cause the principles of the People's Charter to become the law of these realms, believing it to be a just and necessary measure to ensure equal and just legislation. We have been too long engaged in trifles and expediencies. Millions of our fellow men rise up in poverty and perish in crime, whilst mock philanthropy, too regardless of the present, gives promises of hope to future generations.

" But, fellow countrymen, while we are desirous of your aid we shall not despair without it ; our cause is strong in proportion as it is just, and our numbers will swell in proportion as our enemies oppose us. Our National Petition may be indignantly spurned ; our charter at first may have but few supporters, but our second petition will swell in numbers at the injustice ; our energies shall be redoubled at each division that may be made against us ; our third shall embody the numerical power and mental energy of the kingdom, whose determination to have ' justice ' will increase with each refusal, till their irresistible resolution can no longer be controlled by all that power and wealth can purchase.

" These, brethren, are our views, our objects, and our determination. To carry them forward we implore the co-operation of rich and poor, male and female, the sober, the reflecting, and the industrious; we can spare the drunkard from our ranks till reflection shall have made him a more worthy member of society; and, strong in the right and justice of our cause, we invoke the blessing of success."

CHAPTER X.

THIS Address of ours, which was well received by a large portion of the public press, by Sharman Crawford, and other patriotic Irishmen, was replied to by Mr. O'Connell, on behalf of the *Precursors.* It was entitled, "The Reply of the Precursor Society, on behalf of the People of Ireland, to the Address of the persons styling themselves the Radical Reformers of England, Scotland, and Wales." In this reply he deplored our ignorance of the Irish people; contrasted the conduct of Whigs and Tories; charged us with the want of sympathy for the sufferings of his countrymen, and with want of candour in disclaiming leadership; and concluded with charging upon us the physical force doctrine of O'Connor, Stephens, and Oastler. The following was put forth in answer to it :—

"The Working Men's Association to the Irish People, in Reply to an Address on their behalf by Persons styling themselves the Precursors.

"Fellow Countrymen,—The object of the Radical address to you, signed on behalf of a hundred and thirty-six associations, was to show you, notwithstanding Mr. O'Connell's assertion to the contrary, that there were men among us cordially disposed to unite with you to render you 'justice,' as there were others resolved to unite to keep you in the reins of Whiggery *for their own especial advantage,* careless of the beggary and wretchedness of the millions. And we also, in thus addressing you, are no less anxious to secure your co-operation towards effecting one of the greatest objects men can perform on earth to be acceptable to heaven; that of improving those institutions which, according to their purity or corruption, render a nation enlightened, prosperous, and happy, or ignorant, poor and degraded.

"It would appear, however, from the persons who style themselves 'the Precursors,' and who have taken upon themselves to write for all Ireland, that whatever hopes or sentiments animate the great bulk of your countrymen, there are persons among you who do not desire union with men whose objects are 'justice for all classes.' And if we could bring ourselves to believe that these persons represented the national mind of Ireland, and that that mind was so steeped in the opiate of Whiggery as to lay its thoughts and feelings prostrate before one man—though that man's talents were as transcendant as *their* gratitude has been unbounded—we should rather be disposed to despair for her fate than entertain bright hopes of her regeneration.

"The document we refer to is an echo of the Whig press of England—what it fails to answer it does not scruple to pervert. It taunts us with wanting candour, and accuses us of falsehood, and yet itself is made up of the very essentials it condemns. It is, however, what it was intended to be, *a Whig apple of discord;* not only to prevent union between the English and Irish radicals, but, if possible, to divide those already united. It begins by upbraiding us for not having denounced certain individuals for their expressions of violence. In reply to which we beg to inform you that our great object has been to honestly pursue principles rather than to denounce men; we have left abuse to those who are better masters of the art. And even were we so disposed, we could not except that great reprover of his age, Mr. O'Connell himself, who, when denouncing others for impropriety of language, talks of petitioning with 'a million and a half of men of *fighting age*."

From the origin of our Association we have ever discountenanced violence—we have ever declared that the moral power of the people would be the most effective weapon to combat the enemies of freedom, and similar opinions were expressed in the address we sent you. Yet for all these declarations, our character has been belied and our motives impugned, because individuals have been found to attend our meetings who, like Mr. O'Connell, have appealed to the passions rather than to the intellect of men. No man has made stronger appeals to the lower feelings of an assembly than the chairman of the Precursors; his 'bloody and brutal' sentiments, his pre-eminently abusive expressions, and fighting threats, have been more loudly applauded by his select audiences than have similar expressions been by the poor weavers of the north. No persons can more sincerely regret than we do the improprieties of language and threats of violence persons, professing the sacred name of Reformers, have recently indulged in; they have only afforded delight to the enemy, and engendered doubts and recriminations among friends. We are of opinion that whatever is gained in England by force, by force must be sustained; but whatever springs from knowledge and justice will sustain itself. Therefore it is that in our aspirations of freedom we seek to build up her temple *in peace*—to raise up a social and political edifice founded on national enlightenment and justice—a temple in which all classes might freely worship without tax, tribute, or reproach; in which all might unite to devise wisely and execute justly, and where the energies of all should be directed to the solving that great political problem, yet unsolved by any nation—*how shall all the resources of our country, mentally, morally, and physically, be made to produce the greatest happiness for all its members?*

"We confess that our imaginations sicken at any prospect of civil discord, even if oppressors only were to be the victims, and therefore earnestly trust that the edifice we are seeking to rear may never be established upon a foundation of blood, to be cursed by widowed mothers and undermined by the fatherless. But we must confess we greatly doubt the sincerity of those who, while deprecating violence, are continually boasting of the physical force of 'eight millions,' and threatening that 'Ireland alone would afford sufficient force to crush a revolution in England,' and that they '*are as ready to go to battle as any people in the world.*'

"But we are wisely informed by the Precursors that the words 'universal suffrage' have no magic in them. We thank them for this information ; but inasmuch as they are words used by all *honest radicals* to express the extent of the suffrage they desire, defined also, as these words have been, to mean the right of voting to all males above twenty-one, of sane mind, untainted by crime, we think it more honest and straightforward for all (*especially those who have sworn and pledged themselves to universal suffrage*) to retain the well-understood term rather than to adopt the less ingenious Whig phrase of ' the greatest possible extension of the suffrage that can practically be obtained.'

" The extent of the suffrage which ' can practically be obtained ' will depend on the honesty and perseverance of reformers. If they shall ever be induced to give up any portion of their principles to secure any unworthy object or fraudulent position—to gain power, place, or patronage—they will most certainly be induced to make still further sacrifice of principle *to retain what they have gained;* and thus from their miserable position principle after principle must be abandoned, till those who began as practical reformers turn out practical apostates.

" Persons wishing to impose upon the public words without definite meaning, as well as those who are not disposed to adopt radical principles, may have some excuse in coining language to express their desires ; but surely the chairman, at least, of the Precursors has not this excuse, for setting aside his public avowals of having been *sworn* to universal suffrage, *we have his signature attached to a resolution of his own proposing,* pledging himself ' *to support and vote for a Bill to be brought into the House of Commons, embodying the principles of universal suffrage, equal representation, free selection of representatives without reference to property, the ballot, and short Parliaments of fixed duration.*' Nay more, *he was one of the committee for drawing up that Bill, and the Bill that emanated from that committee was the People's Charter.* To that great bond of ' justice ' we mean to keep him ; we shall demand his support and vote for it in the forthcoming session, agreeably to the pledge he has given and the part he has taken ; his differing from its details will not be taken as an excuse, but will rather be attributed to his neglect of duty.

" It would appear that the gentlemen of the Precursors persist in adopting the same unmanly policy towards us as the Whig and Tory press. Finding they could not justly oppose our principles nor answer our arguments—finding that our public appeals in favour of temperance, knowledge, social improvement, and political right, were bringing around our standard good men of all classes, creeds, and opinions, they have endeavoured to enlist public opinion against us by identifying us with the sentiments and opinions of others. ' The Oastlers, Stephens's, and O'Connors,' are charged as being ' our leaders,' notwithstanding we have repeatedly disclaimed leadership of every description. Now, what can be more apparent than the wilful perversion of truth, which repeatedly identifies Mr. Oastler in particular with our proceedings; he has often publicly avowed himself as an ' Ultra Tory,' and to our knowledge has never attended one meeting in favour of our Charter. And Mr. Stephens is more known for his opposition to the new Poor Law than for his advocacy of Radicalism; he has ridiculed our principles and publicly declared his want of confidence in us. But still, as far as either of these gentlemen has sympathised with the infant factory children, and for the poor and oppressed in their respective districts, they are entitled to our honest praise; but as far as their violent language and mischievous advice to violence have been expressed, we deprecate their conduct. And as far as Mr. O'Connor and others have deviated from a just course and followed their example, we equally disapprove of theirs; because we think with that honest patriot, Mr. Sharman Crawford, that ' *when the application of physical force* is held forth as *the moving power* for attaining the reform of our institutions, the aggregation of the *moral power*, which can alone render physical force either justifiable or effective, is destroyed.' But in thus disproving of the language which Mr. Fergus O'Connor has frequently indulged in, we are no ways inclined to gratify the vindictive spirit of Daniel O'Connell by injuring the usefulness of that gentleman, still less to gratify the enemy by dividing the Radicals of North and South. We verily believe Mr. O'Connor to be sincere in his desire to promote the cause of reform, and it is because we think such language highly mischievous to it, that we thus honestly express our opinion.*

" We are told by the Precursors ' that no popular party can possibly be without leaders, that those who do the business are necessarily leaders.' Now let us not be misunderstood—we understand by leadership, the implicit reliance and obedience of any body of men to one man's will—the foolish belief that he of necessity knows more and can do better, under all circumstances for the whole body, than could be done if they deliberated and acted according to the knowledge and judgment of the whole. Now the experience of the past has taught us, that whenever a person is thus elevated *as a leader* he becomes the principal, and generally the vulnerable object of attack. If he can be influenced through his vanity or his avarice, the blind reliance of his followers renders them the secure victims of the enemy. Do you for a moment suppose, that if the vast number of intelligent minds which do honour to your country, had been free from the domination of leadership, and for the last four years were united to devise the best means of politically and socially benefiting your country, that you would have been led for that time in the quagmire of Whiggery for fear of the bugbear of Toryism? That you would be loyally shouting your gratitude because Mr. O'Connell has some *insecure* portion of patronage, and is consequently enabled to drag along with him a train of expectants, who hail him as the idol of to-day, but would as readily bow before other idols to-morrow ?

" We are accused of ' wanting candour ' for condemning equally the two factions of Whig and Tory, and that ' our injustice to the Whigs demonstrates our want of sympathy to Ireland.' We must, however, again confess, that the long catalogue of Whig perfections which the Precursors doubtlessly prepared to move our sympathy, has not

* This passage was amended from my original draft, for the purpose of maintaining union; I doubted his sincerity then, and have had abundant proofs since.

effected its purpose. We think, however, that their *superior candour* should have caused them to have added Catholic emancipation to the list, which the Tories are said to have given to Ireland; but, as we think of the Whigs on the questions of the Reform Bill and Negro Slavery, they yielded to public opinion what in safety and in justice they could no longer withhold. But the Whigs, in yielding, completely marred the benefits of the one, and made us pay a very considerable price for the other. Among all the heinous sins of Toryism, there is not one but its Whig parallel might easily be found, and we conscientiously believe that there are no acts of atrocities which the Tories have inflicted on England or Ireland, that can match those deeds which the perfidious Whigs have inflicted on our Canadian brethren; and shame to Mr. O'Connell—after his profession of sympathy, after his public promises and declaration, that he would use his power and influence to prevent the sacrifice of their constitutional rights—he acquiesced by his absence, in the most despotic act that ever disgraced an English House of Commons in the blackest days of Toryism, and which act, and all the horrible consequences that have followed, might have been prevented if he and his other Whig admirers had been true to justice. Talk of what the Tories did in America, match their deeds if you can with what the Whigs have inflicted on Canada. They have not scrupled to destroy every vestige of their constitutional rights—their selfish and arrogant myrmidons were the first to provoke Canadian resistance to their unparalleled despotism—they then imprisoned their legislators and proscribed and hunted down the best men of the country, they have brutally encouraged ignorant savages to glut their thirst for blood, they have destroyed the freedom of the press, suspended the Habeas Corpus Act, proclaimed martial law, burned their churches, sacked their villages, laid the country in ashes at the fiat of one man, and confiscation and plunder have been the warwhoop of their brutal soldiers. Gracious Creator of human beings! talk of the crimes of Toryism! match Whiggery with Nicholas instead.

" As to the Coercion Act, which Mr. O'Connell denounces as the standing memento of the Grey and Brougham (and he should have added Melbourne) Administration, we think that next to that despotic measure he ought not to forget the barbarous and arbitrary powers of the one that was substituted for it *by his own approval* in 1835; and which, when Sharman Crawford moved for its repeal, Mr. O'Connell pronounced to be ' *a very necessary law.*' We hope that the Irish people will make an analysis of these two acts for Mr. O'Connell's especial perusal.

" We must here, however, make an observation on the absurd notion of gratitude inculcated by Mr. O'Connell and his disciples. It is assumed that because a set of men, called Whigs or Tories, some fifty years or a century ago performed a good action or a dishonourable deed, that we forsooth and our children, must always be very grateful to the party of the one, and cherish eternal enmity against the party of the other, *though not even a relative of the persons who did either of the acts* compose the present faction. This kind of ' gratitude ' may afford Mr. O'Connell an excuse for his present policy, but it is not of that description our ' common sense ' inculcates.

" We think that no course of policy that could have been adopted could have done more mischief to the cause of Radicalism, than has the absurd folly of pulling down and the setting up of parties and factions. We have long since given up this game, and it shall be our policy for the future, *to prevent any faction from possessing political ascendancy in this country*, if we can prevent it, aye, even a Radical *faction* itself, for the principle of Radicalism is opposed to all faction. And in thus expressing our resolve, we think (however contemptible we may appear) we have the power to prevent *the supremacy* of either Whig or Tory Faction. Nor do we want any ' leader ' or party individual to assist us to effect this object.

" Sincerely hoping that you will give up your devoted attachment to party men and measures of every description, that the good and the wise of all classes among you will be united equally against Whig and Tory domination, and that you will urge your representatives to break through the trammels of *political expediency*, and advocate those broad principles of justice, which can alone redeem our common country. We remain with truth and sincerity your fellow-countrymen."

Now there was no doubt of the truth of Mr. O'Connell's assertions regarding the physical force mania generated in many parts of the kingdom by the speeches of O'Connor, Stephens, and Oastler against the New Poor Law; the great injustice was in branding all the Radicals of England and Scotland as the abettors and followers of these men. For it was well known to him that a large section of them had for years previously disclaimed the doctrine of physical force, even when he himself was reminding his countrymen that those "who would be free, themselves must strike the blow." He knew well that the Birmingham Council, the members of our Association, and a number of the Radical and Working Men's Associations of Scotland had repudiated the doctrine, and had exerted themselves in various ways to check its progress. The fact was known to him that a large number of the Radicals of Edinburgh met on the Carlton Hill and passed a series of resolutions condemnatory of the physical force folly, which were warmly responded to by other towns, and were ably supported by the earnest eloquence and abilities of such men as John Fraser, the Editor of the "True Scotsman," the Rev. Patrick Brewster, and numerous others. Indeed Fergus O'Connor must have considered them as highly censurable of himself, for he posted off to Edinburgh with great speed and called a meeting of his disciples together to pass votes of confidence in him and Stephens, and, as he called it, to rescind the Carlton Hill resolutions. But Mr. O'Connell's conduct was the more to be condemned as he had by his desertion and treachery to our cause, coupled with his entreaties and blarneying in favour of Whiggery, caused many of the liberal members of Parliament to stand aloof from our movement whose aid, coupled with his own powerful talents, would have effectually kept back the physical force advocates, and conducted our movement to a successful issue. I had it from Mr. Joseph Hume himself that it was Mr. O'Connell's entreaties to give the Whigs a fair trial *for the sake of Ireland*, that led him and others to stand aloof as they had done.

But the meeting of the Convention was now fast approaching, and so strong was the hope reposed in that meeting by the Chartist body, that the great majority of them manifested the strongest desire to sacrifice their peculiar feelings and convictions for the sake of union. A few hot-brained enthusiasts, however, were not so patriotic; union was naught with them compared with their own blustering harangues about arming and fighting; these and their daily invectives against everything bearing the resemblance of moderation, preparedness, or intellectual and moral effort, served to create constant irritation in our ranks, and ultimately to cause distrust and disunion. On the other hand there were not wanting exciting incidents, opposing preparations, denunciations, and ridicule, on the part of those who opposed our claims, to stir up the feelings and try the patience of poor frail humanity; so that when the gauntlet was eventually cast down we need not wonder at the numbers prepared to take it up in the spirit of resolute and reckless defiance.

CHAPTER XI.

THE General Convention of the Industrious Classes originated with the Birmingham Political Union, as did also the National Rent Fund, the proposal for a Sacred Month, the plan of Simultaneous Meetings, and the first National Petition.*   This last document was, I believe, drawn up by the late Mr. R. K. Douglas, then editor of the *Birmingham Journal,* an able and talented writer, and a keen, clear, eloquent speaker; one, in fact, of the most efficient men delegated to the Convention.   The delegates to this body were, for the most part, appointed by very large bodies of men.   The Birmingham meeting was composed of 200,000, the Manchester meeting of 300,000, that of Glasgow of 150,000, of Newcastle of 70,000, and other towns equally large in proportion to their population. The number of delegates composing the Convention was *fifty-three,* many of them representing several places, with the view to economy.   Of this number three were magistrates, six newspaper editors, one clergyman of the Church of England, one Dissenting minister, and two doctors of medicine, the remainder being shopkeepers, tradesmen, and journeymen.   They held their first meeting at the British Coffee House, Cockspur Street, Charing Cross, on Monday, February 4th, 1839, and subsequently met in the hall of the Honourable and Ancient Lumber Troop, Bolt Court, Fleet Street.   On their first assembling the Birmingham delegates proposed me as secretary, and, though the proposition was at first strongly opposed by some of the physical force party, I was eventually elected unanimously.   This, it would seem, gave great offence to

---

* See a copy of it in the Appendix.

O'Connor, who was not present when the election took place, for at the next meeting he posted up a notice of motion, by the adoption of which he thought he should get rid of me as secretary. It was to the effect that persons accepting any paid office in the Convention should resign their delegation. Finding, however, that I had resolved to offer my services *gratuitously* as secretary, rather than resign my privilege as a delegate, he withdrew the notice he had given.

Not intending in this memoir to give a particular history of all the doings of the Convention, I shall confine myself to a few of the most prominent particulars, sufficient perhaps to show the causes that marred the great object we had in view, *that of creating and extending a public opinion in favour of the principles of the People's Charter.* Soon after our assembling the subject of the Queen's speech from the throne became a question for discussion, in consequence of a passage in it charging some portion of the people with " disobedience, and resistance to the laws." This induced us to put forth an address to the people (drawn up by Dr. Taylor), in which the charge was repudiated, and in which the Whigs were reminded of their own resistance to the laws, for the forcing of the Reform Bill, when Mr. William Brougham and Lord Fitzwilliam in particular publicly declared their resolution of resisting the law by the non-payment of taxes.

The rules and regulations for conducting our proceedings, drawn up by myself, were next agreed to, and a barrister consulted for ascertaining the legality of our objects, whose opinion, though very guardedly worded, seemed satisfactory to the members. On the collection of the petition sheets from different towns it was found that many parts of the country, in which there had been no political organization, had done little or nothing towards procuring signatures. This caused us to delay its presentation for a few weeks, and in the interim to send out a number of our members as missionaries to different parts of the country, with the view of making the principles of the Charter more generally known, and for obtaining additional signatures to our petition. The instructions given

to our missionaries were, " to refrain from all violent and
unconstitutional language, and not to infringe the law in
any manner by word or deed." Mr. James Paul Cobbett,
delegate from Yorkshire, seems to have been alarmed by
this resolution to send out missionaries, and shortly afterwards brought forward a series of resolutions, to the effect
that the whole business of the Convention should be to
present the national petition. This proposal, not being
agreed to by the members, that gentleman gave in his
resignation. The delay, too, in presenting the petition.
gave great offence to the physical force party, and more
especially to the *Democratic Association of London*, at the
head of which was Mr. George Julian Harney, one of the
most indiscreet, if not the most violent, among them, for
he scrupled not to flourish his dagger at public meetings,
in order to give point to his perorations.* This party,
being joined by a few of the most hotheaded and enthusiastic members of the Convention, were very industrious
out of doors in censuring and denouncing us for our delay
at their various meetings, and also created much excitement, division, and loss of time in the Convention by their
insane and foolish conduct. It was to gratify this party
that O'Connor brought forward his motion for calling the
public meeting at the Crown and Anchor, on March 11th,
at which meeting the physical force party displayed such
violence and folly as to cause the Birmingham delegates,
Messrs. Salt, Hadley, and Douglas, to secede from us.
It may be necessary, however, to state that this violent
party were greatly in the minority, both for numbers and
talent, till the resignation of the Birmingham delegates and
other resignations that speedily followed, whose places
were supplied, for the most part, with men of less reasonable views. During the delay that took place in the presentation of the petition, those of the members not engaged
as missionaries employed themselves in the discussion of a
variety of questions brought before them. About the first
of those questions was that of " ulterior measures," or

---

* Our friend Harney has since redeemed his past violence and
folly, by his intelligent writings and moderation in the cause of
right and justice.

measures to be adopted if the petition should be rejected. This was introduced by Bailie Craig, of Ayrshire, but which question it was judged prudent to postpone until after the presentation of the petition. The "grievances of Ireland" also gave rise to a long discussion, but very little practical benefit, as did also "the suffering in the manufacturing districts," "the factory system," the "New Rural Police Bill," and several other subjects. In fact the love of talk was as characteristic of our little house as the big one at Westminster. Among the letters read one morning was one from the London Democratic Association, containing a series of resolutions passed at one of their meetings, to the effect, "that if the Convention did its duty the Charter would be the law of the land in less than a month;" "that no delay should take place in the presentation of the national petition;" and "that every act of injustice and oppression should be immediately met by resistance." A motion that this ultra communication should not be received gave rise to a very long discussion, in which the conduct of three members, Harney, Ryder, and Marsden (who took part in the meeting referred to), was very warmly reprobated and condemned. They having expressed their approbation of the resolutions referred to during the debate, a motion was brought forward at the next meeting by Mr. Whittle, the editor of the *Champion*, to the effect that they should be called upon to offer an apology for, and disclaimer of the resolutions addressed to the Convention. They having refused to do this, a motion was brought forward the next day for expelling them, when they deemed it advisable to make the apology required, after they had thus wasted three days of our time.

Another subject, about this period, which produced great excitement in the Convention, as well as throughout the country, was the conduct of Lord John Russell's Ministry towards Mr. John Frost, of Newport (one of our members), whom they struck from the roll of magistrates for attending two Chartist meetings in London. It was thought, however, that Mr. Frost's straightforward and independent letter to Lord John

Russell, in reply to the charge made against him, formed a more serious offence in the eyes of his little mightiness, than the ostensible one of attending the public meetings. That Mr. Frost's conduct, as a magistrate and a man, was greatly estimated by his townsmen may be judged of by the fact that on the first rumour of his exclusion, a testimonial was transmitted to the Home Secretary on his behalf, signed by most of the leading and influential men of the town, men of all political creeds and opinions.

In the beginning of April Mr. Richardson brought forward a motion, of which he had given previous notice, relative to the right of the people to arm, and in a long speech quoted a great many authorities, ancient and modern, in support of his views. A resolution to the effect " that it was admitted by the highest authorities, beyond the possibility of doubt, that the people of this country had the right to use arms," was finally agreed to, it having been supported by Messrs. O'Brien, Fletcher, M'Douall, Harney, Neesom, and O'Connor, and opposed by Halley, Carpenter, Burns, Rogers, and others.

One day towards the latter end of this month O'Connor got up and called the attention of the Convention to the fact, that in the indictment sent up to the King's Bench against the Rev. Mr. Stephens, the jurors had declared on their oaths, *that the Convention was an illegal body.* On the following day he proposed " that on Monday, the 13th of May, the Convention should commence holding its sittings in Birmingham." No reasonable argument having been adduced in favour of such a motion, and thinking, moreover, that it seemed a cowardly proceeding, I thought it well to propose an amendment to the effect " that we continue to hold our sittings in London till after the presentation of the petition, and until we had come to some vote respecting the introduction of the People's Charter to Parliament." My amendment having been lost by a majority of seven, and other objections having been taken to O'Connor's motion it was postponed to a future day.

On the 6th of May the national petition was taken to the residence of Mr. Attwood, in Panton Square, that gentleman, in conjunction with Mr. Fielden, having promised to present it to parliament on the following Monday.

When all the sheets of this bulky document were united it was found to be *nearly three miles long*, and signed by 1,283,000 persons, all of them, I believe, the genuine signatures of men earnest in their desire for the suffrage, however they may have differed about the means of obtaining it. On our arrival at Mr. Attwood's, that gentleman informed us that he was then doubtful when he should be able to present it, as Lord John Russell's resignation from the Ministry was expected that evening. We informed him that we were desirous that he should present it as early as possible, and that he should also take the earliest opportunity to move for leave to bring in a Bill entitled the People's Charter. This last he refused to do, as he said he did not agree with all the points of it, especially that of electoral districts. A long conversation then took place regarding what he would do in the matter, which, he said, would altogether depend on the manner in which he was treated by the House of Commons when he presented the petition. In fact the issue of paper money was more important to Mr. Attwood than the People's Charter. One of our members, Mr. Vincent, having been arrested on the 10th of May, 1839, on a warrant by the magistrates of Newport, on a charge of conspiracy and sedition, Fergus O'Connor again brought forward his motion for adjourning to Birmingham. The topics of his speech were, the change of ministers; the arrest of Vincent, the safety of the Convention, and the sympathy and support we should have if we adjourned to Birmingham. In this proposal he was supported by many delegates who had previously opposed it, as the change in the ministry had rendered it doubtful when the petition would be presented. There were others who opposed it on the grounds that we had not yet agreed to the project of "ulterior measures," of which so much had been said. And here I deem it necessary to give a brief history of our "Manifesto of Ulterior Measures," for reasons hereafter stated.

As many members of the Convention lodged at the Arundle Coffee House, opposite St. Clement's Church, a number of us were induced to subscribe a small sum for the purpose of retaining the first floor of that place to ourselves, it being a very convenient place for assembling together to talk matters over when we were not engaged in the business of the Convention. As many of the physical force party, on those occasions, as well as in the convention, had talked largely of "ulterior measures," without seeming to entertain any very clear ideas on the subject, many of the more prudent portion thought it necessary to call a meeting of the delegates together in that room for the purpose of talking the matter over and arriving at some definite opinion on the subject, rather than trust to its being hastily introduced to the convention by some hot-headed member without thought or consideration. A meeting of the delegates was therefore called at the " Arundle " for the purpose of talking the subject over among ourselves before it was introduced publicly to the Convention. At this meeting a large number of the delegates attended; a chairman was appointed, and every member present called upon in rotation for his opinion regarding the ulterior measures to be adopted should the prayer of the petition be rejected. As their secretary, I took notes of the opinions given and conclusions arrived at, which in the course of the week I embodied in the form of a manifesto, and laid before them at their next meeting at the same place. At that meeting the Rev. Mr. Stephens attended, and, after the manifesto was read over, he and others were very complimentary in its praise. It was then resolved that we should hold another meeting at the rooms of the Working Men's Association for the purpose of discussing it clause by clause. After it had been thus discussed it was all but unanimously agreed to, the only dissentient being Mr. Halley, of Dunfermline. Being thus far agreed to, it was resolved that we should publicly name a committee the next day in the Convention for considering the subject of ulterior measures. We did so, the committee named being Messrs. Frost, O'Connor, Bussy, Pitkeithley and Mills, together with myself as secretary. The manifesto as prepared was laid before them, and, after some slight verbal alterations, was agreed to, and ordered to be laid before the Convention as their report. Before, however, this could be done, O'Connor had proposed the adjournment to Birmingham, as before described ; so that when the manifesto was brought before the Convention, it was resolved " that the further consideration of it be deferred till we got to Birmingham." To that town we accordingly went on the 13th of May, and were welcomed by a vast assemblage of the people, whose excitement about this period had been greatly increased by the arbitrary conduct of their local authorities regarding the right of meetings in the Bull-ring, coupled with Lord John Russell's letter to the magistracy *offering arms to any association of the middle classes that might be formed for putting down the Chartist meetings.* The day after our arrival at Birmingham the consideration of the manifesto took place, which, after some trifling amendment, was adopted, and ten thousand copies of it ordered to be printed and circulated. At the next meeting O'Connor proposed that in the event of any attempt being made to interfere with the simultaneous meetings, about to be held, the delegates should repair to Birmingham, declare their meetings permanent, and " recommend *the observance of all the measures contained in the manifesto.*" During the Whitsun holidays the delegates repaired to their different constituencies for the purpose of attending the simultaneous meetings, and for ascertaining the opinion of the people *regarding the manifesto.* O'Connor (and others who have since condemned that document) spoke at several of those meetings, but not one word did they say in opposition to, or in repudiation of it at that time, but when I was cooped up in Warwick Gaol he had the impudence to boast that he was the man that prevented the Sacred Month from taking place ! although, as described, he was an active party in recommending it. He subsequently on several occasions endeavoured to persuade his dupes that I was the concoctor of the violent measure, although himself and his disciples were the first to talk of arming, of the run upon the banks, and the Attwood project of *the sacred month.* I mention these facts in no way to disclaim the hand I had in it, although I believe that I did an act of folly in being a party to *some of its provisions;* but I sacrificed much in that convention for the sake of union, and for the love and hope I had in the cause, and I have still vanity enough to believe that if I had not been imprisoned I could have prevented many of the outbreaks and follies that occurred. The following is a copy of the manifesto referred to :—

" Countrymen and Fellow-Bondsmen,—The fiat of our privileged oppressors has gone forth—that the multitude must be kept in subjection. The mask of CONSTITUTIONAL LIBERTY is thrown for ever aside, and the form of DESPOTISM stands hideously before us: for, let it be no longer disguised, THE GOVERNMENT OF ENGLAND IS A DESPOTISM AND HER INDUSTRIOUS MILLIONS SLAVES. Her ' constitutional rights ' are specious forms wanting substance ; her forms of ' justice ' subterfuges for legal plunder and class domination; her ' right of the subject' is slavery, without the slave's privilege ; her ' right of petitioning ' a farce ; her ' religious freedom ' a cheat.

" Fellow-Countrymen,— Our stalwart ancestors boasted of rights which the simplicity of their laws made clear, and their bravery protected ; but we, their degenerate children, have patiently yielded to one infringement after another till the last vestige of RIGHT has been lost in the *mysticism* of legislation, and the armed force of the country transferred to soldiers and policemen. But if there be yet within you a latent spark of that quality which was wont to distinguish Englishmen throughout the globe—of that manly courage with which our forefathers sacredly guarded our island, and arrested with their iron grasp foreign foe or domestic spoiler—you will start from your political slumber, and resolve, by all that renders life desirable, to make your homes happy, your laws just, and your altars free, or peril life in the attempt.

" We will not, however, point out a path in which we are not prepared to lead ; neither will we peril our political rights on any ill-advised proposal, which would give joy to the enemy, but death to our cause. But we are prepared—and we trust that you, our constituents,

14

are also—to peril that life which God has bestowed for no holier purpose than to righteously endeavour to make our country free and our brethren happy. And in thus expressing our determination, we appeal to Almighty Wisdom with reverence, and to impartial posterity with confidence—that we have right and justice on our side.

"Believing that our political burthens and social grievances are the result of exclusive law-making, we have provided for that evil what we conceive to be a remedy —'The People's Charter'—and public opinion has been concentrated in favour of that remedy to an extent unpre-cedented in the annals of our country. We have embodied its principles in a *Petition to Parliament*; those who dared to brave the menaces of employers, the sneers of faction and the power of wealth, have appended their signatures to that petition, and millions who dared not brave starvation and misery to do so, have responded in silence to its prayer.

"The answer, fellow-countrymen, to your 'constitu-tional' and *peaceful* application may now be anticipated. We were prepared on the presentation of the petition for the subtile sophistry and fraudulent assertions of Whig-gery; *but we may now be prepared for the worst;* for we clearly perceive the despotic determination of both Whigs and Tories to maintain their power and supremacy at any risk.

"We see victim after victim daily selected, and silently witness one constitutional right after another annihilated; we perceive the *Whig* and the shuffling *professor of Liberalism* uniting their influence to bind down the millions, and, if possible, to stifle their prayers and petitions for justice.

"Men and women of Britain, will you tamely submit to the insult? Will you submit to incessant toil from birth to death, to give in tax and plunder out of every *twelve* hours' labour the proceeds of *nine* hours to support your idle and insolent oppressors? Will you much longer submit to see the greatest blessings of mechanical art converted into the greatest curses of social life?—to see children forced to compete with their parents, wives with their husbands, and the whole of society morally and physically degraded to support the aristocracies of wealth and title ? Will you thus allow your wives and daughters to be degraded, your children to be nursed in misery, stultified by toil, and to become the victims of the vice our corrupt institutions have engendered ? Will you permit the stroke of affliction, the misfortunes of poverty, and the infirmities of age to be branded and punished as crimes, and give our selfish oppressors an excuse for rending asunder man and wife, parent and child, and continue passive observers till you and yours become the victims ?

"Perish the cowardly feeling ; and infamous be the passive being who can witness his country's degradation, without a struggle to prevent or a determination to remove it ! Rather like Sampson would we cling to the pillars which sustain our social fabric, and, failing to base it upon principles of justice, fall victims beneath its ruins.

"Shall it be said, fellow-countrymen, that four millions of men, capable of bearing arms, and defending their country against every foreign assailant, allowed a few domestic oppressors to enslave and degrade them ? That they suffered the constitutional right of possessing arms, to defend the constitutional privileges their ancestors bequeathed to them, to be disregarded or forgotten, till one after another they have been robbed of their rights, and have submitted to be awed into silence by the bludgeons of policemen ? Hence our modern legislators, fearing that knowledge has even converted soldiers into patriots, are preparing to dispense with their services in England, and to substitute a legion of police, to mar the peace of every village in the empire.

"Men of England, Scotland, and Wales, we have sworn with your aid to achieve our liberties or die ! and in this resolve we seek to save our country from a fate we do not desire to witness. If you longer continue passive slaves, *the fate of unhappy Ireland will soon be yours*, and that of Ireland more degraded still. For, be assured, the joyful hope of freedom which now inspires the millions, if not speedily realized, will turn into wild revenge.

The sickening thought of unrequited toil—their cheerless homes—their stunted starving offspring—the pallid partners of their wretchedness—their aged parents pining apart in a workhouse—the state of trade presenting to their imaginations no brighter prospect—these, together with the petty tyranny that daily torments them, will exasperate them to destroy what they are denied the enjoyment of. Terror will soon give wings to British capital, and it will fly to other climes where security can be found. The middle-class population of our country—the distributors and exchangers of wealth—will be broken down by bankruptcy and insolvency. Our famed commerce, which at present is sustained by a breath, will be destroyed. The wrongs which landlords, farmers and manufacturers, have conspired to heap upon the working millions, will burst into a flame; and the property of our cities, no ways vengeance proof, will be the more in peril by being the basis of legislative injustice.

" This, fellow-countrymen, is a state of things we are anxious to avert, and however the paid libellers of the day may impute to us other motives, we solemnly believe that the Radical Reformers are the only restraining power that prevents the execution of an outraged people's vengeance. We would therefore urge all friends *of peace and order* to declare at once in favour of justice ; and unite with us to obtain that share of political power for the unenfranchised people which cannot much longer be safely withheld. How, we would ask, can those of the middle classes, who are yet standing apart from us, reconcile their conduct with their conscience, when they were parties to a compact with us to contend for the Reform Bill, and promised in return they would make it a stepping-stone to our political rights, while they still ungratefully neglect us ?

" Why will they presumptuously risk the consequences of such selfish conduct ? What fruits do they hope to gain by their exclusiveness ? They are now sowing the seeds of disappointment; we would implore them to beware of the harvest.

" Do they ardently desire the happiness and prosperity of their country ? Do they seek to develope the moral and intellectual energies of the people? Do they aim at cheap and efficient government? Do they desire equal laws justly administered? Do they wish for security for person and property, and to give to industry its honest reward? We, too, are in pursuit of similar objects; *let common interests, then, unite us in the pursuit.*

"We are contending for no visionary or impracticable scheme. The principles of our charter were the laws and customs of our ancestors, under which property was secure, and the working people happy and contented. Nay, these principles are now in practical operation in different parts of the world; and what forms the strongest argument in favour of their general adoption is, that wherever they are in practice the people are prosperous and happy.

"But, fellow-countrymen, both Whigs and Tories are seeking, by every means in their power, to crush our peaceful organization in favour of our charter. They are sending their miscreant spies to urge the people into madness; they are arming the rich against the poor, and man against his fellow-man. The war hounds of their will are trained and loosened for our slaughter; every bulwark of their injustice is fortified against us; and they fain hope that our impatient impetuosity may afford sport for their vengeance, and their triumph over our defeat give stability to their power.

"We trust, brethren, that you will disappoint their malignity, and live to regain our rights by other means— at least, we trust you will not *commence* the conflict. We have resolved to obtain our rights, 'peaceably if we may, forcibly if we must'; but woe to those who begin the warfare with the millions, or who forcibly restrain their peaceful agitation for justice—at one signal they will be enlightened to their error, and in one brief contest their power will be destroyed.

"You appointed us, fellow-countrymen, the humble instruments of your will and determination; we have performed the duty you imposed on us to the extent of our power, and are prepared still further to execute your commands. But, from the numerous communications we have received, we believe you expect us to collect the will and intentions of the country respecting *the most efficient means* for causing the People's Charter to become the law of the land.

"Anxious, therefore, clearly to ascertain the opinions and determination of the people in the shortest possible time, and doubly anxious to secure their righteous object *bloodless and stainless*, we respectfully submit the following propositions for your serious consideration :—

"That at all the simultaneous public meetings to be held for the purpose of petitioning the Queen to call good men to her councils, as well as at all subsequent meetings of your unions or associations up to the 1st of July, you submit the following questions to the people there assembled :—

"1. Whether they will be prepared, *at the request of the Convention*, to withdraw all sums of money they may individually or collectively have placed in savings' banks, private banks, or in the hands of any person hostile to their just rights ?

"2. Whether, at the same request, they will be prepared immediately to convert all their paper money into gold and silver ?

"3. Whether, *if the Convention shall determine that a sacred month* will be necessary to prepare the millions to secure the charter of their political salvation, they will firmly resolve to abstain from their labours during that period, as well as from the use of *all intoxicating drinks ?*

"4. Whether, according to their old constitutional right —a right which modern legislators would fain annihilate— they have prepared themselves *with the arms of freemen to defend the laws and constitutional privileges their ancestors bequeathed to them ?*

"5. Whether they will provide themselves with *chartist candidates,* so as to be prepared to propose them for their representatives at the next general election ; and if returned *by show of hands* such candidates to consider themselves veritable representatives of the people—to meet in London at a time hereafter to be determined on ?*

" 6. Whether they will resolve *to deal exclusively with Chartists,* and in all cases of persecution rally around and protect all those who may suffer in their righteous cause ?

" 7. Whether by all and every means in their power they will perseveringly contend for the great objects of the People's Charter, and resolve that no counter agitation for a less measure of justice shall divert them from their righteous object ?

" 8. Whether the people will determine to obey all the just and constitutional requests of the majority of the Convention ?

" After these simultaneous public meetings the Convention will hold its sittings, when by its deliberations, its missionaries, or otherwise, it will endeavour to ascertain the opinions of the people on all these important questions ; and having thus carefully ascertained the opinions and determination of the country, immediately after the 1st of July it will proceed to carry the will of the people into execution.

" Remember, brethren, our motto is *Union, Prudence,* and *Energy ;* by these combined we shall win the people's charter in spite of the people's enemies. Hoping that you will steadfastly and cautiously observe this motto, we remain your faithful representatives,

" THE MEMBERS OF THE CONVENTION."

---

* This was James Brontere O'Brien's plan.

CHAPTER XII.

ALTHOUGH there was great excitement throughout the country in consequence of the different arrests that had taken place, and the despotic conduct of the local authorities in many counties, the *Simultaneous Meetings* were very numerously attended, and went off very peaceably, the Convention having previously put forth their advice on the subject. During the recess, however, it became a serious question among the more prudent portion of the members, as to the course to be pursued when the Convention resumed its sittings at Birmingham. For though many of them had advocated the possession of arms, as an ancient and constitutional right, and as a means for securing protection and respect, they were far from advising the public exhibition or use of them. Still less were they agreed on the propriety of a general suspension of labour for a month, although they were not adverse to the discussion of the subject, as a threat to our adversaries. In fact, one of the Scotch delegates, Abraham Duncan, very pithily described the policy of this party when he said—"We must shake our oppressors well over hell's mouth, but we must not let them drop in." The withdrawal of their trade and benefit funds, and a run upon the banks, however, they thought perfectly right and justifiable, as it was their own money, and they had the precedent for it from the Whigs. The putting forth of an address, therefore, on this subject was about one of the first measures they adopted on their return to Birmingham; unfortunately coupled with an addenda regarding the sacred month which had much better been avoided. Respecting this *sacred month*, some few of us entertained the opinion, that before committing ourselves (as the Convention subsequently did when I was in prison), by the fixing of any specific time for its commencement; the Convention should fix a day *for one or two trades to cease from labour,* and at the same time call upon the country to raise a fund for supporting them. This we thought would be a mode *of testing the country;* for if persons were not disposed to pay a small sum weekly for such an object, we could not expect that they would agree to cease labouring altogether; and then we should have had a very reasonable excuse for abandoning the project. I had in fact made arrangements for preparing an Address on this subject, to be laid before the Convention on the Monday, but my arrest on the Saturday prevented the accomplishment of my desire.

The following are the circumstances that led to my arrest, and that of my fellow-prisoner, Mr. Collins :—It appears that the middle classes of Birmingham, during the agitation *for the Reform Bill,* were in the habit of meeting in the Bullring, in conjunction with the working classes, during a portion of their dinner hours and in the evenings, for the purpose of hearing the news of the day; when stirring appeals from the newspapers were read, and speeches made regarding the measure then before Parliament. The Reform Bill, however, being past, a great change was soon seen in the political conduct of some of the leading reformers of Birmingham, as well as of other towns. *Municipal reform* had given power and authority to some, and Whig patronage snug places to others. When, however, the agitation for the People's Charter commenced, the working classes, following the example of their former leaders, began to hold their meetings also in the Bullring. But this of course was not to be endured by the ex-reform authorities; what was once right and legal in themselves was denounced as seditious and treasonable in the multitude.* The poor infatuated workies, however, could not

---

* An instance of the extreme measures the middle classes were prepared to resort to at the first reform period was communicated to me by one of the principals engaged to carry it out. When the Duke of Wellington was called to the ministry with the object, it was believed, of silencing the political unions and putting down the reform agitation, an arrangement was entered into between the leading reformers of the North and Midland Counties and those of London

perceive the distinction of the Birmingham authorities between tho two political measures, but continued to meet as usual ; and though several of them were arrested, and held to bail for their obtuseness, their meetings were kept up. At last the governing powers of Birmingham, indignant at such proceedings, sent up to London to their former friends and allies requesting them to send down a strong posse of the new police to assist them. They came down by rail, and were no sooner out of their vans than they were led on by the authorities, truncheon in hand, and commenced a furious onslaught upon the men, women, and children who were assembled in the Bullring, listening peaceably to a person reading the newspaper. This proceeding, as may be supposed, greatly exasperated the people, and speedily a cry was raised for " Holloway," one of their usual places of meeting a little out of town. On their way thither, happening to pass St. Thomas's Church, they bethought themselves of a weapon with which to defend themselves should they be again attacked, and pulled down the railings round the churchyard. Once armed, however, they resolved on again returning to town to wreak their vengeance on the police. On returning, however, they were met by Dr. Taylor and Dr. McDouall, two of our convention, who, after much persuasion, induced them to throw away their arms. Dr. Taylor also subsequently interfered to prevent the ill-usage of one of the police, and very soon after was arrested for having been seen among the crowd.

The morning after this brutal attack, a number of the working classes of Birmingham called at the Convention Rooms, and stated that they were anxious that some public expression of opinion should be made regarding the out-

---

for seizing the wives and children of the aristocracy and carrying them as hostages into the North until the Reform Bill was past. My informant, Mr. Francis Place, told me that a thousand pounds were placed in his hands in furtherance of the plan, and for hiring carriages and other conveniences, a sufficient number of volunteers having prepared matters and held themselves in readiness. The run upon the bank, however, having been effective in driving the duke from office, this extreme measure was not necessary.

rage, and some advice given to them as to what was best to be done respecting their right of public meeting. Feeling most strongly with them, that a great injustice had been inflicted, I drew up and proposed to the Convention the three following resolutions, which were unanimously agreed to, and ordered to be printed. They were signed by myself as secretary, and taken to the printer by one of our members, Mr. John Collins:—

"1st.—That this Convention is of opinion that a wanton, flagrant, and unjust outrage has been made upon the people of Birmingham by a bloodthirsty and unconstitutional force from London, acting under the authority of men who, when out of office, sanctioned and took part in the meetings of the people; and now, when they share in public plunder, seek to keep the people in social slavery and political degradation.

"2nd.—That the people of Birmingham are the best judges of their own right to meet in the Bullring or elsewhere—have their own feelings to consult respecting he outrage given, and are the best judges of their own power and resources in order to obtain justice.

"3rd.—That the summary and despotic arrest of Dr. Taylor, our respected colleague, affords another convincing proof of the absence of all justice in England, and clearly shows that there is no security for life, liberty, or property till the people have some control over the laws which they are called upon to obey."

These resolutions were not posted long about the town before the printer was arrested, who, it seems, was speedily liberated on naming the person who had brought him the manuscript. The authorities then sent for Mr. Salt, one of the members of the Convention who had resigned, with the view of getting him to identify my handwriting. Having so far satisfied themselves, Mr. Collins and myself were next arrested, and brought up for examination before the newly-made recorder, Mr. Hill; and Messrs. P. H. Muntz, Shaw, Clark, Chance and Walker, magistrates of Birmingham. It was rather singular that the recorder was the gentleman whom we had consulted in London a few months previously *regarding the legality of our movement.* As there were no witnesses brought forward against us on this occasion, the recorder adopted the very un-English mode of questioning us, with the view of getting us to make such admissions as should self-convict us. In this course it would appear that he succeeded, to his own and the magistrates' satisfaction, for we were committed to take our trial at the next assizes, the bail required for our appearance being £1,000 each. We were accordingly sent off the next morning to Warwick Gaol till bail could be provided, and in the mean time the magistrates raised every possible objection to the bail offered, even requesting the bail offered for Mr. Collins *to be bound over to good behaviour,* as well as to appear at the assizes. One of my bail, Mr. Watts, of Islington, they at first refused, because he could not give a reference to a banker in town, although he offered to leave bank scrip, and title deeds to the amount of £1,600 in their hands till the trial took place. And it was not till after Mr. Leader, M.P. for Westminster, and Sir William Molesworth had offered to become my bail, that the magistrates agreed to accept the bail first offered, after they had been the means of keeping us in prison for *nine days.*

During this period of our imprisonment a number of other arrests had taken place, and the town of Birmingham kept in a very excited state by the constant aggressions made upon the people by the police. I may here remark that their conduct was subsequently made the subject of a public enquiry by the Town Council of Birmingham, headed by Mr. Joseph Sturge, and the opinion arrived at was couched in almost the very terms of one of the resolutions for which I was imprisoned, namely, " That it was proved that a brutal and bloody attack had been made upon the people of Birmingham, and that it was their opinion that if the police had not attacked the people, no disorder would have occurred, and they considered the riot was incited by the London police." The excitement however was, as I have said, continued from day to day by the constant collisions between the people and the police, aided at times by the soldiery, till, on the evening of the 15th of July, it broke through all bounds. It would seem that the news of our bail having been accepted, and that we were expected into town that evening, had led great numbers of the people to again assemble in the Bullring. The sudden appearance of the police for the purpose of dispersing them, only served to exasperate them into frenzy. In a short time the police were scattered, the gas-lights extinguished, and a rush made upon the shops of several persons in the Bullring, who had rendered themselves peculiarly obnoxious to the people by their recent conduct, and very speedily their shops were in flames. On our return from Warwick towards Birmingham we were fortunately met on the road by Mr. Collins's brother and two or three of his friends, who had come for the purpose of making us acquainted with this lamentable affair. This determined us at once to change our route, so as to enter Birmingham by an opposite direction to that we were going. And fortunately it was for us that we met with those persons, as we should otherwise have entered through the Bullring, and possibly have been charged with the burnings. As it was, the outrage was in a great measure laid to our charge, and the weapons, said to have been taken from persons by the police on that occasion, were brought forward by Lord Campbell and laid upon the table during our trial, as if to prejudice the jury still further against us. On our return to town I drew up a petition to both Houses of Parliament, declaring the indignities to which we had been subjected in Warwick Gaol while we were waiting for trial, *before we were tried or found guilty of any offence.* The one to the Commons was presented by Mr. Leader, and that to the Lords by Lord Brougham, the latter having made a very impressive speech on the occasion. When he came to that part of our petition about my hair being cropped by a common felon, it was received with a derisive laugh by some members of the House of Privilege, which at once was met by a very severe rebuke from Lord Brougham. He said, "I am extremely mortified to perceive that such a statement as this should produce in any part of this House tokens of merriment. I deem it to be the most disgraceful conduct I have ever known in any assembly. I feel almost ashamed to belong to such an assembly. I really am ashamed to belong to a place where any men could hear of such indignities being committed upon the persons of their fellow-creatures, and consider it a fit subject for mirth. It can only, however, I trust, be with very few of your lordships." The following are extracts from our petition :—

"That when your petitioners were removed to the County Gaol of Warwick, they were stripped stark naked in the presence of the turnkeys, and measured in that condition, and examined all over, to discover any particular marks on their bodies, an indignity by them so severely felt that they find themselves compelled to notice it emphatically to your right honourable House.

"That your petitioners were then taken into a room, in which there were not less than eight prisoners, recently brought into the gaol, and with these men, some of whom were in a filthy state, were compelled again to strip themselves naked, bathe in the same cistern of water as the men did, and dry themselves as well as they could on the same towel.

"That a common felon was ordered to crop the hair of your petitioner, William Lovett, and to this indignity your petitioner was also compelled to submit.

"That their shirts were taken from them, and the initial letters of their names, in roman letters an inch long, stamped thereon in indelible ink.

"That your petitioners were then put into a ward where there were 22 prisoners, one of whom was infected with the itch.

"That during each of the nine days your petitioners were confined, they were at five different times, and sometimes more frequently, each day compelled to fall into their exact place among the prisoners in a row in the open yard, to answer to their names, receive their food, to be examined by the doctor to discover if they had taken the itch, and to be exhibited to persons who came to see the prison, when they were compelled to stand bareheaded.

" That your petitioners were limited to the common gaol allowance, and no one was allowed to supply them with any addition thereto.

" That this allowance consisted of a small loaf, which your petitioners suppose might weigh $1\frac{1}{2}$ lb., one pint of oatmeal gruel for breakfast, which was given at nine in the morning; for dinner at 12 o'clock about 2 ounces of cheese, excepting Sundays and Wednesdays, when they were served with a pint of what was called beef soup, in which there was no other appearance of meat than some slimy, stringy particles, which, hanging about the wooden spoon, so offended your petitioners' stomachs that they were compelled to forego eating it; and at 6 p.m. one more pint of oatmeal gruel; while from 12 o'clock on Sundays until 9 a.m. on Monday, your petitioners were not served with any food.

" That in addition to this, the common gaol allowance, your petitioners, in common with all *untried prisoners*, were permitted to expend *three pence* per day in butter, sugar, bacon, eggs, salt, pepper, worsted, thread, or tape; but your petitioners were not allowed to have either eggs or bacon cooked, and had themselves no access to fire to cook them, and did actually eat both eggs and bacon raw.

" That during 11 hours out of the 24, your petitioners were locked up in a vaulted cell paved with brick, at the door of which, to their great discomfort, they were compelled to leave their boots : that in this cell there was neither chair, stool, nor table, the whole furniture consisting of a wooden tub, an iron bedstead with a wooden bottom, a wooden pillow, a straw mattress, two blankets, a rug, but no sheets.

" That your petitioners were, under the penalty of solitary confinement, compelled to make their bed in a particular manner, and each morning fold up the mattress, &c., in a close and compact form, to the exclusion of air, so that, when unrolled in the evening, the smell was offensive to an extent not to be conceived.

"That during two hours each morning, a half-hour before being locked up at night, and once in each day, your petitioners were turned into the yard, and not allowed to retreat into any place of shelter.

"That your petitioners were prohibited from seeing any person, excepting on four days in the week, and then in the presence of the gaoler, at certain fixed times, only for a few minutes, a wicket-gate with spikes on the top of it being between them and their friends.

"That the watch and money of your petitioners, and everything else their pockets contained, were taken from them, and they were not allowed the use of knife, fork, plate, nor any other vessel save a small wooden tub, and a spoon of the same material.

"That no books or printed papers (the Bible or Prayer-book excepted), were permitted : that your petitioners were debarred from the free use of pen, ink, and paper ; no letter addressed to them was permitted to reach them until it had been examined, and every part of the paper which was not written upon carefully torn off.

"That your petitioners were not allowed to write to any person, however necessary it might be, but in a particular room, where other prisoners were also allowed to write, and in which they were locked up, and were compelled to leave their letters open, to be examined before they were dispatched by post.

"That your petitioners at the same time beg to be understood as making no complaint of the personal conduct of the Governor, Mr. Atkins.

"That your petitioners having been thus treated as convicted felons, where the discipline is particularly severe, having been treated with great indignity, having been deprived of all comforts in every respect, limited both in quantity and quality of food, and otherwise treated as shown in this their petition, pray your Right Honourable House to take the same into your consideration as conduct such as no Englishman should be subject to while under confinement pending the production of bail, and *previous to being convicted of any crime*," &c., &c.

It will now be necessary to mention that during the time we had been in prison waiting for bail, Mr. Attwood had brought forward a motion in the Commons—" That the House resolve itself into a Committee for considering the prayer of the National Petition "—the Petition itself having been presented on the 14th of June. Mr. Attwood's speech on this occasion was mixed up with many of his currency crotchets, and the motion was but feebly supported by the Liberal Members, many of them contenting themselves with a silent vote; while Lord John Russell, in his opposition to it, scrupled not to introduce all kinds of false and virulent charges against the petitioners; among others charging them with the desire for an equal division of property. The motion was lost by a majority of 189.

The Convention, now having re-assembled in London, resumed the discussion regarding the sacred month; and finding Mr. Attwood's motion rejected, a great number of their body arrested and bound over for trial, the Government justifying the onslaught that had been made upon the people, and the police and authorities actively engaged in every possible way in putting down the meetings of the people, came to a resolution—" That in their opinion *the people should work no longer after the* 12*th of August,* unless the power of voting for Members of Parliament, to protect their labour, is guaranteed to them." This resolution, I heard, having been come to in a very thin meeting, produced much dissatisfaction among the absent members, many of whom were then engaged with their constituents in different parts of the country. Further enquiry also proved that the Convention had been grossly deceived, regarding the preparedness of the people in many districts, by the false and exaggerated statements of many of their correspondents. These accordingly led to a re-discussion of the subject, and on the 6th of August, the proposal for the observance of a sacred month was abandoned, and on the 6th of the following month, on a motion by Mr. O'Brien, the Convention was dissolved.

As before stated, Mr. Collins and myself were bound over to attend the Warwick Assizes in July, 1839, as were

also Dr. Taylor and G. J. Harney. The charges against
the two last were, however, ultimately abandoned. The
first cases tried were those of the persons charged with the
riot and burnings in the Bullring, four of whom were condemned for death, but eventually transported. My trial
took place on the 6th of August, before Mr. Justice
Littledale; Mr. Collins' having taken place the day
before. The three resolutions, already referred to, were
charged against us as *a seditious libel*; my offence being
for writing them, and my colleague for taking them to
the printer. It had been arranged between us, while we
were in prison, waiting for bail, that we should both
defend ourselves; myself to defend the right of public
meeting—which had been outraged by the police—as well
as the principles involved in the charge against us; and
Mr. Collins to bring forward the whole proceedings respecting the Bullring, and the attack upon the people.
When, however, Mr. Collins arrived at Birmingham, his
friends dissuaded him from this course, and advised the
retaining of Serjeant Goulbourne to defend him. This very
unfortunate advice, which diverted my friend Collins from
his resolution, was to me a source of great annoyance, as it
obliged me to make fresh arrangements, and to collect new
matter so as to embrace, as far as possible, the whole case.
Some of my friends, also, were influenced by it, and began
to think that I was too presuming in seeking to defend
myself; and several of them quoted to me the old adage:
"That he who defends himself has a fool for his client."
But recollecting a saying of Lord Lyndhurst, on John
Cleave's trial, that "that was an adage made by the
lawyers," I was not much influenced by it. When also I
arrived at Warwick, Serjeant Goulbourne did all he could
to dissuade me from making "*my political speech*," as he
called it, and to leave the both cases to him. But I was
firm in my determination to have my say; being satisfied
that there were points to be defended that no counsel would
contest, and more especially a Tory one. This resolution
of mine would seem to have led to two indictments being
prepared, that against Mr. Collins being brought on first,
probably in compliance with the request of the learned

Serjeant. In point of justice, however, my case should have been the first, as I was evidently the chief offender, being the writer of the libel. But, after the learned Serjeant had made the defence of my colleague *a mere party question of Whig and Tory*, and had done his best to excite the ire of the Attorney-General, Lord Campbell, and after the condemnation of Mr. Collins for the minor offence of taking the copy to the printer, it will be seen that I had no possible chance of escape, whatever I might urge in my defence. But it may be asked, how do I know that Serjeant Goulbourne made the defence of Mr. Collins a *mere party question?* If further evidence is wanted than is contained in his own speech on that occasion, I will state it. It would seem that the learned gentleman was very anxious to rake up all the ultra-Whig speeches made by Lord Campbell during the agitation of the Reform Bill to fling against him on this occasion, without reference to the fate of poor Collins. He accordingly wrote a note to the Secretary of the Conservative Society at Coventry, requesting him " to send him a file of the papers of that period, stating in his note that having to defend the Chartist Collins (about whom he cared little)," it was *a glorious opportunity of having a slap at the Whigs.*" The person to whom the note was entrusted to take to Coventry not finding the person to whom it was addressed, in his way back, by some mischance, fell into the water. The wet and torn note, taken from his person—by some mis-understanding—was given into the hands of Mr. Collins just as he was removed from the dock, who in the excitement and bustle of the moment, put it in his pocket. Some months afterwards, in rummaging his pockets, he found the remains of this wet note, and showed it to me, by which we discovered another proof to convince us how lamentably our case had been injured by Serjeant Goulbourne making it a mere party question.

I need scarcely to state, that when my case came on I had but little, if any, chance of escape. In the first place I had not a fair jury; for several of them, on the eve of my trial, had been heard to express themselves very strongly against us; two of them in particular to *wish all the Chartists were hanged.* This fact was communicated to me by several persons who heard them say so, but, being given to believe that *I could peremptorily challenge any person on the jury,* I neglected to bring my witnesses into court, as required in cases of *misdemeanour,* so that I was left to the mercy of men who would have substituted hanging for imprisonment if they had had the power. In the next place the Attorney General had very unjustly caused to be spread out on the table a display of weapons of various kinds, said to have been taken from persons in the Bullring, and by his handling and referring to them during his address, evidently sought to connect me with the riots and burnings that had taken place there. And, to add to the difficulties of my defence, I had to examine, as I best could, most of the witnesses we had provided—a duty which Mr. Collins had entrusted to Serjeant Goulbourne, whereas he only called two persons to speak to the character of my colleague. When my defence had been concluded, the reply to it was made by Mr. Balguy, in the absence of the Attorney-General; and at the conclusion of the case the jury, as may be supposed, hesitated not a moment in finding me guilty. I was therefore immediately taken from the dock, and, in that feverish, excited state, thrust into my cell without shoes on the cold brick floor. The next day I was brought up for judgment with my friend Collins, and both of us were sentenced to twelve months' imprisonment in the County Gaol.

In the course of the week, the clergyman visited the prison for the purpose of questioning new prisoners regarding their religious persuasion; of which, I believe, a register is kept. How far any such record of the religion of prisoners is to be depended upon may be judged of by the following :—We being new comers, some of the old stagers told us, as a valuable piece of information, that when we went into the parson's room he would ask each of us our name, trade, and religion; and that "if we told him we were *Catholics,* the old codger would not ask us another word;" that having been the plan they had adopted themselves to prevent any unpleasant questioning respecting the Church they attended, or the creed they professed. We were cautioned, however, not to make a

mistake in giving our *trade* for our religion, as a prisoner
had done shortly before. It seems he had been schooled
to give his replies in the order in which the questions were
generally given; but some variation having been made in
the questioning, the prisoner, when asked what religion he
was, said he was " *a pearl-button maker.*" This advice to
us, though kindly given, I did not avail myself of; I merely
said that I was of that religion which Christ taught, and
which very few in authority practised, if I might judge
from their conduct; but whether I was registered as
Protestant, Catholic, or Infidel I know not.

On the morning after my trial, when my little bucket of
gruel was served out to me, I took up a black-beetle in
about the first spoonful; this, together with the feverish
state in which I was, caused me to take a loathing against
this part of my prison fare. I therefore tried to satisfy
my appetite for a few days with a little bread soaked in
cold water for breakfast, and a morsel of bread and cheese
for dinner. But this diet in a short time brought on a
horrible diarrhœa, under which, I believe, I should have
speedily sunk had not my weakly appearance attracted the
notice of William Collins, Esq., the member for Warwick,
one of the visiting magistrates, on his going his rounds
through the prison. Being too weakly to stand, I was re-
clining on a dust-bin in the yard as he passed through.
Seeing me look so ill, he came up to me and kindly questioned me about my health, and at once ordered me to be
taken into the hospital. As soon as I recovered a little I
was again ordered down to the yard, when Mr. William
Collins very kindly undertook to lay before the magistrates
of the county any request we might choose to make to
them. We accordingly wrote, that as we found it impos-
sible to preserve our health on the kind of food allowed to
us, we begged to be permitted to purchase a little tea,
sugar, and butter, and occasionally a small quantity of
meat. Also that we might have access to a fire to warm
ourselves, the use of pens, ink, and paper, and be allowed
to retire to our cells to read and write. This request the
magistrates refused to comply with, without they had a specific authority from the Secretary of State. Mr. Collins

then offered to take up to town for us a memorial to Lord John Russell. We accordingly memorialised his lordship that we might receive the like indulgences that had been granted to Wooler, Edmonds, Maddox and others, imprisoned for a similar offence in the same prison, who had been placed *on the debtors' side*, allowed to purchase their own food, and to have the free use of pens, ink, and paper. A reply to this was verbally given to us by the Rev. John Boudier, one of the magistrates, to the effect that we were to be allowed the use of pens, ink, and paper, until, in their opinion, we abused the privilege, but not the other indulgences. He said, at the same time, that " he had no hesitation in saying that any application from us to the visiting magistrates would have received much more attention but for *our highly-coloured petition!* " This, in fact, constituted our chief offence in the eyes of these gentlemen. They hated us, and did all they could to punish us when they had us in their power, for having presumed to expose the treatment we received *before trial*, as well as for the expense that exposure cost them; for, owing to that, they were obliged to erect a new and more convenient bathroom, and to provide coarse sheets for the prisoners, instead of the old filthy blankets, which stank so abominably that Mr. Collins and myself were obliged to throw open our cell window, and shake them up and down for upwards of an hour before we could bear to lie down in them. And if this speech of Mr. Boudier is not sufficient to show their animus towards us, the manner in which they acted during the whole time they had it in their power will serve to confirm it. During our incarceration one petition and memorial after another were presented in our favour—the Working Men's Association sent two memorials, another was presented by the people of Birmingham, one by my wife, and another by Mr. Francis Place, who was indefatigable in trying to obtain an amelioration in our condition. Mr. Warburton, M.P., also very kindly interested himself on our behalf; and Mr. Thomas Duncombe very nobly brought our case before the House of Commons, together with that of other political offenders. To all of which the authorities turned a deaf ear, the only favour granted being that alluded to, together with a pint of tea instead of the prison gruel. Whenever the magistrates were applied to for any little mitigation of our severities, they invariably contended that they had no power without the sanction of the Secretary of State; and when he was memorialised he referred us to the visiting magistrates. Their reply to him was accompanied with the certificate of the prison surgeon, which was generally of the same character—" I find the prisoners in good health, and do not consider an increase of diet called for at present." Even when I was so weakened by the diarrhœa as not to be able to sit upright, he certified that I was suffering from a mere attack of the bowels common at that season of the year. My friends, not satisfied with these certificates, sent down Dr. Black to examine the state of my health. His report regarding my sinking state was laid before the Marquis of Normanby (the Secretary of State during the latter part of my imprisonment), who forwarded it to the visiting magistrates, but still they remained inexorable. Thus were we kept by them for the first six months of our imprisonment without a bit of animal food, nor should we, I believe, have had any during our whole term had we not found out some facts connected with the making of the prison soup, which we turned to our advantage. The facts were these :— The prisoner who cooked the soup and gruel for the prison being taken ill towards the end of his term, was sent into the hospital at a time when Mr. Collins and myself were both there ill. From him we learnt not only the mode in which the soup was prepared (being parboiled and pounded up into mere fibre), but also *the quantity of meat put into it,* he having had the weighing of it, and knowing also the proportion according to the number of prisoners. Some short time after our recovery we were visited in our cell by T. Galton and —— Bracebridge, Esqrs.—two of the visiting magistrates—to whom we complained of the great hardship of being deprived of animal food. Mr. Bracebridge having expressed surprise at this, Mr. Galton said, " But you have meat in the soup, half-a-pound twice a week." We replied that we had reason for believing that they did not put that quantity in it.   At this he seemed a little excited, and asked very earnestly if we intended to make that an allegation.   We replied that we had been informed by the cook, who had the weighing of the meat, that for the last week he cooked, there were but from 34 lbs. to 35 lbs. of meat to make soup for a hundred and thirty odd prisoners, being little more than a *quarter of a pound for each.*   At this statement Mr. Galton seemed surprised, and was very particular in writing it down.   The next day, Jan. 2nd, we received a visit from Sir Eardley Wilmot.   He said that he wished to see us, that he might be enabled to say so, if he should have to defend the visiting magistrates, as he expected he should when Mr. Duncombe brought forward the subject of Dr. Black's visit.   He told us that it was of no consequence what Dr. Black or any other medical man said, the surgeon of the prison excepted, he being responsible. He had seen, he said, the Marquis of Normanby about three weeks ago on some other business, when our case was mentioned, and that he told him then that whatever he ordered, if even for the opening of the doors, it should be done.   But he thought the Marquis would be very careful of interfering with prisoners in England, as he had burnt his fingers with them in Ireland.   We then reiterated the old complaint of being kept without animal food, when he very roughly replied that prisons were not places of relaxation or pleasure, and that he had not come to argue with us. We then told him that we were desirous of ascertaining his opinion regarding the power given to the visiting magistrates by the following clause from the prison rules :—" No prisoner who is confined under the sentence of any Court, nor any prisoner confined in pursuance of any conviction before a justice, shall receive any food, clothing, or necessaries, other than the gaol allowance, *except under such regulations and restrictions as to the justices in general, or Quarter Sessions assembled, may appear expedient,* with reference to the several classes of prisoners, *or under special circumstances to be judged of by one or more of the visiting justices.''*   He replied that the magistrates certainly have the power by that clause to grant us any indulgences, but that they did not choose to exercise it, and he added that a prison was a place of punishment, and not for indulgence. We then pressed upon him the fact of our diet not being such as was specified by the rules, a copy of which we produced (having taken the precaution of bringing one in with us). He asked us if they contained the rules for the dietary. We said they did, and referred to them. He asked for what class of prisoners. The governor, who was present, said that the dietary was the same for all alike. We then pointed out to him that the rule stated *half-a-pound of meat twice a week, and soup,* whereas we had no meat. He then asked of the governor whether these were the last regulations? He said no. We reminded him, however, that the copy we were referring to was a copy of those presented by the magistrates, and printed by order of the House of Commons, when our petition was presented. He said that the rules ought to be hung up in the prison. We replied that they were the same as those we showed to him. He then asked the governor whether these were the rules he went by? He replied *that they were not;* that they *had been altered about two years ago,* so as to reduce the quantity of meat in the soup *to a quarter of a pound* instead of the *half pound.* He added that the late surgeon, Mr. Birch, had always contended for the half pound of meat, but that *the present surgeon, Mr. Wilmshurst, said that that quantity made the soup too rich !* After this exposure of the doings of the magistracy, Sir Eardley all at once began to assume a very kind and sympathising tone towards us, and said that he had no doubt but that twelve months' imprisonment to persons like us, was a far greater punishment than two years would be to many others. He also wrote off a letter the same evening to the Marquis of Normanby, in which he professed great sympathy for us, yet, nevertheless, justified the magistrates in their treatment of us ; contending that they had no power by the rules to act otherwise than they had. At the same time, he hoped his lordship would relax the rules in our favour, so as to make the last six months of our confinement less rigid. The Marquis, in his reply to him, pointed out the same clause of the rules that we had, to show that the magistrates had the power to grant indulgences to prisoners, and not him; and that he thought, that, in my case at least, whose health had been represented to be delicate, some relaxation might have been reasonably made. To maintain, however, their own obstinate opinion of the rules, and at the same time get out of the invidious position in which this reply had placed them, they resolved on a provisional improvement of the dietary *of all the prisoners in the gaol,* giving them an addition of the *two half pounds of meat in a solid form,* which caused great rejoicing throughout the prison. This change was a great blessing to both of us; and without it, I believe, I should never have survived the term of my imprisonment. As it was, I became so weak and emaciated towards the conclusion of the term that the surgeon was induced to allow me a more nourishing kind of diet during the last few weeks of my imprisonment to keep me from sinking altogether. As for my fellow-prisoner, Mr. Collins, who was of a more robust constitution than myself, he, from being a stout, portly person when he entered, became so thin, before the animal food was allowed to us, that he could easily put his hat within the waistband of his trousers. It would be tedious to recount the various annoyances to which we were subjected, by the orders of our very severe disciplinarians, the magistrates, during our imprisonment. The few letters addressed to us were invariably opened, and those we sent out scrupulously examined, to see if they contained a sentence savouring of freedom, which, if they did, were prevented from going altogether. A letter to my poor old mother was kept back altogether, because I said something in it of better men having suffered in the cause of liberty. My wife was only allowed to see me twice during my imprisonment, and that in the presence of the turnkey, who heard every word spoken. We were not even allowed to have a razor of our own to shave ourselves, but to submit to the operation of the prison barber, one of the prisoners. One of whom who shaved me for some time was the notorious Jem Bradley, who, with some others, was, I understand, subsequently hanged in Australia for the number of murders they had committed. I had not, however, any cause to com-

lain of Jem's conduct towards me, but having heard him
n one occasion describing to the prisoners how he threw a
oman down who had offended him, and then *kicked her in
ie face and eyes,* I had some scruples in trusting my face to
im in future, and managed to bribe him with some of my
read for the loan of his razor to operate on myself. A
w weeks before the termination of our imprisonment
e were informed by the magistrates that the govern-
ient was disposed to remit the remaining part of our
ntence, providing we would be bound for our good
ehaviour for twelve months. This we refused to do,
ad were kept our full term. The following letter con-
ains our reasons for this refusal :—

" Warwick Gaol, May 6th, 1840.
To the Right Hon. the Marquis of Normanby, Her
Majesty's Secretary of State for the Home Department.
" My Lord,—The Visiting Magistrates of the County
aol of Warwick having read to us a communication, dated
Vhitehall, May 5th, and signed S. M. Phillips, in which it
stated that your lordship will recommend us to her
[ajesty for a remission of the remaining part of our
ntence, provided we are willing to enter into our own
cognizances in £50 each for our good behaviour for one
ar, we beg respectfully to submit the following as our
iswer :—That to enter into any bond for our future good
nduct would at once be an admission of past guilt; and,
owever a prejudiced jury may have determined the resolu-
ons we caused to be published, condemnatory of the
tack of the police, as an act in opposition to the law of
bel, we cannot yet bring ourselves to believe that any
uilt or criminality has been attached to our past conduct.
Ve have, however, suffered the penalty of nearly ten
onths' imprisonment for having, in common with a large
ortion of the public press and a large majority of our
untrymen, expressed that condemnatory opinion. We
ave been about the first political victims who have been
assed and punished as misdemeanants and felons because
e happened to be of *the working class.* We have had our
ealth injured and constitutions greatly undermined by

the treatment already experienced, and we are disposed
suffer whatever future punishment may be inflicted up
us rather than enter into any such terms as those propos
by your lordship.

"We remain your lordship's most obedient servants,
"WM. LOVETT,
"JOHN COLLINS."

I may here state that when pen, ink, paper, and a fe
books were allowed to us, I commenced the writing of
little work entitled, "*Chartism, or a New Organization
the People*," which was published when we came out, in o
joint names.   The chief object of this work was to indu
the Chartists of the United Kingdom to form themselv
into a National Association for the erection of halls ar
schools of various kinds for the purposes of education-
for the establishing of libraries; the printing of tracts; ar
the sending out missionaries; with the view of forming
enlightened public opinion throughout the country
favour of the Charter, and thus better preparing the peop
for the exercise of the political rights we were then co
tending for.   The writing a little of this work daily, wh
I was well enough, contributed very much to relieve t
tedium and monotony of my prison life, although, as w
hereafter appear, it was the means of bringing down up
my head censures unmitigated and unparalleled.   Beii
very doubtful whether such a work would be allowed
pass the prison gates, we contrived to smuggle out a co
of it, with the view of getting it published on the day
our liberation.   But the friend to whom it was sent, wis
ing me to unite in another project—the Corn Law Agit
tion—threw cold water on the proposal, so that i
publication was greatly delayed, to our ultimate loss.

In the brief sketch I have given of our treatment
Warwick Gaol, most persons must be struck with t
immense power for evil which our unpaid magistra
possess—a power to obstruct all mitigation of sufferin
and to give, if they choose, a two-fold severity to the la
For let two persons, in two different counties, be tried f
similar offences before the same judge, and condemn

under the same Act to suffer similar penalties, owing to the power possessed by the magistracy, the punishment of the one person may be two-fold more severe than that of the other. In the one prison the diet may be poor and scanty, the silent system enforced, the discipline severe, and measures the most arbitrary and despotic adopted for the enforcement of it ; while in the other prison kindness of treatment and an ample supply of food may render imprisonment comparatively light. Thus it is seen that magistrates, by having the making and enforcement of our prison regulations, have a power to increase the severity or to neutralize the power of the law ; a power in fact greater than is possessed by Queen, Lords, or Commons. In fact, our whole prison discipline seems calculated to make bad worse, instead of improvement or reformation. The instruction of the poor boys in Warwick Gaol was entrusted to an ignorant turnkey, and the deprivation of food the means adopted for quickening the remembrance of the tasks imposed on them. As for the adults, they were allowed to instruct each other regarding the best means of making and passing bad money, and for becoming more expert and successful depredators. We heard one of them instructing another, whose time had nearly expired, *how to rob his own mother,** the conditions being that he was to send in to him a pair of shoes, with some of the silver between the soles ; and yet we were obliged to be silent for our own safety, they being our daily companions. But Warwick Gaol was provided with a clergyman to teach these poor neglected wretches *their religious duties*. His power for good may be judged of when I state that I have seen him from the pulpit point out to the gaoler poor wretches for unavoidably *coughing*, after they had been kept standing in the cold yard for nearly half-

---

* His mother kept a greengrocer's shop, and when she went to market with her horse and cart she placed her little bag of money in one corner of it, behind the bags and baskets, and this being known by her unworthy son, he instructed the out-going thief to rob her, on condition of his sending him a portion of the money between the soles of a new pair of shoes, as shoes and articles of clothing were admitted.

an-hour, without their hats, in the winter season ; and for which trifling offence they would be locked up in the refractory cell for a certain period. And the nature of this cold, dark cell may be imagined when I state, that I knew a boy of the name of Griffiths, of the age of 17, locked up in it for three days and nights in the month of February, for having quarrelled and struck another boy, and when he came out he was so swollen as hardly to be known ; he had several holes in his feet, and *two of his toes festered off.*

While my friend Collins and myself were thus squabbling and ruminating in Warwick Gaol, important events were taking place outside, of which a few imperfect scraps of information occasionally reached us through the new prisoners admitted into our yard. The trial of our friend Vincent, I may observe, took place a few days before our own, and ended in his incarceration for twelve months. His treatment was also severe, and his jury equally prejudiced against him as our own ; for in a petition describing his mode of treatment, it is deposed that one of his jury, in rejoicing at his capture, had been heard to declare, that *he would give nine-pence to buy a halter for hanging him without judge or jury.* Our trials were speedily followed by those of McDouall, Brown, O'Brien, Richardson, Fenning, Richards, O'Connor, Crabtree, Frost, Carrier and Neesom, all members of the Convention, and by a host of others in different parts of the kingdom ; the political prisoners incarcerated in the prisons of England and Wales in the years 1839 and 1840 being 443, besides many others subsequently. But the most serious of all the events that happened during our imprisonment was the Newport outbreak, and the transportation of John Frost and his companions. Of the cause of this unhappy affair I had no opportunity of learning while in prison ; but soon after I came out I made enquiries, and from a person who took an active part, in matters pertaining to it, I learnt the following :—That the chief cause that led to the outbreak was the treatment pursued towards Vincent in particular, as well as of the Chartists generally. That Mr. Frost, having done all he could to effect an alteration in Vincent's treatment, came to London. That, in company with two or three members of the Convention, on complaining of the conduct of the authorities, he said he had great difficulty in restraining the Welsh Chartists from endeavouring to release Vincent by force. On this one of the parties present said, if the Welsh effect a rising in favour of Vincent, the people of Yorkshire and Lancashire, he knew, were ready to join in a rising for the Charter. This seems to have been the origin of the affair, but nothing further was done until both parties had gone back and consulted the leading men in their respective districts; Mr. Frost, it would seem, having taken upon himself to consult the Welsh, and Peter Bussy, the people of Yorkshire and Lancashire. Soon after a meeting was convened at Heckmondwick, where about forty delegates attended from the surrounding districts; three of them being members of the Convention, and my informant one of them. At this meeting they were informed of the intended rising in Wales, and in the discussion that ensued respecting it—while several thought the rising premature—they were very general in their determination to aid it, by an outbreak in the North. From another communication made to me by Mr. J. Collins—who had it from one of the parties—it would seem that in anticipation of this rising in the North—a person was delegated from one of the towns to go to Fergus O'Connor, to request that he would lead them on, as he had so often declared he would. Collins's informant was present at this interview, and described to him the following conversation that took place :—*Delegate.*—Mr. O'Connor, we are going to have a rising for the Charter, in Yorkshire, and I am sent from ———— to ask if you will lead us on, as you have often said you would when we were prepared. *Fergus.*—Well, when is this rising to take place? *Delegate.*—Why, we have resolved that it shall begin on Saturday next. *Fergus.*—Are you all well provided with arms, then? *Delegate.*—Yes, all of us. *Fergus.*—Well, that is all right, my man. *Delegate.*—Now, Mr. O'Connor, shall I tell our lads that you will come and lead them on? *Fergus* now indignantly replied, " Why, man! when did you ever hear of me, or of any one of my family, ever deserting the cause of the people ? Have they not always been found at their post in the hour of danger ? " In this bouncing manner did Fergus induce the poor fellow to believe that he was ready to head the people ; and he went back and made his report accordingly. But the man subsequently lost caste among his fellow-townsmen, for bringing them a false report—Fergus having solemnly assured them that he never promised him anything. No sooner, however, did he find out that they were so far in earnest as described, that he set about to render the outbreak ineffectual; notwithstanding all his previous incitements to arming and preparedness, and all his boast and swaggering at public meetings, and in the columns of the " Star," he is said to have engaged George White to go into Yorkshire and Lancashire, to assure the people that no rising would take place in Wales ; and Charles Jones he sent into Wales, to assure the Welsh that there would be no rising in Yorkshire, and that it was all a government plot. When Jones arrived at Mr. Frost's house, he found he had already left for the country, for the purpose of conferring with the leaders in different districts, and was directed where to find him. On his meeting Mr. Frost, and telling him his errand, he was informed that Mr. O'Connor's message had come too late ; that the people were resolved on releasing Vincent from prison ; and that he might as well blow his own brains out as try to oppose them or shrink back. He then urged Charles Jones to go back to Yorkshire and Lancashire and tell the leaders what the Welsh had resolved on doing. Jones being short of money for the journey back, Mr. Frost gave him three sovereigns, to aid him in getting back as fast as possible. Before, however, anything could be done in the North, the Welsh Chartists had congregated together, to the amount of some thousands, and, amid a drenching storm in November, had marched on with the object of releasing Vincent from prison. The result is well known ; they were met at Newport by the soldiery, a skirmish ensued, ten people were killed and nearly fifty wounded, and Mr. Frost and several others speedily arrested. When the news of this disaster reached Yorkshire, the Chartists there were exasperated beyond measure, to find that they had been misinformed respecting the Welsh. They, therefore, resolved that they would have their rising—as previously projected—and that on the following Saturday ; Peter Bussy, one of the delegates to the Convention, having been appointed to be their leader. Peter, however—although one of the physical force party—seems not to have relished this prominent position, for he was very suddenly taken ill. The Chartists of Bradford, however, were resolved to see for themselves whether Peter was ill or not, but on searching his house he was not to be found ; he was gone, it was said, into the country for the benefit of his health. His little boy, however, in chattering among the customers, let the truth out—for Peter, be it remembered, kept a beer-shop and huckster's shop combined. "Ah, ah!" said the boy, " you could not find father the other day, but I knew where he was all the time ; he was up in the cock-loft behind the flour sacks." This being soon noised about, Peter was obliged to wind up his affairs, and soon embarked for America. Fergus also, apprehensive of being called upon to set an heroic example, in those rising times, thought it a timely opportunity for visiting Ireland, so that by the time he came back most of the foolish outbreaks were over. Having been back for a short time, and keeping very silent, many of his disciples called upon him to make some exertions in favour of Mr. Frost and the other Chartist prisoners ; when he deemed it necessary to bestir himself, and offer a week's receipts of the *Star* towards the expenses of their trial.

16

CHAPTER XIII.

On our release from prison, which took place on the 25th of July, 1840, we were welcomed by a large number of people in the town of Warwick; delegates also having been sent from many towns to greet our entrance into Birmingham, the people of that town also having made arrangements for a public procession and a festival on the occasion. My health, however, was in that state that I was obliged to decline this generous invitation, as well as a number of others I had received from different parts of the country, and to set off into Cornwall as soon as possible, to try as a restorative the air of my native place.   The members of our Working Men's Associations, the Combination Committee, and Cabinet Makers, having conjointly made arrangements for giving a public dinner to Mr. Collins and myself, I did manage to attend that before I set off. The dinner took place at White Conduit House, in a large tent, on August the 3rd, when upwards of 1000 persons sat down to dinner.   Mr. Wakley, the member for Finsbury, took the chair; Mr. Duncombe, the other member, and a great number of friends attended; and Mr. Richard Moore officiated as secretary.   There was also a ball in the evening.   I must also gratefully acknowledge the further kindness of my friends, composing the Working Men's Associations, the Combination Committee, the Cabinet Makers, and other kind friends who exerted themselves in various ways to procure subscriptions for the support of my wife and daughter, while I was in prison. They had also been so far successful among my friends in different parts of the country that in addition to their support, they had raised sufficient to pay my expenses down into Cornwall, as well as a few pounds for helping me into a small way of business when I returned. Before, however, I went down to Cornwall, Mr. Collins and myself made arrangements for the printing and publishing of " Chartism," the little work already referred to. The first edition of it sold off during my stay in Cornwall; and it having been very favourably reviewed by the Press, we were induced, in consequence, to *stereotype* the second edition; but this not selling (in consequence of the clamour subsequently raised against us by the O'Connorites) caused us to lose by the transaction.

I may state, also, that I was no sooner out of prison than I had a variety of claims made upon me on account of the *Charter Newspaper*. This was a paper devoted to the interests of the working classes, and originated in a proposal made to our Combination Committee by Mr. William Carpenter, its first editor. It was conducted for some time by a committee chosen by the subscribers, and the paper and printing found by a printer and paper merchant, in consideration of the number of persons who had agreed to purchase it. It was carried on, I think, for nearly twelve months, but the speculation not answering the expectation of the printer, he gave up the printing of it, and the committee consequently dissolved. Myself and another, however, had allowed our names to be entered *as sureties at the Stamp Office*, and we had not formally withdrawn them when I was sent to prison. The publisher, however—very unjustly to us—thought fit to carry on the paper on his own account; and our names standing at the Stamp Office, rendered us liable for a great variety of debts he incurred on it. The other surety not being so well known to the creditors as myself, when I came out of prison I was dunned in all directions for these debts; and claims for a considerable amount were sent down to Cornwall after me. As may be supposed, this was to me a source of great trouble and difficulty, but eventually some of the creditors were induced to relinquish their claims, some of the debts my friends subscribed together and paid, and others I paid myself, or compounded for, as I best could.

As regards my journey, I may state that the bracing

effects of my voyage down, the kindness of friends and the salubrious air of Cornwall, in a few months greatly served to renovate my shattered constitution; although I may now conclude that I shall never fully recover from the debilitating effects produced on my health by my treatment in Warwick Gaol.

Having been depicted by the opponents of Chartism in the blackest colours, I was regarded as something monstrous by many, and I must mention a little anecdote in proof of it. Riding on the top of an omnibus towards my brother's house, I got into conversation with a gentleman beside me on the subject of mineralogy, he having some specimens with him. I said I wanted a few of a peculiar kind, but I did not know where to meet with them, when he told me he thought he could supply me if I called on him. I thanked him, and said I would do so. A little time before I got down I gave him my address in exchange for his own; but when he saw my name, he said " What ! William Lovett, the Chartist?" "Yes, I replied, the same individual." "Why," said he, scrutinizing me very earnestly, "*you don't look like one ;*" evidently believing that a Chartist was something monstrous. "Well," I said, " as you gave me an invitation to call on you without knowing me, now you do know that I am a Chartist, your invitation had best be cancelled." " Not so," he replied good-humouredly; " we met on scientific grounds, and I do not trouble myself about politics, and if you call I shall be glad to see you." I did so in a short time, when he showed me his collection, and I purchased a few specimens of him. He proved to be a Superintendent of the Wesleyan Ministers of that district, and I doubt not a very estimable man, for all his notions about Chartists.

Not possessing strength to work at the cabinet business, I was induced, on my return to town, to open a small bookseller's shop in Tottenham Court Road, conceiving that to be a business by which I might earn my bread, and which my wife could manage, and by which I might have some time to devote to politics; but here I was again doomed to disappointment. But although I had not much business in my shop, I was kept busily engaged otherwise;

for I was very soon elected a vestryman of St. Pancras, and soon after one of the guardians of the poor. Soon after I opened my shop, I also received a letter from Mr. Samuel Smiles, the author of the " Life of Stephenson," and other admirable works, offering me the situation of sub-editor to the *Leeds Times*, he being then the editor of that paper. Not liking, however, to leave London, and thinking that I might be able to earn a livelihood by my bookselling business, I respectfully declined his kind offer. Not many months after I had opened my shop I received also a requisition, signed by a number of persons, requesting me to take some active steps for the formation of an association *upon the plan set forth in our little work* entitled " Chartism." I accordingly drew up the following address, and Messrs. Collins, Hetherington, Cleave, Rogers, Mitchell and others having appended their signatures to it, copies of it were forwarded to leading radicals in different parts of the country, inviting their signatures previous to its general publication—the same means, in fact, which we formally adopted with our Irish address :—

" To the Political and Social Reformers of the United Kingdom.—Brethren, in addressing you as fellow-labourers in the great cause of human liberty, we would wish to rivet this important truth on your mind :—*You must become your own social and political regenerators, or you will never enjoy freedom.* For true liberty cannot be conferred by acts of parliament or decrees of princes, but must spring up from the knowledge, morality, and public virtue of our population. Be assured, fellow-countrymen, that those who have hitherto been permitted to rule the destinies of nations, who in their madness or folly have cursed the land with wars, cruelty, oppression, and crime, will ever maintain their power and ascendancy while they have ignorant and demoralized slaves to approve of and execute their mandates. Though revolution were to follow revolution, and changes were to be continually effected in our constitution, laws, and government, unless the social and political superstructure were based upon the *intelligence* and *morality* of the people, they would only have exchanged despotism for despotism, and one set of oppressors for another.

"If, therefore, you would escape your present social and political bondage, and benefit your race, you must bestir yourselves, and make every sacrifice *to build up the sacred temple of your own liberties*, or by your neglect and apathy bequeath to your offspring *an increase* of degradation and wrong. You cannot suppose that those who revel in the spoils of labour, and live by the wretchedness they have created, will be instrumental in promoting the political and social improvement of the people. They may talk of liberty while they are forging your fetters; may profess sympathy while they are adding insult to wrong; and may talk of instructing you while they are devising the most efficient means for moulding you into passive slaves; but they will contemptuously spurn every proposal for esta-blishing *equality of political rights and social obligations*—the enduring basis of liberty, prosperity, and happiness.

"Let every man among you, then, who is desirous of seeing the bounties of heaven made subservient to human enjoyment, who is desirous of seeing our land blessed with peace and human brotherhood, and the intellectual and moral capabilities man is endowed with springing forth in all their usefulness and excellence, anxiously enquire how he can best aid the holy cause of man's social regeneration and political freedom.

"Tracing most of our social grievances to class legis-lation, we have proposed a political reform upon the principles of the People's Charter; we have made it the polar-star of our agitation, and have resolved by all *just* and *peaceful* means to cause it to become the law of our country. Believing it to have *truth* for its basis, and the *happiness of all for its end,* we conceive that it needs not the violence of passion, the bitterness of party spirit, nor the arms of aggressive warfare for its support; its principles need only to be unfolded to be appreciated, and being appreciated by the majority, will be established in peace.

"But while we would implore you to direct your undivided attention to the attainment of that just political measure, we would urge you to make your agitation in favour of it more efficient and productive of *social benefit* than it has been hitherto. We have wasted glorious means of usefulness in foolish displays and gaudy trappings, seeking to captivate the sense rather than inform the mind, and aping the proceedings of a tinselled and corrupt aristocracy, rather than aspiring to the mental and moral dignity of a pure democracy.

"Our public meetings have on too many occasions been arenas of passionate invective, party spirit, and personal idolatry, rather than public assemblies for calmly deliberating and freely discussing national or local grievances; or as schools for the advancement of our glorious cause, by the dissemination of facts and inculcation of principles; as it is by such teachings that our population will be prepared *to use wisely* the political power they are now seeking to obtain.

"We are, therefore, desirous of seeing these means applied to a higher and nobler purpose, that of developing the mental and moral energies of our population, *to the great end of their political freedom and social happiness.* For as no earthly power *can prevent an intelligent people from obtaining their rights,* nor all the appliances of corruption *permanently enslave them,* we are anxious, above all things, in seeing them instructed in their political rights and social duties.

"Although the attainment of political power is essential to enable them to improve to any extent their physical condition, yet we believe that a vast increase of social enjoyment might be effected (despite a corrupt and degrading government), if sobriety and moral culture were more generally diffused. And, therefore, we are desirous of seeing our political teachers disseminating unpalatable truths against drunkenness and immorality of every description, and, by precept and example, endeavouring to rescue our brethren from *the thraldom of their own vices,* and from *servilely imitating the corruptions and vices of those above them.*

"As also the children of to-day will, in a few years, be called upon to exercise the rights and duties of men, it becomes our paramount duty to qualify them for their future station, and not permit them to be moulded to the several purposes of priestcraft, sectarianism, and charity-mongers; but *to devise, maintain, and execute a wise and just system of education*, calculated to develope all the powers and energies God has given them, to the end that they may enjoy their own existence, and extend the greatest amount of happiness to all mankind.

"With no disposition to oppose the associations already formed, but with an anxious desire to see all those interested in the social and political improvement of their fellow-men united in one general body to effect it, we propose that such an association be established, and that the following be its objects :—

"National Association of the United Kingdom, *for Promoting the Political and Social Improvement of the People.*

"1. To establish in one general body persons of all creeds, classes, and opinions, who are desirous to promote the political and social improvement of the people.

"2. To create and extend an enlightened public opinion in favour of the *People's Charter,* and by every just and peaceful means secure its enactment; so that the industrious classes may be placed in possession of the franchise, the most important step o all political and social reformation.

"3. To appoint as many *missionaries* as may be deemed necessary to visit the different districts of the kingdom, for the purpose of explaining the views of the association, for promoting its efficient organisation, for lecturing on its different objects, and otherwise seeing that the intentions of the general body are carried into effect in the several localities, according to the instructions they may receive from the general Board.

"4. To establish *circulating libraries,* from a hundred to two hundred volumes each, containing the most useful works on politics, morals, the sciences, history, and such instructing and entertaining works as may be generally approved of. Such libraries to vary as much as possible from each other, and be sent *in rotation* from one town or village in the district to another, and to be lent freely to the members.

" 5. To print from time to time such *tracts* and *pamphlets* as the Association may consider necessary for promoting its objects ; and, when its organisation is complete, to publish a monthly or quarterly national periodical.

" 6. To erect *Public Halls* or *Schools for the People* throughout the kingdom, upon the most approved principles, and in such districts as may be necessary. Such halls to be used during the day as *infant, preparatory,* and *high schools,* in which the children shall be educated on the most approved plans the Association can devise, embracing physical, mental, moral, and political instruction ; and used of an evening by adults for *public lectures* on physical, moral, and political science ; for *readings, discussions, musical entertainments, dancing* and such other healthful and rational recreations as may serve to instruct and cheer the industrious classes after their hours of toil, and prevent the formation of vicious and intoxicating habits. Such halls to have two commodious play-grounds, and, where practicable, a pleasure-garden attached to each ; apartments for the teachers, rooms for hot and cold baths, for a small museum, a laboratory and general workshop where the members and their children may be taught experiments in science, as well as the first principles of the most useful trades.

" 7. To establish in such towns or districts as may be found necessary *normal* or *teachers' schools* for the purpose of instructing school-masters and mistresses in the most approved systems of physical, mental, moral, and political training.

" 8. To establish on the most approved system such *agricultural* and *industrial schools* as may be required for the education and support of the *orphan children of the Association,* and for instructing them in some useful trade or occupation.

" 9. To offer premiums, whenever it may be considered advisable, for the best essays on the instruction of children and adults, for the best description of school-books, or for any other object promotive of the social and political welfare of the people.

" 10. To devise from time to time the best means by which the members, in their several localities, may collect subscriptions and donations in aid of the above objects,* may manage the superintendence of the halls and schools of their respective districts, may have due control over all the affairs of the Association, and share in its advantages, without incurring personal risk or violating the laws of the country.

"Submitting those objects for your serious consideration, and resolving to make every possible effort to establish such an association, we remain your devoted servants in the cause of human liberty and social happiness," &c., &c.

This address was no sooner issued than it was denounced by O'Connor and the writers in his paper, the *Northern Star*, as a " new move," concocted by Hume, Roebuck and O'Connell for destroying his power, and for subverting his plan—that of the " National Charter Association," and his land scheme. All who appended their names to it were condemned as " traitors, humbugs, and miscreants," and

---

* If the number of persons who signed the National Petition belonged to such an association by paying a less sum even than *a penny per week each person*, they would be able to effect the following important objects *every year* :—

	£
To erect *eighty* district halls, or normal or industrial schools, at £3,000 each	240,000
To establish *seven hundred and ten* circulating libraries at £20 each	14,200
To employ *four missionaries* (travelling expenses included) at £200 per annum	800
To circulate *twenty thousand tracts per week*, at 15s. per thousand...	780
To printing, postages, salaries, &c.	700
	£256,480
Leaving for incidental expenses	120
	£256,600

myself in particular came in for a double portion of abuse.
A number of those who, approving of the plan, had appended their signatures to it, bowed and cringed most
basely under this storm of vituperation; and the only
reward they got from the *Star* for withdrawing their
names from our address was to obtain the designation of
" rats escaping from the trap." Votes of censure and denunciations innumerable assailed us from every corner of
the kingdom where O'Connor's tools and dupes were
found, but fortunately for me and my friends they had not
power in proportion to their vindictiveness, or our lives
would have been sacrificed to their frenzy. Among the
most prominent of our assailants in London was a Mr. J.
Watkins, a person of some talent and, I believe, of some
property, who preached and published *a sermon* to show the
justice of assassinating us. An extract from this very popular discourse (for it was preached many times in different
parts of London) will serve to convey its spirit:—" The
interest of Chartism demands that we be firm friends, and
as firm foes. No truckling, no time-serving, no temporising, no surrender to the enemy, no quarter to traitors.
Despots show no quarter to traitors, except quartering their
limbs. What was the sentence on poor Frost?—to be
hanged by the neck; but to be cut down while yet alive,
his bowels to be torn out before his own eyes, and his
limbs to be severed from his breathless, bleeding trunk.
If Frost was a traitor to government, he was true to us,
and if such was to be his fate, shall traitors to the people—
the worst of traitors—be tenderly dealt with—nay, courted,
caressed? No, let them be denounced and renounced; let
us prevent their future treasons, and make examples of
them to deter future traitors. Washington hanged Major
Andre in spite of his most urgent intercessions—hanged
him for being a spy—and who will say that Washington's
example should not be followed? We are in a warfare,
and must have martial law—*short shrift, and sharp
cord.*"

All kinds of ridiculous charges were made against us in
the *Star,* and every species of insult and abuse poured
forth against every person who presumed to defend us, but

seldom an argument in our favour was admitted into the columns of that paper. Although those poor frenzied dupes who had been blindly intoxicated with the falsehoods of O'Connor were for the most part too cowardly to have recourse to personal violence, they exercised their powers in various ways to injure all those who were favourable to the "new move," as they designated our plan. Many were the persons whose business they ruined by their persecution, and many were those who left their country in consequence; and as far as they could injure my own business they did so. My respected friend, Mr. Neesom, who at one time was a zealous, physical force O'Connorite, but who had seen cause to change his opinions, and to append his signature to our address, was one who was persecuted by them most relentlessly. Living at Spitalfields, in the midst of the most virulent of them, and his newspaper business and his wife's school greatly dependent on them, these were speedily shut up, his life often threatened, and he and his wife, in their old age, obliged to seek elsewhere for a livelihood. Regarding the " National Charter Association " referred to, I may observe that on my return from Cornwall I received an invitation to join it, but refused, on the grounds of its illegality, at the same time referring them to an Act of Parliament, in which it was shown that all who belonged to them incurred the risk of transportation. Mr. Collins also about the same time called the attention of the editor of the *Northern Star* to the same subject; and the editor, writing to Mr. F. Place for his opinion, was shown by him also the illegality of this association.

To return to the address referred to, which had excited all this hostility, I must state that eighty-six persons having appended their signatures to it, in testimony of their approval, induced us to take further steps for the promotion of our object. With this view we issued the following address to the Political and Social Reformers of the United Kingdom :—

" Fellow-Countrymen.—In addressing you on subjects connected with your political rights and social duties, we are no ways anxious to proclaim our actions or our sacrifices in the cause of the people; we merely demand that justice for ourselves which we have suffered in seeking to establish it for others—*the justice of being heard patiently, and judged impartially.*

"Having been mainly instrumental in embodying in the *People's Charter* those political principles which, for a great number of years, were cherished by all true reformers, but which previously divided and distracted them by being separately contended for; and many of us having also suffered persecution and imprisonment in defence of its principles; we thought ourselves entitled, *in common with others,* to put forth our views and opinions respecting the best means of causing that measure to become the law of the land.

"Conceiving that the past conduct of a number of those who professed to subscribe to the just principles of the Charter was wanting in that integrity, honesty, and justice, which are necessary qualifications to secure the co-operation of the wise, and the confidence of the good; and believing that the falsehood, exaggeration, and violence of those who were active to scheme, but too cowardly to act, had led to the sacrifice and incarceration of hundreds of victims, by which means our cause had been retarded and defamed, we felt anxious *to redeem by reason what had been lost by madness and folly.*

"We accordingly, about five months ago, put forth a proposal for forming a National Association, as set forth in a pamphlet, written in Warwick Gaol, entitled 'Chartism'—a plan embracing such objects as, in our opinion, were best calculated to unite the elements of Chartism, and secure the co-operation of all benevolent minds who were desirous of benefiting the great mass of the people politically and socially.

"In publishing that plan, we explicitly stated that *we had no wish to interfere with the societies then in existence;* our object being to form a general association for certain explicit purposes. These purposes being, first and foremost, to create and extend an *enlightened public opinion* in favour of the People's Charter, among persons of all creeds, classes, and opinions, by the means of missionaries, lecturers, circulating libraries, tracts, &c. And in order to secure proper places of meeting for those purposes, we proposed a systematic and practical plan for the erecting of *Public Halls for the People* in every district of the kingdom; by which means our working-class brethren might be taken out of the contaminating influences of public-houses and beer-shops—places where many of their meetings are still held, in which their passions are inflamed, their reason drowned, their families pauperised, and themselves socially degraded and politically enslaved.

"Seeing, also, that vast numbers of our infant population are the neglected victims of ignorance and vice, creating on the one hand the evils we are seeking to remove, on the other—seeing that the selfish, the bigoted, and the fanatic, are intent on moulding to their several purposes the infant mind of our country; and that the different parties in the state have for several years past been devising such national schemes of instruction as shall cause our population to become the blind devotees and tools of despotism— we urged on our brethren the necessity of remedying and averting those evils, by adopting a *wise and General System of Education* in connection with these Public Halls; such a system of instruction as shall develope in the rising generation all the faculties which God has given them, to the end that they might enjoy their own existence, and extend the greatest amount of happiness to others.

"In proposing this plan, we impressed on our brethren the necessity of devoting to those ennobling purposes those means which had previously been wasted in frivolous efforts and childlike displays. We urged them with all the earnestness which the importance of the subject merits, that all who would place freedom on an enduring basis, to adopt such a course of agitation in favour of our Charter as should unite in one bond of brotherhood the wise and benevolent of all classes, who would be intent on cherishing and propagating the noblest principles of freedom among young and old, so that the most substantial fruits might be gathered from that political power we are now seeking to obtain.

" This proposal, while it was warmly greeted by the Press, and received the commendations of a great number of intelligent minds among all parties, was met with falsehood, intolerance and bitterest rancour, by the most prominent organ of Chartism, *The Northern Star*. Its proprietor and editor jointly denounced it as a production of Messrs. O'Connell, Hume and Roebuck! as a plan intended to destroy Fergus O'Connor's political supremacy and subvert one which he had previously concocted. *Education* was ridiculed, *Knowledge* was sneered at, *Facts* were perverted, *Truth* suppressed, and the lowest passions and prejudices of the multitude were appealed to, to obtain a clamorous verdict against us. We were denounced by them and their hired partisans, as 'thieves, liars and traitors to the cause of Chartism,' as persons who 'if a guillotine existed in England would be its just victims.' Nay, a *sermon!* has been preached by one of those professors of freedom to show the necessity for *privately assassinating us.*

" As far as we have been able to obtain insertion for a vindication of our conduct, through the channel by which we have been calumniated, we have called, but called in vain, for *proofs* of their base assertions. As far as they have dared reply to us, they have proclaimed themselves false, intolerant and reckless in the eyes of every reflecting man; and when the eyes of their dupes shall have been opened, they will be ashamed of the virulence they have displayed against men whose only crime has been the publication of *a rational plan* for the attainment of the People's Charter.

" Strong in rectitude of our principles, and more than ever convinced of the necessity of that plan, we pity those who have so vindictively assailed us. Their vanity has inflamed their intellect, their prejudices have darkened their understanding, and toleration and charitable feeling have been blotted from their minds. Believing themselves supremely wise, they spurn with Gothic ferocity all knowledge, truth, or justice; and, judging from their actions, they seem to think that liberty can only be realized by violence and proscription.

"But while these are the characteristics of the most ignorant and noisy portion of the Chartist body—persons who, without thought or judgment, are empty professors of our principles to-day, but worshippers at any other shrine to-morrow—we believe that the great bulk of our Chartist brethren is composed of men whose conviction in favour of the Charter has sprung from observation, enquiry, and patient investigation regarding the causes of political injustice and social misery. Men of this description may be deceived and misled for a season by mystification and falsehood; but their minds, bent on enquiry and ever open to conviction, will soon penetrate the flimsy veil which has been drawn over their understanding.

"To men of this character we confidently appeal; and we ask them whether the best means of obtaining the Charter, and the placing of our liberties on the securest foundation, do not form proper and legitimate questions of enquiry for every man in the United Kingdom? Or is it that the solving of these questions forms the exclusive prerogative of any particular individual or party among the people?—thus practically exemplifying in conduct the exclusive and despotic principles which they seek to over-throw, and bidding fair to render Chartism a by-word and derision.

"Holding the principles of democracy, we will yield to no man's dictation; we believe that both England and Ireland have been cursed by *man-worship*, to the sacrifice and delay of that freedom we are now contending for; and because we have dared honestly to assert our opinions, we have incurred the highest displeasure of all those whose vanity expects the homage of a crowd, peculiar patronage, and exclusive power. But warring against such selfish folly and mischievous authority, whether displayed in the courtly aristocrat or the social oppressor, we shall ever exert our humble powers to prevent *individual or social despotism* from being introduced into that just state of things which all good men are now contending for, and which, if they be united in one bond of brotherhood, no power can much longer prevent, delay, or subvert.

"Our calumniators have falsely asserted that we are for

delaying the franchise on the grounds of ignorance. So far from this being true, we have reiterated and published in various forms the contrary of this doctrine. We insist on the *universality* of the franchise on the broad principles of *personal* and *conventional rights.* *Personally,* as no man has a right to enslave or starve another man into submission to his will, which is done by arbitrary and exclusive laws. *Conventionally,* as every man living under the laws of society ought, in right and justice, to have a vote in determining what those laws should be. But while *as a right* we thus insist on our just share of political power, we are desirous of seeing the most *effective steps taken to gain it,* and of seeing our brethren *preparing themselves to use that power wisely when they shall have obtained it;* and not to be half a century exercising the franchise, and at the end of it still find themselves the sport of cunning schemers and wily politicians.

"First, then, as regards the best means of obtaining our Charter.—We are of those who are opposed to everything in the shape of a physical or violent revolution, believing that a victory would be a defeat to the just principles of democracy; as the military chieftains would become—as all past history affirms*—the political despots; and as such a sanguinary warfare, calling up the passions in the worst forms, must necessarily throw back for centuries our intellectual and moral progress. Believing that the attainment of the Charter would be an instrument of benefit to all—the only means through which the corruptions, monopolies, and evils of our Government can be removed, and that those who are interested in their continuance are few compared with the population—we think that all that is necessary for the carrying of that measure is, soberly and rationally, to convince all classes of our population how far it is *their interest to unite with us,* in order that we may peaceably obtain it; for a combined people have always numerous means for the attainment of their object without violence.

"But it is not the *mere possession of the franchise* that is

---

* With the exception, I believe, of Washington.

to benefit our country; that is only *the means to a just end—* the election of the best and wisest of men to solve a question which has never yet been propounded in any legislative body—namely, *how shall all the resources of our country be made to advance the intellectual and social happiness of every individual?* It is not merely *the removing of evils*, but *the establishing of remedies* that can benefit the millions; and in order to check the natural selfishness and ambition of rulers, and induce them to enact just and salutary laws, *those who possess the power to elect must have knowledge, judgment, and moral principle to direct them*, before anything worthy of the name of just government or true liberty can be established.

" Of what benefit would be the franchise, or what description of Government would be established by those, who, too ignorant to investigate, not only clamorously oppose, but if they had power, would even sacrifice all who differ from them? Happily, however, for the progress of humanity, those neglected and maddened unfortunates are few compared with the vast numbers of our countrymen, whose sound sense and generous feeling prompt them to investigation, improvement, and peace.

" But, notwithstanding this feeling prevails at present, the political and social condition of our country is such as to demand the consideration and combined energies of all who are anxious for peace, prosperity, and intellectual and moral progress. Taking into account the vast extent of social misery, which class legislation has mainly occasioned —viewing the contentions of factions for supremacy, and their desire to perpetuate the corruptions and monopolies by which they exist—seeing the deeply-seated wrongs and extended poverty which prevail, and which, if not speedily removed or mitigated, may madden our population into a state of anarchy and direst confusion—a consideration of this state of things should call forth the benevolent feelings of reflecting men among all classes, and should prompt them to be united, in order to investigate and remedy our political and social evils, and to place the liberties of our country upon a sound and lasting foundation.

"Having thus stated the intolerant conduct pursued against us, and briefly expressed our reasons for our opinions, we call upon men of sense and reflection to decide between us, at the same time inviting all who think with us to join the National Association."

Shortly after the publication of this address (in October, 1841), a number of persons residing in London, approving of the objects of the National Association, resolved to form themselves into a distinct and separate body for the purpose of individually and collectively promoting them in their locality, and for carrying out such portions of them as their funds would enable them to do. This body was designated "The London Members of the National Association."* It held its first meeting at the Globe Coffee House, Shoe Lane. Its first secretary was Mr. Henry Hetherington, and on his resignation, Mr. Charles Westerton, a gentleman who subsequently, as church-warden at Knightsbridge, rendered great service to the Liberal cause by his opposition to *Puseyism*.

About one of the first efforts of this Association was the establishment of a cheap weekly periodical, entitled " The National Association Gazette." It was edited by my eloquent and much-esteemed friend Mr. J. H. Parry (now

---

* The persons who took, more or less, an active part in the National Association were the following :—Henry Hetherington, Wm. Lovett, John Cleave, Henry Vincent, Henry Mitchell, James Watson, John Collins, Richard Moore, James Hoppy, Charles H. Neesom, James Savage, H. B. Marley, Joseph Turner, Arthur Dyson, Stephen Wade, R. W. Woodward, George Bennett, Isaac F. Mollett, Charles Tapperell, C. H. Simmons, A. Morton, John Alexander, Charles Westerton, W. J. Linton, Benjamin Huggett, C. H. Elt, H. Beal, J. Peat, J. Newton, J. H. Parry, Wm. Statham, John Statham, Wm. Saunders, Thomas Wilson, J. Kesson, James Stansfeld, Sidney M. Hawkes, Wm. Shaen, Henry Moore, John King, Wm. Addiscott, R. McKenzie, George Cox, Abram Hooper, Richard Spur, G. Outtram, Thomas Scott, J. Jenkinson, Thomas Lovick, W. H. Prideaux, Henry Mills, John Mottram, James Lawrence, John Lawrence, Capt. Walhouse, John Bainbridge, Wm. Dell, John Parker, Henry Campkin, Thomas Donatty, J. J. West, J. Dobson Collett, T. Beggs, J. Corfield, F. Rickards, Charles M. Schomberge, W. H. Ashurst, H. Taylor, J. Beasley, A. Davenport, Wm. Hyde, Wm. Crate, J. Tijoue, &c.

Mr. Serjeant Parry), a gentleman whose acquaintance (originating with the starting of that little publication) I warmly cherish, and whose many acts of friendship and generosity towards me I shall ever have cause to remember. This gazette was continued for many months, and by its able management did our cause great service; but from its being an unstamped publication, and in consequence not able to embrace the news of the week, it never had a large circulation.

The repeated interruptions of public meetings, by the violent portion of the Chartist body, having excited strong prejudices in the minds of the *Middle Classes* against our principles, led us to put forth the following address to them :—

"Fellow-Countrymen,—The political partisans of our respective classes have in too many instances succeeded in awakening our mutual prejudices; and selfishness and distrust on the one hand, and violence and folly on the other, have ripened animosities and fostered the spirit of exclusiveness, to the dissevering of those links which ought to be united for our common weal; while a selfish, corrupt, and oppressive few have flourished and triumphed by reason of such prejudices and dissensions.

" Seeing the result of those evils in the social degradation, the commercial ruin, and political oppression of our country, we are anxious to see a mantle of oblivion cast over past differences, and to see the wise and good of all classes resolving, *that in future they will labour and reason together to work out the social and political regeneration of man.*

" Amid the multiplicity of opinions entertained by a large portion of your class regarding the causes of commercial depression and social misery, we are desirous of laying before you the views entertained by a numerous body of our working-class brethren, in order that you may be induced, if possible, to examine their merits without prejudice, and reasonably discuss their efficacy to promote the great end which, we trust, we are all aiming at—namely, the peace, prosperity, and happiness of our native land.

" In tracing the monopolies, the trading and commercial restrictions of which we complain, we find them originating in the selfishness and party power of legislators. When we ask the origin of those burthens which paralyze our domestic energies, and prevent us from coping with other nations, we find that they have sprung from the cupidity, the fears, and selfishness of law-makers. When we investigate the origin of pauperism, ignorance, misery, and crime, we may easily trace the black catalogue to exclusive legislation, and the restrictive and intolerant laws which have been enacted to block up every avenue to knowledge, by which means the mass of society have been left to grope in ignorance and superstition; and, goaded by the poverty corrupt legislation has occasioned, they have been rendered still more desperate by the sanguinary and cruel laws which class legislators have made to hedge about their individual interests.

" Satisfied, therefore, that most of those evils can be traced to unjust and selfish legislation, we have pushed our inquiries still further, and we find their chief source *in our present exclusive system of representation.* The franchise being confined to a small portion of our population, and that portion controlled and prejudiced to an incalculable extent by the wealthy few, the legislators and governors of our country have not been a representation of the mind and wants of the nation, but of the political party through whose influence they owe their power. Thus it is that restrictive laws are maintained, that selfish measures have originated, and class interests are supported, at the expense of national prosperity and individual happiness.

" To remedy a state of things thus prejudicial to your interests and ours, the class to which we belong have embodied in a document, called " The People's Charter," such principles and means of just and equal representation as we believe will best secure the object we are aiming at— *just and honest legislation.*

" To a calm consideration of that measure of justice, and to the creating and extending an enlightened public opinion in its favour, we would especially direct your attention, so that by a cordial union of the Middle and Working Classes the *originating cause* of all the evils of which both parties complain may be speedily removed. We would implore you, fellow-countrymen, to think deeply and seriously of the multitude of human beings, destined for high and noble purposes, who are, year after year, sacrificed by class legislation, while professing reformers are busily occupied with *the effects* of political and social wrongs, and leaving *the originating cause* in all its contaminating rottenness.

" We are the more induced to call upon you at this time to examine the merits of the Charter, as we understand that some philanthropic individuals* among you, dissatisfied with our present representative system, are about to propose to you some modification of the suffrage short of that which we believe *essential for just government*—such, indeed, as is embodied in the People's Charter. If it can be shown that the principles of that document are *unjust*, we shall be found as ready to abandon as we are now resolved to maintain them. If it is not so universal in its character as to place *woman* upon the same footing of political equality with *man*, propose it to us as the terms of your union, and we engage that most of our brethren throughout the kingdom will readily declare their adherence. If its details are defective, show us in what respect they can be amended, so as to better carry out its principles, and our brethren will not be slow to adopt improvements.

" But a determination, deep, resolute, and extensive, has gone forth; and persecution and suffering have only served to strengthen conviction and rivet our adherence, that we will no longer waste our energies in combating with *mere legislative effects*, while *the cause of such effects* remains to generate more evils. It was a conviction of the folly of such conduct, rendered still more evident after the passing of the Reform Bill, that led us to embody in our document what we believe *essential to just legislation*, believing that though our efforts to secure it might be difficult and prolonged, yet the attainment of it forms the only hope of our political and social salvation.

---

* The Complete Suffrage Party.

" Many of you who agree with our principles may probably tell us that the intolerant and mischievous conduct of a large portion of the Chartist body, has engendered timid fears and hostile prejudices, which it is necessary to conciliate by standing apart from the name and principles of the Charter. Shall just principles be set aside because bad men have espoused them, or foolish ones diverted them to an unwise purpose? If the principles of Christianity itself had been tried by the conduct of its professors, where would be the records of its moral sway, and its triumphs over the barbarism of man?

" Come with us, then, and declare at once for the Charter! Do not, we pray you, seek to get up what will be considered a *counter agitation*, generating distrust where we believe benefit is intended, but which will only serve to keep those asunder whose union is essential to secure the benefits our starving brethren need, whose disunion is the life-giving principle of our aristocratical oppressors, but destruction and death to the principles of true democracy.

" Say that you disapprove of the folly, the violence, and intolerance of hundreds of professing Chartists, and thousands will honestly respond to such a declaration! Say that you condemn the insane threats which have been ignorantly hurled against those rights and interests which experience has proved necessary for the security of our social fabric, and the well-disposed of all classes will unite with you to form a wall of adamant to protect all just laws and good institutions.

" Say, then, that you will make common cause with us upon the broad principles of right and justice contained in our Charter, and the kind and generous feelings which distinguish our countrymen will respond with gratitude. The anger which pinching poverty has excited would then give place to hope, and intelligence, being made the basis of our agitation, would brighten as it extends; we should then become efficient to promote all good, and powerful to guard it.

"Trusting that you will respond to the wishes of your suffering countrymen, we remain, your fellow-citizens," &c., &c.

CHAPTER XIV.

THE second National Petition, which was put forth by the National Charter Association in 1842, having given great offence to a considerable number of the Scotch Chartists, on account of the question of the *Repeal of the Union* being introduced into it, was also for the same reason rejected by the members of our Association. They therefore adopted the following *Remonstrance* to the Commons House of Parliament instead thereof :—

"The REMONSTRANCE of the undersigned inhabitants of this kingdom respectfully showeth—

"That we have just cause of complaint and remonstrance against you, who, in the name of the Commons of Great Britain and Ireland, profess to represent, watch over, and legislate for our interests. That as the ancient and constitutional custom of *public petitioning* has, by your acts, been rendered a mere mockery, we are thus induced to substitute *a public remonstrance against you*, it being the legitimate means by which any portion of the people, whose political rights have one by one been legislated away by their rulers, can appeal to the public opinion of their country ; a tribunal by whose will representation is alone rendered constitutional, and for whose benefit alone government is established.

"We justly complain of your utter disregard and seeming contempt of the wants and wishes of the people, as expressed in the prayers and petitions they have been *humbly addressing to you* for a number of years past. For, while they have been complaining of the unequal, unjust, and cruel laws you have enacted—which, in their operation, have reduced millions to poverty, and punished them because they were poor—you have been either increasing the catalogue, or mocking them with expensive and fruitless commissions, or telling them that 'their poverty was beyond the reach of legislative enactment.'

"While they have been complaining that you take from them three-fourths of their earnings by your complicated system of taxation, and by your monopolies force them into unequal competition with other nations, you have exhibited a contempt for their complaints in your profligate and lavish expenditure at home and abroad, and by a selfish pertinacity in favour of the monopolies you have created for your own especial interests or those of your party.

"While they have been praying that our civil list may be reduced in proportion to the exigencies of the state, and, at a time like the present, when bankruptcy, insolvency, and national destitution prevail to an extent unparalleled in history, that Her Majesty and her Consort should be made acquainted with the necessity for dispensing with useless and extravagant frivolities; yet you, in ready compliance with the wishes of the ministry, have gratified such extravagancies at the expense of want and wretchedness, when, if you had been loyal to your queen or just to your country, you would have shown her the necessity for retrenchment in every department of her household.

"While the humane and considerate portion of the population have been demonstrating to you the evils of ignorance and the source of crime, and have been entreating you to apply to the purposes of education and social improvement, the enormous sums which you inhumanly employ in punishing the victims of your vicious institutions and culpable neglect, you have gone on recklessly despising the prayers of humanity and justice, augmenting your police, increasing your soldiers, raising prisons, and devising new means of coercion, in a useless attempt to prevent crime by severity of punishment, instead of cultivating the minds, improving the hearts, and administering to the physical necessities of the people.

"While the intelligence and humanity of our countrymen have been loudly expressed against sanguinary and cruel wars, barbarous means for brutalizing the people and perpetuating bull-dog courage under the name of glory; you, who profess to watch over our interests, have, in order to gratify aristocratic cupidity, selfishness, and ambition, been supporting unjust and uncalled-for wars, by which thousands of human beings have been led on to slaughter and to death, and through which our enormous debt will be increased, and the stigma of cruelty and injustice left upon our national character.

"While our brethren have been praying for religious freedom, you have allowed a State Church to take from them upwards of nine millions per annum, independent of the evils it inflicts on them by its troublesome imposts, grasping selfishness, and anti-gospel, persecuting spirit.

" While our brethren have been contending for the free circulation of thought and opinion, through the channel of an unshackled press, as a means by which truth may be elicited and our institutions improved; you have been imposing the most arbitrary measures to check public opinion, retard freedom of enquiry, and to prevent knowledge from being cheaply diffused.

" While our social evils and anomalies have repeatedly been brought before you, you—whose duty it was to provide a remedy—have looked carelessly on, or have been intent only on your interests or your pleasures. Your own commissioners have reported to you, that thousands of infant children are doomed to slavery and ignorance in our mines and factories, while their wretched parents are wanting labour and needing bread; and that wives and mothers, to procure a miserable subsistence for their families, are compelled to neglect their offspring and their homes, and all the domestic duties which belong to their sex; that thousands of skilful mechanics are starving on a few pence, which they obtain for fourteen hours' daily toil; that vast numbers, anxious to labour, are left to linger and perish from cold and hunger; that in Ireland alone *two millions three hundred thousand are in a state of beggary and destitution;* and that misery, wretchedness, and crime, are fast spreading their deteriorating influence, and gradually undermining the fabric of society.

"Nor is your misgovernment confined to this country alone, but its baleful influence is felt in every part of the world where British authority is known. Throughout our dominions you have permitted rights the most sacred to be invaded, in order to provide resting-places for aristocratical fledglings. You have disregarded the constitutions you have given, violated the promises you have made, and, spurning the prayers and petitions of our colonial brethren, you have trampled upon every principle of justice to establish your power and feed your ravenous lust for gain.

"You have therefore shown *by your acts* that you do not represent the wants and wishes of the people; on the contrary, self, or party considerations, are seen in almost every enactment you have made, or measure you have sanctioned. So far from representing the *commons* of this country, or legislating for them, the majority of you have neither feelings nor interests in common with them. It is seen by your proceedings, that while the supposed rights of every class and party can find advocates among you, *the right of labour is left to find 'its own level.'*

"Is the justice of titles questioned, the wisdom of ecclesiastical law doubted, or a repugnance shown by conscientious men to support the church they dissent from? *The Church* can always find zealous defenders among you. Is the expensive and unjust administration of *the law* complained of, together with all its technical and perplexing absurdities? its wisdom and propriety is at once demonstrated by your host of legal advocates. Does any one presume to question the propriety of our very expensive *military* and *naval establishments,* or to doubt the justice of flogging as a means of discipline?—he will soon find a regiment among you prepared to combat his opinions. Is the justice questioned of allowing the *landowners* to tax the people of this country to the extent of seventeen millions annually, to support their own especial monopolies —the corn laws, &c.?—eloquent advocates will at once be found among you to plead for the vested rights of property. In short, bankers, merchants, manufacturers, and all interests and professions can find advocates and defenders in the 'Commons House,' excepting *the common people themselves.*

"That there are some well-intentioned and benevolent individuals among you, we readily admit; but far too many of those who profess liberal and just principles think more of the safety of their seats, and the prejudices of their associates, than they do of taking any active measures to carry their principles into practice. Instead of boldly proclaiming the dishonesty, hollowness, and injustice of your present legislative system, the party cry of Whig and Tory is too often the substance of their speeches—the cheat and phantom, which you all used to silence the timid and divert the ignorant.

"That you do not represent the people of this country may be further seen from the fact, that those who return you are not more than *a seventh part* of the adult male population. For by the last returns that were laid before you, while in Great Britain and Ireland there are about 5,812,276 males *above twenty years of age*, the registered electors are only 812,916; and it is practically proved, that of these electors only about nine in every twelve *actually vote;* and of these nine, many possess a plurality of votes.*

"On analysing the constituency of the United Kingdom, it is also proved that *the majority* of you are returned by 1,58,870 registered electors, giving *an average* constituency to each of you of only 242 electors.

"It is also proved by the returns that have been made, that 39 of you are returned by less than 300 electors each; 43 by less than 400; 20 by less than 500; 34 by less than 600; 34 by less than 700; 20 by less than 800; 18 by less than 900; and 23 by less than 1,000 registered electors.

"It is also notorious that, in the Commons House, which is said to be exclusively *the People's!* there are *two hundred and five persons who are immediately or remotely related to the peers of the realm!*

"That it contains 3 marquises, 9 earls, 23 viscounts, 27 lords, 32 right honourables, 63 honourables, 58 baronets, 10 knights, 2 admirals, 8 lord-lieutenants, 74 deputy and vice-lieutenants, 1 general, 1 lieutenant-general, 7 major-

---

* This was in 1842.

generals, 22 colonels, 32 lieutenant-colonels, 7 majors, 67 captains in army and navy, 12 lieutenants, 2 cornets, 53 magistrates, 63 placemen, and 108 patrons of church livings, having the patronage of 247 livings between them. And there are little more than 200 out of the 658 members of your house who have not either titles, office, place, pension, or church patronage.

"These facts afford abundant proofs that you neither represent the *number* nor the *interests* of the millions, but that the greatest portion of you have interests foreign, or directly opposed, to the true interests of the people of this country.

"Setting aside your party changes and rival bickerings, important only to those among you who are in possession of the public purse; with a knowledge of your past actions, and with these notorious facts before us, as plain-speaking men, claiming the freedom of speech as our birthright, we hesitate not to declare that, individually and collectively, you have all been tried by the test of *public utility*, and, with few exceptions, have been found wanting in every requisite for representatives of an intelligent and industrious population.*

---

* The Representaties of the People, as described by the *Morning Post*, Jan. 18th, 1835 :—

"The most confused sounds, mysteriously blended, issued from all corners of the House. . . . At repeated intervals a sort of drone-like humming, having almost the sound of a distant hand-organ, or bagpipes, issued from the back benches; coughing, sneezing, and ingeniously extended yawning, blended with other sounds, and producing a *tout ensemble* which we have never heard excelled in the House. A single voice, from the ministerial benches, imitated very accurately the yelp of a kennelled hound. . . . At one time you would have thought, from the rapidity with which they rose up and sat down again in their seats, that they had been trying some gymnastic experiments. . . . One Honourable Member imitated the crowing of a cock so admirably that you could not have distinguished it from the performance of a real chanticleer. Not far from the same spot issued sounds marvellously resembling the bleating of a sheep, blended occasionally with an admirable imitation of the braying of an ass. Then there were coughing, yawning, and other vocal performances, in infinite variety, and in most discordant chorus."

" The wide extent of misery which your legislation has occasioned, and the spread of information which your decrees could not suppress, have called up inquiring minds in every portion of the empire to investigate your actions, to question your authority, and, finally, to condemn your unjust and exclusive power.

" They have demonstrated to their brethren that the only *rational use* of the institutions and laws of society is to protect, encourage, and support all that can be made to contribute *to the happiness of all the people.*

" That as the object to be attained is *mutual benefit,* so ought the enactment of laws to be *by mutual consent.*

" That obedience to the laws can only *be justly enforced* on the certainty that those who are called on to obey them have had, either personally or by their representatives, a power to enact, amend, or repeal them.

" That all who are *excluded* from this share of political power are not *justly included* within the operation of the laws. To them the laws are only *despotic enactments,* and the assembly from whom they emanate can only be considered an unholy, interested compact, devising plans and schemes for taxing and subjecting the many.

" In consonance with these opinions they have embodied in a document, called ' The People's Charter,' such just and reasonable principles of representation as, in their opinion, are calculated to secure *honest legislation* and *good government.* That document proposes to confer the franchise on every citizen of twenty-one years of age, who has resided in a district three months, who is of sane mind, and unconvicted of crime.

" It proposes to divide the United Kingdom into 300 electorial districts, containing, as nearly as may be, an equal number of inhabitants, each district to send *one* member to Parliament, and no more.

" It proposes to take the votes of the electors by ballot, in order to protect them against unjust influence.

" It proposes that Parliament be chosen annually.

" It proposes to abolish money qualifications for Members of Parliament.

" It proposes that Members of Parliament be paid for

their services, and, moreover, contains the details by which all these propositions shall be carried into practice.

"This document, being so just in its demands, has already received the sanction of a vast portion of the population ; and petitions in its favour have already been laid before you, containing a larger number of signatures than probably have ever been obtained in favour of any legislative enactment. And though indiscretion among some of its advocates may have retarded public opinion in its favour, we are confident that the conviction in favour of its justice and political efficacy has taken deep root in the mind of the nation, and is making rapid progress among all classes not interested in existing corruptions.

" That you may see the wisdom and propriety of timely yielding to such opinion in favour of a better representative system, and that you will speedily declare in favour of the People's Charter, or, by resigning your seats, prepare the way for those who will enact it as the law of these realms, is the ardent *prayer* of us, the undersigned inhabitants of this kingdom.''

The signing of this Remonstrance was delayed till towards the end of the sessions, in order that it might not interfere in any way with the signing of the National Petition. The motion, however, founded on that petition, by Mr. T. S. Duncombe, *that the petitioners be heard by counsel at the bar*, having only received the support of fifty-six Members, caused a great number of the working classes to avow a resolution that they would never again pray or petition the House of Commons in any form. Our Remonstrance was, however, signed by a considerable number of people, but, the end of the session approaching, it was deemed desirable to postpone its presentation till the next session ; but, other matters respecting our hall interfering, the project was abandoned. Among the persons who testified their approval of this document was the late persevering and consistent Reformer, Joseph Hume, who, in a letter to the Lambeth members of our Association, thus wrote :—" The principles of reform as set forth in the Remonstrance of the National Association are such as would place the people in their proper state, to protect their property and interests against the rapacity and monopolies of the present system; and I hope to see the Middle Classes soon join with the millions of industrious men in a constitutional agitation for their rights."   I deem it but just to record this opinion of Mr. Hume in favour of what may be called extreme views of Radicalism, as O'Connor and his disciples were not sparing of their abuse of him, on account of what they called his Whig principles.   That, like too many other reformers of that day, he was often led to support the Whigs for fear of the bugbear of Toryism may be admitted; but I believe that no man was ever more persevering in seeking to carry the principle of reform into every department of the State than was Mr. Hume.   And certainly, of all men, whose efforts to free the *Working Classes* from the enthralment of the infamous *combination laws*, he is the most worthy of honour, and of their grateful remembrance.

CHAPTER XV.

IN January, 1842, Mr. Joseph Sturge, whose benevolent labours in the cause of humanity and freedom are so notorious, commenced his exertions in favour of what was called "*Complete Suffrage*." His first effort was the preparing of a Memorial to the Queen, earnestly entreating her to retain in her service and take to her councils such Ministers only as would promote in Parliament that full, fair, and free representation of the people in the House of Commons to which they were entitled by the great principles of Christian equity, as well as by the British Constitution; as, according to Blackstone, "*no subject of England can be constrained to pay any aids or taxes, even for the defence of the Realm, or the support of Government, but such as are imposed by his own consent, or that of his representative in Parliament.*" *

This Memorial having been sent to our Association for signatures, it was resolved to give it all the support in our power; although, at the same time, we felt bound to express our opinion, that neither a full nor fair representation of the people could be obtained till the essentials of the People's Charter were enacted as the laws of the realm. Soon after this, being at a Public Meeting at the Crown and Anchor, on the suffrage question, I was invited, with Messrs. Hetherington, Parry, and others, to meet some of Mr. Sturge's friends in the refreshment-room, to talk over this subject. After some very excellent speeches, there given, by Mr. Miall, Mr. Crawford, Mr. Spencer and others, Mr. George Thompson, the chairman, called upon

---

* I have since heard that this Memorial was first mooted at a meeting of the Anti-Corn-Law party.

me for my opinion. I told them that my definition
Complete Suffrage was found in the People's Charter;
the principles of which I thought to be essential to secu
the just representation of the people. I very briefly ga
my reasons in proof of this, and urged on them a f
discussion of the subject. Shortly after this meeting
received a letter from Mr. Sturge, informing me that
Provisional Committee had been formed at Birmingha
and that they intended to call a Complete Suffra
Conference on the 5th of April, 1842.

This conference, composed of eighty-four persons, bc
of the middle and working classes—appointed for the m
part by those who had signed the Memorial referred to
met at Birmingham at the time specified. Mr. J.
Parry and myself were appointed by the members of o
Association to attend it, and Mr. C. H. Neesom and N
Charles Westerton, two other of our members, were a
delegated—the former from the district of Spitalfields, a
the letter from Knightsbridge. The members of our Assoc
tion, conceiving that there was little chance of a cord
union being effected between the two classes without t
recognition of the Charter, on behalf of which so ma
sacrifices had been made by the working classes, we
anxious to bring this document forward as one of the fi
subjects for discussion. But the Business Committ
objecting to this course, the consideration of it was delay
till other matters had been discussed. These were t
essential principles that were thought to be requisite i
securing a full, fair, and free representation of the peopl
these were accordingly discussed, and after a very long a
earnest debate, we were gratified in seeing most of t
principles of our Charter adopted. On the third da
therefore, according to the arrangement previously agre
on, I brought forward the following motion :—

"That this Conference having adopted such just prin
ples of representation as are necessary for giving to
classes of society their equal share of political power, a
as the People's Charter contains such details as have be
deemed necessary for the working out of such principl
and has, moreover, been adopted by millions of c

brethren as an embodiment of their political rights, this Conference, in order to effect a cordial union of the middle and working classes, resolve in *a future conference* (in which the working classes may be more fully represented) to enter into a calm consideration of that document among other plans of political reform, and, if approved of, to use every just and peaceable means for creating a public opinion in its favour." In the lengthened discussion which arose on this resolution, it appeared that considerable prejudice existed in the minds of many of the middle class members against the Charter; though the resolution did not call upon them to agree to that document, but only to take it into consideration, among other plans of reform, at a future conference. However, to conciliate this feeling against us, without any deviation of principle, we Chartists eventually modified the resolution as follows, fully believing that the majority would not be opposed to a fair discussion of the Charter at the next conference:—
" That this conference having adopted such just principles of representation as are necessary for giving to all classes their equal share of political power, resolve at some future period to call another conference, in which the whole people may be fully represented, for the purpose of considering any documents which embody the necessary details for the working out of the above principles." This having been adopted, the conference next agreed to a plan, constitution, and rules for the formation of a new society, entitled " The National Complete Suffrage Union;" and, after some few other business resolutions, concluded its sittings, it having lasted four days.

This effort to effect a union between the two classes was to some extent successful; for a great many local Complete Suffrage Associations were formed in many towns. Great numbers of the working classes were, however, kept aloof from it, by the abuse and misrepresentations of the *Northern Star;* and others who, so far, approved of the principles of the Union, were not disposed to forego their own agitation for the Charter to join it till they had tested it by another conference. In the meantime, however, the members of the Union were not idle; tracts were printed, lectures given, meetings held, and, to the best of my recollection, two motions introduced into the House of Commons on the subject of the Suffrage by Mr. Sharman Crawford.

In September 1842, a special meeting of the Council of the Union was called at Birmingham to arrange, among other matters, for the calling of the next conference. Now, as O'Connor (notwithstanding his hostility to the Union) had boasted largely of his intention to get the working classes fully represented in the next conference, if he spent half he possessed;—which in reality meant that he would get it packed with his own disciples, if possible;—it became a question, with those who wanted a fair conference of the both classes chosen, how it could be best prevented. In talking the matter over with my friends, I suggested that this could be best done by one-half of the representatives being chosen by electors, and half by non-electors; and that if they interfered with each other's meetings the election should be void. This plan being approved of, I drew up the following Address and took it down to Birmingham to submit it to the Council, which, after some discussion, was adopted:—

" The Council of the National Complete Suffrage Union, to Political Reformers of all shades of opinions.

" We address you, fellow-countrymen, deeply impressed with the moral obligation of men and citizens, whose duties have been imposed on us by an authority greater than princes or rulers, commanding us to " do unto all men as we would wish them to do unto us," consequently requiring us to lend that aid which ourselves would desire, to extricate from their condition the millions of our brethren, who, by the oppression or neglect of rulers, are plunged in the lowest depths of misery, groping in ignorance, and daily sinking in crime.

" Though we believe that that great Christian obligation calls *upon all men* to assist in freeing their brethren from the power of the oppression, yet, at this crisis, we address ourselves especially to you, the Reformers of the United Kingdom; because it is for you—the active and intelligent spirits of progression—you who desire to see justice established where injustice is enthroned—it is for you, in your energy and self-sacrificing resolution, to determine whether our country shall rise in freedom, knowledge, and happiness, or sink, as a land of beggared serfs, beneath the paralysing power of a corrupt and selfish oligarchy.

"In thus addressing you, we desire not to arouse your passions, we would only awaken the nobler feelings of justice, humanity, and Christain duty; considering our cause too sacred to be promoted by violence, or benefited by wrong.

"To you we need not depict the widespread misery of our country. Most of you are familiar with it, in all its sickening forms, and vast numbers of you are already its victims. But we ask you, with all the sober earnestness of men and Christians, whether you will unite with us in one general bond of brotherhood—and by persevering peaceful and energetic means, resolve, at any personal sacrifice, to stay the progress of our national debasement—to check the ravages of starving poverty—to remove the drag chains of monopoly, the over-burdening pressure of taxation, the progress of crime, the race-destroying curse of war; and under the blessing of Heaven, free our country from the accumulating evils of corrupt and selfish legislation?

"Fellow-countrymen, we are not desirous of interfering with your present local arrangements, but we call upon you to meet us in the spirit of truth and justice, to determine with singleness of purpose, *what is best to be done to effect the political and social deliverance of our country?* and, having once determined, to concentrate all our energies to the accomplishment of such a glorious consummation. This, we think, can be done without the amalgamation of societies, between whom differences of opinions and modes of action exist; this can be done legally, constitutionally, and effectively. All that is necessary for its accomplishment is union, energy, and self-sacrifice, *on all points of agreement*, and forbearance, toleration, and Christian charity, where differences of opinion prevail.

" But, in the election of representatives to meet in such a conference as we contemplate, all party spirit must be excluded ; all efforts for forcing *individual views* through the power of numbers must be avoided ; a victory obtained by such intolerant, overbearing policy would be defeat to our object—that of having a *fairly-constituted* NATIONAL CONFERENCE, a body in whom all shades of reformers, among the middle and working classes, may place confidence, and under whose peaceful and legal guidance we may unitedly contend, till we have secured the blessing and fruits of freedom.

" We are also desirous that the ensuing conference shall be the means of effecting a better understanding and closer union between the middle and working classes than has hitherto existed ; feeling convinced that, so long as the enemies of the people can keep them divided, so long will they both be victimised by a corrupt and liberty-hating aristocracy. We call, therefore, upon the middle classes to send *their representatives* to confer with *those of the working classes*, to see how far they can remove the state of animosity, apprehension, and disunion that prevails ; how far arrangements may be made to secure our mutual objects *speedily and peaceably*, and thus free ourselves from the grasping insolence of faction, guard against the storm of anarchy, be secure against military despotism, and unitedly raising up the intelligence and virtues of the democracy on the basis of free institutions, hasten the consummation of that happy period when ' our swords shall be beaten into ploughshares, and our spears into pruning hooks,' and when every man shall sit down in peace and security to enjoy the fruits of honest industry.

" Having been appointed to make arrangements for the calling of a conference, to consider the details essential for the carrying out of the principles on which the National Complete Suffrage Union is founded ; and as its paramount object is to effect a union between the middle and working classes, to secure the just and equal representation of the whole people, we think it our duty to submit such propositions for the consideration of the conference as may be best promotive of that end.   We, therefore, submit the following propositions for the consideration of the confer-ence, which we call upon you, the Reformers of the United Kingdom, to elect :—

" ' 1. To determine on the essential details of an Act of Parliament, necessary for securing the just representation of the whole adult male population of the United Kingdom of Great Britain and Ireland ; such Act to embrace the principles and details of complete suffrage, equal electoral districts, vote by ballot, no property qualification, payment of members, and annual parliaments, as adopted by the first Complete Suffrage Conference.

" ' 2. To determine what members of parliament shall be appointed to introduce the said Act into the House of Com-mons, and in what manner other members of the house shall be called upon to support it.

" ' 3. To endeavour to ascertain how far the friends of unrestricted and absolute freedom of trade will unite with us to obtain such an Act of Parliament, provided we re-solve to use our newly-acquired franchise in favour of such freedom of trade, and to vote only for such as will pledge themselves in its favour.

" ' 4. To devise the best means for maintaining competent parliamentary candidates pledged to our principles ; the most effectual means by which assistance may be rendered to them in all electoral contests ; and also the best means for registering the electors and non-electors throughout the kingdom who may be disposed to promote our objects.

" ' 5. To consider the propriety of calling upon the municipal electors to adopt immediate measures for secur-ing the election of such men only to represent them in their local governments as are known to be favourable to the principles of complete suffrage.

" ' 6. To call upon our fellow-countrymen seriously to con-sider the great extent to which, in various ways, they now willingly co-operate with their oppressors, and to ascertain how far they may be disposed to prove their devotion to the cause of liberty, by refusing to be used for the purposes of war, cruelty, and injustice, and particularly by the disuse of intoxicating articles.

" ' 7. To express an opinion as to the duty of the people

giving their countenance and support to all those who may suffer from espousing their cause.

"'8. To determine the best legal and constitutional means for energetically and peaceably promoting the above objects; for checking all kinds of violence and commotion by which the enemy triumphs; for disseminating sound political knowledge; for spreading the principles of sobriety, peace, and toleration throughout the country, and by every just and virtuous means preparing the people for the proper exercise of their political and social rights.

"'9. To devise means for raising a national fund for the purpose of promoting the above objects, as well as to protect all persons, who, in their peaceful prosecution of them, shall become victims of unjust laws or despotic ordinances.'

"And in order to convince the middle classes that the working population have no ulterior object inimical to the general welfare of society, we advise that they meet in the forthcoming conference on terms of perfect equality to discuss these important propositions, feeling convinced that our principles need no other aid than their own intrinsic excellence; having truth for their basis, and the happiness of the human family for their end, and affording the best guarantee for the security of private property, which we regard as sacred and inviolable, equally in the poor man's labour and rich man's possessions.

"We, therefore, advise that public meetings be called, by advertisement or placard, of not less than four days' notice, in every town throughout the kingdom, inviting the inhabitants to elect representatives to hold a National Conference at Birmingham, on Tuesday, the 27th of December, 1842, for the purpose of deciding on an Act of Parliament for securing the just representation of the whole people; and for determining on such peaceful, legal, and constitutional means as may cause it to become the law of these realms.

"That two representatives be sent from the smaller towns and boroughs, having less than 5,000 inhabitants, and four from the larger ones, excepting that London, Edinburgh, Birmingham, Manchester, Glasgow, and Liverpool, may send six representatives, but no more.

"That one-half of the representatives shall be appointed by the electors, and half by the non-electors. The meetings for such purposes to be held separate, unless that both classes can agree in having all the representatives chosen at one meeting, which we earnestly recommend; but where they do not so agree, the two classes are not to interfere with each other's meetings, otherwise their election shall be declared void.

"That, should the authorities interfere or trespass on this constitutional right of public meeting, so as to prevent any meeting from being held, the leading men of the two classes shall then cause nomination lists to be made out, recommending their respective candidates; such lists to be publicly notified, and left in public situations to receive the signatures of the inhabitants; those having the greater number of signatures to be declared duly elected.

"That the places sending representatives make arrangements for defraying their expenses.

"That as our Irish brethren are prohibited, by exclusive and oppressive laws, from sending representatives to such a conference, we especially invite, and will receive as visitors, all who approve of the object of our meeting, and who share the confidence of the people of that country.

"Should the police or the authorities of any town, in their desire to stifle public opinion, wilfully interrupt or unjustly interfere with the right of public meetings called for legal subjects, we advise that the people in those places cause proper evidence to be taken of such interruption, so that the question may be tried in our higher courts of law; and that Englishmen may learn whether those rights, of which they are proud to boast, *the rights of publicly assembling, and reasonably declaring their opinions*, are sacred and inviolable, or whether they depend on the fiat of some local magistrate, or on a portion of those who hate liberty, or on a servant of the government armed with staff and sabre.

"Believing that the above objects are perfectly just and legal, being in conformity with our ancient constitutional usages, being the only rational and proper means for ascertaining the public opinion of the country upon any great question affecting the general welfare, we especially invite your co-operation and support. We remain your friends and fellow-citizens, the members of the National Complete Suffrage Union," &c.

The plan for electing representatives to the conference, as set forth in this Address, though agreed to by the council, was not, as might be supposed, approved of by the O'Connorites, who took every opportunity of denouncing it as anti-democratic and unjust. The Complete Suffrage party, however, instead of defending it as a fair and just mode for choosing a deliberative assembly, where reason and argument were to prevail instead of the power of numbers, foolishly gave way, on this very important point, at almost the first meeting they attended after its publication. The result was that O'Connor immediately began his preparations for securing a majority in the conference, recommending as candidates those of his own party to every town where he thought their election could be secured. The middle classes among the Complete Suffrage party, finding that they were likely to be outnumbered by the O'Connorites, and being, moreover, prejudiced against the charter, adopted a plan by which they thought they should get rid of Fergus and his party without ultimate injury to their union. They, therefore, got two legal gentlemen in London to prepare a bill, founded on the principles they had adopted, and which they designated " The New Bill of Rights," intending to give that *the priority of discussion* at the forthcoming conference. This course was not only unwise—as it proved—but was also unjust, for although myself and Mr. Neesom *were members of their council,* we were never made acquainted with their intentions or proceedings until I was shown the bill in print. I then expressed to Mr. Sturge my great regret at this course of proceeding, as I thought that the putting forth of this measure in opposition to the charter would destroy all chance of union between the two classes, as myself and others who had joined them could not with any consistency vote for their " Bill of Rights " in opposition to the charter, and that I believed that the majority of the working classes would not desert the document they had so long fought for for this new measure the council had prepared.

When, therefore, we had forwarded to us the programme of the conference, as prepared by the council, and found by it that they proposed to bring forward " the Bill of Rights " *for priority of discussion,* those of our friends who had been delegated from London met together to determine what was best to be done. In looking at the programme it was seen at a glance that on the Bill of Rights being proposed some of the O'Connorites would propose an amendment in favour of the charter, on which we, if true to our principles, would be compelled to vote. It was, therefore, recommended to me that, when this measure was proposed, I should do all I could to induce them to withdraw it, or otherwise to propose the People's Charter as *an amendment,* as by this course a breach might possibly be avoided, which otherwise was sure to take place.

This second conference, consisting of 374 members, met at Birmingham on Tuesday, Dec. 27th, 1842, according to the arrangement made. After some minor business regarding the letters received, and the election of members, they proceeded to consider the most important part of their programme, this new bill. When, therefore, my friends Mr. Thomas Beggs and Mr. John Dunlop had proposed the resolution, " That the bill to be presented by the Council of the National Complete Suffrage Union be taken as the basis of discussion," I rose to urge on the Complete Suffrage friends the necessity for withdrawing that part of the resolution if union were to be maintained. I endeavoured also to remind them, that I was induced to modify my resolution regarding the charter at the last conference, on the understanding that its details would be discussed at the present one; and I informed them that if our friends were not disposed to do this I should consider it my duty to propose, that the People's Charter be taken as the basis of discussion as an amendment to the resolution proposed. It being then, however, near the time of adjournment, the conference broke up its sittings to give our Complete Suffrage friends sufficient time for considering the proposal made to them. The next morning, they not being disposed to yield the point regarding their bill, I proposed the following amendment, which O'Connor seconded :—

" That the document entitled the People's Charter, embracing as it does all the essential details of just and equal representation, couched in plain and definite language, capable of being understood and appreciated by the great mass of the people, for whose government and guidance all laws ought to be written ; and that measure having been before the public for the last five years, forming the basis of the present agitation in favour of the suffrage, and for seeking to obtain the legal enactment of which vast numbers have suffered imprisonment, transportation, and death, it has, in the opinion of this meeting, a prior claim over all other documents proposing to embrace the principles of just representation ; it is, therefore, resolved that we proceed to discuss the different sections of the People's Charter, in order to ascertain whether any improvements can be made in it, and what those improvements shall be, it being necessary to make that document as clear and as perfect as possible."

To this there were two other amendments proposed—one to the effect "that neither of the bills proposed take priority, but that both be laid on the table ;" and the other, " that the Bill proposed being founded on the Charter, it was not necessary to discuss any other document."   Previous to the vote being taken, I informed the Conference that in my anxiety for union I had made the following propositions to the leading members of the Complete Suffrage Union :—
" That both the propositions *for priority* should be withdrawn ;" " That the two documents (the People's Charter and the Bill as proposed by the Council) should be laid on the table ;" " That the clauses of the two documents should be read and discussed alternately ;" " That thus having extracted all that was valuable in both, and formed a Bill, that this Bill should go forth to the country without any other title than ' A Bill to provide for the just representation of the people.' "   But, I regret to say, that this reasonable proposal was not acceded to, those gentlemen rather wishing that the motion and amendment should go to the vote.   The vote being consequently taken, there appeared for the original motion of Mr. Beggs 94, and for my amendment 193.   After this decision the minority left

the conference and met at another place to discuss their Bill; and the majority continued their sittings to discuss the details of the Charter; to which some slight amendments were made, and ordered to be printed for the consideration of the people. I may here state my conviction that the split was not so much occasioned by the adverse vote, as from the strong resolve of the minority to have no fellowship with Fergus O'Connor; but they did not, in my opinion, adopt the straightforward method to effect it.

CHAPTER XVI.

IN returning to the subject of the National Association I may state that efforts were made in some few places to form local bodies, similar to those of the London members, but they did not enroll sufficient numbers to make them effective. Our London Association, however, continuing to increase, it was deemed advisable to look out for a larger place of meeting. A large building, known as Gate Street Chapel, Holborn, being to be let about this period, it was thought to be a very desirable place, if we could raise the means for putting it in substantial repair, for, having been long unoccupied, it was in a very dilapidated state. Some few wealthy friends having been consulted, among others Mr. J. T. Leader, who promised us £50, it was resolved to take it for the purposes of the National Association. Four of our members were accordingly selected as persons in whose names it should be taken, and forty others subscribed to a legal document, agreeing to pay each a pound annually, should the means not be forthcoming to pay the rent, rates, and taxes, for which the four were legally responsible. It was accordingly taken on a lease of twenty-one years, we agreeing to rebuild a portion of one of the walls, and to otherwise put it in good repair. It having been also taken on the understanding that it should not be used for socialist purposes, as the chief object of our Association was to unite persons of all creeds and opinions in favour of Chartism, the members deemed it necessary to come to the following resolution :—"That the hall shall *not be used for purposes of controversial theology.*" This was subsequently made one of our fundamental rules, as was another, " That no intoxicating drinks should be allowed on the premises." It was also agreed that the hall should " be *managed by twelve directors,*" four of them to be those of us who were legally responsible for rent, &c., four to be chosen by the forty guarantee members, and four on behalf of the London members. I deem it necessary to state this, as the divided management and the rule regarding the letting of the hall were constant sources of contention, and contributed in no small degree to weaken the efficiency of the Association. This, however, was not felt to begin with, as all our efforts were directed to the raising of the means, and the fitting up of the place. The repairing and fitting it up, together with the furniture, cost us upwards of £1,000 to commence with; £600 of which were paid by subscriptions raised from members and persons favourable to our objects, leaving about £400 unpaid, a debt which, during the existence of the Association, was a constant source of embarrassment to the directors, and, finally, was one of the chief causes that led to the dissolution of the society. For, owing to the enthralment of this debt, we were unable to meet the expenses necessary for public meetings, lectures, schools, periodicals, newspapers, &c., essential for creating an interest sufficient for the public to join us, or for retaining a great number of those who had; and many of our officers were frequently obliged to subscribe together to pay pressing debts.

The National Hall, capable of containing nearly two thousand persons, was opened in July, 1842, with a public festival. It was devoted to public meetings, lectures, concerts, and classes of different kinds, to most of which the public were admitted on reasonable terms. Our coffee-room and library were for the use of members, although the public were subsequently admitted when business was not being transacted. Among the most prominent and talented of our lecturers were Mr. J. H. Parry, Mr. W. J. Fox, Mr. Thomas Cooper, and Mr. P. W. Perfitt. The lectures Mr. Fox delivered there have since been published in three volumes.* Soon after our

---

* It is here necessary to state that we were induced to engage Mr. Fox in consequence of a kind and generous offer made to our Association by a philanthropist, whom I shall designate A. B., that he would contribute £100 a year towards the lectures if the Association would give a like sum, a proposal which was readily agreed to.

opening, being desirous of establishing classes for the teaching of music and dancing, we applied to the magistrates of Middlesex for a licence, but were refused on account of our Chartist principles; these worthies, doubtless, conceiving that Chartists should not be allowed to sing or dance under the ægis of authority. Although these same discriminating guardians of the principles and morals of the people, very shortly after licensed a place, at no great distance from us, where pugilistic contests were publicly given for the amusement of the people, and where girls of the town were admitted to their dances as an attraction, free of payment.

Owing to our embarrassing debt, we were not able to establish, what we all desired, a day school for children, but in 1843 we managed, with what apparatus we could afford, to open a Sunday School upon a small scale. Free admission was given to all who came cleanly in clothing and person; the education given being reading, writing, arithmetic, grammar, and geography, with such other kinds of information as was in our power to bestow. It was kept open for about four years, and was conducted by myself and such of the members as we could induce to sacrifice their time to Sunday-teaching after the toils of the week.

The great exertions made by the people of Ireland in this year, in favour of the Repeal of the Union induced our Association to send them a very excellent address on the subject, written by Mr. C. H. Elt. A few weeks after Mr. O'Connell, at a meeting at the Corn Exchange, Dublin, in noticing this document, was pleased to make a very severe attack upon me, which induced me to put forth the following reply :—

"Sir,—A few weeks ago the National Association, of which I am a member, deemed it advisable to put forth an address to the people of Ireland on the subject of their present agitation. That address was couched in respectful terms, and expressed no other wish than the welfare of that country, however it might differ from you as to the most efficient means for its attainment. As the representative of Ireland you promised to reply to it, but the only fulfilment of that promise was a sneering doubt regarding the existence of the Association from which it emanated, and an unjust attack upon me, as the person whose signature was attached to it as Secretary.

"Sir,—It would seem that this mode of answering arguments is peculiarly characteristic of you, of which I have lately seen so many examples, as to be induced to pity it as a natural infirmity ; and this last attack of yours would have been unnoticed by me had you not charged me *with political dishonesty*, had you not accused me of *uniting with your self-important countryman Fergus O'Connor.* To rebut these accusations, and to show that I could not have acted otherwise than I did act at the Birmingham Conference without being politically dishonest, are the chief inducements for thus publicly addressing you.

"Sir,—It is somewhat singular, after your 'minute enquiries,' that you should not have heard of the National Association, seeing that you were the first to publicly praise it in Ireland, about two years ago, and for which praise of yours the Association was contemned by that luminary the Northern Star and its august chieftain as a '*new move*,' chiefly of your concoction, and was consequently denounced and condemned by all the faithful vassals of Fergus throughout the kingdom.

"But, sir, I am not going to defend the merits nor prove the existence of the National Association ; the men who compose it will not yield to you in their desire to benefit mankind, though they doubt the propriety of effecting it by threats, abuse, and individual calumny ; and if the Address represented only the person whose signature was attached to it, if it did not merit an answer, at least did not deserve your slander.

"The public papers represent you as saying, that you could not think me politically honest, because I joined Fergus O'Connor against Joseph Sturge. Now, sir, this is not true. The Council of the Complete Suffrage Union deemed it advisable to draw up their plan of Complete Suffrage in a Bill which they called a 'Bill of Rights :' and at the last Conference brought forward a resolution for giving that Bill priority of discussion. I, *who with you and others*, had framed the People's Charter, and who had frequently at public meetings pledged myself never to cease agitating for it till it should become law, I who had joined the Complete Suffrage movement as a Chartist, *regarding the Charter as my definition of Complete Suffrage*, and having moreover been induced to believe that the Charter would become the chief subject of discussion at the Conference, could not allow that same Charter to be passed over, or superseded by another Bill. Therefore, after saying all I could to do away with the question of priority, so as to admit both Bills to be fairly discussed, and finding it unavailing, I proposed a resolution expressive of my opinion on the subject, which resolution was seconded by Fergus O'Connor. Now, how this can legitimately be construed into ' *a union* ' *with him*, or how this conduct of mine can any ways be considered ' *dishonest*,' I leave the public to determine. But, sir, let me briefly contrast this adhesion of principle with your conduct as regards the People's Charter, and let the public then determine who ought in justice to be accused *of political dishonesty*.

"In 1838 a meeting was convened by the Working Men's Association for the purpose of inducing professors of Radical principles to adopt and contend for some definite plan of reform. At that meeting you, among other Members of Parliament, attended, and after much discussion (which took up two evenings), a series of resolutions were agreed to, pledging you and others to draw up, and introduce a Bill embodying Universal Suffrage and all the other essential points of Radical Reform. The resolutions thus agreed to were subsequently signed by you and others, which signatures I have still by me to remind you, if you need it, of your perfidy to Chartism. When Mr. Cleave and myself waited upon you the morning after the meeting, to obtain your signature, you gave us the names of several of the Irish Members who you thought would also sign them, and by your conversation induced us to believe in your sincerity. The Bill thus promised was subsequently drawn up; you attended the

Committee when it was finally adopted, you suggested amendments, some of which were adopted, some rejected, and were in all respects a party to it. The Bill thus prepared and agreed to was the *People's Charter.*

" But, previously to our commencing any active agitation in its favour, your Whig friends had given you power and patronage in Ireland, which seems to have greatly influenced your views of Chartism. You began by accusing the English Chartists of a desire for blood, although, as the originators of the Charter, we declared from our first meeting in its favour, that we were opposed to force, and desired only to create and extend an enlightened public opinion in its favour.

" Your ex-favourite O'Connor (who had hitherto burked the Charter in his *Star*), with the Rev. Mr. Stephens and others, finding Chartism becoming popular, and likely to be more profitable to them than the anti-Poor-law movement in which they had been engaged, began by denouncing us as ' moral-force humbugs,' and having means at their disposal for tramping the country, began to undermine the good that had been effected, by their unmeaning threats and vaunting rhapsodies.

" You cunningly seized the advantage thus given you ; you began your fulminations against the whole Chartist body ; you condemned all because of the conduct of the few ; the Marplots of our cause you held up as our *leaders ;* and your loyalty to Whiggery became so rampant as to cause you to offer the whole force of Ireland to put down and extinguish that which you had helped to kindle.

" We, still wishing to undeceive you (not knowing the Whig game you were playing), sent an Address to the Irish people signed on behalf of 136 different Associations, clearly setting forth our principles, disclaiming leadership of every description, repudiating the doctrine of force, and earnestly beseeching the people of Ireland to join us in our just and peaceable object.

" But no, you persisted in your opposition to Chartism, your threats of force to put it down called forth feelings of retaliation ; your talents, your energies, were fearfully wielded on the side of oppression ; persecution begat bitterness, treachery, defiance, till at last the best feelings of some of the best men in our ranks were carried to a point beyond which reason cannot extenuate, nor our calmer judgment approve of.

"Sir, it is my deliberate conviction that you are mainly responsible not only for the persecutions and sufferings which thousands have undergone for the sake of Chartist principles, but also for the political policy, and subsequent oppression, of the last six or seven years. If you, instead of joining the Whigs in their persecution, had been true to your professions, and had sincerely laboured for the equal representation of the people, as is proposed by the People's Charter, we should never have heard of the violence, the folly, and intolerance, which the enemy has so successfully introduced into our ranks. Your bitter invectives caused some of the best men in the country to doubt, to desert, or regard us with horror; so that those who wished to establish the Charter, by conviction of its justice, were soon left in the minority by those who found their profits extended by excitement, and their vanity gratified by being regarded as political saviours by a famished and oppressed people.

"You talked of my joining O'Connor against Joseph Sturge, thus seeming to possess great anxiety for the cause of Complete Suffrage. You talked largely, legally, and patronisingly, respecting it in its infancy; but what practical steps have you ever taken to render it effective? None.

"You talked of it as you formerly talked of Universal Suffrage, making it the flourish of some flowery harangue, but still regarding it as a beautiful theory, too good to be practised even in your newly-proposed '*Domestic Legislature.*' If you were sincere, you had the means of making Complete Suffrage the opinion of Ireland as much so as your present Repeal project; which you have fondled into being as the bugaboo of Toryism, and which, there is every reason to believe, you would again strangle if it stood in the way of your individual supremacy.

"Sir, whatever may be your aspirations, be assured that with some advantages of talent in your favour), O'Connor and yourself will afford parallels in history of two lawyers the most popular in their day, because the most eminent in the art of political gulling. Of two professing reformers equally skilled in the art of retarding all social improvement, and of checking all political reform. Men, who stood chieftains in their arena by vituperation and blarney; who silenced their opponents by denouncing them, and who retained no colleagues but subservient lackeys who daily trumpeted their virtues and their sacrifices. Men, who, scorning every elevating sentiment, continually appealed to the passions and prejudices of the multitude, setting man against his brother man till the intolerance, bitterness, and persecution they had engendered, aroused all good men to unite to restrain the evil and prevent the further demoralisation of their brethren. Sir, I have seen sufficient of your proceedings to know that these sentiments, expressive of my opinion of you, will be construed into a 'Saxon's hatred of Ireland,' and opposition to her just rights. But, though I yield to no man in an ardent desire to see the wrongs of Ireland redressed, I cannot help believing that you, by your conduct for many years past, have mainly contributed to keep both England and Ireland in political bondage.

"In support of your miserable instalment principle you dragged the people of the two countries through the quagmire of Whiggery for years; to maintain your paltry patronage, you encouraged the Whigs to acts of despotism they dared not otherwise perpetrate; till the nation, sickened of their perfidy, was glad to embrace Toryism as the least of two tyrannies.

"But, sir, so long as the people of any country place their hopes of political salvation *in leadership of any description*, so long will disappointment attend them; and if the people of Ireland would have 'justice,' they must relinquish their leading-strings, and win it for themselves, they must build up their own liberties, or they will never be truly free. The principle of political right, and knowledge to use it wisely, must go hand-in-hand, otherwise no change of masters will benefit them; they will be cheated and enslaved by their 'Domestic Parliament,' as they have been by their 'Imperial' one."

In September, 1843, I received a very kind letter from Mr. A. H. Donaldson, of Warwick, and Mr. J. Mason, of Birmingham, two members of the National Charter Association, requesting me to allow them to nominate me for the Secretaryship of O'Connor's newly-proposed Association, his well-known *Land Scheme*. Having, however, no faith in the originator, or in the scheme, I gave them the following reasons, publicly, for refusing :—

" Dear Sirs,—I beg to acknowledge the receipt of your kind letter of yesterday, expressive of your regret of the circumstances which have kept me from your union, and requesting that I would give my consent to your nomination of me as Secretary of your newly-proposed Association. My good sirs, if I could perceive any change in the circumstances you refer to, calculated to render any union effective, no personal feelings should stand in the way of my cordially uniting, in any rational measure, for carrying out the great object for which I have so long laboured, the just representation and social happiness of my fellow-men. But I will be frank with you, though I have every reason to believe that this frankness will be construed with personal feelings against individuals. But still, as you have referred to the subject, this shall not prevent me from stating my opinions regarding an individual as introductory to my reasons for not complying with your request. Whatever may be the merits of the plan you are met to discuss, I cannot overlook O'Connor's connection with it, which enables me at once to form my opinion as to any good likely to be effected by it, and which at once determines my course of action. You may or may not be aware that I regard Fergus O'Connor as the chief marplot of our movement in favour of the Charter; a man who, by his personal conduct joined to his malignant influence in the *Northern Star*, has been the blight of democracy from the first moment he opened his mouth as its *professed advocate*. Previous to his notorious career there was something pure and intellectual in our agitation. There was a reciprocity of generous sentiment, a tolerant spirit of investigation, an ardent aspiration for all that can improve and dignify humanity, which awakened the hopes of all good men, and which even our enemies respected. He came among us to blight those feelings, to wither those hopes. Not possessing a nature to appreciate intellectual exertions, he began his career by ridiculing our '*moral force humbuggery,*' as he was pleased to designate our efforts to create and extend an enlightened and moral public opinion in favour of Chartist principles. By his great professions, by trickery and deceit, he got the aid of the working classes to establish an organ to promulgate their principles, which he soon converted into an instrument for destroying everything intellectual and moral in our movement. Wherever good was to be undone, principles to be uprooted, and honest men's reputations to be undermined by calumny, there he posted, like the spirit of evil, to gratify his malignancy; and the *Star*, a mere reflex of the nature of its master, only sought to outvie him in his attacks upon everything good in democracy, or to place Toryism once more in the ascendant. By his constant appeals to the selfishness, vanity, and mere animal propensities of man, he succeeded in calling up a spirit of hate, intolerance, and brute feeling, previously unknown among Reformers, and which, had it been as powerful as it was vindictive, would have destroyed every vestige and hope of liberty. I refer not to those persons who, from feeling and conviction, believed that liberty might be won by force, and who, with all the enthusiasm of their nature, were ready to die for the cause they had espoused; but I refer to that brutal spirit which denied the free utterance of thought, and which, had it possessed power, would consequently have silenced every opposing tongue. The men who, in the time of persecution and danger, had stood courage-proof, were among the first victims selected by this physical-force blusterer and his brawling satellites; no means, however despicable, no lie, however hollow, were neglected to destroy all those who dared to think, or who refused to bow to the golden calf, who had deified himself as the only object worthy of Chartist worship. The credulous were therefore fed from week to week with forged and slanderous romances against individual character and

reputation ; the envious were gratified in the work of persecution, and the unthinking captivated with the man who,
according to his own professions, had lost class, station, and
fortune in their cause ; and they therefore readily joined
in the warwhoop of the *Northern Star* till they had driven
thousands into exile, and had consigned many noble-
hearted victims to an untimely grave.   Did any man, or
body of men, venture to assert that they had equal rights
with others, to proclaim their views, or to agitate for their
principles, their motives were at once impugned by this
great ' I am ' of Chartism, they were crucified in the
columns of the *Star*, and the fawning pack of intolerants
who, from gain or fear, were its zealous retainers, were
hounded on to hunt and clamour down those presumptuous
sticklers for individual right and freedom of action.   Nay,
so inconsistent and blind have those professing democrats
been, that while they have joined O'Connor in his endeavours to put down every other kind and shade of agitation,
except Chartism as defined by the Star, they have been led
away and befooled by a hundred crotchets which he has
set up for the purpose of bringing new readers to his
paper.   Need I allude to his recent panegyrics on Dan,
and his unsuccessful attempt to divide the honours of
' repeal ' with that illustrious deceiver of the working
classes ; or to his still more recent project, ' *The Land*,'
and his six-acre scheme, which I understand is to form the
prominent object of your new organisation.   The conduct
and character of this man, which I have thus briefly referred to, have prostrated all hopes of success of any plan
which he may be connected with ; and I fear that my
Chartist brethren will never redeem their cause from the
odium which he and his satellites have cast upon it till they
relinquish his pernicious counsels, return to the just and
rational course of agitation which he caused them to swerve
from, cultivate tolerant and brotherly feelings in their
ranks, invite the co-operation of the wise and good of all
classes, and instead of trusting to leadership of any description endeavour to work out their own political salvation.   For myself, I will have nothing to do with such a
man as O'Connor, not only believing him to have done

irreparable mischief to our cause, but knowing him to be politically and morally dishonest; I believe he will still further injure every cause he may be connected with. With no other feelings towards you but those of personal respect, I must nevertheless decline your offer for nominating me for your secretary."

In June, 1844, the late Emperor of Russia paid a visit to this country, with the object, it has since appeared, of getting our Government to consent to his possession of Turkey; a piece of information, kept back by our rulers from the people, with which they ought to have been at once acquainted, and the dangers at the same time pointed out to them of the contemplated aggression. Had this been done, the probability is, neither the Menschikoff mission nor the Crimean war would have taken place, nor all the horrible consequences that have since ensued. It was, I believe, our courtly *shillyshallying with a tyrant* that induced him to believe that he could bully the Turks out of their possessions, without any other danger than a few paper pellets from the diplomatists of Europe. Rumours of his coming having reached the members of our Association, we resolved on calling a public meeting, to lay an account of some of his atrocious deeds before an English audience. It so happened that about the same period Joseph Mazzini was induced to believe that his letters had been opened at the Post Office, and that in consequence of such a nefarious act the Austrian Government had obtained information which led to the sacrifice of a number of Italian patriots, the Bandean Brothers especially. How to ascertain positively this letter-opening business became a question In furtherance of it I was requested—among other friends of Mazzini's—to write a letter to him, and to fold it up in such a way, with some small matters inside, that if it were opened I should be perfectly assured of it. I accordingly wrote a letter to him, stating the rumours I had heard of the Czar's intended visit, and wishing to know whether he (Mazzini) knew anything positively of his coming, as we intended to get up a public meeting on the occasion. This letter was folded up and put in the post-office, in presence of Mr. Hetherington, and it having been brought back from Mazzini's as he received it, was again opened in Mr. Hetherington's presence. Before, however, it was opened, we were both satisfied, from its appearance, that the seal had been broken, and when opened we had proof positive. Others having discovered, in a similar way, that their letters to Mazzini were opened, presented a petition to Parliament on the subject. Mr. Thos. Duncombe, having patriotically taken up the matter, was successful in bringing to light the whole of this *Grahamizing system,* a proceeding which was very properly reprobated from one extremity of the kingdom to the other.

The Emperor Nicholas having arrived, and having been very courteously received at Court—lauded by the Royal Society as " the friend of science "—and otherwise toadied and flattered by a large portion of the public press, our Association put forth the following bill for the calling of a public meeting :—

" *Nicholas of Russia in England !*—A public meeting will be held at the National Hall, on June 6th, 1844, for the purpose of ascertaining how far the people of England are prepared to welcome to their country the Russian Emperor Nicholas.

" He, who by butcheries and cruelties unparalleled effected the subjugation of unhappy Poland ; and when he had massacred, tortured and expatriated her bravest sons and defenders, and extinguished every vestige of freedom, amid the silence of destruction proclaimed that ' *Order reigns at Warsaw.*' He, who not satisfied with his brutal conquest over a brave people, has since sought to extinguish their name and blot out their memory. By his despotic edicts he has closed the Universities of Poland, abolished her schools, forbidden her language, destroyed her religion, commanded that her children should be brought up in that faith which makes the emperor equal with God ! and enforces his horrible mandates with the knout, with death, or banishment to the mines of Siberia.

" He, who has pursued with vengeful cruelty every brave spirit who, seeking the elevation of his brethren, has dared to strive against his despotism. Torture, lingering captivity in grated cells, banishment and death; women publicly flogged and tortured to death for favouring the escape of their relatives; thousands of virtuous females forced from their parents and handed over to gratify the lust of his soldiers; black atrocities like these form but a small portion of the catalogue of his iniquities.

"Englishmen! It is said that this active, scheming, wily tyrant; this chief personification of European despotism; this despiser of human right, and persecutor of all who dare defend it, has been invited to the court of St. James's. Can it be possible that Englishmen who talk of sympathy with the wrongs of Poland, and talk of Jewish emancipation, will welcome to the Royal table the direst oppressor of Poles and Jews?

"Englishmen! You who love liberty, hate tyranny, and are loyal to your country, be on your guard against foreign corruption; be especially vigilant when tyrants like Nicholas are invited to your country; and above all urge your Queen to guard against the contaminating influence of despotism."

The numbers who attended this meeting were sufficient to fill to overflowing two other public meeting rooms besides the National Hall, which was crowded to excess. The following resolution, being one agreed to on that occasion, will serve to show that we were intuitively right in our apprehension of the Czar's visit, which after ten years of secret diplomacy has recently been made manifest.* "That the people of England have just cause for suspecting that some infringement on the rights of humanity or public liberty is contemplated when a tyrannical and despotic sovereign visits their country; and it behoves them earnestly to watch lest those in power betray the trust reposed in them, to gratify the desires of such a man as Nicholas."

In the same year the fire-brained son of Louis Philip, Prince de Joinville, with the war ministry of Thiers,

---

* This was his attack upon Turkey, which led to the Crimean War.

together with a number of other combative animals on both sides of the Channel, exerted themselves in various ways to stir up a quarrel between England and France; two countries which of all others ought to be allied in the cause of peace, liberty and progress. Knowing the incalculable evils that would inevitably result to the working millions of the two countries by such a contest, we deemed it our duty to do all we could to allay the bad feeling that was being excited, and with that view issued the following " Address to the Working Classes of France on the subject of War " :—

" Brethren,—By this title we presume to address you; for though the channel divides, *just principles* and *mutual interests* should unite us, and though, at this crisis, bad men would foster prejudices and strife between us, the spirit of Christain brotherhood should recall us to our duty, and cause us to spurn all those who would urge us to break every moral obligation, and plunge our respective countries into a ferocious and devastating war.

" We are, for the most part, *working men* who now address you—men, who intent on the political and social improvement of our brethren, conceive we have some claim to the attention of those of our own class upon any subject of mutual and vital importance; and considering war as paramount for evil, in its demoralising effects, as well as for retarding the intellectual, moral, and physical progress of mankind; we deem it our duty to invite you, fellowmen, in the spirit of fraternity, to a calm consideration of its evils as respect ourselves, our countries and our race; and would urge your co-operation in appealing to the higher and nobler feelings of our brethren, to devise means for extinguishing this destructive spirit, which has cursed our race from the beginning of time.

" We are induced to make this appeal to you, the working classes of France, in particular, as the warlike spirit has of late been sought to be fomented between us, by those who have either party views to promote, exclusive interests to protect, or who, like vultures, hope to thrive on the carnage of war.

" The press, too, of both countries, with few exceptions, for some time past has unhappily been administering to our combative feelings ; and by sallies of wit, boastings, and threatenings, seeking to fan our old (and we trust never to be revived) animosities into a flame of destructive war. Nay, to the disgrace of those who shared in it, we have seen professed followers of Him who preached forgiveness and mercy, vindictively inciting those they could influence to revenge the real or supposed insult to an individual, by plunging whole nations into war.

" The prevalence of this insane conduct has caused us to appeal *to you, the Working Millions—you,* by whose industry the munitions of war must be raised—*you,* who are mainly selected to be the tools and instruments of warfare—*you,* who must perform the bidding of some aristocratic minion, were it to war against freedom abroad or to exterminate your brothers at home—*you,* who have most cause for lamenting the sacrifices and bereavements of war—*you,* who must bear (and are now bearing) the burthens in peace which past wars have inflicted—*to you we appeal,* who with the working millions of England, must bear the brunt and sacrifices of war, and of you we ask for a verdict condemnatory of the strife which the parties we have alluded to are seeking to foment.

" We address you, the *working-classes,* because we believe that *the interests of our class are identified throughout the world.* Our interests are evidently in the peaceful cultivation of our lands, the feeding of our flocks, in the ingenuity and extent of every manufacture and production capable of administering to human happiness ; the reciprocal interchange of our commodities, the full enjoyment of the fruits of our labour ; and the cultivation of freedom, intellect, morality, religion and brotherly affection among all the nations of the earth ; in all these we believe there is *an identity of interests,* and when the majority of our brethren have knowledge to perceive it, the advocates of national strife will be few, and the trade of war will fail to bring either glory, honour or fame.

Can men so readily forget the enormous expenditure of money, and immense sacrifice of life, wasted in the last wars between your country and ours, that they are so anxious to renew them? The Revolutionary War and the war against the empire have already cost England £2,229,830,000, and the destruction of more than 700,000 human beings, and if to this amount we add the sacrifices made by your country, we should imagine that such a holocaust of life and wealth sacrificed to the demon of war, sufficient to glut the sanguinary appetites of men to all posterity. Does not every generous mind already revolt at the record of blood between two nations said to be foremost in civilisation and refinement? and shall the page of history be still further defiled with the atrocities of war between people who ought *to lead the world to freedom by their intellectual and moral greatness?* Forbid it every tongue! condemn it every mind devoted to human happiness!

"Imagine, fellow-workmen, that the wealth and human energies sacrificed in our last wars had been devoted to the instruction, comfort and happiness of our neglected, ill-used, and unhappy fellow-labourers, what imperishable and glorious results might now be realised. What schools, what colleges, what smiling happy villages, might be covering the soil beneath which repose the dust of beings once madly incited against their fellows, to glut the vengeance, or gratify the vanity of those the world is still taught to worship as 'heroes.'

"We would also direct your attention to the amount *annually* expended by our respective countries in consequence of the demoralizing spirit of war. The annual war expenditure of England at present is £14,513,916; of France, £20,418,730, an enormous amount annually drained from the sinews of our brethren, and used to enslave and degrade them. Yet the only excuse for this mischievous and useless warlike array, is the mutual fear or jealousy entertained by one country of another: *mutual folly,* which it is high time the common sense of our brethren condemned and scouted, not only as a pernicious waste of the fruits of their industry, but as an instrument for perpetuating national feuds and political slavery. If England and France were to set an example to the world, if two powerful nations united in amity, relying on the interests, energies, and affections of their people to repel all who dared assail them, we should soon witness *the holiest of all national alliances*, one for promoting the peace and happiness of the world.

" But those who would excite your prejudices, remind you of the evils which our country has inflicted on France. They condemn our rapacity and lust of power— they point with jealousy to our colonies, and with envy to the extent of our commerce: and for past ills would fain invoke present retaliation.

" Now, fellow-men, we are not of those who would frame an apology for injustice, and we also condemn, and have the burthen of our debt to remind us of, the monstrous injustice of warring against the rising liberties of your country. We have also great cause for lamenting all the wars which our aristocracy have waged for the preservation of " their order," as for providing resting-places for their children and dependants; and would greatly rejoice if every colony of England were *self-governed*, and attached to us by no other tie than that which should unite all countries—that of enlightened self-interest, and the brotherhood of man. We class our late wars in China and Affghanistan with the war you are now waging in Algeria, as *unjust wars;* the power of might being immorally exercised in all, as it always is when force and destruction take the place of reason and justice.

" But our object is not the mere condemnation of particular wars, but of all war; believing *war in principle* to be *vengeance in practice,* a vice equally opposed to our *morality* and condemned by our *religion;* its tendency being to deteriorate the nobler faculties of man, and strengthen those which level him with the brute. It stands the most formidable impediment to the civilization of our race, rendering nearly nugatory the best devised efforts for elevating humanity; for, by polluting the youthful mind with tales of blood, by stamping public approbation on deeds of vengeance, and idolizing *as heroes* those who have excelled in crime, we sap the very foundations of virtue, and offer the highest premium to vice.

"Be assured, fellow-men, the evils of our age cannot be remedied by the sword; the steady *increase of knowledge* is the harbinger of freedom to the millions, and *individual and national morality* must be the basis upon which political and social prosperity must be founded. The arts of peace are fast preparing a highway to the world's happiness; the ingenuity of invention and triumphs of genius are fast breaking down the barriers which separate nations; gothic prejudices are yielding before human sympathies; the productive classes are fast learning the lesson of human reciprocity, and eventually the freedom of nations will be placed on a foundation not to be endangered by official folly, or destroyed by the whim of a despot.

"And shall this promise of good be marred by the ill-intentioned or unreflecting? by those who plan battles on paper, and prefer fighting by proxy; who talk of national 'honour' being purified by '*blood!*' who invoke the specious name of 'glory' to induce our brethren to leave their peaceful pursuits, their homes and relatives, to deal destruction and death against those who have given them no just cause for resentment? Let but the united voices of the millions proclaim it *madness*, and the civilisation of the world is secure.

"Unhappily for the cause of peace and human progress, State and Church are combined in favour of war. We have seen your bishops and ours bless its flags and symbols! invoke the Deity for its success, and pour out their thanksgivings for victory! But, fellow-workmen, though the highest authority may sanction, *it cannot establish the justice of crime.* The principles of religion and morality stand out broadly in condemnation of war, and to these we would refer you, against all power and all authority.

"In furtherance then, of this sacred cause, in the spirit of brotherhood, in the love of peace and hatred of war, we respectfully submit the following propositions for your consideration, amendment, or approval, hoping that they may form a preliminary bond of fellowship, to unite us for every good object tending to advance the intelligence, morality, freedom and happiness of mankind :—

"'1. That we, the working classes of France and

England, respectfully present our different legislative bodies with a solemn *Protest against all war*, as being in principle opposed to morality, religion, and human happiness.

"2. That we request them to use their influence with the nations of the world, to establish *a Conference of Nations;* to be composed of three or more representatives, chosen *by the people* of their respective countries, to meet annually, for the purpose of settling all national disputes that may arise, by *arbitration,* without having recourse to war.

"3. That we urge on them to devote the enormous sums now expended in war and warlike preparations to the *education* and *improvement of the people* of their respective countries.

"4. That we impress on them the necessity of setting *an example to other nations,* of that justice, forbearance, morality and religion, which they preach the necessity of to their own people.

"5. That we earnestly beseech them to set the bounds of justice *to their acquisitions of territory,* and seek to amend their institutions, and improve the condition of their people.'

"Should you concur with these propositions, or with others more effective, for the just and peaceful accomplishment of the object aimed at, we shall be ready to co-operate with you; excepting that we do not desire to enter into any new agitation short of our primary object, The Political and Social Improvement of the People.

"But it is not on our rulers alone we should rely for support or sympathy in this great cause, *but on our own combined intellectual exertions.* We have too long relied on others for effecting our political and social redemption; each and all must labour in this grand work, and every individual must be religiously impressed with the necessity of exertion and sacrifice to effect it. The increasing progress of knowledge is rendering opinion powerful, and it lies with the millions to make that opinion conducive of good to themselves and posterity. Let us therefore, brethren, begin by directing our own thoughts to the

20

examination of great principles, and honestly proclaim them bad or good, regardless of consequences to ourselves.

"If, on examining the principles of peace and war, we think the former should be extended and the latter condemned, we should commence our reform at the source of pollution, and begin with our children. We should remember that the warlike tales and toys of the nursery are the seeds of strife and battle; and that *our admiration* of warlike splendour and gory "*glory*" is fitting instruction for moulding our sons into soldier slaves, or tyrant chieftains.

"Instead of stamping our approbation on the *heroes of war and oppression*, let us seek to generate a more ennobling opinion in favour of those who have contributed to the intellectual greatness or physical happiness of their country; then indeed would Art contribute her best efforts to elevate and dignify humanity, instead of representing the mementoes and horrors of war, to brutalize and degrade it.

"Nor must we, in our pursuit, forget the power we possess to render the *press* one of the most powerful instruments for human benefit, instead of being, as it too often is, the ally of power and corruption. Let us wisely discriminate and generously encourage that portion of it which maintains its exalted character, as the proclaimer of *truth* and asserter of *right*, and thus shall we gradually lead it onward to perform its highest duties—*the improvement of human institutions* and *the perfecting of human character*.

"Sincerely hoping that your country and ours may long be cemented in fellowship, that our people may unitedly seek to secure the peace and tranquillity of the world, that our rulers may effect timely reforms, and apply the vast resources of our fair countries to the happiness of our brethren, and that we may all fast progress in knowledge, morality, and universal brotherhood, is the ardent hope of the members of the National Association."

This address was translated both in France and Switzerland, and, from letters we received from friends, I am induced to believe that it had a very fair circulation in those countries. But, although it was very generally commended by our own press, it did not altogether escape censure. The *Liverpool Journal* put forth an article in reply to it, entitled " An Apology for War," which was replied to by another from our Association, entitled " *An Apology for Peace.*" Wishing, however, to compress these pages within reasonable limits, I shall give but two paragraphs from it :—

" But looking to the black record of our race with feelings of pity and regret to think that so many nations should have risen up to be swept away by the scourge of war, to think that highly-gifted man should be urged, tiger-like, to prey upon his brother, and to destroy and desolate his brother's home ; looking, we say, *to the past* as the necessary phases of ignorant and degraded humanity, we would appeal to the intellectual light, the moral and religious feelings *of the present,* and would ask our countrymen, *is there no other road to individual and national liberty but the gory road our ancestors have trod ?*

" If *war* is the only path to civilization, what a *mockery is it to preach up the religion of Christ.* If brute force is to be the instrument of human happiness, why talk of cultivating the mental and moral nature of man, the more he partakes of the nature of the savage the better will he be prepared for the work of war and destruction."

In the latter end of this year (1844), I took part in the formation of a society entitled, " The Democratic Friends of All Nations," its chief object being to cultivate a brotherly feeling among the people of different countries, by meeting together at stated periods for the purpose of friendly conversation, and for rendering assistance to those who were driven from their country for seeking to advance the cause of freedom. It was chiefly composed of refugees from France, Germany, and Poland, to which were joined a few English Radicals. Their first public " Address to the Friends of Humanity and Justice among All Nations " was written by myself. I was given to understand, how ever, that the following portion of it gave great offence to *the physical force party*, and caused many of them to stand aloof from the Association during the short time that I continued a member of it :—

" Not that we would incite you to outbreaks or violence, for we have faith in the mental and moral combinations of men being able to achieve victories for humanity beyond the force of armies to accomplish. What is wanting are men armed in all the moral daring of a just cause, and resolved at all risks to pursue and achieve their righteous object. Let but the same daring mind and resources which have so often warred with tyranny, and so often been worsted in the conflict, be once *morally applied and directed*, and citadels, armies, and dungeons will soon lose their power for evil.

A cheering prospect to encourage you to espouse the cause of humanity is seen in the extent of mental light which is so rapidly being diffused among the productive classes. They are gradually awakening to a sense of the wrongs inflicted on them by exclusive institutions and privileged orders, and are beginning to declare that they, too, *are brethren of the same common family.* Many of them may have mistaken the *forms for the principles of true democracy ;* may have had too much faith that others would accomplish that freedom for them which each individual must strive to attain, and may still have too much confidence in arms and sinews, and too little reliance on mental and moral effort. But the spark of mind once kindled is inextinguishable ; it will spread silently and surely to the destruction of old errors, time-worn institutions and gothic privileges, till the mind-illumined ranks of labour shall rise up in all their moral grandeur to declare them vain and puerile, and that henceforth *the brotherhood of man shall be their rule and motto*, and that the heroes of their veneration shall be the wise, the good, the true, and useful, who have laboured to redeem the world from slavery, oppression, ignorance, and crime."

From an Address to the Chartists of the United Kingdom, put forth by the National Association in 1845, in consequence of the anti-democratic conduct of O'Connor and his disciples, I extract the following :—

"Amid this state of disunion and despondency we deem it our duty to address you, for we cannot be brought to believe that you would *knowingly consent to be the instruments of your own slavery.* We are persuaded that numbers of you have been deceived by sophistry, and led by falsehood to injure the cause you have so warmly espoused. We seek to call you back to reason; we have no interests apart from yours; we may honestly differ from you regarding the best mode of effecting our object, but we are all equally agreed on the necessity of its attainment.

"For, amid the present distracted state of our cause, we have the strongest faith *in the justice of Chartist principles.* We still believe that those who have once espoused them will always cherish them, and we still hope that you, the Chartists of the United Kingdom, will yet arise *in your mental and moral might,* purified from past errors, and will unitedly and ardently strive for the attainment of those rights proclaimed by the Charter, by conduct which shall win the esteem of the wise and good of all classes, so that, ere long, Government will be powerless in opposing your claims.

"We would ask you, then, in all sincerity, whether the conduct we have referred to is in accordance with your professions of democracy? *Democracy,* in its just and most extensive sense, means *the power of the people mentally, morally, and politically directed, in promoting the happiness of the whole human family, irrespective of their country, creed, or colour.* In its limited sense, as regards *our own country,* it must evidently embrace *the political power of all classes and conditions of men,* directed in the same wise manner, *for the benefit of all.* In a more circumscribed sense, *as regards individuals,* the principle of democracy accords to every individual *the right* of freely putting forth his opinions on all subjects affecting the general welfare; the right of publicly assembling his fellow-men to consider any project *he may conceive to be of public benefit*, and the right of being heard patiently and treated courteously, however his opinions may differ from others.

" We regret to say, fellow-countrymen, that in almost all these particulars the principle of democracy has been violated by a great number of professing Chartists. What would *you* think of your arguments and resolutions *in favour of the Charter* being continually met by speeches and amendments in favour of any one political measure? Of every public meeting you got up being invaded by your opponents, and your proceedings drowned by clamour? Would you not justly denounce them as despots, thus to assail and obstruct your right of public meeting, by constantly introducing a subject foreign to the object for which you had assembled? And is it just, we would ask, to do that to others which you yourselves would condemn?

" Be assured, fellow-men, that such proceedings can never serve our righteous cause ; and the proof is afforded in seeing that those who have indulged in it are only powerful for mischief; are the disgust of all reflecting Chartists, the dupes of the enemy, and blind to their best interests ; not only disgusting their friends, but affording their enemies plausible arguments of their unfitness for the suffrage. We can readily believe that some persons may find their interests promoted by such insane proceedings. But surely you who desire to see the Charter the law of England, can never suppose it can be realized by such disgraceful means. We would ask the thoughtful and considerate among you, whether such conduct has not driven from our ranks hundreds of intelligent and active individuals, who, in different localities, once formed the stay and strength of our cause? Nay, are not hundreds to be found who lament the loss of parents and friends sacrificed by violence and folly, instigated by those same individuals who are still the fomenters of strife and disunion?

" Judging from their conduct towards the middle, the trading and commercial classes, persons might be led to suppose that the Charter was *some exclusive working-class measure*, giving license for abuse, threats, and violence, instead of a measure of justice for uniting all classes in holy brotherhood for promoting the common good of all. That the working classes too often experience wrong and injustice from persons in all those classes, as well as from those who possess the political power of the state, is admitted ; but surely those evils can never be redressed by such conduct. No, friends ! There is a principle of goodness, of right and justice, pervading universal humanity. To that principle we must appeal, that we must cultivate, that combine, if ever we hope to see political justice established.

"Be assured that those who flatter your prejudices, commend your ignorance and administer to your vices, are not your friends. 'Unwashed faces, unshorn chins,' and dirty habits, will in nowise prepare you for political or social equality with the decent portion of your brethren, nor will the ridiculous title of 'Imperial Chartists' prepare you for the far better one of 'honest democrat'? Empty boastings, abusive language, and contempt for all mental and moral qualifications, will rather retard than promote your freedom ; nay, if even you possessed political power, would still keep you the slaves and puppets of those who flourish by popular ignorance.

"But it is for you, *the reflecting portion of the Chartist body*, to determine whether renewed efforts shall be made to redeem our cause from its present position ; whether the enemy shall continue to avail himself of those means hitherto so successfully applied to divide us ; whether we shall continue to be pitied by the good, feared by the timid, and despised by all those who batten on the fruits of our industry ; or whether we shall purge and purify our ranks of those who now disgrace it, and by a combination of the wise and good, once more rise into vitality and strength."

CHAPTER XVII.

IN the following year, 1846, great excitement was called forth by the newspaper press of England and America regarding the disputed territory of Oregon. Perceiving the lamentable results that would inevitably follow from a quarrel between two countries so connected by trade and commerce, by associations of country and ties of blood, we thought it advisable to do all in our power to allay the bad feeling sought to be created. Knowing that the industrious millions in both countries would have to bear the brunt and burthen of war, we endeavoured to influence this class by the issuing of the following " Address to the Working Classes of America on the War Spirit sought to be created between the two countries " :—

"Working Men of America.—By our alliance of blood, of language, and religion, as well as by every aspiration we feel for the mutual freedom, peace, prosperity, and happiness of our respective countries, we would address you as *brethren*, in the assurance that, as brethren, our interests are identified, and in the hope that no other spirit than that of brotherhood may long continue to exist between us.

" But the hostile threats and warlike preparations, the jealousies and prejudices now sought to be fomented by the interested, thoughtless, and immoral of your country and our own, have awakened us to a deep sense of the dangers which threaten the peace and welfare of the *working classes of all countries*, evils which we believe our mutual understanding and wise and determined resolutions may timely avert.

" You, fortunately possessing political power to restrain

the unjust acts of your rulers, are, we fear, too apt to believe that the persecutions, encroachments, and insolence which for ages past have characterised the aristocracy of England towards most nations of the earth, have been shared in by the great body of the industrious classes ; who, unhappily, for the most part, have hitherto had *neither voice nor vote in the matter.*

" That the power and influence of our aristocracy over the minds and consciences of men, their perversion of every principle of morality and precept of religion to uphold their power and monopolies, have often enabled them to enlist great numbers of our unreflecting brethren to fight their battles and espouse their cause, we readily admit; but these we conceive, should be *pitied* rather than *blamed,* as the deluded victims of selfish and hypocritical men ; persons who have perverted justice and truth for gain, and the religion of peace and goodwill for the purposes of war, contention, and strife.

" Within the last few years, however, knowledge has been rapidly extending its influence among the industrious millions of England ; universal right is now asserted, and is progressing, despite persecutions and sufferings ; anomalies, corruptions, and vices in Church and State are being exposed ; unjust privileges and monopolies decried ; and mental and moral worth fast allying itself to the cause of humanity and justice. Thus knowledge, extending and combining, is fast calling forth mental light and political power, tending to the good of our country, such as our State Church can no longer mislead, standing armies restrain, nor aristocratic influence avert.

" This progressive improvement towards a higher state of civilization and happiness to which all good men are looking forward with delight, our aristocratic rulers would gladly mar, and nothing but war and national commotion would favour the accomplishment of their wishes. With the high-swelling cant of " individual glory " and " national honour," the din and dazzle of warlike preparation, they would speedily intoxicate *the unreflecting.* They would then be enabled to turn the national mind from all social and political improvement to the prospect of foreign battles, and brilliant (though expensive) victories. Our present moral and intellectual progress, the advance of trade, commerce, and the peaceful arts of life would be stayed and obstructed by the unholy scourge of war, and thousands of our brethren having their worst passions loosened and excited, would be transformed into savage demons thirsting for blood.

" We beseech you, Working Men of America, do not permit yourselves to be drawn or seduced into war, and thus afford the enemies of our liberties and the haters of yours, a pretext and opportunity to produce those lamentable results ; nay, it may be to jeopardize the rights and liberties which you now enjoy. Your country has long been an asylum for persecuted freedom throughout the world, and your democratic institutions inspire the hopeful and struggling among all nations ; but while your Republic offers a beacon to cheer and animate the friends of human rights and equal laws, it at the same time sends forth a light that despotism would fain extinguish. For be assured, the despots of Europe would gladly cast aside their petty contentions to form another unholy alliance against the growing Republic of America ; and though their combined power might fail to crush your liberties, they would not fail in desolating your shores, and in destroying great numbers of your people.

" What, too, has prevented the further development of *your national resources?* the cultivation of your fertile soil? the increase of your capital? the progress of your commerce? and the further prosperity of your people? What, but the same power that has retarded *our* liberties, paralyzed our manufactures, crippled our commerce, and pauperised and impoverished our country? What but the selfish, monopolising aristocracy of England? who, by their prohibitory laws, their imposts and burthens, have raised up barriers of injustice and enmity to prevent the prosperity of both countries.

" Despite their maddened efforts, however, those barriers are fast yielding to the progress of thought : the knell of monopoly and injustice is sounding, and the prospect of political righteousness and social happiness is lighting up with hope the cheeks of our famished and pauperised population. Working men of America, do not, we pray you, by any unwise proceedings on your part, retard or prevent the consummation of such prospective happiness, the fruits of which you will not eventually fail to share.

" We fain hoped that Republican America was free from that mania of kings and princes, the grasping after territory and dominion. Think you that any amount of *real power or advantage*, either to you or to us, could be gained by the possession of such an inhospitable and savage region as that now disputed by your rulers and ours? Think you that the *strength* of England is augmented by her dominion over her colonies, most of which she must keep bristling with bayonets to keep down her half-rebellious progeny? It is true they may form objects of solicitude to the scions and offshoots of our aristocracy, enabling them to eat the bread of idleness, but to the mass of the English people they are far more burthensome than profitable. Surely the disputed question regarding the territory of Oregon, might be amicably settled *by arbitration*, the peaceful and just mode of arranging all such matters, without plunging our two countries into war, and, it might be, the whole of Europe also; and with such an unfortunate event, all its destructive consequences —a state of desolation and misery it would take centuries to repair.

" And surely you, the working classes of America, cannot so readily have forgotten the lessons of your greatest statesmen and profoundest philosophers respecting the evils and consequences of war; nor can we suppose that you have less regard for those great principles of morality and religion, which unitedly condemn it as one of the monster evils that afflict our race.

" Working men, this military and warlike spirit must be curbed and kept in subjection, if ever we desire the civilization and happiness of our race. Men, indeed, cannot be called *civilized* who will consent to be made the tools and playthings of statesmen, or who delight in the playing of soldiers on their own account. The constant appeals to the individual vanity and mere animal propensity of the soldier, and the narrow spirit of nationality sought to be engendered, are antagonistic to the mental and moral development of our nature, and the broad and ennobling principles of universal brotherhood and peace.

" How much longer will the labouring population of the world submit, that that wealth which is accumulated by their incessant toils, anxieties, and privations, shall be applied to the keeping of thousands in idleness and vice; with no other object in view than that of still making them toil for the drones of society, or the going forth at the bidding of their rulers to murder and destroy? For, in our desire for human progress, we could wish that what is called " *honourable warfare*," and " *glorious victories*," were properly designated to be NATIONAL CRIMES! For were they for the most part stripped of their gloss and glory, *and tried by our moral or Christian code*, one of them would exhibit an aggregate of crime, comprising murder, robbery, and devastation—more black and atrocious than could be found in the collected annals of a century.

" The *war-spirit* already excited between our two countries has prepared the way, and given a pretext to our rulers to inflict additional burthens on our working-class population. Already they have announced their intention of adding, under the name of a militia, upwards of 40,000 soldiers to our present army; to take our brethren from their homes and avocations; and while, on the one hand, they cause us to pay upwards of *ten millions annually* for our clergy to preach to them *the religion of peace and brotherhood*, to impose additional taxes on the other hand, *for the purpose of imbuing their minds with the spirit of war and vengeance.*

" This additional number of human beings, who by their skill and labour could raise food, clothing, and habitations to bless the half-starved millions of our country, are to be taken—many of them from their wives and children—for *three years*, to be drilled and disciplined in the arts of destruction ; and, it is said, to be kept apart from their fellow-citizens in *military barracks*, doubtless lest sympathy and interchange of thought should disqualify them for their brutal profession.

" This burthen, too, will, in all probability, as usual, fall upon *the Working Classes* for the most part ; for should they seek, *by fine or substitute*, to avoid being taken from their homes and families, the poorest labourer, on his shilling per day, will have to pay equally with the wealthiest person in the kingdom : the consequence will be, that *wealth* will in most cases procure exemption, and the sons of poverty be left to their fate.

" Such, friends, are the first-fruits of this warlike excitement here, about a portion of territory of little use to either country, and which, perhaps, in strict justice, belongs to neither. But why should we, the industrious classes, year after year, and age after age, thus submit to injustice ? We, whose interest is in the peaceful cultivation of our respective countries—in the production of the conveniences and arts of life—in the peaceful interchange of our commodities—and in the intellectual and moral development of ourselves and children—why should we, who have no quarrels or disputes with one another, be thus continually made *the victims or tools* of those who delight in contention and profit by war ?

" Fellow-men ! deeply impressed with the wickedness, injustice and misery, that always flow from such contentions, we would call upon all good men, but more especially on you, *the Working Classes of England and America*, to use every intellectual, moral, and political means you possess, to extinguish that spark of national animosity which is now sought to be fanned into a flame ; and to be prepared to make any personal sacrifice to prevent the direful calamity of war between the two countries. On this subject we have morality, christianity, and justice on our side ; and if our firm and peaceful conduct should call forth the power of the law or the strength of the oppressor, we had better far be martyrs in the cause of right, than suffer ourselves to be coerced into the shedding of human blood, and the retarding of the civilization of our race.

" We trust, however, that this dispute of our rulers may be speedily settled *by arbitration ;* and earnestly hope that the growing intelligence of the age may lead men to perceive *the demoralizing and deteriorating effects of soldiers and armies*, and to perceive that *war is more fatal in its moral and physical effects than the plagues, earthquakes, and tornadoes of nature.* That so impressed they will speedily free themselves from the evils and expenses of Standing Armies, garrisons, and ships of war—that they will soon seek amicably to settle their national disputes by a *Congress of Nations*, freely chosen by the people of their respective countries—and that, through such instrumentality, universal peace and human brotherhood may be established, freedom extended, commerce promoted, and the arts, industry, and civilization of *each* be made to contribute to the welfare of *all.* In the ardent desire for fellowship and peace, and in the hope that both our countries may advance in knowledge and happiness, and seek to promote the happiness of all others, we remain, your brethren, the Members of the National Association."

This Address was widely circulated, both in England and America, and was warmly commended by the peaceful portion of the press, in both countries. Our Aristocratic Statesmen, however, evinced a far greater alacrity in providing for a contest against *Republican America* in support of this paltry territory than they did to check the wholesale encroachments of *barbarous Russia*; although they knew Nicholas's intentions years before his base attack upon Turkey. The Lords Lieutenants of Counties were at once written to regarding the enrolment and training of the Militia; and the newspapers, in their interest, informed the people that the *ballot* was to be renewed, and that the half of those enrolled were to be called on for duty for *three years.* Now, beyond our desire to be at peace with America, we had seen enough of former *ballotings for the Militia* to allow of us remaining silent, when preparations were being made for restoring this unjust and obnoxious system. We accordingly put forth our reasons against it, and by public meetings and otherwise called forth a strong expression of the working classes against the measure proposed. The war feeling that was sought to be excited, also called forth the reprobation of many public bodies, and a great number of addresses were exchanged between the peace-fully-inclined in both countries, calling loudly for arbitration, and these happily led to this peaceful means being adopted for settling the question in dispute.

I have mentioned, in a former part of my story, that, owing to an embarrassing debt, our Association was not able to accomplish the establishing of *a Day-School for Children;* one of the most important objects set forth in our prospectus. In the beginning, however, of 1846, a kind friend (who, not liking to be talked of as the doer of good deeds, shall be designated A. B.), made a proposal to the Association, through Mr. Francis Place, for the establishing of a day school in the hall under my superintendence and management; he agreeing to provide the necessary desks and apparatus for the opening of the school, as well as to pay the *fixed salary of the schoolmaster.* Indeed, the proposal was first made to myself, to the effect that I should conduct it; but having then some distrust of my own abilities for a teacher, I was fearful of undertaking the task. I readily agreed, however, to superintend it as I best could; and hence the proposal was made to the Association in the form stated. The majority of our members having highly approved of the proposal, arrangements were speedily made, and certain alterations effected in the hall for carrying the plan into execution. As soon, however, as it became known that such a school was to be established, an application was made to Mr. Place and myself by a person offering himself as a schoolmaster, for the conducting of the school, he understanding us to have the appointment. In the note which he sent to me, stating his qualifications, he said he had written to Mr. Place more fully on the subject. I accordingly went down to Brompton to Mr. Place, in order to ascertain his opinion on the subject, as well as to express to him my own, which was to this effect:—That as we wished to establish *a secular school* upon a broad and liberal basis, such as might embrace children of either Christians, Jews, or Infidels, I thought we should do wrong in giving it either a Sectarian or an Infidel character, as we should assuredly do if we placed at the head of it the person who had applied to us, he being an avowed Atheist. That as one of the objects of our Association was to embrace persons of all creeds, classes, and opinions, in favour of our political views, and as our own members were of various religious opinions, I thought we should be acting unjustly to them, as well as thwarting our objects, were we to stamp our school as an Infidel school. Therefore, without entering into the question of the applicant's merits or demerits, I thought him a very improper person to appoint as schoolmaster. As, however, he (Mr. Place) was the person through whom the proposal was chiefly made, and as he was greatly my senior, I should leave him to decide on the answer that was to be given to the applicant. On my return home, I also mentioned the subject to several members of our committee, and they concurred with me that the applicant was not the kind of person whom we ought to appoint as schoolmaster. By leaving the answer altogether to Mr. Place, however, it appears that I did wrong; for he neglected to give any answer for or against the appointment, so that when I met the person some days after (it might be weeks), I was greatly annoyed to find that no answer had been given to his application. I told him, however, the steps I had taken in connection with it, and the opinions I had expressed to Mr. Place regarding him. He said it was very possible that his appointment might have affected the school, as I apprehended, but that he was then very indifferent about such a situation, as he was about to start a new periodical. On learning from me that we had not yet been suited with a teacher, he referred me to a person whom he thought would suit us, one, he said, who had some experience as a schoolmaster. Some weeks after this explanation had taken place, a few of our members, who were greatly prepossessed in favour of the applicant referred to, made a charge against me of a dereliction of duty in not answering his letter, as before stated. Their motion, however, after a warm discussion, was lost by a very large majority. But regarding this as one of a series of insults I had lately received from the same parties, I was induced to resign my situation as secretary to the Association. This resignation delayed the opening of our day school for nearly two years.

In 1846 I became a member of the Council of the Anti-Slavery League, of which Mr. George Thompson was president, and Mr. Robert Smith, secretary. This association was formed on the occasion of Wm. Lloyd Garrison, Frederick Douglas, and Henry C. Wright's visit to England, three noble champions of the poor slaves. I am induced to believe that the chief object of their visit was to impress upon religious bodies that slavery was a heinous sin, and ought to be abolished; and also to urge on them the necessity of withholding fellowship from the religious bodies of America, who were the advocates and abettors of slavery. Among the religious bodies of England and Scotland, they endeavoured to influence the Evangelical Alliance on behalf of the slave, but were unsuccessful. They accordingly got up a public meeting on the subject at Exeter Hall, where the mock Christianity of this body was treated rather freely. Our League having strongly condemned the conduct of some of these bodies, who, for the sake of filthy lucre, and the subscriptions they were in the habit of receiving from the religious slaveholders of America, persisted in recognising them, regardless of the millions of their fellow-men in slavery; and hence we were noways popular with them. We, however, employed Frederick Douglas for a short time as our missionary, and his and George Thompson's very eloquent discourses called forth great sympathy on behalf of the poor slave. Lloyd Garrison, also, while he was in London, gave a very eloquent lecture on slavery at the National Hall.

During our friends' visit, I recall to memory a very delightful evening spent with them and other friends, at the house of Mr. J H. Parry. On that occasion we had not only a very interesting account of the Anti-Slavery movement and its prominent advocates in America, but our friend Douglas, who had a fine voice, sang a number of negro melodies. Mr. Garrison sang several anti-slavery pieces, and our grave friend, H. C. Wright, sang an old

21

Indian war song. Other friends contributed to the amusement of the evening, and among them our friend Vincent sang "The Marseillaise."

In this year, also, I became acquainted with Mr. George Gill, of Nottingham, a gentleman whose liberal and patriotic benevolence led him to establish, in that town, the People's College, devoted to the purposes of education; the People's Hall, intended for meetings, lectures, and classes of instruction for the working classes; also a place called the Retreat, consisting of several comfortable cottages, for aged people, rent free. I had previously drawn up for him a constitution for his college, and in 1856 I received an invitation to come down to Nottingham to draw up a constitution for the People's Hall. He was very infirm at the time, and exceedingly deaf, but having made myself acquainted with his wishes, I prepared the document. This, having received his approval and that of his son, and late partner, was sent off to his lawyer to be engrossed. My old friend, however, died before it could receive his signature, but his son, I hear, has since honourably carried out his noble father's wishes.

Being out of employment, as before stated, I was recommended by my friend, Mr. Prideaux, to William and Mary Howitt, and was shortly after engaged by them as the publisher of their journal. This very excellent little periodical had a very fair circulation at first, and bid fair to pay well, but a dispute between Mr. Howitt and John Saunders, the editor of the *People's Journal* regarding the conduct of the latter, caused the circulation to fall off. In the meantime Mr. Howitt became involved in pecuniary difficulties, by reason of his former connection with the *People's Journal*, so as eventually to lead to the discontinuance of his own journal, and the loss of what property Mr. Howitt possessed. Fortunately, however, William and Mary Howitt possessed a mine of mental wealth that trouble and difficulty could not altogether deprive them of, although these greatly operated for a season to injure the health and spirits of both of them. They have now, however, by great industry and unwearied application in their pursuits, mastered their enemies and their troubles, and have since delighted their readers by the production of many very excellent works, one of which, " Land, Labour, and Gold," recently published by Mr. Howitt, a work descriptive of Australia and Van Dieman's Land, forms a picture of governmental stupidity and official incapacity in relation to these fine countries, which will make future generations wonder why their ancestors were such patient, plodding animals, to be so begulled and befooled as they have been. In expressing this opinion, I may add, that it is now many years since my first acquaintance with these very estimable people, and, the more I know of them, the stronger is my appreciation of their worth and excellence and goodness of heart.

During the time I was the publisher of *Howitt's Journal* I had not much time to devote to politics; although I continued to take part occasionally in the proceedings of the National Association. Perceiving, however, the variety of efforts that were then made in different directions in favour of Political and Social Objects of Reform, it struck me that the realization of most of them might be easily accomplished by some plan of co-operation, if persons could be induced to engage in it. I, therefore, put forth the following " Proposal for the consideration of the Friends of Progress " :—

" Fellow-Countrymen,—Millions of our brethren, from their ardent desire to promote such changes, social, political, moral and religious, as they conscientiously believe will remove, or greatly abridge, the present lamentable amount of poverty, misery, vice, and crime, may all justly be considered *friends of progress.*

" Knowing that vast numbers of those friends are actively engaged in their respective societies, as well as individually, in forwarding each their peculiar views, too often midst difficulties and discouragements ending in disappointment, and destructive of future efforts, I have long been desirous of seeing some combined effort made, by which—as I conceive—all the various objects of reform which they are separately in pursuit of, may sooner be realized than can possibly be effected by individual or isolated effort; while, at the same time, they are cultivating principles of peace, union and brotherhood, which doubtlessly form the best foundation for social happiness and national advancement.

"To effect any great improvement in this country, politically or socially, we have learnt from experience the great effort that is needed, as well as the great amount of money that must be spent before public opinion can be formed and concentrated so as to influence our legislature in favour of even *one* measure of reform; and yet *very many are needed* to effect our social and political salvation.

"Owing to this slow and tardy process of reform, misery, vice and crime are perpetuated; thousands are born and die in ignorance and vice; and thousands, too, often lose health and hope in the continuous and protracted struggle to make men wiser, better and happier than they found them.

"This slow progress for good is evidently to be attributed to the great variety of measures advocated by different bodies of reformers; also by the contentious feelings too often engendered in their onward progress, and the consequent difficulty of uniting our brethren in favour of any one object; and, above all, in the great difficulty of abrogating *old laws, or instituting new ones* necessary to effect or facilitate the reform desired by any particular body of Reformers, or portion of the people.

"But as all those various classes of Reformers *are equally the friends of progress,* all zealous and desirous of benefiting their fellow-men, and, it may be, all equally active in promoting the especial object they have espoused, it will be useless to call upon any of them to give up their particular object in favour of any *one* measure that may by some persons be considered more practical and important than another; for such appeals have frequently been made, and as often disregarded.

"As measures of progress, they are all doubtlessly important, if not equally so; and as they are all equally desirous to check evil and promote good, and, it is presumed, *anxious to live to see the realization of some of the objects they are contending for,* the question arises whether upon *the good Samaritan principle,* of each helping his fellow-man, they can be brought to unite, the sooner to *realize the objects they are severally in pursuit of,* and thus carry forward, simultaneously, all those measures necessary for accomplishing the greatest good in the shortest possible period.

" In reflecting on the difficulties in the way of progress it has struck me that something might be done to facilitate such a desired object, in the formation of a GENERAL ASSOCIATION OF PROGRESS ; in which might be combined *all those measures of social and political reformation for which societies are established, or mankind individully are now in pursuit of;* as well, indeed, as any other measure calculated to aid the great cause of mental, moral, and political progression.

"Anxious that something should be done in favour of some combined effort for the progress of humanity, I have presumed to address you, as well as to direct your attention to the following proposal, as an outline explanatory of my views on the subject, which may be improved or altered by any persons disposed to promote or aid such an undertaking :—

" PROPOSAL FOR FORMING A GENERAL ASSOCIATION OF PROGRESS.

" Its first object being to unite in one General Union of Progress all those who are now separately, or in small bodies, seeking the attainment of the following *political* and *social* objects. Secondly, to devise some *practical measures* for unitedly promoting and realizing such objects in a shorter time than can possibly be done under present arrangements ; and this without interfering in any way with the internal regulation of any present association.

" POLITICAL OBJECTS OF ASSOCIATION.

" 1st. The *Equal and Just Representation* of the whole people.

"2nd. The Abolition of all *State Religion;* and the right of conscience and opinion secured.

"3rd. The *Absolute Freedom of Trade;* and the abrogation of all Custom and Excise Laws.

"4th. The *Abolition of all Taxes upon Knowledge:* such as the tax and securities on newspapers, stamps and advertising duties, taxes on paper, books, pamphlets, &c.

"5th. The *General Reduction of Taxation;* and a more rigid economy of its expenditure.

"6th. *Direct Taxation on Property;* and the abolition of all *in direct* means of raising a revenue.

"7th. The *Abolition of all Political Monopolies* and *Unjust Privileges.*

"8th. The *Legislative Improvement, Impartial Execution* and *Cheapening* of *Law and Justice* for the whole people.

"Social Objects of Progress.

"9th. *General Education for the Whole Population;* provided by *all* and carried out and enforced *by all*, with the least possible government interference.

"10th. The promotion of *Scientific Institutions—Schools for Adult Instruction*—and *Libraries* for general circulation among the whole population.

"11th. The *Promotion of Temperance, Sobriety, Cleanliness* and *Health* amongst all classes; and the securing of places of rational recreation for the people, *apart from intoxicating drinks.*

"12th. The devising means by which the working and middle classes may have *Comfortable Homes*, and be gradually unabled to become *Manufacturers, Traders,* or *Farmers,* on their own capital.

"13th. To labour for the *General Abolition of War, Slavery* and *Oppression,* and the promotion of *General Civilisation* and *Christian Brotherhood* throughout the world.

"Sketch of the General Organization.

"That any number of individuals uniting, or already united, to promote any of the above objects, may become members of the Association of Progress by complying with the following conditions :—

"1. That they be united for one or more of the objects specified, and be *classified* (for purposes hereafter mentioned), *in classes of one hundred persons* in each class.

"2. That they individually subscribe 2d. each towards a general fund *weekly ;* the same to be collected by one of their own body, and paid into the District Bank of the Association.

"3. That they signify, by resolution, that any sum their class may secure by lot (or otherwise) shall not be divided, or applied otherwise than for *their declared object.*

"4. That they appoint one of their own members towards forming *a Committee for the district ;* such committee to see that the sums collected by the classes within the district are paid into the bank, as well as for promoting the objects of the Association within their respective districts.

"General Committee.

"That each District Committee appoint two members annually to form the *General Committee of the Association;* such Committee to meet in London (or other large town alternately) for the division and application of the money thus raised, according to the rules agreed to ; as well as for promoting the general objects of the Association by all just and peaceful means.

"Application of the General Fund.

"That the fund so raised be annually divided by the General Committee into portions of £2,000 ; such portions to be appropriated *by lot* (or any other approved means) among *the different classes of the Association,* and immediately handed over to those who may be so successful ; the same to be applied by them in promoting the declared objects without any further intervention.

"Such is a mere outline of the plan proposed. It will be seen that I have sought to include under the head of *Political* and *Social* Reform all those measures which are now advocated and contended for by different bodies, as well as others, which I deem desirable and necessary, before right, knowledge, and happiness, can be effected for our fellow-men.

"I have not thought it necessary to enter into the details of rules and regulations, as those can be best matured by such persons as may be disposed to form such an association.

"As, however, a mere outline of the plan is set forth, it may be necessary to explain that the chief object of classification *into hundreds* is for the appropriation of the fund raised ; as well as to afford facilities for persons not included in any existing association to form part of such an Association of Progress. As, for instance, 100 men, known to each other, may unite for the purpose of building themselves comfortable habitations—for raising means to take a farm—to commence manufacturing or trading—or for any social or political object embraced by the Association ; and in this manner may obtain £2,000 capital to commence with, or forward their undertaking. Or if they are not successful *directly*, in a pecuniary sense, they will by their union be *indirectly* benefited *by the reforms they would unitedly be able to effect.*

"If in this manner the friends of progress were only combined to the extent of *one million*, that number paying 2d. each per week would raise money enough to give £2,000 capital *to 216 different classes every year.*

"The mere pecuniary advantages, however, would be trifling, compared with the great and paramount object, A UNION OF ALL THE FRIENDS OF PROGRESS ; all aiding each other in the spirit of Christian brotherhood, the better to accomplish the reforms they are anxious to effect ; acting in concert for the promulgation of their respective views and objects ; seeking to smooth down those contracted, prejudiced, and contentious feelings, which now so much impede the progress of reform ; and uniting hearts and minds to remove the poverty, misery, and oppression of their land, and to extend the blessings of peace, prosperity, knowledge and happiness among all the nations of the earth."

Being, as I said, very busily engaged at this period, as the publisher of *Howitt's Journal*, no other steps were taken by me beyond the putting forth of the proposal; but I still entertain the hope that the day is not distant when some such general organization of the friends of progress will take place.

In the year 1848, the year of revolutions and commotions; of frightened despots and elated and hopeful people; our Association issued the following "Address to the French" :—

"Citizens of the French Republic,—As members of an Association formed for promoting the Political and Social Improvement of the Millions, we feel that we should be wanting to the great cause we have espoused, if we failed to extend our fraternal sympathies towards you at this important crisis; especially when more than sympathy is shown by many of the privileged of our country for the perjured despot you have recently scared from his throne —a man whose regal career has been a continuous warfare on human rights, and whose last effort to grind your liberties in the dust has made your streets flow with the blood of his victims.

"Abhorring such acts, we rejoice at his downfall—we conceive that a man so criminal should be left to the corrodings of his own conscience till repentance of his misdeeds shall have purified his heart, and caused him *to proclaim his own fallen example as a warning to the despots and oppressors of mankind;* to teach them the hollow foundation which courtiers and armies afford for the stability of thrones based on unrighteous power.

"But, fellow-men, while we rejoice in your victory, we deeply deplore the fate of the slain, and sympathise with the condition of the wounded; and we earnestly hope that your liberties will be consolidated, and that our liberty, and that of the world's, will be speedily effected without any further effusion of human blood.

"For we would fain hope that this last great example you have exhibited to the world *will teach wisdom to its rulers,* and cause them to proclaim a new era for humanity by liberalizing their institutions, and freeing their people; will prompt them to redeem the past by their future exertions to promote the improvement and happiness of their race; and, instead of relying on forts and armaments, and influences of corruption, to rely on the power and stability they can build up in the hearts and minds of a free people.

"But, whatever may be the course or disposition of *rulers*, the *people* of all countries have imperative duties to perform, in preparing themselves intellectually and morally, FOR THE COMING AGE OF FREEDOM, PEACE, AND BROTHERHOOD—an era when national jealousies shall be buried with the despotisms and privileges which have engendered them—when separate countries, brought nearer and nearer by the grand achievements of human inventions, cemented in friendship by ties of fraternity, freedom, and commerce, shall dispense with soldiers, armies, and war; when nations bound in amity shall vie only in promoting happiness and refinement at home, and civilization abroad; and when every individual shall have learnt that his highest earthly duty is to labour for the happiness of others, with the same zeal as he would seek to promote his own.

" The privileged and the powerful may smile at these aspirations, having only seen humanity through the distorted medium their own oppressive laws and enslaving institutions have engendered; but we have faith to believe that in the heart of lowest vice, there are chords of sympathy that may be struck to raise the fallen victim up in all the majesty of God's great image. We judge from man's better nature, when quickened by instruction, matured by kindness, and inspired by freedom; and strong in our hopes we hail every effort tending to that great end, when our faith shall have become a reality.

"People of France! You have proclaimed your country a Republic, and your political object *freedom for all*. In this your great resolve we are hopeful of the future, and hasten therefore to extend to you our sympathies. We respect your form of government; we cordially approve of your object; we have faith in the good men you have selected for consolidating your liberties; and our earnest prayer is that you may have the virtuous conduct of every French citizen to govern, guard, and guide your

Republic to a successful and lasting issue—to the forming of a commonwealth, *strong* in the intelligence and morality of your people; *secure*, by pursuing a career of peaceful improvement; *beloved at home*, for the happiness you shall diffuse; and *respected abroad*, for the practical virtues you shall exhibit of the government of a true democracy.

"But amid our hopes and congratulations we would fain mingle our fraternal advice and respectful warnings; feeling that liberty is one, and the common cause of nations identical in the great brotherhood of man. Have faith, we implore you, in the righteousness of your object, and in the great and good men you have chosen for realising its consummation.

"Respect the opinions of those who differ from you; abolish all jealousies and distrust of power, wealth, and influence; and, by peaceful, kind, and courteous conduct, resolve to convert even your enemies into friends. Trust more to your individual virtues than to your collected armies, for the consolidation and security of your Republic.

"Dignify honest labour, industry, temperance, and frugality, with national approbation; everywhere diffuse a knowledge of your political and social obligations; and make the instruction of your children your paramount object; for by so acting you will build up your liberties on a foundation, firm, lasting, and impregnable.

"Brethren of France! we also take this opportunity of assuring you that the millions of our country cherish no other feelings towards you than those of kindness and regard; and no other desire than to see our two countries cultivating a free and friendly intercourse, and heartily promoting the peace and civilisation of the world.

"The hard-working, industrious millions of our brethren, destitute of political right, overburthened by taxation, and deprived of their earnings for the benefit of idlers, are also desirous of obtaining *their* liberties, and trust that their moral energies will ere long enable them to achieve them. They are now earnestly watching every step in your progress, and hopefully believe that your future career will be a beacon to cheer them, and not a brand to deter. *Your success* will help their enfranchisement.

"That your onward course may be prudent and peaceful; that your Republic may be established by the united voices of France; and that the wisdom of your rulers and the virtues of your people may make it a glorious example to the nations of the world, is the sincere prayer of your English brethren, the members of the National Association."

This Address was translated by our estimable friend Dr. Bowring—now Sir John Bowring—whose signature was attached to it, as one of our honorary members; he having generously come forward when the Association was first formed with a very handsome present of books for the library, and was otherwise a kind friend to the Association. The original document was engrossed and forwarded to the ambassador of the Republic in London, and a copy forwarded to M. de Lamartine, but the receipt of it was never acknowledged.

Unhappily the hopes which we cherished regarding the Republic of France were but shortlived; the selfish impatience of the middle classes in refusing *temporary relief* to the working classes, whose labours had been suspended by the new order of things, led to excitement and disorder— the crude and startling proposals put forth by the Socialists and Communists regarding the rights of property, caused all who had anything to lose to pray for despotism as the least of evils—the unseemly squabbles and daily contentions of the representatives of the people disspirited the hopeful and emboldened the daring—the fighting propensity of the Celtic race, their warlike idolatry, and the ignorance and superstition of the peasantry, were unhappily antagonistic to freedom—all these unitedly prepared the way for priestly and imperial despotism to extinguish liberty with false and hypocritical representations, a drunken soldiery, and a river of human blood. Unhappy France! thrice gloriously to free herself from the bit and bridle of kingcraft and priestcraft, but her people not appreciating the blessings of Freedom, to thrice again submit their backs to the burthen, their mouths to the bridle, and their sides to the spur.

CHAPTER XVIII.

In this year (1848) I cherish, with feelings of the warmest gratitude, the remembrance of a numerous company of kind friends, who assembled at the National Hall, to present to me a public testimonial, as a mark of their respect for my public services. The testimonial comprised a handsome silver tea-service, and a purse of one hundred and forty sovereigns. A very kind and warm-hearted Address, written by my esteemed friend Mr. William J. Fox, M.P. for Oldham, and signed on behalf of the subscribers by my earnest and sincere friends Mr. J. H. Parry as *chairman*, and Mr. J. F. Mollett as *secretary*, was likewise presented to me on the same occasion.* I estimate that testimonial the more so, because I believe that the friends with whom it originated, as well as the subscribers generally, were prompted at that particular period by the purest and noblest feelings to extend their kindness towards me in the manner described.

---

* " The testimonial this day presented to William Lovett is intended both as an expression of gratitude for public services, and of respect for private worth. The Subscribers rejoice to feel that they cannot distinguish between the Patriot and the Man; but find that the selfsame qualities of integrity, purity, firmness, zeal, and benevolence, which have secured to William Lovett the lasting attachment of those who know him, have also been the characteristics of his political career. Whether enduring the loss of his goods, for refusing to be coerced into military service; or that of his liberty, for protesting against the unconstitutional interference of the police with the people; whether founding the Working Men's Association, for the attainment of political rights, or the National Association, for the promotion of social improvement; whether embodying the principles of democracy, in the memorable document called the People's Charter, or shewing the means of redemption in his work, entitled 'Chartism, a new Organisation of the People;'

Shortly after this event, our day school (so long post-poned) was opened in the Hall ; our generous friend, A. B., not only furnishing the desks, books, and apparatus required for the opening, but also the fixed salary of the schoolmaster. The introduction to our prospectus states that "the object in forming this school is to provide for the children of the middle and working classes a sound, secular, useful, and moral education—such as is best calculated to prepare them for the practical business of life—to cause them to understand and perform their duties as members of society—and to enable them to diffuse the greatest amount of happiness among their fellow-men." I may add that it is now upwards of nine years since our school was opened, during which time our kind friend A. B. has handsomely contributed towards its maintenance, without which assistance it could not, I believe, be kept open ; the small payment of the children not being sufficient to pay the salaries of the teachers and assistants, together with the rent and out-goings of the place.

About this period I put forth a small pamphlet, entitled "Universal Suffrage in the Moon." The merits of this little work, however, I deem it necessary to state, I have no claims to, it having been written by a friend, who

---

whether cultivating, by instruction, the intellectual and moral nature of destitute children, or by numerous addresses from the above-named Associations recommending Peace, Temperance, Justice, Love, and Union, to erring multitudes and nations ; in labours which will make themselves known, by their results, to posterity, or in unrecorded scenes of friendly and domestic intercourse, WILLIAM LOVETT has been ever the same ; and may this memorial now presented to him serve as an assurance that the feelings of his friends, admirers, and fellow-labourers in the cause of humanity are strong and unchanging, like the truth of his own character, public and private, by which those feelings have been produced.

"It is the fervent wish of the Subscribers that his future life may be long, happy, and successful, as his past has been true, honourable, nd beneficent.

"Signed on behalf of th Subscribers,

"J. HUMFFREYS PARRY, Chairman.
"J. F. MOLLETT, Hon. Sec."

was desirous of its being published in my name, from the belief that it was more likely to be circulated among the working classes; an idea, however, which was not realized.

The last political association I was actively connected with was the *People's League,* which originated in the following manner:—Soon after the outbreak of the French Revolution, in 1848, the members of the National Association were desirous that we should make another effort to unite the Radical Reformers of the United Kingdom in favour of the Charter. I was therefore requested by them to prepare an Address, such as I might deem likely to be promotive of that object. It having been suggested that such an Address was likely to be more effective if we could obtain the sanction of the members of the "National Alliance,"* and some of the leading reformers among the middle classes, such as Mr. Hume, Cobden, Miall, and others, I was requested to see some of these men and confer with them on the subject.

I accordingly drew up a brief proposal for the formation of a new political association, to be entitled the People's League, having the following objects:—

"1. To obtain the just and equal representation of the whole people, as set forth in the *People's Charter,* with such alterations or amendments in its details as may here after appear necessary.

"2. The *reduction of our National Expenditure* in every department of the State.

"3. *The repeal of all Customs and Excise Laws* and all *indirect* means of raising a revenue.

"4. The substitution of *a Direct Tax on Property,* in an increasing ratio upwards, according to its amount."

This proposal readily met with the support of the committee and secretary of the Alliance; but Messrs. Hume and Cobden, while they expressed themselves favourable to our views of reform, were fearful that the Middle

---

* This was a political association, with political objects similar to our own.

Classes could not be got to unite in any plan for its attainment. The chief point dwelt upon by both of them was, that O'Connor and his disciples had, by their folly and violence, made the name of *Chartist* distasteful to that class. Mr. Hume, however, being exceedingly anxious that something should be done at that crisis, requested me to leave the above proposal with him, as he wished to submit it for the consideration of some of his friends belonging to the "Free Trade Club." I did so, and when I called again he informed me that he had got about fifty of his friends to agree to certain resolutions in favour of Financial Reform and Household Suffrage. This not coming up to our views of reform, *our Proposal* was subsequently modified in the form of the following "Address to the Radical Reformers of the United Kingdom" :—

"Fellow-Countrymen,—Desiring the peace, prosperity, and happiness of our country, we deem it our duty to address you at this eventful period, believing that correct views, just feelings, and *a cordial union among all classes of Reformers*, would be the most effective means of peacefully removing all unjust obstructions to our national prosperity; and would form the best security for the advancement of our people.

"But, in inviting your aid in the formation of such a union, we deem it necessary to declare that we are opposed to every description of outrage or violence, and that we have no feeling inimical to the present constitution of the realm. We only wish the Commons House to be a true representation of the industry, intellect, and good feelings *of the whole population*—that our reforms should be peacefully and justly effected—that the security of person and property should be maintained—that our trade, commerce, and enterprise should be justly extended—our brethren improved and educated—and that our country should progress *politically* and *socially* as the first among the nations of the world.

"We have faith also to believe that all this can be effected by *peaceful and moral effort;* as our combined industrial energies, our united capital, *our moral courage*, our *intelligence* and *will* alone, give strength to our state, and constitute the only power of our rulers.

"But, judging from the legislative effects and burthens of the last few years, we have just cause for apprehending that the longer reform is delayed, in every department of the state, the more difficult will it be to effect it—the more destructive will be its results to the middle and working classes, and the greater will become the danger lest an impoverished and oppressed people overturn, in their frenzy, the accumulated wealth, power, and improvement of ages.

"For should our present system of privilege and corruption be prolonged, we may confidently predict that our *Manufacturers* and *Traders*, overburthened by taxation, cramped by monopolies, and fettered by exclusive laws, will, year after year, find it the more difficult to compete with less-burthened countries; and that their markets, being thus restricted, will afford less profits on labour and capital, and will cause less employment for our continually-increasing population.

"Our ingenious *Artizans* and industrious *Mechanics* and *Labourers*, compelled to strive with each other for such limited employment, would inevitably bring down their present inadequate wages to the subsistence point; and with that would speedily come the fast deterioration, the pauperising and destruction of our country's hope and pride, her intelligent and industrious people.

"Our *Shop-keeping* and *Middle Classes*, chiefly dependent on the consumption of the industrious millions, would most assuredly sink with them; as, in addition to their loss of business and profits, they would have to sustain the burthen of that pauperism and misery such a state of things would engender.

"With an unemployed and impoverished people would come turbulence and disorder—for a people steeped in misery will not always listen to the dictates of prudence—and, to escape such a state of commotion, *the capital,* the enterprise, and the intellectual stamina of our country, would wing their way to other lands, as we have seen in the case of unhappy Ireland.

" But, fellow-countrymen, with all our apprehension of the future, we need not to point beyond present evils to afford abundant cause for awakening your sympathies and stimulating your benevolent resolves.

" Misery, starving wretchedness, and ill-requited toil have been proclaimed by our rulers to be the daily lot of millions of our working-class brethren. Over-burthening taxation, restricted trade, debts, bankruptcy, and insolvency, are making rapid inroads on the industrial energies and previous accumulations of our middle and upper classes; and yet, amid all this social deterioration, our rulers are adding burthen to burthens, and seem resolved to perpetuate them.

"The Commons House, which ought to be a true representation of the wants and wishes of the whole people, and composed of men whose aim and object it should be to reduce and keep down our present extravagant expenditure, and to determine how the mental, moral, and industrial energies of our people should be developed and extended, so as to add to the prosperity and happiness of all, seems but a mere instrument in the hands of our privileged orders for maintaining the monopolies, perpetuating their unjust powers, and taxing our population.

" For the present franchise, being so limited and unequally distributed, and the means of bribery and corruption so extensive, the legislative efforts of the few representatives of the people in that House are generally neutralised, or rendered hopeless, by the overwhelming power of aristocratic nominees, army, navy, and mere privileged representatives.

" Fellow-countrymen, the intellectual and moral energies of Reformers have for years been contending against this power of corruption. Thousands of lives have been sacrificed, and millions of money have been spent, in striving to make the House of Commons an instrument of progress —an organ for effecting the welfare of our country. To move every reluctant step it has ungrudgingly been compelled to take, a social tornado has been required; and, that subsiding, it has again sought to retrace its progress, and to again build up and strengthen its oppressive powers.

" Believing, therefore, that the House of Commons must truly and justly represent the *whole people* before it can become effective for lessening our burthens, removing restrictions and monopolies, or for helping onward the intellectual, moral, and truly religious progress of our people, we invite the good and true among all classes to unite with us for the forming of a PEOPLE'S LEAGUE ; the chief object of which shall be to obtain the equal and just representation *of the whole people,* as set forth in the *People's Charter,* with such alterations and amendments in its details as may appear necessary.

" But, in adopting the principles of this document, we deem it necessary to state, that we adopt it in the spirit of those with whom it originated, whose object it was to create and extend an enlightened public opinion in its favour, and to endeavour to unite all good men for peacefully obtaining its legislative enactment.

" At the same time, we repudiate, with all earnestness and sincerity, the violent language and mischievous conduct which selfish and unprincipled individuals have associated with that measure of political justice—persons who have sought to maintain their notoriety and to acquire an ascendancy over the multitude by lauding their vices and administering to their intolerant and persecuting spirit. By which malevolent conduct they have fostered and perpetuated divisions between the different classes of society, given support to oppression, delayed the cause of reform, and consequently prolonged the poverty and misery of the millions.

" Hopeful, however, that the time is now arrived for a union of all true Reformers, and having full faith that there is sufficient intelligence, moral energy, and true feeling among our countrymen for restraining all acts of violence and folly, and for peacefully effecting all those reforms necessary for the prosperity of our country, and the elevation and happiness of our people, we resolve to attempt the formation of such a union, and invoke the blessing of Heaven for our success."

This Address, meeting with the approval of the Committee of the National Alliance, as well as of our own

Association, was printed and sent forth to a great number of the leading Radicals of the country; accompanied with a circular (signed by a number of well-known Reformers) inviting them to attend a *friendly conference* on the subject, at Herbert's Hotel, Palace Yard, on the 3rd of May. The circular, however, had no sooner been issued than some of our leading friends, who had appended their signatures to it, began to raise doubts and state difficulties about the extent of the suffrage we had proposed in our Address; so that when the conference took place a considerable modification was made from our first proposal, and from what I and several of my friends, thought to be essential for the basis of a union calculated to call forth the spirit of the country. And what rendered it the more mortifying was, that the objections came from ultra-Chartists, and not from the more moderate Reformers; our friend Vincent having been about the first to raise doubts and difficulties. The conference was, however, attended by about 300 persons; and, after much discussion, a resolution was agreed to in favour of *universal suffrage;* the subject of the People's Charter having been deferred till some future conference. In fact the resolution agreed to, forming the basis of the union, was a great falling-off from the basis of the Complete Suffrage Conference held at Birmingham in 1842; and the result turned out as I anticipated; we failed in securing the co-operation of the millions, and only received a very lukewarm support from some few of the Middle Class Reformers. The League, however, was formed, and some few hundreds joined it, among those myself; hopeful that it might grow in numbers and improve in principle. The plan of organization having been agreed to, the first object was to appoint a deputation to wait upon the leading members of the Free Trade Club to impress on them the superiority of *Universal* over *Household Suffrage* as a practical and conservative measure—the gentlemen of the Club having recently declared in favour of the latter.

"An inaugural meeting was next called at the London Tavern on the 24th of May, for the purpose of submitting our views to a larger body of Reformers, Colonel

Thompson having been appointed our chairman; but the O'Connorites—headed by Ernest Jones—having forged admission cards to a large extent, interrupted and broke up the meeting in disorder.

An Address, written by Mr. John Robertson, was next circulated to a wide extent, setting forth the defective state of the franchise, showing the steps taken by the League for its improvement, and invoking the people to join in a peaceful and powerful demand for their enfranchisement. A subsequent one, written by Mr. Thomas Beggs, was put forth by the Executive Committee, inviting attention to the object of the League, and calling for active sympathy and support. These, as well as a great number of private efforts, having failed to call forth the spirit of the country, and that pecuniary support necessary to meet the ordinary expenses of the League, caused the secession of a large number of the members of our Council in the following September; among whom were Dr. Price, Mr. Miall, Thomas Box, Charles Gilpin, Stafford Allen and others.

A number of us, however, indignant at the effort made by the Whigs at that time to stifle the reform movement, determined to keep together; to greatly economise our expenditure, and to use every means in our power to keep up the agitation for the suffrage. The Whigs, having effected a triumph over O'Conner and his boasting physical force followers by their blundering demonstration on the 10th of April, and having, moreover, exposed the frauds and fallacies in connection with the " Monster Petition " presented about that period, resolved to crush, if possible, the right of petitioning altogether. The Government had previously rendered the right of petition nearly a nullity, by preventing the members presenting them from explaining or supporting them; and now they thought to effectually silence the public voice by raking up an old law of the Stuarts, which declares that political petitions shall not have more than *twenty signatures.* And this, be it remembered, was effected by *Whig Reformers.*

I ought to have stated before this, that the first secretary to the League was Mr. Robert Lowery; the second, my friend Mr. Thomas Beggs; but he having resigned, I was appointed their *Honorary Secretary.* Shortly after my appointment I was requested to prepare an " Address to the People of London," on the subject of petitioning for the suffrage in the form the Whigs allowed. The following is the Address agreed to :—

" Fellow-Citizens,—We live in a city distinguished for its wealth, enterprize and commerce, above most of the nations of the earth. Our public.buildings are numerous and costly, and the mansions of our wealthy citizens vie in elegance and magnificence with those of princes. Our shops are gorgeous in the display of splendid and ingenious merchandise; our warehouses overflow with every description of productions; our freighted ships are seen on every sea; and in every part of the world our manufactured produce affords ample proofs of the industry and ingenuity of our untiring people.

" But what, fellow-citizens, has been the power that has most contributed to the raising up and supporting of this our wealthy and populous city? What was the power that chiefly sustained her in her numerous struggles against feudal freebooters, despotic kings, and grasping courtiers? What, but *the spirit of freedom*—that noble resolution to guard, at any sacrifice, the fruits of honest industry—that undaunted determination which so often aided *the right and protected the oppressed*, in the teeth of base rulers, furious chieftains, and armed retainers?—and *that spirit, that power*, in proportion as it manfully resisted the attacks of despotism, or withstood the cajolery of kingly or aristocratic domination, made our city wealthy, and her citizens prosperous.

" And be assured, fellow-citizens, that in proportion as that spirit of freedom is allowed to decline among us, to be usurped by open foe, or undermined by plausible pretensions, so assuredly will our trade languish, our power diminish, and that superstructure raised by the combined industry and freedom of our forefathers fall to ruin and decay. The concentrated rays of healthful activity, which serve to render a city prosperous, must beam upon it *from without;* but if the chill of poverty and oppression is once allowed to extinguish the outward sun, the warmth of city life will soon become exhausted. On the activity, the wages and consumption of the millions, the prosperity of our manufacturing and distributing classes depend; but on the profitable interchanges *of all* must our towns and cities rely for their prosperity.

"And are there no alarming symptoms now stirring, warning us both from within and from without—symptoms which should serve to recall the freedom and independence of the past, and awaken our apprehensions of the future? In our *social arrangements* is not a spirit of reckless gambling fast usurping the trade of honest, plodding industry? and a course of chicanery and fraud, ending in bankruptcy, becoming too frequent and too fashionable to be thought dishonourable? Are not the fearful and increasing evils of pauperism, vice, crime, and disease annually displayed in facts and figures, giving us dreadful warning of social disorder? Is not the gulf fast widening between the different classes of society? and have not the careless indifference, the hauteur and oppression of the rich too long left the poor a prey to their own misery and heart-burning meditations? Are not the substantial realities and real pleasures of wealth—the means of promoting knowledge and rewarding goodness—fast being exchanged for the empty pride of distinction, or the ambition of a name?

"And, *politically*, are not the mass of our industrious people, the bound, padlocked, and plundered serfs of our aristocratic factions?—this coalition, this league of political despots and social spoilers, whom General Foy once described as " a band of those who wish to consume without producing, live without working, occupy all public places without being competent to fill them, and seize upon all honours without meriting them.' Is not the grasping and despotic power of this class, their annual drainings, their monopolies and exclusiveness, the searing blight which everywhere prevents industry from blossoming, and cankers commerce in its bud? Yet this is the class whose unrighteous power you are daily taught to uphold as necessary to your country's salvation! persons for whom places must be found, and taxes paid ; for whose dominion armies must be raised, battles fought, spoils won, and men bleed ;—and for all of which you, and your children, must not only toil and pay, but the labour of generations unborn must be mortgaged to give them cause for remembering this aristocratic race.

" Under the specious plea of upholding the Crown and dignity of England, the two aristocratic factions have gradually been undermining our institutions, and robbing us of the rights and liberties our forefathers wrested from their despotic progenitors. They have graspingly monopolised the best portion of our possessions at home and abroad, and have dexterously shifted every burthen from their own shoulders on to those of the people. They have made church, army, and navy, their especial property and instruments—have filled the people's house (for the most part) with the vassals of their will—have selfishly stripped royalty of its possessions, and (judging from their conduct) would fain usurp its power.

" Where, fellow-citizens, are these institutions our fathers once gloried in ? All the great provisions of Magna Charta, the Petition of Right, the Habeas Corpus Act, the Bill of Rights, and the Act of Settlement, with numerous other constitutional privileges, have, one after another, been gradually undermined and nearly rendered a nullity by these two factions ; who now, through their corrupt organs, call upon us to bless God for our invaluable political blessings ! And this, too, at a time when they have nearly deprived us of the last of our political rights—the right even of the criminal at the bar, the right of making our grievances known and our prayers for justice and redress public and notorious.

" In addressing you, fellow-citizens, we beg to assure you that we are no destructives, seeking to undermine society —to destroy our institutions—or to subvert the monarchy. But we deem it our duty to declare, that society is not safe while honest industry fails in procuring bread—that our institutions are in danger while the prison is sought for as an asylum—and that the monarchy has more to fear from the oppressive rule and grinding exactions of our aristocracy, than from those of their victims, whom despair and poverty have rendered desperate.

" The people of England are far from being changeful in their character ; for even their turbulence oftener proceeds from justice outraged, or rights deferred, than from any anxious desire for other institutions. Their humble homes and kindred hearts are more entwined with their lives and aspirations than is seen among the mere roving exquisites of fashion, or lords of millions grasping still for more.

" As for the Monarch of England, she has more true hearts in huts and hovels than are found in court circles or lords' mansions. With the former she is respected as a monarch, and esteemed as a woman ; and could she but contrast their honest feeling with that of those ' Ins and Outs ' of place, profit and preferment that hover round her person, she would soon see on whom reliance could be placed if she ever needed protection. For recent examples are not wanting to convince her of the faithlessness of courtiers, and the insecurity of armies.

" But in thus declaring our opinions of aristocratic rule and dominion, we desire it to be understood that it is not *the men* but *the system* we condemn—it is not against their rank or possessions we so much complain, as against their oppressive and unjust power ;—they, in fact, may be said to constitute ' The State.' For them England has warred, and is still warring against freedom at home and abroad—for their benefit and domination, and not for the support of the monarchy, are our present expensive establishments maintained—and by *their laws, their monopolies, their rule*, has England been pauperized, and her people enslaved.

" Need we remind you, fellow-citizens, that the organs of this class, taking advantage of the strife now waging on the Continent of Europe—between the despots who would bind and the victims who would escape their thraldom—are now seeking, by every perversion of fact and sophistry of argument, to alarm your fears and awaken your prejudices, the more easily to make you the instruments of your own slavery. They would fain make you believe that your social and political salvation are dependant on standing armies and aristocratic sway!! and they sneeringly denounce all those who remind you that these have ever been the instruments of oppression in all ages; and that the warlike spirit they have engendered is the chief evil which continental liberty has now to cope with.

"Those who tell you that the freedom and happiness of England will be best promoted by endeavouring practically to carry out the great lessons of the Gospel, in seeking to promote peace, extend knowledge, and *do justice to all our brethren*, are made the scoff of those venal instruments, who do the bidding of our oppressors. The *landed aristocracy* of England, they would fain cause you to look up to as your hereditary fathers and best defenders; and would teach you to despise all those who by the industrial arts of trades and manufactures, and the peaceful intercourse of commerce, have scattered far and wide the blessings of knowledge, and enriched this land of oaks and acorns with the multifarious productions of the globe. Exceptions they would doubtlessly make, where accumulated wealth was necessary to enrich an empty title, or where intellectual greatness was willing to forswear the gifts of nature to become the willing puppets of *their order*, but even then the feudal pride would be manifest in the blending.

"Fellow-citizens, and you who make up the two million inhabitants of this great metropolis, it is for you to record your verdict against this social and political injustice; and, though humble ourselves, in all but earnestness of purpose, we implore you to do so by the remembrance of the past, by the gloom and despair of the present, and by the hopes of a brighter future.

"It is evidently *your interest* as it is *ours*, to live in free and friendly intercourse with all nations; but our *aristocracy* are constantly fomenting fresh quarrels, devising new conquests, demanding more soldiers, and fresh sacrifices of our fellow-men.

"It is surely your desire,—as it is our own,—that our industrious people should be fully employed in raising productions to supply their famishing and destitute brethren at home, or to exchange for commodities which all classes desire from abroad ; but our aristocracy, by their lavish expenditure in armies, navies, and in every department of the state, are continually abstracting from the productive energies of the country; and, by their monopolies and quarrels, have called forth a host of competitors, who are constantly limiting our exchanges with the nations of the world.

" It is your and our interest to retain in our own hands the largest amount of our own earnings ; but our aristocracy demand by far the largest share to support them in their idle extravagances, their expensive pomp, power, and dominion.

" If, then, you would promote your own interest, and seek to diffuse the greatest amount of happiness among your fellow-men, you will join your voices and will add your exertions to those of others, in peacefully promoting such a reform in this country, and especially in the Commons House of Parliament, as shall prevent this grasping aristocracy from much longer impoverishing our country and degrading our people. This great work against a powerful and continually-increasing body is not to be effected *by partial or party measures;* the heart and soul of the kingdom must be enlisted in the struggle to secure such reform peacefully and effectively ; and to do this the suffrage *must be personal—must be universal.*

" We need not here stop to define this measure, nor to afford additional arguments in favour of its justice. It is now notoriously understood as pertaining to every man of full age and sound mind, having a fixed residence and untainted by crime. The *right of it* is founded on the great brotherhood of humanity, is based on the justice of all conventional arrangements, and is such as our moral and Christian codes inculcate and approve.

" While, however, we feel bound, by every principle of political morality, ardently to contend for the legislative enactment of this great right, we are most anxious to obtain it *peacefully* and *constitutionally.* But it behoves every lover of peace, order, and progress, to be prompt in the exercise of those means, as, year after year, our aristocratic factions are blocking up those constitutional channels through which our social grievances may be made known, or political reforms effected. Almost the last right-left us, *the right of petition*, has gradually been curtailed and restricted; and the legislative shearing of the last session has almost rendered it a nullity. But under this last constitutional rag the friends of peaceful political progress should speedily rally; lest this, too, be struck down by some aristocratic fiat. And, poor and scanty as it is, such an act would be a matter of solemn moment, as there are fearful facts on record of evils occasioned by the stifling of the public voice, and by the blocking up all peaceful channels of constitutional redress.

"Believing, then, that multitudes in this great city are anxious to see our social and political wrongs redressed, and sufficiently imbued with the spirit of their forefathers to abide by this constitutional right of petitioning, we would respectfully urge them *still to get up petitions*, though they be '*limited to twenty signatures*,' according to the provision of the despotic law of the Stuarts, which has recently been raked from oblivion by our fair-promising, but liberty-hating Whigs.

"We, therefore, earnestly request that they will, in brief and clear language, record their opinions on the great question of *universal suffrage*, the only effective measure that can allay the increasing discontent of the millions—the only radical cure for those political corruptions and social burthens which exclusive legislation has generated, and which our aristocratic rulers seem resolved to maintain.

"We will not call upon them to petition in this or that form, or for those points and details which we deem essential to make the suffrage effective. Let each petition be in accordance with the views of those who sign it; but let the occupant of every apartment, the inhabitant of every street—let each and all record their signatures upon this great and growing subject. A general expression of the feelings of the metropolis, couched in respectful language, and to every signature the address carefully appended, would be the best reply to those who proclaim the people's political satisfaction with things as they are, as well as the best rebuke to those who have driven us to such a mode of petitioning."

Several hundreds of these "Score Petitions," as they were called, were forwarded to us for presentation to Parliament; but the mass of the Chartist body, discouraged by the result of their different petitions to that House, seemed doggedly resolved to petition it no more, but to wait the chances of events, the conflict of parties, or the pressure of circumstances, for the attainment of that "justice" which their prayers and petitions had failed to secure for them. Thousands of the most enterprising and thoughtful among them—men who, by their industry, skill, and economy, had accumulated the means of emigration—shook from their feet the dust of their unjust and ungrateful country, and are now enriching other lands with their labours.

The tools of our aristocracy are often prone to talk of the bad feeling and ingratitude displayed by a large portion of the American people, as well as by many of our Colonists, towards the mother country; forgetting that these feelings had their origin in their own base ingratitude; they having refused to acknowledge (save as serfs and instruments) the men who, by their skill and labour, had contributed to their country's greatness—men who, when ground down and forced from the homes of their fathers, with the bitter remembrance of their past treatment, have very naturally stirred up hearts to sympathise with them, among those into whose ears they have told their tale of wrong.

I may here state that the People's League lingered on, without being able to do anything very effective, till September, 1849, when it was dissolved, since which time I have chiefly devoted my energies to Education.

Some efforts, however, having been made in this year, by a portion of Middle Class Reformers, in favour of Household Suffrage, induced me *individually* to put forth an appeal to them on this question, entitled " Justice safer than Expediency." In this I endeavoured to show that justice was likely to be compromised, and misery and discontent prolonged by the course they seemed disposed to adopt; and that it was an expedient as foolish as it was unjust to give the right of suffrage *to the tenement* and *not to the man.* That while Household Suffrage *would embrace the ignorance* that might be found in cot and hovel, *it would exclude the intelligence* of clerks, mechanics, and professional men who live in lodgings, and single men who live at home with their friends. That it would also carry with it the thousand legal quibbles of house, tenement, land, rating, and taxing, which have rendered the Reform Bill a nullity; and which have wasted a countless amount of time and money in the vain attempt to unravel their legal and technical mysteries. And that they might be assured that the adoption of a Household Suffrage would not settle the great question of representative right; for the excluded class would keep up and prolong the agitation, and be more and more clamorous as the injustice towards them would be the more apparent.

CHAPTER XIX.

In this same year I published in *Howitt's Journal* an "Address to the People of the United Kingdom on the State and Condition of Ireland."* The following extracts will convey its character :—

"Fellow-Countrymen,—We presume to address you on this important subject because we conceive that we have, 'each and all,' a common interest in all that concerns our country or our race; and because we believe that we shall all be wanting in our moral and political duties if we remain apathetic when starvation and misery abound, or keep silent when *justice* is withheld, or *wrong* about to be perpetrated on any portion of our brethren.

"And, without undervaluing the exertions that have recently been made to mitigate the wretchedness of Ireland—and feeling a deep interest in the warm and generous sympathy that from the hearths and homes of England has been extended to relieve the starving people of that country—we, nevertheless, believe *that justice is about to be withheld, and wrong perpetrated* towards the millions in both countries, *unless the voice of England shall unite with that of Ireland in a demand for Justice, and not Charity.*

"Fellow-Countrymen,—We have no desire to lacerate your feelings with the horrible details of starvation, outrage, and revenge, which years of oppression have engendered, and famine and despair recently aggravated; but we would direct your attention to the necessity that exists for your thoughtful enquiry and earnest resolve, so as to prevent, if possible, an annual recurrence of this unparalleled misery.

---

* This was the year of the famine.

" You have seen that our rulers, instead of providing effective remedies to prevent a recurrence of these evils, are content in administering mere palliatives or doles of charity, which are to be extracted from the industrial energies of *the many* to support the unjust privileges of *the few*. An additional burthen of eight millions is to be placed upon the back of industry—the blight of heaven— producing starvation to thousands—is to be made a pretence for improving the fortunes of absentee idlers, and maintaining domestic spoilers in their unjust possessions— the canker is still to be left to prey upon the heart of Ireland—English industry must continue to bear the burthens the disease engenders, and Parliament must again, session after session, be engaged in the old routine of *coercion* or *delusion* for Ireland.

" Seeing, then, this system of injustice, and having so long felt its baneful results, is it not high time to demand from our rulers that those annual legislative tinkerings for the evils of Ireland shall speedily be put an end to, by a measure that shall at once be just and comprehensive ?—a reform aiming at *the elevation and enlightenment of the people, and the prosperity and happiness of the country*, instead of permitting *the unjust privileges of individuals* to stand in the way of all just reformation, and to retard the improvement *of a nation*.

" The *causes* which have produced, and which serve to perpetuate destitution, periodical famine, and misery in Ireland, and *the means that can be devised for the improvement of that portion of our brethren*, are questions in the solution of which all are interested, physically and morally, from the poorest labourer in the kingdom, whose scanty wages are dependant on the causes which bring competitors from Ireland, to the possessors of wealth and affluence, whose capital is often wasted or rendered profitless by reason of the wrongs inflicted on that unhappy country.

" Forming, therefore, a portion of those interested in the peace and prosperity of our Irish brethren, and urged by a sense of duty to endeavour to stimulate your enquiries and active interference in their behalf, we respectfully submit for your consideration *what we conceive to be the causes* which have mainly contributed to the deplorable condition of that country, and at the same time to suggest *such remedies* as we conceive would greatly mitigate the misery of the people, and form the means of gradually elevating their social condition.

"The primary cause of most of the evils which afflict Ireland, we humbly conceive can be traced to the legislative and executive power having hitherto been vested in the *few* instead of the *many*, those few having legislated for, and governed Ireland for their own individual interests and aggrandisement, instead of seeking to improve the country and elevate her population.

"That by virtue of this unjust power the few have gone on gradually extracting the wealth and productive capital of the country—too often to spend out of it, in supporting their extravagances and debaucheries—till they have beggared and pauperised the greatest portion of the people.

"That these evils have been greatly augmented by *the Established Church of Ireland*, to support which the people have been unjustly taxed and cruelly treated; and which Church has only served to perpetuate religious feuds and animosities, instead of uniting the people in the bonds of charity and human brotherhood.

"This state of destitution, misery, and religious antagonism, has naturally engendered strife, violence, and frequent commotion; to subdue which Ireland has been still further drained and coerced, till she is nearly converted into one great arsenal of soldiers and policemen.

"That this turbulent state of things has gradually driven out *the trade and commerce of Ireland*, nearly annihilated *her manufacturing and trading classes*, and left few others than victims and their oppressors.

"That instead of the resources afforded by trade and commerce to employ her continually-increasing population, the greater portion of them have been *thrown back upon the soil*, for their miserable subsistence of potatoes, which has increased the competition for land to a degree to which no other country affords a parallel.

"That this rife competition has been greatly augmented, and the evil extended by the present rent and profit-grinding system; with its land-agents, underletting, minute divisions, and short and uncertain tenures; which in their operation prevent farming from being carried on successfully, so as to employ labourers at decent wages, or to increase the capital of the country.

"That this struggle for a subsistence out of the soil has placed the millions of Ireland, both farmers and cotters, in a state of wretched dependence on their landlords, too many of whom are regardless of every principle of humanity and justice; and who, when the people are likely to become burthensome or troublesome, scruple not to turn them out upon the world to starve and die.

"That these conjoint evils have depressed the energies of the people, and paralysed the hand of improvement, which, joined to the neglect of education, have fostered feelings of enmity between the two countries, when sympathy and union are essential for the progress and emancipation of both.

"Fellow-countrymen, we have thus endeavoured to trace some of *the prominent causes* which we think have produced the present misery of Ireland; but whether we have traced them correctly or not that misery exists, and is such as demands prompt and efficient redress. The evil of a destitute and famishing people maddened by oppression, and filled with despair, is not to be depicted in all its naked hideousness; but our imaginations may form some conception of the mental and physical wretchedness that must be concealed, in secret and in sorrow, from the soul-harrowing records which have recently been proclaimed through a thousand channels.

"In venturing, fellow-countrymen, to suggest such *remedies* as we deem necessary in the present state of Ireland, we do not conceal from ourselves the difficulties which stand in the way of such being rendered effective, nor do we expect to escape censure for presuming on a task which has perplexed abler heads. But we put forth our suggestions in the hope of leading you to the investigation of the subject, so that, ere long, still more effective measures may be devised, and your combined efforts force them on the attention of our rulers, as being far better means for securing the peace of Ireland than wretched Charities or Coercion Bills; for it is to you, the industrious millions, that the people of Ireland must ultimately look for redress, and not to political parties or class interests.

"The remedies we conceive should embrace:—

"*First,* means to provide for the pressing and immediate wants of the destitute, the aged, and infirm.

"*Secondly,* means to check the deteriorating process, by which farmers are converted into cotters, and cotters eventually turned out of their wretched holdings, to become mendicants or starve.

"*Thirdly,* to open up other sources of employment than that of the present wretched system of agriculture, so as to prevent those contentions and crimes, which have their origin for the most part in the present competition for land.

"*Fourthly,* to remove the chief cause of religious strife and contention, and provide for the general education and improvement of the people.

"To provide for the pressing wants of the people, the landowners of Ireland, we respectfully conceive, should at once be made responsible to the claims of justice, *by the enactment of a just and comprehensive Poor Law;* a law by which their property should be directly taxed to meet the wants and necessities of their respective districts; and which law should be administered in a humane and just spirit, instead of being made exclusive and degrading.

"To improve the present state of agriculture in Ireland, and to give the farmer some reasonable chance of increasing his capital, *some legal enactment is necessary to do away with the present sub-letting system, and its deteriorating evils; and to compel landlords to grant leases of not less than fourteen years, free from all unreasonable restrictions, and at the same time to secure for the tenant at the end of his term a fair equivalent for what improvement he may have made on his farm.*

"To provide for great numbers now dependent on casual

labour, and often in extreme destitution, the waste and unreclaimed lands of Ireland, amounting to upwards of 5,000,000 of acres, now nearly profitless to the owners, and injurious to the country, should be appropriated by Government, and improved and applied by them to meet the wants of the people.

" That the superfluous, wealthy, Established Church of Ireland—a lasting source of national contention—should be removed, its existence being as unjust in principle as its tithe gleanings and merciless exactions have been anti-religious and criminal in practice, and its land and re-venues, producing an annual income of nearly £2,000,000, should be applied to the improvement of the country, leaving only a suitable income to each clergyman where there are actual congregations.

" That the property and income-tax should be extended to Ireland, and the revenue raised from that, and the sources referred to, be applied for the next ten years at least to the reclaiming of waste lands, the making of im-proved roads, the establishing of mines and fisheries, the improvement of harbours, the erecting of schools, and for promoting other national improvements.

" That the reclamation of the waste lands and all other national improvements should, in our opinion, be placed under the superintendence and direction of a General Board in Dublin, and as many district boards as may be found necessary throughout Ireland : such boards to be ap-pointed by Government, and composed *of such competent persons as have the confidence of the Irish people*, without reference to their creeds, class, or political opinions.

" In putting forth the suggestions we shall probably be reminded of our proposed interference with ' the rights of property.' We may be told that a Poor Law to relieve the destitution of Ireland, would swallow up the landed revenues of that country; that an appropriation of the waste lands of that country would be a monstrous and unjust confiscation ; and that the lands and revenues of the Established Church should be held as sacred and inviolable as any other property in the kingdom.

" To all such assertions we would reply, that all property

originating in conventional arrangements, and founded on *public utility*, must be ever tested by that standard; and when the wants of starving millions, and the luxuries of a selfish few, are so tried and tested, justice and humanity will find little difficulty in settling the question. And as the rich and powerful have hitherto found, in their legislative appropriations of waste and common lands, no very formidable obstacle *in the claims of the poor man to his share and property in the village green or common*, we can discover no just obstacle in the way of legally appropriating the waste lands of Ireland to relieve her famishing people. And as to the property of the Irish Church, that too, must yield to the claims of utility and justice. It had its origin in cunning, fraud, and force; it has changed its possessors with the opinions of the times, or the power of rulers, and it must speedily yield its unjust accumulations to the better fulfilment of its mission; that of '*relieving the poor and binding up the broken-hearted.*'

"In our proposals we have suggested that for the next ten years the revenue raised from the sources referred to, should be solely devoted to the improvement of Ireland, and applied under the direction of those who possess the confidence of the people, who, having means at their disposal, would doubtlessly seek to call forth new energies and improved habits among their present forlorn and destitute countrymen. Such an arrangement, we believe, would not only be advantageous to Ireland, but to the people of this country also; for the people of Ireland, on perceiving a just and comprehensive plan of reform being carried out under the direction of their friends and advisers, would, we believe, cordially cooperate with the Government to render it effective; so that our labour market would soon have fewer competitors, our present expensive establishment of soldiers and police for the ruling of Ireland might be dispensed with, and all classes peacefully bent on the improvement of their country, would soon cause capital, trades, and manufactures to take root there; which, with extended education and increased freedom, would speedily spread peace and happiness where contention, misery, and desolation dwell."

Since this was written many of the suggestions contained in it have been carried into effect, with many benefits resulting from them. Other beneficial reforms would doubtlessly have taken place, but for the impractical projects of Irish politicians, directing people's minds away from real grievances, to such projects as a Repeal of the Union, Fenianism, Home Rule, &c. The Home Rulers, however, have one special grievance to complain of, in common with the people of England, Scotland, and Wales— that of the great difficulty of having local matters readily attended to by the General Parliament. This grievance I think, ought to be at once redressed, and that by having the kingdom divided into districts, to each of which should be referred for legislation all local matters pertaining to the district. The General Act of Parliament, for establishing such kind of Home Rule, should, however, carefully name the various subjects of which these district legislatures should take cognizance; taking care that no locality should have it in its power to restrict public liberty, or the right of public meeting, speaking, writing, or printing, nor meddle with the rights of property, nor interfere with religious liberty, and the right of conscience, nor have power to interfere with the education of the people, other than Parliament prescribes—all such subjects, and many more, should be matters of legislation and control by the whole Kingdom through the General Parliament.

Stopping at Birmingham for a few days in this year with my kind and amiable friends Mr. and Mrs. Goodrick— he being now Alderman and Justice of the Peace—whose cordial hospitality, and warm and generous friendship, for a great number of years I shall ever remember with feelings of gratitude, my attention was directed to some peculiar doctrines on the "Peace Movement," in a periodical entitled the *Family Herald*.* As one of the advocates of that important movement—conceiving it to be, not a sectarian, a party, or merely a national question, but

---

* Mr. Cobden first pointed this out to Mr. Joseph Sturge, and he wished me to write an answer to it.

a question of universal humanity, embracing all nations, yet existing on the earth, and concerning all that are yet to be—I deemed it my duty to reply to it as I best could. A note, however, by the editor, expressing his wish to steer clear of controversy, determined my friend George Goodrick to get it printed in a pamphlet form. It was entitled " The Peace Principle—the Great Agent of Social and Political Progress." It being of a controversial character, I shall refrain from making any quotations from it. From a kind letter which I received from Mr. George Combe respecting it, I think it well to extract the following as evidencing the philanthropic, and hopeful disposition of the man :—

"But the prevalent religious creeds do not recognize man's moral character with sufficient force and faith to give the religious members of the community confidence to act on it as a natural truth. Hence we have armies with Christian chaplains going to battle in the name of God, not in defence of their own soil, which would be justifiable, but to conquer nations half the globe distant, and the public at home applaud their achievements. There is no remedy for this, that I see, but to preach and teach the true nature of man and his relations to the physical creation and to God ; and when these are understood soldiers will be disbanded and ships of war discontinued, as no longer necessary. It appears to most people utopian to expect such a day to arrive; but so did your ancestors and mine think it utopian to imagine that a day would ever come when the walls of Carlisle and Berwick-upon-Tweed might be dismantled, and Englishman not fear Scot nor Scot fear Englishman, and yet *we have lived to see that day.* What has been practicable betwen England and Scotland, is perfectly practicable between England and France, and so with all other nations, whenever they have experience, as the English and Scotch have, how much more it is for their interest and moral welfare to live in peace than to fight. But all this is your own doctrine," &c.

It will now be necessary to mention, that on my resignation of the secretaryship of the National Association in 1846, its business was carried on for a short time by a Sub-Committee, and eventually by my friend Mr. Neesom, who was subsequently appointed Secretary. The Secretary and General Committee, having however, experienced great difficulty in carrying on the business by reason of the large sum of £434 then owing by the Association, being under the necessity of frequently subscribing sums of money out of their own pockets to meet pressing difficulties ; resolved in April, 1849, on advising the members to transfer the hall to the trustees, who were legally responsible for rent, taxes, and other outgoings. This proposition having been adopted by the members, and there being no other alternative than that of carrying it on, or giving it up to our landlords ; I was requested, on the part of the then trustees, to undertake its future management. The large debt was a serious difficulty in the way at first ; but with the help of my testimonial money, already referred to, and by the aid and assistance of Messrs. Mollett, Neesom, King, McKenzie, and other kind friends, the difficulty was lessened year after year, and has been long surmounted.

For the first eighteen months of the establishment of our school I could not devote much time to its superintendence, being employed, as I have stated, in the service of Mr. Howitt. As soon, however, as I was at liberty, I applied myself to the task of making it as efficient as possible, by the introduction of such subjects as I conceived indispensable to a good school. The subject of *Social Science*, or "the science of human well-being," my kind friend, Mr. William Ellis (the founder of the Birkbeck Schools), kindly undertook to introduce into our school, in connection with several others in which he gave lessons on this very important subject. I may here state, that my acquaintance with this clear-headed and kind-hearted man, formed a new epoch in my life—for my attendance at his various lectures, and the many interesting conversations I had with him, gradually dispersed many of my social illusions, and opened my mind to the great importance of this science, as forming the chief and secure basis of morality, of individual prosperity, and national happiness. In fact, the little knowledge I was thus enabled to glean regarding social science, was the means of enabling me to concentrate and apply my previous knowledge in a manner I could never otherwise have done. I may further state, that few persons have done more for promoting a sound, useful education among our people than this earnest good man : not only by building and supporting a great number of schools, but in writing many admirable schoolbooks, and by personally teaching in various schools the important subject of social science, or human well-being. To him, in fact, is due the high honour of first introducing the teaching of this important subject in our common schools, and in simplifying what at one time was considered a very abstruse subject, so that children can readily comprehend it. It is, however, to be greatly regretted that this important subject is not yet generally taught, and until it is made a most necessary part of education, I fear society will have to pay the penalty of this neglect, in the social wrecks so many of our people become. For, being turned out of their schools without any notion of the conditions to be fulfilled for securing *well-being*, nor any knowledge of the duties they owe to society, social or political, we need not wonder at the ignorant blunders so many of them make. In most of the schools, however, established by Mr. Ellis—and known mostly as the Birkbeck Schools—this important subject is taught, as well as a knowledge of their own nature and the laws of health ; a knowledge also of the existences around them ; and a large amount of elementary science – in fact an education that will cause them to remember with gratitude the lessons received at school. I may here name a few schools, which I can remember, built, or supported, by Mr. Ellis, though it is difficult to give a complete list, as many of his good deeds in this particular is known only by himself. The first established—after our own—were the schools at the Mechanics' Institute, formerly conducted by Mr. John Runtz. Another one near the Hall of Science, City Road, formerly conducted by Mr. Cave. One at

Cambridge Road, Mile End, under the management of Mr. Pike. Another fine school built by him at Kingsland, conducted by Mr. James Runtz. Other fine schools built by him in Peckham Fields, under the management of Mr. Shields. Another built by him in Gospel Oak Field, conducted by Mr. Teither. Another established in Westminster, under the direction of Mr. Runtz. In addition to these, he has given thousands towards building or supporting other schools, under the control of others.

Conceiving all education to be defective which did not seek to impart to children some knowledge of their own physical, mental, and moral nature, I was desirous of having the subjects of *Elementary Anatomy* and *Physiology* taught in our schools; but not being able to succeed in getting either of the masters I had engaged to prepare themselves for teaching these important subjects, I resolved to set about the work myself. Not having had much school instruction, and having devoted myself, for the most part, to political and social matters, I found the task of qualifying myself to teach those difficult subjects by no means an easy one. I had just read sufficient to perceive the great importance of physiology, but had little or no idea of it scientifically when I began. The first work I got hold of on the subject was an old copy of "South's Dissector's Manual," which, with its technical phraseology and long Latin names, puzzled me exceedingly—for of Latin I knew nothing. It at first gave me the headache and the heartache, and I almost began to despair of even understanding the subject, much less of being able to teach it. I persevered in my task, however, day after day, and gradually obtaining a little mental light regarding its perplexities, I began at last to take a pleasure in my work. Subsequently I obtained the loan of other works more easily to be understood, and having eventually prepared a set of brief lessons, such as I thought I should be able to make children understand, I set about devising such diagrams as I thought essential to make a beginning. I was fortunate in meeting with Mr. Tuson, at that time draughtsman of the University College, and having explained to him, and given him rough sketches of what I wanted, he drew for me my first set of diagrams. Having formed a class of boys, and another of girls, I commenced my teaching, and was gratified as I proceeded to find that even the youngest in the class took an interest in the lessons, and very readily mastered the rather difficult names of the bones, muscles, &c. When I had taken my young ones through their first course, I was greatly encouraged to persevere in my work by Mr. George Combe, of Edinburgh, who, in hearing me give a lesson to my class of girls, was pleased to make some very complimentary observations respecting their knowledge of the subject. At the suggestion, also, of Mr. Ellis, and at the request of three of the masters of the Birkbeck Schools, I formed classes for teaching elementary anatomy and physiology in those schools ; and subsequently opened a class at our hall for giving what information I could on the subject to the teachers and assistants belonging to them. Having so far progressed, I thought it might aid others who might be disposed to teach these important subjects, and be the means of introducing them into other schools, if I printed the lessons I had prepared, accompanied by coloured drawings of the diagrams I had used. This idea induced me to write a more *advanced series of lessons* to print with them, in addition to others on diet, intoxicating drinks, tobacco, and disease. When I had prepared them, I thought it advisable to have the opinion of some experienced physiologist regarding them before I ventured their appearance in print. I accordingly wrote a note to Dr. Elliotson (who had manifested great kindness towards me on several previous occasions), informing him of what I had written, and requesting him to favour me by his perusal of it. He very kindly undertook to do this, and was pleased to express his warm approbation of my performance, at the same time correcting some few inaccuracies I had made. The work thus prepared, entitled, " Elementary Anatomy and Physiology, for Schools and Private Instruction," is now nearly through its second edition;* has been favourably reviewed

---

* A third is prepared, but I have no means of printing it.

by the press, and has found its way, as a text-book, into many schools. Among them I may name the Herriot Hospital Schools of Edinburgh, the directors of which kindly sent me a vote of thanks for the use of my diagrams for illustrating Dr. Hodgson's very able lectures on the subject given to the pupils and teachers of that institution. Since, also, I commenced the teaching of those two sciences to the children of our own and the Birkbeck Schools, those subjects have been introduced into the boys' school of the London University, and the subject has recently been taken up by the Directors of the School of Design, who have published a set of large diagrams, prepared by Mr. Marshall, for illustrating them.

In May, 1849, I was examined before a Select Committee of the House of Commons on the question of establishing " Public Libraries for the People ;" a subject first submitted for the consideration of the House by Mr. William Ewart. I need scarcely state that my evidence was in favour of this laudable object ; and among other means which I suggested for the improvement of the people was that of opening our Museums and Galleries of Art and Science on Sundays.

In March, 1850, I was invited by the Bishop of Oxford, and Mr. Henry Cole, to form one of the " Working Class Committee of the Great Exhibition." My time being fully occupied with my physiological teaching, as before described, I was unwilling at first to accept of a situation, the duties of which I might not be able to attend to. But having expressed myself warmly in favour of the Exhibition, the Secretary requested that I would allow my name to be appended to the list, although I might not be able to give as much attendance as I could wish. With that understanding I formed one of a Committee of five and twenty, consisting of persons of all creeds, classes, and opinions ; among whom were Lord Ashley, Chas. Dickens, W. M. Thackery, Rev. J. Cumming, Chas. Gilpin, Sir J. Walmsley, Hy. Vincent, Thos. Beggs, Robt. Chambers and other well-known personages. The objects which this Committee were called together for were the following :—

1st. To take means for informing the Working Classes throughout the United Kingdom of the nature and objects of the Exhibition.

2nd. To assist in promoting the visits of the Working Classes to the Exhibition.

3rd. To ascertain what means exist for accommodating the Working Classes in the metropolis during their stay, and to publish the information accordingly.

These objects, which would have entailed on the Committee a large amount of labour, could not be carried out without money, which it was suggested should come out of the *General Fund*, our Committee to be considered a Branch of the General Committee for these specific objects; for we thought it unwise to appeal to the country for funds for this particular purpose, and the more so unless we had authority so to act. It would seem, however, that there was some aristocratic prejudice, on the part of some of the General Committee, against acknowledging us as a branch or part of their fraternity; which, being taken in dudgeon by some of us, caused us to vote for our own dissolution; the motion being proposed, as far as I can remember, by Mr. Chas. Dickens.

The second schoolmaster, whom I had engaged for our school, having resigned his situation for another business in 1851, and I finding it difficult to get another *trained teacher*, on account of the school being a secular one, I resolved—(having now acquired some little experience in teaching)—to undertake the management of the school myself, with the aid of an assistant-master. The school, being a large one, entailed on me much mental and physical labour; the more so, as I had not only to devote myself to the acquisition of new branches of knowledge, but to digest and simplify that kowledge as much as possible, in order that it might be understood by the children. Liking the work, I entered upon it with some little enthusiasm; and, if I might judge from the satisfaction expressed by parents, and the increased numbers of the school, I believe I gave satisfaction. Unfortunately, however, my bodily strength did not keep pace with my mental effort; for fits of illness frequently interrupted my labours during the time

I conducted it. I may also add, that of all the kinds of labour I have undertaken, physical and mental, that of teaching I have found the most wearing to the system.

I may here state that in addition to the elements of such sciences as I was able to teach in my school, I introduced a mode of teaching *spelling*, that I think might be useful in most schools; and that is the teaching of it *as a game and amusement*,—by means of small cards, with two words on each, and graduated according to the class,—instead of teaching it as an irksome and disagreeable *task*, as it was in my boyhood.

In 1852 my poor old mother died at the age of 74, she having laboured and toiled hard up to within a few weeks of her death. She had buried her husband—a miner—some few years before, by whom she had two sons, John and Thomas, both living; the former a shopkeeper, and also in a small way of business as carpenter and wheelwright, at Fraddam, near Hayle; and the latter, a builder and surveyor, at Penzance. They are both married, and have families; and are both intelligent and industrious men. I need scarcely say that it gave my poor mother great satisfaction to be surrounded by her three sons in her dying moments; for I was fortunate enough to arrive about two days before her death. Although dead, poor woman, she yet lives in the memory of her children as the best and kindest of mothers; and, I believe, in that of her neighbours as one who was ever ready with acts of kindness and words of cheering consolation. Soon after my return from Cornwall I was laid up with a severe attack of bronchitis, having taken a severe cold on my journey back. The prevalence of the east wind and cold weather having prevented me, with my weak lungs, from going out of doors during a period of three months, I availed myself of this leisure time to finish a little work I had commenced some years before, on " Social and Political Morality." I had long conceived the idea that there were *moral principles* (apart from those enjoined by religion) which formed the basis of our social and political arrangements; although I had not a very clear notion of those principles, and of the reasons by which they were to be enforced, till I had acquired some knowledge of *Social Economy.*   Having by that study satisfied myself, that national liberty, social prosperity, and individual happiness, have their origin, security and stability, *in the morals of our population,* I thought I might be the means of directing some portion of my fellow countrymen to the study and practice of this important subject, if I put it before them in a clear and intelligible form.   It was with this hope that I commenced my labours, which I occasionally pursued from time to time when leisure served me, till the time of my confinement from illness, when I made an effort to complete my work.   This little book was published in 1853, and I may here add that, while I have every reason to be satisfied with the manner in which it was spoken of by the press, by Mr. Cobden, Mr. Hume, Mr. Fox, and others, I regret to say that it was not circulated so as to effect the object aimed at.

About this period, too, I have to record a debt of gratitude, which I owe to my respected friend Mr. Thomas Beggs, and a few other friends, who were kind enough to raise £70 to pay up an insurance of £100, which I had commenced some time previous, in the Temperance Provident Institution, so as to afford some little aid to my wife should I die before her.   This kindness I cherish with grateful feelings, for my prospects then were not very favourable.

Beyond the daily routine of my school, and the many difficulties and annoyances I met with in the carrying on of the hall in Holborn, I have very little to say of my proceedings for the next two years.   In 1856, however, when the lamentable disasters and loss of life in our war with Russia, owing to *incompetent management,* had induced the public to believe that some system of examination was necessary in the appointment of persons to office, I thought they did not carry back their principle of examination far enough.   I therefore drew up the following Petition to the House of Commons which Mr. Roebuck presented for me.   The idea, however, of such self-exalted personages as legislators, being brought to the same test of examination as " puir folk " for the Civil Service very much excited the risibility of some of them. But after all their laughter it is very probable that, in our progress to perfection, " to this complexion must they come at last ;" for the rising generation are not likely to be always contented with the wasteful and blundering management of aristocratical fledglings ; with the law-making of interested cliques ; or with the shortcomings of those who have only their money-bags to bribe their way to place and power.

"*A Higher Intellectual and Moral Standard for Members of Parliament.*

" To the Honourable the Commons of Great Britain and Ireland in Parliament Assembled. The petition of William Lovett of 16, South Row, New Road, London, humbly sheweth—

" That your Petitioner is one among a large number of his countrymen who believe that your Honorable House is exclusively and unjustly appointed by a select and trifling number of electors, compared with those who ought in right and justice, to have (through their representative) a voice and vote in the enactment of the laws they are called upon to obey, and in the expenditure of that revenue to which they contribute their part.

" That in the opinion of your Petitioner this restricted mode of election, coupled with the inefficient qualification for membership, have caused the Commons' House to be, in a great measure, composed of the representatives of parties and factions ; of persons whose interests in too many instances have been opposed to the general welfare and prosperity of England.

" That in the neglect of their public duty, or in the pursuit of their own interests, they have, Session after Session, allowed their country to be governed by the two aristocratic parties of Whigs and Tories, whose incompetent and selfish administration, in various departments, has within the last few years led to a lamentable sacrifice of human life, and to a wanton and lavish expenditure of the resources of the nation.

"That the chief and prominent cause of so lamentable a neglect of public duty is evidently to be traced to the want of some higher standard of intelligence, information and morals, for those who are chosen to make the laws and rule the destinies of our country, than that which now prevails, for (with a few honourable exceptions) the possession of wealth, party interests, title, and privilege, are the only qualifications thought of.

"That in order to redeem the folly of the past by a wiser future, it is necessary that means be at once adopted through the instrumentality of which the future legislators and rulers of our country may be properly prepared and qualified·for their important duties, so that the wisest and best of our countrymen may be chosen to govern and direct us; and by which the titled pedant, the purse-proud, ambitious, and the selfish deceiver of the multitude may be prevented from being placed in a position to waste their country's means, and to retard its prosperity, enlightenment, freedom, and happiness.

"That for the better instruction of the Legislators and rulers of England, and for a more conscientious discharge of their duties, it is necessary that the *property qualification* for Members of Parliament be at once abolished, and *an intellectual and moral standard* substituted instead thereof; as intellectual and moral fitness for the proper performance of legislative and administrative duties are of far greater importance than any property considerations.

"That, as a means of eventually securing persons intellectually and morally qualified to become the Legislators and rulers of England, it is necessary that the intellectual and moral requisites for these important offices should be publicly set forth in an Act of Parliament, and a Public Court of Examiners appointed, before whom all persons qualified and aspiring to become Members of Parliament, or to fill any other important office in the State, might present themselves for examination.

"That an examination of candidates should be made before the said court, at stated periods, and all such as should be found fully qualified should be provided *with a*

24

diploma to that effect, and hereafter no candidate should be eligible to offer himself as a representative of the people in Parliament, or to fill any important office in the State unless he possessed such a diploma of his competency.

" That members of the Legislature, possessing such diploma, who should have diligently attended to their duties in Parliament for the term of *seven years*, should— on a vote of the House—be entitled to have their names inscribed on a list of 'Persons Competent to Share in the Government of their Country,' and in the choice of Cabinet Ministers, Secretaries of State, Ambassadors, and all important public servants, her Majesty should be respectfully informed, that save such, no others possessed the confidence of Parliament.

" Your petitioner therefore prays that the *property qualification* for Members of Parliament be abolished, and *an intellectual and moral qualification of a higher standard than now prevails be substituted in lieu thereof;* that a Public Court or Courts of Examiners be held at stated periods, before whom persons desirous of becoming Legislators, or of taking part in the government of their country, may present themselves for examination. That all such persons as may be deemed qualified be presented with *a diploma to that effect,* and that no candidate be eligible to sit in Parliament, or to fill any important office in the State, without he possesses such a diploma of his competency. That Members of Parliament possessing such diploma who have diligently performed their parliamentary duties for seven years, be entitled (on a vote of the House) to have their names inscribed on a list of 'Persons Competent to Share in the Government of their Country,' from which list Her Majesty's Ministers, and all important public officers may be chosen; and as such means for securing intellectual and moral fitness in legislators and rulers would remove all apprehensions of ignorance, violence, or party having any undue ascendancy in Parliament, the franchise may be universally extended, and every means safely taken for securing a full and free representation of the whole people of these realms, granting which your petitioner, as in duty bound, will ever pray."

Towards the end of this year was published a little poem of mine, entitled " Woman's Mission." This was written about fourteen years previous to its publication, in compliance with the request of my kind friend, Mrs. Goodrick, of Birmingham, at whose house I was then staying for a short time for the benefit of my health. It was written, for the most part, during my visit, and I believe was greatly helped to its completion by her kind encouragement, and shrewd and sensible remarks thereon. One of my poetic friends (Mr. Thomas Beggs) having seen it some years after it was written suggested that I should make an effort to render it more complete than it was ; the measure of the early part of it not being accordant to rule. My school duties and other matters prevented me from doing this until the time referred to, and I believe it would not have then been published had not my generous friend, Mr. Isaac F. Mollett, kindly taken upon himself the charge of printing it.

CHAPTER XX.

THE following year (1857) was to me a period of great trouble and anxiety, occasioned, for the most part, by my connection with the National Hall. A publican having taken the premises adjoining to it, resolved to obtain our premises, if possible, for a music hall, in connection with his public-house. To this end he employed a scheming house-agent to assist him, one who boasted to me that he had travelled upwards of a thousand miles before he could find out the proprietors, and settle with them about the sale of the hall. These were three Quaker brothers, of Bristol, their agent to whom I paid the rent being another Quaker, living in London. This last had told me many months previously that he thought the proprietors were disposed to sell the hall, and promised to obtain all the particulars respecting it for me; for though I had no means of purchasing it myself, I had a friend that would have purchased it on account of the schools held in it. The house-agent referred to, however, found out the proprietors, and in some way arranged with the agent that I should know nothing about it till the bargain had been concluded. The publican having thus got possession of the premises, commenced a series of annoyances and persecutions in order to obtain occupancy, for I had upwards of six years of my lease unexpired. Having just paid off the debt on the hall, and laid out a large sum in putting a new flooring in it and repainting it, I was hopeful that if I could retain it for that period I should be somewhat indemnified for the outlay, labours, and sacrifices I had made during the time the management had been thrown upon me. I had also two large schools in it, and was doing some good, and that was a strong motive for inducing me to retain possession. This, however, was not to be, for the publican first began by threatening to stop up the passage leading to the hall, as it ran under his premises, and we had had to obtain the consent of the previous occupant for flooring and covering over a part of it. His next plan was to get a surveyor to examine the premises, and to make out a report unfavourable to their safety. But, singular enough, while the surveyor and the publican were going over the premises, to make out this report against their safety, the surveyor was, at the same time, giving him hints, and telling him how he might alter it for a music hall; and assured him that the beams of the roof were sufficiently strong to bear chandeliers. This curious conversation was overheard, and made known to me by Mr. Henry Mills, the hall-keeper, a man on whose veracity I place the greatest reliance.

With this false report, however, in his possession, he represented to the Commissioners of Police that the premises were highly unsafe, and that as we were about to have a large public meeting in it of the unemployed, who were in the habit of meeting in Smithfield (which was a great falsity), that we ought to be restrained. A magistrate's warrant was accordingly issued, and the police surveyor sent to examine the premises. He accordingly ordered that, before the place should be occupied again, a certain portion of the east wall should be taken down, and piers built up from the foundation to the roof on one side. I not having the means for accomplishing such extensive repairs went, in my dilemma, to see my kind friend A. B., who had for so many years been a friend and supporter of the school. He told me that if I entertained any hopes that these repairs would enable me to keep on the schools, and to carry on the business of the hall as usual, that he would lend me the means for completing them. This induced me to engage a builder to commence the repairs required, which, when the publican heard of, he did all he could to induce the police surveyor to condemn the end of the building nearest to his own premises also. Failing in this, as well as in an effort to obtain possession of the magistrate's warrant, so as to turn me out of the place on the plea of insecurity, he sent a person to again threaten me with the blocking up of the passage. I told him that he might do his worst, as he had done hitherto, and that the law must take its course. In the course of a few days, however, he sent a person to inquire what I wanted for the remainder of my lease. I told him that I did not wish to give up the premises, as they were well occupied. Having, however, in the interim consulted a lawyer friend, respecting my right of way through the passage, I found that my case was doubtful, and that I should have but a poor chance if I let it pass into a court of law, as *the right of way* had been abandoned by the people who had the place before us (they having had another entrance) and our right not having been established by the usage of twenty years. Then it was that I thought it well to give up the struggle, and to let my lawyer negotiate for me. This ended in my receiving £600 for the remainder of the lease and fixtures, and £159 for the builder's acccount for repairing the wall. Subsequently I received £70. 14s. 6d. for the school furniture and apparatus at a public sale, and these conjointly formed my final receipts. When I had repaid out of this money all sums due for repairs, rent, salaries, loans, legal and other expenses, there remained in my hands the sum of £290 11s. 2d. on account of the hall. Thus after labouring for about fifteen years to establish and uphold this place did it pass out of our hands to be converted into a gin-palace. Thus was an institution for the education of about three hundred children, and for the instruction and improvement of the great numbers that attended the lectures and classes held in it, obliged to give way to an institution for corrupting the rising generation; for I hold that no more efficient means for corrupting a people can be found than that of blending their amusements with the means of intoxication. It will be remembered, from what I have already said, that the magistrates of Middlesex refused to grant a music license to our Association when we first opened the hall because, forsooth, we were Chartists; persons who aimed at freeing, instructing, and soberising the people, by excluding all kinds of intoxicating drinks from among them; but no sooner did the hall pass into the hands of a publican than a license was not only readily granted by the magistrates, but some of their body, together with brewers, publicans, and their disciples, met to drink, revel, and rejoice in it, and to express the great gratification they felt that so glorious a change had taken place. Everything of course that will divert the people's attention away from all social and political improvement is by all means to be encouraged by those who live by their ignorance and prosper by their vices. Hence we see, in all parts of the country, how readily magistrates license places of amusement in connection with public-houses, and how numerous they have become in the course of a few years. It needs, in fact, little discrimination to perceive that all and every project calculated to divert our young men's attention from all intellectual pursuits, and from all efforts for their social and political improvement, meet ready patronage, praise, and encouragement from those in power and authority. When I left the hall, however, I was hopeful that I might soon meet with another place to enable me to carry on my schools as formerly, and I got my desks and other school apparatus warehoused with that hope. But after keeping them for about four years and having failed in getting any place likely to suit me, I disposed of them by sale, as I have stated. In the meantime, my kind friend A. B., having recommended me to the Treasurer and Superintendent of St. Thomas Charterhouse Schools—the Reverend Mr. Rogers—as a teacher of elementary anatomy and physiology, and my services being accepted, I continued for nearly eight years to teach these subjects there to the best of my ability when health permitted. Subsequently I taught the same subjects for nearly two years, at Mr. W. Richardson's Grammar School, Gray's Inn Road.

My educational efforts having been interfered with at the hall in the manner described, I thought I might possibly be able to render some service to the cause in another way. Having felt as a teacher the great want of books suitable for enabling me to teach the outlines of science to those committed to my care, I thought I might be able to prepare a few elementary works, adapted for imparting that description of knowledge to children; and I thought also they might possibly be found useful to working men who like myself had not had the advantage of a scientific education. I know that many will be found to smile, if not to sneer, at the notion of working men being taught anything of *science;* beings who are only expected to labour and be content in the situation in which they are placed, and to be obedient and humble to all their betters. But entertaining the notion that the wealth, happiness, and security of a country depend more on the general enlightenment, good conduct, skill, and industry *of the many,* than on the superior attainments of the *few,* I am for the education and development of all the powers God has given *to all* without reference to the class they belong to, or the station in life they may hereafter fill. And until that broad principle of education is recognised and acted upon *justice* will not be rendered to the millions, nor will the productive and manufacturing powers of our country be developed to the extent that they would be if this were done. With these notions I have laboured and shall continue to labour to the extent of my poor abilities to impart the outlines of science to the rising generation, believing that it can be easily done, and that it will do more towards enabling them to understand their own nature, to know their duties to society, and the means of making them good and useful members of society, than much of what now goes by the name education.

The first, then, of the elementary books I prepared was one on astronomy, a science that I think all should know something about, at least of its great outlines. For in contemplating the heavens of gorgeous grandeur and boundless extent—filled with suns and worlds innumerable—the mind is filled with the most delightful imaginings regarding their nature, origin, and extent; and is lifted far above all superstitious grovelling on becoming acquainted with the great facts the science of the heavens unfolds. It has been in this region of inquiry above all others that the human mind has been expanded to the achievement of its grandest and proudest triumphs ; for in striving to grasp the mighty magnitudes, the rapid motions, the unfathomed distances, and the laws that govern the majestic movements of the orbs above him, man has not only unravelled thread by thread the veil of mystery and error, but has made his knowledge of the heavens his noblest guide on earth ; enabling him to push his fearless course across the trackless ocean, to spread his bounties, extend his knowledge, improve and bless his brethren, and finally, let us hope, to link the whole world together in amity. My next little work was one on geology, a subject which I think of the highest importance, as from the wide field which it opens out for man's investigation, observation, and thought in every department of nature— from the curious and wondrous records which it unfolds of an immeasurable past—from the facts which it presents of a ceaseless, ever-changing present—and the curious speculations which it affords of the new races and still more advanced forms that may people the future—there is perhaps no other science so well calculated to captivate and expand the intellect, and to excite our imagination, our wonder, and delight; and " *Knowledge and Thought*," says the great and noble-minded Humboldt, " *are at once the delight and prerogative of man and form a part also of the wealth of nations.*" Independently, however, of the blessings that spring from knowledge, the study of nature, in all her boundlesss fields, not only serves to gratify the natural thirst and curiosity which every reflecting person has to know the purposes, the uses, and properties of the existencies around him ; and the strong desire which he has to trace the past and to question the future ; but such studies serve also to solve, or cast a flood of light to illumine, a thousand subjects otherwise dark, perplexing, and mysterious. In throwing open the stony records of geological science, the attentive student may read for himself— " without the aid of translators or commentators "—a true illustrated history of the various animal and vegetable tribes that lived and flourished on our globe countless ages before the mighty Alps that now lift their rocky summits above the clouds, were ejected from the molten caverns of the earth, and long before the fossilised stones, of which the hoary pyramids are built, were upraised from beneath primeval ocean. In those records, formed beneath the waters, may he find entombed the stony forms and distinctive features of earth's first living things. Here may he trace upwards through miles of strata, which it may have taken millions of ages to form, the successive races and ever advancing forms of animal and vegetable life; these " commencing with the simple polype, the arm-footed mollusc, the humble trilobite, and sea-weeds of the lowest forms; and advancing upwards to the succession of fishes, reptiles, birds, and mammals, up to the being *man*, and the trees, fruits, and plants on which he depends for his subsistence." These observations are made with the view of showing my working class brethren the great necessity for the cultivation of this important branch of science; not only for the great material benefits that flow from it, but for the mental pleasure it affords to all those who are anxious to know something of the world they inhabit —of the changes that have taken place on its surface— and of the beings that peopled its land and its waters before *man*, the savage, the oppressor, the slave, or the benefactor of his species, made his appearance upon earth. Entertaining also the strong conviction that man has hitherto been oppressed and enslaved because he lacked the strength and power which *knowledge* alone can give, I am anxious to see the masses of my countrymen striving to acquire and disseminate it by every means in their power; for they may rest assured that every increase of useful knowledge will be found an addition to their pleasure—will give them an increase of power for the abolition of evil—will add to their social and political usefulness—will give them greater means for producing and extending the means of happiness—and will create among them the desire to be the friends and benefactors of the various nations of the world. And amongst the different kinds of knowledge taught, and to a great extent appreciated in the present day, I know of none more valuable than *scientific knowledge*, including, of course, the sciences of social and political life. Not that any one person can be expected to master many sciences, but I hold that all men might be able to master the *great outlines of many sciences*, if they were taught them at school, and that without more mental effort than is now given to teach them the Old and New Testament History, the History of the Churches, Creeds, Collects, Catechisms, Church Formulas, the Geography of Palestine, and much of what is now designated *religious teaching*. That I am not singular in my opinion, that many of these subjects might be well exchanged for a more essential kind of knowledge, I would refer to the *Report of the Educational Commissioners of* 1861. In speaking of the then syllabus of the training colleges of the country, they say :—" But we feel bound to state that the omission of one subject from the syllabus, and from the examination papers, has left on our minds a painful impression. Next to religion, the knowledge most important to a labouring man is that of the causes which regulate the amount of his wages, the hours of his work the regularity of his employment, and the prices of what he consumes. The want of such knowledge leads him constantly into error and violence, destructive to himself and to his family, oppressive to his fellow workmen, ruinous to his employers, and mischievous to society. Of the elements of such knowledge we see no traces in the syllabus, except the words ' savings' banks and the nature of interest,' in the female syllabus. If some of the time now devoted to the Geography of Palestine, the Succession of the Kings of Israel, the Wars of the Roses, or the Heresies of the Early Church, were given to Political Economy, much valuable instruction might be acquired, *and little that is worth having would be lost.*" The lines I have italicised myself. Again they say,—" We think also that the present list of alternative subjects, omits some which are so important that the question whether they should not be made *compulsory*, in all cases, *at the expense of sacrificing some of what we have described* as the elementary subjects, well deserves the attentive consideration of the framers of the syllabus. These are the principles of Physiology, in so far as they are necessary to explain these rules which affect the preservation of health." To show the opinions of others, of what is at present taught in those colleges and schools, I will adduce a portion of evidence given in the same report; one, by the Principal of a training college, and the other by one of Her Majesty's Chaplains in Ordinary. The first of these, Mr. Robinson, of York Training College, says, " To use a very significant and very intelligible expression, the great feature of the course of study pursued in training colleges is *cram*. In such subjects as Old Testament History, outlines of English History, there is necessarily an immense preponderance of names, dates, and facts, which have to be *remembered*, but not digested." The Rev. F. B. Zincke, Her Majesty's Chaplain, says, " A very large portion of the whole school period is usually spent in reading the Holy Scriptures, and in committing to memory the Bible History and more or less of the sacred text. All the while everybody knows how little good in most cases results from all these efforts and sacrifices." To which I may add an extract from Mr. Foster's evidence taken from the same report. " The efforts of the teachers (says Mr. Foster) whom I met with appeared directed chiefly to the facts of Scripture History, stimulated hereto by the usual tenor of the Inspector's Examition." Now it requires very little argument to cause thoughtful enquirers to perceive that *science*, in preference to such teaching, affords the only means for making children acquainted with their own physical, mental, and moral natures ; a description of knowledge which would prove the best safeguard of their health, as well as the best security for clearly knowing and understanding their moral duties. It needs, too, no laboured argument to prove that a knowledge of *science* can alone enable them to understand the various great and important questions of social life ; while, at the same time, it would cause them to clearly perceive the sure and certain path that leads to their own *well-being* and that of all their brethren. Science, too, may be said to form the foundation of all those arts, appliances, and inventions that supply the wants, and minister to the comforts and happiness of civilized life. And the proof of this is perhaps more evident in our own day than in any past period of our history; for to what do we owe our vast increase of capital, our extended trade and commerce, our rapid transit by sea and land, and our varied and multiplied means of comfort and enjoyment, but to the investigations, contrivances, and labours of a few thoughtful, plodding, persevering men, whose wondrous achievements had their foundation in a knowledge of nature, and of nature's laws? In fact, *science* throws open to every enquirer the whole extensive laboratory of Nature—displays before him her immense stores of varied materials fitting for every purpose—stimulates his ingenuity by showing him her countless contrivances, from the most minute to the most stupendous—calls forth his inventive and constructive powers by teaching him the simplicity and efficiency of her wondrous laws—awakens whatever latent genius, whatever feelings of hope or ambition may be in his nature, and bids him energetically and industriously labour to apply all those means and resources for the benefit of his country and his race. And among those who have availed themselves of those teachings, and who have laboured in compliance with these injunctions, there are surely none who stand higher in the roll of earth's benefactors than those who have sprang from the ranks of labour. But great as has been our country's share in the glorious work of human advancement, and justly proud, as we may be, of the men whose labours have made our country, so far, "*great, glorious, and free,*" we must gird up our loins for renewed efforts in the race of invention and improvement, if we would still maintain our position, and enjoy the advantages we derive from it. Other nations than our own are fast applying our inventions, and stimulating their people to improve and extend them; and we, too, must, by every means in our power, strive to stimulate the latent genius and slumbering energies that, doubtless, now lie buried in the minds of our people beneath an incrustation of ignorance, prejudice, and vice, if we would continue to extend our improvements, our inventions, and means of production, and maintain our ascendency for the advancement of our own and the world's happiness. But can we wonder at the extent of ignorance that still prevails in society, when our people are taught nothing at school regarding themselves, nor of the social duties necessary for realizing the means of happiness for themselves or others; nor of the why or wherefore of the political institutions under which they live? Can we wonder at the vast numbers of our fellow men being content with mere animal indulgences, while they have the means of procuring them, without regard to present duty or future consequences, when they are taught little or nothing at school of the rules of conduct that are necessary for their well-being? Need we be surprised that thousands of our women are deficient of every moral requisite to fit them for wives or mothers; many of them not being able to cook a decent meal, to make or mend their own or their children's garments, nor even in many cases to keep them clean! when the chief requisites of their school education—if they get any—are to be able to parrot over the catechism, to say a few prayers or collects, to sing a few hymns, or to mumble over a chapter in the Bible; or, if wealthy, to acquire a few of what are called "accomplishments?" I know that "*religious education*" is thought by some to be the great thing necessary. But is this, that so often goes by the *name of religion*, much other than one great sham? I should have no objection to see the essentials of religion made a part of education; but not the mere form and shadow of it. True religion, in my opinion, is a question essentially *of duty*, and not of *mere belief*. A religion of mere belief can effect little good, neither can it continue to satisfy the mind of an intelligent enquirer. For being founded on mere *belief*, it must be more dependent on external circumstances than on deep moral convictions; for the firm belief on any creed or religious notion to-day, may be easily swayed and carried away captive by the stronger evidence of to-morrow. Hence, we need not be surprised to learn that thousands of persons of deep and earnest faith in some belief or form of religion, which they have in a manner inherited without investigation—and being ignorant of all the great facts of history, and of the science and phenomena of nature—become doubters or apostates to their faith as soon as those facts and that science and phenomenon are made clear to them. Some of them thus convinced—as we have recently seen—are content to suffer the greatest obloquy and sacrifice rather than forego their earnest convictions; while others, with less honesty, stifle their convictions, and make their religion a thing of interest, fashion, or expediency. But when our religious convictions are based on *duty*, when we are clearly led to perceive that a certain and conscientious *course of conduct* is necessary to be observed by every individual in this world to secure individual happiness and human well-being, we have a hopeful and stable religion, urging us from day to day, and from year to year, to use our best efforts for the enlightenment, moral elevation, and general improvement of humanity. The deep religious conviction that our duty to our brethren is their elevation and improvement, from their cradle to their grave, in order that they may be qualified to help on the great work of human progress, and be made participators in all that can make our earth a home of abundance, comfort, peace, love, and kindness to one another, is a religion stable, cheering, and practicable; a religion insuring happiness here, and best qualifying us for the future state of happiness in store for those who have performed their religious duties. But a religion *of belief and saving faith*—often despising works—and of forms, ceremonies, and church and chapel-going, one day in seven, is attended with less trouble, and less sacrifices, than a religion of duty; a religion, such as should cause them to feel that they have a personal religious duty in promoting and supporting *the education of all our people*, and to see that they are so taught as to be able to read and understand something of the great volume of nature, so trained as to know, and readily perform, life's duties to the extent of their abilities, and so qualified that they shall be able to surround themselves with the means of happiness, and to bless others by their labours. Such a *duty*, however, is never thought of by those who have been taught to regard the masses as mere tools and instruments of labour; whose only education should consist of such schooling as shall serve to make them contented, humble, passive, and obedient serfs. They think that they have strictly performed their religious duties towards them, when they have given a donation or subscription to the village or district school, and think themselves laudable Christians if they have whiled away their leisure hours in teaching little children their notions of religion in a Sunday or Ragged School. They never think it *a religious duty* to endeavour to check pauperism, vice, and crime *in the bud* by taking care of the thousands of young, neglected, and destitute children, and so placing and training them that they shall grow up to be a blessing to themselves and others.* No! they must first receive their street education or pilfering-schooling to qualify them for a reformatory or a prison;† or, escaping these, they must pass from one degree of wretchedness to another till they find a refuge in the workhouse, and then they will grudgingly pay their rates for their support, or give them in their zeal their Bible and Prayer Book. Do the great bulk of our so-called *religionists*, who exhibit such zeal to convert the heathen, think it *a religious duty* to instruct, elevate, and improve the vast numbers of our adult population, whose education has been neglected? Do they endeavour, according to their abilities, to give them sound practical lessons on life's duties, and to aid them by personal acts of kindness in want, sickness, and affliction? No! With the exception of a few Good Samaritans here and there— the majority of them exercise their charity as they do their religion—*by deputy;* and that in such a manner as

---

* Since this was written the School Boards are gradually remedying this grievous evil.

† Dr. Croly asserts, on good authority, that there are, in this metropolis, 16,000 children trained to crime, 15,000 men living by low gambling, 50,000 by constant thieving; 5,000 receivers of stolen goods, and 150,000 men and women subsisting by other disgraceful means. There are also not fewer than 25,000 beggars; so that there are more than 250,000 persons in the London district, of all ages and sexes, who prey upon the honest and industrious part of the community.—"The Builder," of June 16th, 1860.

to destroy all self-reliance in the recipients, and to foster hypocrisy and cant. Does the religion of *duty* influence our so-called Christian manufacturers, traders, and dealers, so as to prevent gross adulterations, spurious articles, false weights and measures, and the trickery and deceit so many of them have recourse to? Does the religion of *duty* prevent great numbers of them from obtaining vast sums of money—under *false pretences*—for carrying on their various schemes and companies, and for obtaining extravagant means for their gluttony and dissipation; or for building up fortunes to which they have no just claim? Are the pillars of the Church among the wealthy of our land influenced *by duty* in the application of their wealth? Do they bring up their children to be useful members of the community, to become wise examples, and intellectual and moral workers to help on the world's progress; or do they rear them up in extravagant luxury, idleness, and uselessness? Do they apply their surplus means for the improvement of society, and to raise up the downfallen; or do they waste them in feasts of boundless luxury and wasteful profusion—in hunting appliances and game preserves, in horse-racing, betting, and gambling; or in bribing their way to power, and subjecting the multitude to their will? Or does the religion *of duty* prompt even our clergy to denounce the horrible sin of bribery; to hold up, as they ought, the briber to scorn, or to preach against wickedness in high places? When we have so much reverence expressed for what they call *religion*, either by individuals or by bodies of men, it is well to put a few questions, and to test them by the only practical part of it worthy of consideration; for if all *religious duty* is to be put aside in their life and conduct, their *belief* or *faith* in any particular creed or religion is not worth a grain of mustard seed. What, for instance, is the religious belief of our bishops worth, when their conduct is anything but Christian?* Take one or two facts only in proof of this. They are said to divide among

---

* Since this was written, I have read of one honest, outspoken bishop—Dr. Fraser, of Manchester.

them the sum of £155,000, or more, annually, averaging
about £5,535 a-year each, independent of the splendid
palaces they live in and the influence and pickings that
belong to their order.*   This extravagance, too, is shared
among them while, according to a statement made a few
years ago by the Secretary of the Poor Clergy Relief
Society, "there are more than 5,000 curates of the
Church of England whose incomes do not average
£80 per annum, and about a like number of beneficed
clergymen whose clerical incomes are under £150 per
year.   That some of them with large families can
only afford two meals a day, and animal food only
once a week; and that they have scarcely a decent coat
themselves, and that their children have no clothes to
enable them to go to church on Sundays."   In 1869, a
poor clergyman, not far from Oxford, told his own tale in
the *Daily News.*   He said that his living was but £70 a-
year, on which to bring up a family of six children, and
that then, in his old age, he had to pay a curate £40 a-
year to do the service for him.   Surely such abundant
means of luxury and profusion possessed by the heads of
a Church, who profess the religion of Him who said that
it was easier for a camel to pass through the eye of a
needle than for a rich man to enter the kingdom of
heaven,† that they should take no thought for the morrow, and that even if they had two coats they should
charitably dispose of one of them—surely these men

---

* According to their own returns, published in 1845, twenty-six
of them divided between them £212,562, averaging £8,175 per
annum.—"Standard of Freedom," 1849.

"The Church property (said the Chancellor of the Exchequer) is
worth £90,000,000."—The "Daily News," Jan. 14th, 1874.

According to returns made to Parliament in 1867, there had been
£139,799 spent on the palaces of five bishops.

† A few of the riches gathered by the Prelates of *the Church of
Ireland alone*—Fowler, Archbishop of Dublin, died worth £150,000;
Beresford, Archbishop of Tuam, £250,000; Agar, Archbishop of
Cashel, £400,000; Stuart, Archbishop of Armagh, £300,000; Knox,
Bishop of Derry, £100,000; Stopford, Bishop of Cork, £25,000;
Percy, Bishop of Dromore, £40,000; Cleaver, Bishop of Ferns,
£50,000; Bernard, Bishop of Limerick, £60,000; Hawkins, Bishop

show by their conduct that they have little faith in the religion they profess. As for their poorer brethren—the men who chiefly perform the real work of the Church, many with great zeal and earnestness—the prelates show by their anti-Christian conduct that they have neither charity nor common humanity towards them. Yet these are the men *who talk so much about religion*, and the necessity for extending it, by preaching sermons in theatres, music-halls, streets, and highways, while with soft speech they dun the minister by dozens, and with eager hands clutch at every opportunity of preferment, and at every means for advancing their worldly power and aggrandisement. These are the men, too, who resist all reform in the Church, all progress in the State. We have recently seen how pertinaciously they have resisted any alteration being made in the old Church ritual—a compilation which their predecessors mostly borrowed from Catholicism, in order that recent converts from that creed might the more readily adopt it. Instead of listening to the true friends of the Church, who would reform in order to preserve, and would make their ritual more in accordance with sound Protestantism and the spirit of the age, they—like children over their house of cards—cry out against anyone touching their frail fabric, lest the whole fall to the ground. Yet, among these so-called *Protestant Bishops*, are to be found men who have connived, or looked with complacency, at the Popish follies carried on within the churches they rule over—places where altar-pieces, holy roods, candlesticks, tapers, and fine dresses, are thought to be the great essentials of religion; where confession, and all the mummeries and mischief of Catholicism are in full swing, and where Protestant ministers work with such zeal to rebuild all that our great Reformation was effected to destroy, that they have made the bridge already comparatively easy from Protestantism to Popery;

---

of Raphoe, £250,000; Porter, £250,000. This large amount, of nearly two millions, over their luxurious living, was gleaned from such a poor country as Ireland. The fortunes left by English Prelates are, I doubt not, still larger.

a bridge, too, that it is thought very fashionable to pass over.* But folly, superstition, and mental darkness with these men are not of importance; it is the progress of intelligence, wisdom, and mental light they dread; and, such is their zeal for the Church—with themselves at the head of it—that they have ever sought to block up every cranny by which intellectual light might enter. We have lately witnessed their zeal in this particular :—A few of the most enlightened and learned men of the Church conceived that they might do some service to society by putting forth their views on certain religious questions in the form of Essays. Now, without taking into account the opinion entertained by most of the reflecting minds of our age, that "*Truth can only be elicited by free discussion,*" and that "*It is for the interest of society that truth shall prevail,*" these men were justified in putting forth their views and opinions by the exhortation of the Scriptures themselves, for St. Paul has exhorted us to "Prove all things, and hold fast that which is good." But what conduct was pursued towards these men by the heads of the Church? Did they try to answer them? No; they had recourse to persecution, they appealed to *Church-made law;* and, when they had got *a lawyer* to expound how far the opinions of these men were in accordance with their oracles—instead of in accordance with the truth—and had to some extent obtained a verdict against them, then it was that all who sought favour or preferment put forth answers in profusion. How far any of them have succeeded in disproving *the truth* of what was stated by the Essayists let any competent judge determine. But though they succeeded in obtaining the verdict of the Church against these men, they did not silence the truth; for very speedily one of their *own order* entered the lists as a champion in the cause of *truth*—shamed into it, according to his own confession, by the questions put to him by an

---

* Popery has made rapid strides in England within a few years. There are now said to be here 1,893 Catholic Priests; 1,453 Catholic Churches; 86 Monasteries; and 286 Convents.

untutored Zulo of Africa. But his efforts, too, to free his religion from ancient error and to establish what he believed to be *the truth*, were in like manner assailed by the vindictive vituperations of bigotry and fanaticism. The *law* was at once appealed to, instead of honest inquiry; and when they failed to crush him by that costly engine, they brought the combined power of priestly wrath, from all parts of the world, to denounce and silence him if possible. But these cowardly proceedings, so foreign to justice, so repugnant to the gentle and forgiving spirit of Christianity, have only served to promote inquiry, and to kindle the love of truth in many minds, instead of stifling or retarding it. Instead of honestly investigating whether the statements put forth by their brother bishop were true or not; whether they were opposed to or in accordance with the truths of science, and the great laws of the universe, or whether the statements in these old Jewish books might not possibly be "*unhistorical*"—the mistaken notions, traditions, myths, and speculative crudities of a half barbarous people, who thought themselves the only favourites of heaven, although acting very irreligiously towards the nations around them;—instead of such sober investigations, they threw all intelligent inquiry to the winds, spurned the Christian kindness of the religion they profess, and had recourse to that persecuting spirit they are so prone to condemn in those who made martyrs of persons of their own faith. But this vindictive persecuting spirit forms no part of *true religion*; and if all those who dare question the assertions, acts, and morals, contained in these old Jewish books are to be subject to the persecution of the clergy, then must the Great Founder of their own religion be condemned. For Christ Himself is said to have repudiated the revengeful laws and questionable morals found in these old records; for he said that " instead of an eye for an eye, and a tooth for a tooth," he had brought to mankind *a new religion*, that of the forgiveness of enemies, of love to one another, and of doing good even to those who hate them, despitefully use them, and persecute them. These opinions of mine will doubtless procure for me the title of *infidel*, the great bugbear which priestcraft has set up to frighten and deter, if possible, all those who presume to question its infallibility—the only substitute that free inquiry has left it, with the exception of the Ecclesiastical Court—in lieu of the rack, the dungeon, and the ancient burnings of Smithfield. This bugbear, however, is fast failing them, and the day is not distant when men will laugh at it and eventually despise it. If, however, an earnest desire to see our National Church made a great and efficient instrument for the religious instruction, moral elevation, and improvement of our people, and to see it purged and purified of the follies and superstitions that now keep so many thoughtful and earnest men apart from it, and so changed in character that they may be brought to regard and rally round it for the intellectual light and moral and religious life it diffuses through the land—if such desires merit reproach, I am content to bear the name of infidel. But to the great end I have indicated, the Church must become *truly National*, must become practically religious ; and must *cease to be under the dominion of a bench of Bishops*. The Church and the Church Property truly belong to the whole people, and should not be made the monopoly of a few wealthy families and of an irresponsible hierarchy, whose half papal creed, selfish desires, and bigoted opposition to all reform, either from within or from without, have driven thousands into the arms of Dissent, and whose selfish appropriations and divisions of its revenues outrage all principles of justice, all feelings of true religion. The Church, belonging to the people, should, I conceive, be placed under the control and government of *the People's Representatives in Parliament*, and under the management of the minister responsible to them—say a Minister of Education and Religion, as the two functions could be well blended. But, to prevent either him or any of the clergy or servants of the Church from running counter to the wishes of the nation, as ascertained through their representatives, there should be a clear declaration of the principles and requirements of a National Church ; of the duties of its Ministers, its Government, and Management ; as well as the mode to be adopted for reforming or improving it from time to time, clearly laid down by Act of Parliament; and the present Canons, Articles, and Liturgy, together with the whole machinery of Ecclesiastical Law, thoroughly reformed or consigned to the monkish limbo whence most of them originated.* Now, without presuming to say what the national will might be regarding the extent of such reform, I may, as one of the people, rightfully put forth my views regarding what I conceive should be done to make our Church a great and efficient instrument for the elevation of our people. In the first place, I would do away with the present manifest injustice of giving to one servant of the Church *fifty times* greater means of providing for himself and family than another; and, as little difference would exist in their labours if they were fairly divided, I would give as nearly as may be an equal support to all of them. And as Archbishops, Bishops, Deans, and all such grand offices could be well dispensed with, under the government of a Minister of Religion, their present exorbitant revenues, together with the large benefices now monopolised by a few, would—if equally and justly dispensed—give a comfortable maintenance to every Church Minister. By such change, however, I by no means contemplate the deprivation of any of the present servants of the Church of just means of support; I would only apportion the present revenues and possessions of the Church more in accordance with justice, and with the spirit and principle of the Christian Religion. The next great requisite is the abolition of the religion of form and ceremony—of parroting repetitions, denunciatory liturgies, and mere metaphysical preachings, which for so many hundreds of years have been barren of any results worthy of the name of Christianity—and the substituting in their place the great practical lessons taught by Christ;—the teaching of our population, in plain, simple, earnest language, the great moral and religious duties they are bound to perform—individually, socially, and politically—in order to secure the wellbeing, righteous conduct, the peace, prosperity,

---

* Lord Chatham used to assert that we had a Popish Liturgy.

and happiness of society, and of the great Brotherhood of
man.* Such teaching, too, to be enforced by clear reasoning and demonstrative proofs, so that none should fail to
comprehend their meaning or importance. Their lessons,
too, enforced with all the outspoken truth of the Great
Teacher, meant equally for all men, of all classes and in
all stations, from the idle, improvident, and dissipated
workman, to the fraudulent, adulterating producer, the
unjust and truthless dealer, the seeker of wealth by
questionable means and crooked paths, up to the corrupt,
selfish legislator who bribes his way to power, and the
Emperor, King, or President who takes delight in contention and war. Nor should the labours of our Clergy
end here; for they should strive to kindle intellectual
light, in order to ensure moral or religious results worthy
of the name. Remembering that ignorance is the gan-
grene ever festering the heart of society, poisoning the
happiness of social life, and causing most of the improvidence, dissipation, vice, and crime, that curse our country,
they should sedulously seek to remove the far-spread
ignorance from which these evils spring. Why then,
should not some portion of the Sunday—the only day the
great bulk of our population have at their disposal—be
devoted to their instruction by their Church Minister?
Not merely in teaching them their moral and religious
duties, but in enlightening them regarding the world they
inhabit, the numerous diversified existences they are surrounded by, the great facts and phenomena of nature, of
the mighty wonders of the orbs above them, and of the
great laws of the universe in all their might and magnifi-

---

* A BISHOP'S CHRISTIAN CHARITY.—Bishop Moriarty, of Ireland,
in speaking of the heads of the Fenian Conspiracy, said :—" Oh !
God's heaviest curse, His withering, blighting, blasting curse, is on
them. I preached to you last Sunday on the eternity of hell's torments. Human reason was inclined to say that it is a hard word,
and who can bear it ? But when we look down into the fathomless
depth of this infamy of the heads of the Fenian Conspiracy, we
must acknowledge that eternity is not long enough, nor hell hot
enough, to punish such miscreants."—*The Express*, February, 1867.

cence ? * Why should the great majority of their congregation continue to live in the midst of beauties which they see not, be surrounded with wonders which excite not their curiosity—beings for the most part struggling merely to live, and living merely to labour ; at best, patient toiling drudges, walking in mental night amid the full blaze of intellectual day ? Are these people, whose labours bless our land with abundance, to be always regarded as the mere spokes and cogs of our great social machine without any consideration of the intellectual powers now folded up within them ? Must ignorance continue to engender ignorance and produce its annual crops of vice and crime, while our clergy—whose duty, above all men, should be to diffuse mental light through the land—are restrained by their ecclesiastical tether to the narrow circle

---

* Anecdote of Euler, told by Arago, in the Chamber of Deputies, 1836.

" ' Euler,' he said, ' was eminently pious. One Sunday afternoon, a celebrated preacher of one of the Berlin Churches said to him,— " Alas ! the cause of religious truth is lost—faith no longer exists. Would you believe it," said the preacher, " I pictured creation in all its poetry, in all its marvellous beauty, I cited the philosophers of old, I quoted the Bible itself ; half my audience slept, the others left the Church !" ' Try the following experiment ' said Euler—' instead of quoting Greek philosophers to convey an idea of the vastness of creation, tell your audience *of the facts Science reveals to us.* Tell them that the sun is 1,200,000 greater than our earth. Tell them that the planets are worlds ; that Jupiter is fourteen hundred times larger than our earth ; describe to them the wonders of Saturn's ring. Tell them of the stars, and convey an idea of their distance by the scale of light. Tell them that *light traverses eighty thousand leagues per second.* Tell them that there exists not a star whose light reaches us in less than three years. Tell them that, from several, the light only attains our hemisphere in thirty years—and then, from positive facts pass on to the great probabilities of scientific discovery. Say, for instance, that certain stars might be visible millions of years *after their annihilation,* because the light they emit requires several millions of years to reach our earth, &c., &c.' Next Sunday, the great Euler awaited his friend's arrival with impatience. He came, but depressed and profoundly afflicted. 'What !' exclaimed Euler, 'what has happened ?' 'Ah !' replied his friend, 'I am most unfortunate. My congregation forgot the respect due to God's holy temple—do you believe it ? *they cheered me.*' "

of forms and ceremonies, and the putting forth of old drowsy inanities, the endless repetitions of which neither enlighten nor improve? Our clergymen have all received a liberal education—though not always the best—such as with little study and application would qualify them for this great work, were they freed from the trammels that now bind them and found it to be a portion of their duty. Imagine, then, our twenty thousand clergymen to be earnestly employed in the great work I have indicated—of teaching our people their moral and religious duties, and enlightening them by every means in their power—do you think the future century of the Church would be so barren of good results as the last? Do you think we should have so many thousands of Dissenters leaving it by reason of its creed, forms, and barren teachings? Do you think we should witness so much ignorance, improvidence, drunkenness, vice, and crime in the land, if our clergy, with the means they have at their disposal, had been engaged in enlightening our people and in teaching them their moral and religious duties, in place of their parroting services and metaphysical moonshine? Should we have the strange anomaly we now witness of Prisons, Reformatories, and the increase of outrageous crimes, rising side by side and spreading widely, with the rising up of new Churches, new Schools, and the formation of new Missions, if our clergy had been employed in teaching our people *their duties* instead of Creeds and Catechisms? Seeing, then, these shortcomings and silly ritualistic doings of our National Church, is it not high time to effect a reformation in its teachings or to apply its vast revenues to more useful purposes? I must confess that, while entertaining the strongest repugnance to our present Church system, I would prefer an Act of Parliament for its reformation rather than one for its disestablishment or its abolition, seeing what a glorious instrument for progress it might be made.

Christianity, as taught by Christ himself, appears to me to be a very plain, simple, and practical religion, which all who can read and rely on their own common sense may readily understand, without expounders or commentators. It is, to "love God with all our heart, our soul, and strength, and to love our neighbours as ourselves;" on which two commandments, said Christ himself, "hang all the laws and the prophets." Now, in what better manner can we show our love to God, or to that great Power to which all suns, worlds, and all existences are to be attributed, and all laws for their guidance, and all means for their support and maintainance ordained, than by diligently seeking to acquire a knowledge of those wonders and existences, of the laws that govern and minister to their harmony, and in endeavouring to obey and live in accordance with those laws by every effort of our will? In what better way can we show our love to God than in seeking to promote the happiness of the creatures he has formed; and more especially of the most intellectually endowed of all his creatures, the being—man? Can we be said to love God when we allow man to be brought up in perfect ignorance of the wonders above him, around him, and within him; and to be reared up in the midst of our civilization a perfect savage, without even the virtues of a savage? Can we be said to love God when we allow millions of our fellow-creatures to pine in want and wretchedness, while abundant means for their comfort and happiness are wasted in our costly and mischievous institutions? Can we possibly perform the Christian duty of loving one another and our neighbours as ourselves, while all our political and social arrangements are made for securing the power, ascendancy, and luxury of the few, instead of the necessity, comforts, and happiness of all? Can we be said to love our neighbours, and at the same time be intent on preparations for destroying them—in taking men from their peaceful pursuits, uniting them at home and abroad for the purposes of war and oppression, and in devising the most perfect instruments and schemes for their destruction—and for no other reason than that kings and rulers may maintain their power and ascendancy? In fact, the religion of Christ, of peace, love, and kindness, and of doing all we can to promote the happiness of our fellow-men is shown, by the practice of the greater portion of its adherents, to be a mere Utopia—a thing to be talked about, and made the subject of much eloquent cant, but too good for every day's practice. Hence, soon after its nativity, priests, scribes, and rulers set about to make it more in accordance with their own interests, by gradually blending with it hearsay opinions and fabulous matter foreign to its purity. Subsequently the relics of paganism formed a part of Christian worship, as well as Judaism, or the laws and customs and the recorded sayings and doings of a half-savage people; and these old Jewish records have ever formed texts, incentives, and apologies for barbarities innumerable, opposed to the religion of Christ. War has ever met with countenance and apology in these old records, despite the assertion of Christ that his mission was one of peace, brotherhood, and forgiveness of injuries; and slavery, bigamy, concubinage, oppression, vindictiveness, and cruelty have countenance and apology in their pages. And, in our own day, what is the Christianity sought to be established in our Protestant churches? Is it not to set up anew the old Pagan and Papal decorative sensuous religion? a religion in which ornamental crosses and altar-pieces, candles and incense, fine windows and splendid vestments, shall serve to captivate and gratify the senses, while musical intonations, bowings and genuflections, metaphysical sophistry, foppery and folly, shall captivate the reason. Such progress, too, towards Catholicism has already been made in our country as to call forth the congratulations of the Pope! The establishing of convents and monasteries is openly advocated by some of our Protestant Churchmen, and priestly confessions practised by others; and, if the united voice of reason is not soon proclaimed against these mischievous follies, and some practical means adopted to check it, we shall soon have the worship of saints and relics, and the sale of indulgences, promulgated in our Protestant churches by the degenerate sons of our great forefathers who effected the Glorious Reformation.

I have already stated that I am strongly opposed to what is called disestablishment, or to the notion of having the greater portion of the immense revenues of our Church and our numerous churches and cathedrals divided up between the different religious parties into which our

Church is at present divided. For such would only enable them more effectually to build up a priestly domination in each of them : to aid them to disseminate and perpetuate among their flocks gorgeous worship, stupid forms and ceremonies, sour and narrow creeds, bigoted prejudices, and sectarian animosities, instead of the broad and beneficent doctrines of love and brotherhood and universal charity taught by Christ. I am also desirous of seeing the vast number of educated men belonging to our Church Establishment, who are not tainted with the follies of the day, employed in the glorious mission of teaching and training our people, morally and intellectually, to aspire to a higher and nobler life ; helping them to progress onwards in all that can be made to improve and dignify humanity, and exhorting them to live together in peace and harmony instead of being split up into different sects, each content in perpetuating their own contracted views, in nursing their own spiritual pride, and in binding down the minds of their followers to the creed and notions of their particular church. If we had a Church truly National-governed *by the whole people* through Parliament —its principles and laws clearly laid down, the duties of its ministers clearly defined, and all of them intent on enlightening our people and teaching them their moral and religious duties—we should have a Church loved for the good it diffused through the land, and one that would broaden in its religious sympathies, and its benevolent and enlightened teachings, with the progress of opinion and the spirit of the age.

It is under our Church system as it is, however, that the education of our people has hitherto been chiefly entrusted ; and the Church party now boast that " she has *two-thirds of the Voters of England under her direct teaching,* and that it will be her own fault if she do not imbue them with her principles and secure their allegiance to her cause." * This boasting, however, comes with a very bad grace from the Church party, when we know how resolutely at first they opposed all education of the common people, under

---

* See the Monthly Paper of the National Society, for June, 1873.

the plea that it would create a spirit of independence among them, and lead them to disregard their pastors and masters and those placed in authority over them. But when they failed to prevent the spread of education, then it was that they bestirred themselves to set up rival establishments, so as to direct the stream of knowledge *churchwards*. We have seen, from the Education Commission Report, how defective their teachings have been ; vast numbers of their schools having failed to give even the simplest elements of knowledge to their pupils, notwithstanding the large amount of money they obtained from the educational fund. Since the Government have bestirred themselves to establish a National System of Education we have seen how the clerical party have striven to mar it, or to make it an instrument they can turn to their own interests. And this rivalry and proselytising of church and chapel will continue until education is made general and secular, and *free to all our people.* But to effect this the Working Classes should bestir themselves, and resolve to have vote and voice in determining how their children shall be educated. Failing to do this they should organise themselves and take the education of their children into their own hands, which they could effectively do by a very trifling payment weekly a plan for doing which I submitted to them upwards c thirty years ago.

CHAPTER XXI.

HAVING prepared a set of diagrams for the illustration of natural history while I conducted the school in Holborn, I thought I might now, in my leisure time, be able to prepare a text-book for the teaching of this important science to children; as well as to aid my working-class brethren to acquire it. I thought at first to confine it to the vertebrated animals; but, as I proceeded with my task, I found the subject so important that I determined to treat of the invertebrated animals also. In giving but a brief account of some animals, and their distinguishing characteristics, the subject has swelled out to a larger bulk than I at first anticipated; but thinking it would be imperfect if further abridged, I have persevered as I began; which was to give somewhat full particulars regarding each sub-kingdom, class, order, genera, and family, with a concise account of each animal and its known habits. In the prosecution of this work I have hitherto laboured about four years, and it is far from being finished; and if I live to finish it, I cannot see my way to its publication. I am now in my sixty-fourth year, and from my weakly constitution cannot expect to live many years; but while I live I must keep doing something, though it be but trifling. I know not what, indeed, I should have done for many years past for my subsistence had it not been for the kindness and munificence of my friend, A. B., who has continued to me a part of what he allowed to the school in Holborn. though I have been enabled to render no other services for it than in teaching elementary physiology and anatomy at St. Thomas Charterhouse Schools, which I did at his desire, and taught there between seven and eight years. My friend was also so very kind to me that he would not receive the money I obtained from the sale of the desks and school property when the schools were broken up, but insisted on my putting it in the bank against a rainy day. Such kindness, indeed, has been rarely witnessed towards a stranger as that which I have received from my noble-hearted friend. But while I know that all this kindness is extended towards me freely and ungrudgingly, it does, however, jar upon my feelings to think that, after all my struggles, all my industry, and, I may add, all my temperance and frugality, I cannot earn or live upon my own bread in my old age. Perhaps few persons have worked harder, or laboured more earnestly, than I have; but somehow I was never destined to make money. When I was in work my earnings were never great, and, consequently, I could never save much. The few pounds I was able to save at various times, tempted me to venture into business on three different occasions, but all my ventures proved failures. Perhaps I had not the tact and talent for business, and perhaps my ultra-political principles were much against my success.

Some time has now elapsed since I made an entry in this book, my time having been taken up in teaching and in writing my Natural History. During this time the gigantic war in America has been brought to a close, but not to that peaceful settlement of affairs that I think it would have been brought to if President Lincoln had lived. Happily, by his noble conduct, and the determined energy of the men of the north, the poor negro has been freed from his bonds and can no longer be bought and sold in the market. But as long as he is placed politically or socially at the mercy of his former masters, they will hate him and use him much the same as the planters of Jamaica have their former slaves. They will grind him down, and oppress him by local laws and unjust combinations; and when they have goaded and maddened him to rebel, they will delight in hunting, hanging, and destroying him, as the *twenty million rewarded planters* of Jamaica have recently done. Fortunately for the poor American negro, as well as for the cause of humanity and justice, a great number of the representatives of the North are true to those principles, but they are thwarted in their efforts by President Johnston, and by many of his government, and whether the contest now taking place between them will end in giving negro-hating despots the power of again rebuilding slavery in some form or other, or will end in the determination of the people to crush it out for ever, is for the future to solve. And this contest between the representatives of the people and their President in America, as well as the recent contest between the right divine King of Prussia and the Prussian Parliament, and of the perjured doings and despotic acts of Louis Napoleon, brings forcibly before us a very serious and important question—*Of what real use or benefit to a people are emperors, kings or presidents?* There are times, doubtless, that occur in many states, when a man, fitted to perform a particular duty, might be wisely placed in the position to perform it, unfettered by those who are not so qualified, as Washington was by the American people, or as Lincoln was when he proved himself worthy of their confidence. But the question most important for the consideration of a nation is—not that an individual may not be appointed to perform particular duties, but whether when placed in that position he shall possess the power to control and mar and run counter to the wishes of the nation, and turn its power and resources to his own advantage—power to foment foreign or domestic quarrels—power to plunge a nation into war—to prevent just laws and wise measures—and set at defiance the wishes of the people, as expressed through their representatives? The people of most civilised countries have won for themselves, after many struggles, the great principle of representation, and the establishing of one or two assemblies or houses of parliament, the representative principle being more extensively practised in America than in any other country. This assembly, parliament, congress, or whatever other name it may assume, so appointed by the people, should, in my opinion, be *the sole controlling power and head of the state.* In most civilised countries, heads of departments are appointed by the king, or head of the state, such as the Minister of the Home Department, the Minister of the Colonies, the Minister of War, &c. These men, and the persons under them, perform the *real executive duties of the government*, as the representatives of the nation perform *the duties of legislation*, and the devising of means for the support of the state. Seeing, then, that these men—usually called the *ministry*, or the government—really do perform the work of the state, and are more or less responsible to parliament, why should not parliament have the power of appointing them, and of making them responsible to them alone, and through them to the whole nation? And why should not the concurrence of the majority of such ministry, in any general measure of national policy or execution of the law, be as effective, if put forth under the seal of the state, as if they were signed by a king or president, and counter-signed by ministers? Such ministers, too, would be more likely to be the *élite* of the nation in wisdom and intelligence, if chosen by parliament, and responsible to them alone, than if they were chosen by a king, or president, from among his partisans and supporters, or from among the factions he delighted to honour and uphold. The expenses of emperors and kings, and the lavish expenditure of courts forms no inconsiderable items in the balance-sheet of most nations; but these are trifling when compared to the evils which these useless state appendages have inflicted and continue to inflict, on the nations of the world. What is the tale history unfolds to us of the proceedings of emperors, kings, popes, princes, and rulers, from time immemorial? Is it not a long catalogue of wars, contentions, and cruelties abroad, and of persecutions, waste, profligacy, exactions, and poverty for the masses at home? Here, on the one hand, we have seen an individual's pride or obstinacy kindle the flame of war, and by the choice of reckless ministers involves a country in expense and loss incalculable—there a despotic, cunning schemer obtains the power, through prejury, of making a state-paid army his tools for the enslavement of the nation—there a pompous king asserts his divine right of governing and setting his parliament at defiance—and so throughout the world have nations been kept in submission, and constrained to do the bidding of individual despots, which their own, or their father's follies originally set up in authority over them.* I know most of the courtly arguments in favour of those state chieftains; such as the necessity of concentrating the national will in one person as an executive head—of the benefit of united energy and power free from conflicting councils—of the necessity for individual despotism on great and important occasions, &c. To all of which I would reply —that inasmuch *as one man* seldom possesses the knowledge, the wisdom, and the experience *of many,* we have a better chance of ascertaining the best mode of achieving any given object, of arriving at the truth on any given question, of reconciling different and conflicting interests, and of acting justly for the whole nation, *by consulting many men*—and these men enlightened—than in trusting to one individual, and that individual often ignorant, self-willed, conceited, and ambitious of securing his own ends and aims. But some urge the necessity for a king or president to refer to in cases of war, as if the deliberation and judgment of the majority of the ministry would not be preferable to that of a single individual. Others contend for the necessity of an executive head to dissolve or prorogue parliament, or call it together, as if all such matters could not be provided for by an Act of Parliament, and carried out by the Minister of the Home Department for the time

---

* While we in England have a very expensive government, we have escaped numerous evils for many years past by having a very worthy and intelligent woman for our executive ruler; aided also as she was for many years by a very intelligent and worthy husband; yet it requires very little foresight to perceive that there are evils arising from kingly power, and aristocratic rule to be dreaded in the future, beyond what Englishmen have had yet to grapple with. Even in Republican America the appointment of her President is a gigantic evil. For what a revolution it occasions in the peaceful pursuits of men; what contentious feelings and apprehensions it awakens, and what immense means of bribing are afforded him, in giving him the right of appointing almost every officer in the state.

being. Nations, however, like individuals, are fast progressing in knowledge; they have already in some of them seen the necessity for limiting the power of their rulers; for placing various checks to control them, and in some for setting aside the arrogant titles of kings or emperors, for that of *president*, and they will doubtless some day see the necessity for dispensing with them altogether. Nations, I believe, once freed from kings and emperors would seek to live in peace and amity with one another. Disputes would doubtless arise between them, but being free to act they would soon come to some peaceful mode of arbitrating and settling their differences; for we all know how generally adverse the people of a country are to war, unless indeed the *war spirit* is first excited by false reports and representations, and they are hounded on by the interested tools and organs of government. Instances might here and there arise when people and rulers entered into war with equal energy, as in the late war in America, as their very existence as a free government depended on the issue, for it was a question of the supremacy of slavery or freedom. But war has ever been the sport and hobby of kings, and conquest and dominion their greatest delight; and what misery and wretchedness, what holocausts of lives, what destruction of property, and what mountains of debt bear testimony to their doings? But they are equally the enemies of progress and human happiness in *war or peace.* Every effort that may be made by their own people, or by those of the nations round them they can control, in favour of liberty, in favour of free speech, a free press, or in favour of obtaining a greater share of the blessings of their own industry, these state chieftians regard as treason and rebellion against themselves, and relentlessly strive to crush it in the bud. Why have those great and evident blessings, the liberty of the press, the right of freely speaking and writing men's thoughts to one another, the right to make and freely exchange their productions, and the right of having voice and vote in the making of the laws they are called upon to obey been of so slow a growth? Is it not that those kingly rulers and their aristocratic abettors have warred against them for centuries, and are still warring with all their envenomed hostility and terrible power?   Under the plea of protecting from foreign enemies the countries they rule over they have gradually accumulated the most formidable means for keeping their own people in subjection.   The possession of those means and instruments of destruction gives birth to the desire and excuse for using them, and hence the wars they have fomented.   These warlike powers they have gone on augmenting in all the nations of Europe till the annual expense for supporting them has outrun the power of many of them to pay ; and constant indebtedness, frequent loans, and increased taxation—often beyond the power of their people to pay—is their condition from year to year. And where, as in our own country, the energies, industry, and economy of our people enable them to produce an annual amount of wealth unexampled in the world's history, and thus enable them to bear up under those great burdens, is it not at the sacrifice of comforts which our toiling millions ought to share in, and in the perpetuating of debts for our posterity, that it is monstrously unjust to contract?   We call ourselves a Christian country ! boast of the Christian truths we spread through the length and breadth of the land, and of our great efforts to spread them among the benighted countries of the world. We also vaunt of our high civilisation, and of the spread of knowledge, morality, and religion among our people; and yet with all this Christian feeling, morality, and intelligence we spend about *twenty-eight millions annually in warlike preparations.** The so-called Christian and civilised nations of Europe have been engaged for years past in devising the most deadly instruments for destroying one another, without a Christian doubt being raised by bishops or clergy against the wickedness of it, or of any attempts being made for staying the insane, immoral, and anti-Christian folly.†   A sceptic observer might be disposed to

---

* We spend also £25,500,000 for interest on the debt of former wars.

† There are no fewer than 6,220,000 men under arms in

think that they were all interested in the increase of vice and wickedness throughout the land, seeing that they were paid so well to preach against it; and that if they began to work in earnest, and to strike at the root of the evil among the great and powerful, these annual crops of vice and misery would not be forthcoming, and then their occupation would be gone.

The subject of the extension of the suffrage has again occupied the attention of the country for several months past, and though the modicum of political power proposed to be given to the working classes is but partial, compared to what it ought to be, it has excited the strongest feelings of opposition from ultra-Whigs and Tories. But the age of political exclusiveness, and aristocratic rule has seen its zenith, its decadence is beginning, and whether it shall gradually fall and silently moulder away, or be precipitated like an avalanche into the valley of political oblivion, will depend on the conduct of the ruling few to read the signs of the times clearly. The working millions are beginning to perceive the rights that belong to them, and to feel the power they possess; and when they begin to unite and organise themselves for peaceably securing them, their rights will soon be realised. Numbers, however, of the reading and reflecting part of them, perceiving that the chances were few of their ever obtaining their political rights, or the means of comfortable support for themselves and families under our aristocratic rule, have already flitted to other countries; and numbers of others are

---

Europe, and the yearly cost of men and armaments is upwards of 500,000,000.—Speech of I. W. Pease, M.P., May 21, 1867.

Russia's contribution to the French Exhibition was a monster cannon, every shot it fired costing 5,000 francs, and warranted to kill 500 men per shot.—*Star*, March 30th, 1867.

A formidable cannon, weighing 100,000 lbs., has been cast in Prussia for the Great Exhibition, but its weight has given rise to some difficulty in transporting it, the railway directors being afraid of the damage it might do to the line.—*Public Opinion*, Mar. 30, 1867.

The Chassepot ball inflicts a small hole on entering the body, but on the opposite side it tears away the flesh to the size of a man's hat.—*Star*, Aug. 27, 1868.

looking to America, Australia, and other countries as havens of refuge where the labourer is welcomed, where comforts await him, and where he will be placed on a footing of political and social equality with others, and acknowledged as a man, and to those countries they are hastening as fast as they can collect the means to convey them thither. Vast numbers of men, in my time—the most thoughtful, useful, and thrifty of our countrymen—have taken their departure, and are now enriching, and rendering powerful other countries; and the stream of emigration will continue to flow until justice is done to those who remain. The scarcity of labour is beginning to be felt, and will soon make a great change in our country, and this, perhaps, our rulers may see when too late. The remedying, however, of this state of things will chiefly depend on the future wisdom of our working classes, coupled with the just feelings of the middle classes, for the aristocratic few will never learn wisdom till it is too late. Among the most hopeful signs of our day is the disposition evinced, and example set on the part of some of our capitalists and manufacturers to co-operate with, and to share the profits of their establishments with their workpeople. These experiments, if justly carried out on both sides, cannot fail of being productive of the best results, and of bringing about that great desideratum— the union of capital and labour in the work of production, with *a unity of interests*—for, with that union the salvation of our country will be peacefully secured, whether it be effected by the working classes on their own account or by other classes co-operating with them. Such a system of co-operation would do away with the strife between capital and labour, and effect the saving of vast means that are now wasted. It would also give the workman increased means of comfort, and awaken his perceptions to the necessity for increased industry, knowledge, and thrifty habits, and for the necessity of higher and nobler acquirements, and for taking more enlightened views of his country and his race. The influence of the more enlightened and experienced persons united with him in the undertaking is also likely to be more effective in doing away with the evils of drunkenness, waste. and improvidence that unhappily prevail among them, than when they had separate and opposing interests; and the intelligence and good conduct of their associates are likely to be effective examples. But, to return to the subject of the suffrage, and the claims of the working classes to possess it, and to have a fair share in the election of representatives, these are numerous and unanswerable. They and their forefathers have converted our land of swamps, bogs, and forests into a blooming garden. Our roads, rails, bridges, and canals bear witness to their mighty labours. Our towns and cities, villages, and hamlets were raised chiefly by their skill and labour; and by their industry are daily supplied with every necessary for the wants and comfort of their inhabitants. Our ships, that traverse every ocean, attest their industry, and bear witness to their skill and daring courage. Our trade and manufactures exhibit their inventive and constructive power, and attest their skill, ability, and plodding industry throughout the length and breadth of the land. Their labours have given wings to trade and commerce, which convey the means of happiness to millions in every clime, and will eventually serve to cement the nations of the world in bonds of brotherhood. And if these testimonials to the right of suffrage fail to convince a haughty few, they can display a long list of right noble names, " of Nature's true nobility," to render contemptible those who, often without merit, were christened and *called noble* by the voice of kings and princes.

I have just completed my work on " Zoology for Schools," which has taken the best portion of my time for the last six years. It has been to me a work of immense labour; though, on attempting the task, I could not boast of much scientific knowledge of the subject; but in teaching it in my school I felt the necessity of some such work, and I thought I might glean an amount of information, suited to my purpose, from authors who never designed their works as school books, acknowledging, of course, the source from wherever I obtained it. Dr. Gray, of the British Museum, gave me several books, and lent me several others, which were of great service to me. He was kind enough also to look over my manuscript, and to express himself favourably respecting it. I begin, however, to think that I have been labouring in vain for many years past; for, having consulted several publishers, either personally, or through my esteemed friends Mr. William Howitt, and Miss Eliza Meteyard, I cannot get my Zoology or Geology published; some of them saying that the one is too voluminous, and that the other would be too expensive to get up; and some do not care to print them, as science is not much taught in our schools.* I, however, submitted them to several practical teachers, as well as to scientific friends, and I was encouraged by them to think that my works might be useful, but I laboured without a due consideration of the means of bringing them before the public. Well, I laboured for the best, and must bear my disappointment with patience. I now begin to believe that I should never have got my " Elementary Anatomy and Physiology," nor my " Social and Political Morality " printed, if I had depended on the publishers; for who among them would have cared to bring out the works of an old Chartist? It so happened, however, that at the time they were published I had the means of paying for the printing of them myself; and thus, of giving the public the opportunity of judging of them, as well as enabling me to introduce the teaching of physiology into our Birkbeck Schools.

After I had finished my Zoology—not liking to be idle—I wrote a little work, entitled, " The A B C of Social Science in Twenty Lessons, addressed to the Working Classes by a Working Man." This I was induced to write from the singular notions on the subject often circulated among working men. Here, too, the want of means prevented me from printing it, for Social Science for schools is not a subject to tempt publishers, even if you offer it for nothing, which I did. This little work may be said to have had its origin in the teachings and writings of my

---

* Two kind friends at Manchester also sought to procure a publisher for me in that town.

estimable friend Mr. Wm. Ellis, for it was he, who, many years ago, first pointed out to me the value of this important science, and urged me to the teaching of it in my schools, he having given the first lessons. During the summer of 1868, I, however, got Mr: George Potter, the editor of the *Beehive*, a working-class paper, to print my social science in it weekly, a lesson each week. About the same time I also commenced writing for the *Beehive* a series of papers entitled, "Memorandums for Future Reformers."

CHAPTER XXII.

In the beginning of 1869 I had another severe attack of bronchitis, and during the time I was confined to my room I employed myself in making a model of a *District Hall*, or permanent voting place, as well as the model of a *Self-Registering Ballot Box*, both of which were intended to illustrate a cheap, just, and efficient mode of electing Members of Parliament. For by the present expensive method of electing them few working men's candidates would have a reasonable chance, nor would poor yet competent candidates of other classes ; whereas by my plan the only expense they need incur would be *the paying for their own printing.* When the *People's Charter* was published in 1838, I made a rough sketch of a Self-Registering Ballot Box, and the interior of a District Hall, for the front page, but I had no leisure before the time stated to make models to show their operation. My friend Mr. Allen made for me a working drawing for the Hall, and a Mr. Keissler, a German, made for me part of the mechanism of the ballot-box. The model of the hall took me about three months to complete, and when finished I was permitted to exhibit it in the South Kensington Museum, but unfortunately the Council would not allow me to exhibit the ballot-box side by side with it, to show its operation. I think it was considered by them too political.

The following description will convey what it is intended to illustrate by these two models :—

" That for the purpose of obtaining an equal representation of the whole people in the Commons House of

Parliament, and for preventing as far as possible the undue influence of great and wealthy families, or of individuals who would seek to control the voter in his choice, the United Kingdom be divided into a sufficient number of *Electoral Districts*, each containing, as nearly as may be, an equal number of inhabitants, and each returning *one Representative* to Parliament and no more.

"That all persons of legal age, sound mind, and untainted by crime, who have occupied any house, lodgings, or apartments in a house, for three successive calendar months, be eligible to vote for the representative of the district they live in, and for no other.

"That preparatory to every General Election the Returning Officer of the district should cause *a printed form* to be sent round to every householder in the district, requesting him or her to fill up the same with the names of all persons of the age of twenty-one, or upwards, who shall have resided there for three months or more ; and from which forms, when returned, he should cause a list of electors to be made out.   That after proper publicity being given to this list, he should hold open Courts of Adjudication in his district for the purpose of hearing and deciding on all objections, and from the list thus revised he should cause a *Voter's Certificate* to be sent round to every person qualified to vote.

"That to secure Members of Parliament possessing high intelligence and good moral character, all persons seeking the high honour of legislating for a nation, or for filling any other important office of state—should be required *to pass an examination*, showing that they possess the requisite knowledge and ability, and should *hold a diploma to that effect* before they should be entitled to offer themselves as candidates, or take their seats in Parliament, or be appointed to any important office.

"That *the knowledge requisite for Members of Parliament*, or for other important offices, should be clearly set forth in a special Act of the Legislature, and the mode pointed out by which persons seeking such high honour, or place of trust, should present themselves before *Public Examiners*, which Government should appoint to meet at stated times and places; and all persons who should prove their ability and fitness before such examiners, according to the said Act of Parliament, should receive from them a diploma to that effect.

"That every nomination for a Member of Parliament should be made by *a written requisition*, delivered to the Returning Officer, and signed by at least one hundred electors belonging to the district, who in recommending their candidate should be required to certify to his moral character, and also that he holds a *diploma* of having passed an examination, proving that he possesses the requisite knowledge and ability required by law.

"That to prevent all undue influence bribery and corruption in the election of Members of Parliament, the votes of the electors should be taken by *Ballot.* The present expensive, unjust, and bribing mode of *canvassing for Members*, should be abolished by law, and persons punished for having recourse to it. All Committees, or other meetings, for the election of Members held at *public-houses* should be done away with, as having heretofore been the cause of much undue influence, drunkenness, riot, and disorder.

"That to do away with the present disgraceful and costly mode of electing Members of Parliament, which excludes *the Representatives of the Working Classes*, and of all other persons, however competent, who have not the means of purchasing their way to power, it should be the duty of Parliament to enact that a sufficient number of *District Halls*, or commodious buildings be erected in every voting district to be used as permanent hustings or voting places, which may be used, when not needed for the elections, for the purpose of public meetings, lectures, evening schools, concerts, or other district purposes. That all candidates for seats in Parliament should *have the free use of such halls* during the election, such as the use of the large hall below, or the balcony and ground in front—from which to address the electors in their turn—and the use of the Committee Rooms above according to lot; so that the only expense needed to be incurred by Members would be that of printing their own bills and circulars. The erection and repair of such halls should be paid for by the inhabitants of the district and managed by them, as well as any income arising from the letting of them.

"That previous to the day of any Parliamentary Election, the managers should cause the large room in each District Hall to be fitted-up with moveable fittings; and should provide a sufficient number of *ballot-boxes*, one for each of the candidates nominated, and formed on a plan for securing secresy of voting, as well as for *registering each vote given*, so that the Deputy Returning Officer might be able to announce the state of the poll at the end of the election, without the great disadvantage of counting the votes.

"That the Returning Officer of each district should be required to appoint a *deputy* for each voting place on the day of election, to see that the voting is conducted orderly and fairly, and to cause all persons to be arrested that attempt to vote unfairly, or seek to promote disturbances. It should also be his duty to provide the accredited friends of the candidates with seats immediately behind him, where they might see that the voting is conducted properly. He should also show them the register of each ballot-box before and after the voting, and should cause the correct numbers given for each candidate to be posted up outside the building.

"That every elector entering the hall on the day of election should be required to show his voter's certificate to the Registration Clerk, and if it be found correct he should be allowed to pass on towards the voting place, and receive from the deputy's assistant a balloting ball, when he should enter the balloting place, and with all dispatch drop it into the box of his favourite candidate; the name and colours of the candidate being placed on each box to guide him. After he has thus given his vote he should pass out of the balloting place by another door, where a turn-table and officer should be placed. The table before the deputy, outside the screen, should be on an inclined plane, and the channels from the balloting boxes so arranged that the ball, in whatever box deposited, should roll down the middle of the table in front of the deputy to be ready for the next voter, and thus, should any elector make use of any other balloting ball than the one given to him, it would roll out and lead to his detection before he left the room.

"That any person convicted of registering himself in more than one voting district, of froging or using any forged voter's certificate, of trying to vote in any other district than his own, of trying to vote unfairly or injuring the ballot-boxes, or of going from house to house or place to place to canvass for the votes of electors, or in any other way contravening the Electoral Act, should for the first offence be subject to one year's imprisonment, and for the second imprisonment and the loss of his electoral rights. Also that any candidate employing persons to canvass for him, or should seek to secure his election by bribery, or by intimidating or using any undue influence over an elector, or otherwise contravening the Electoral Act, should be subject to one year's imprisonment and the loss of his seat for the first offence, and for the second imprisonment and the loss of his electoral rights and disqualified for ever after to sit in Parliament.

"That in order to obtain properly-qualified persons as legislators, men disposed to devote their sole time and attention to their Parliamentary duties—instead, as at present, often dividing their time between their private business and their Parliamentary duties, or in regarding their seats as passports to fashionable society—Members of Parliament should be paid for their services by a writ on the Treasury the same as any officers of state."

A very important reason for the adoption of this plan, for electing Members of Parliament *free of expense*, or nearly so, is this—that Members at present are too often disposed to forego their own honest convictions to support a ministry, and often to back them up against the opposition in support of measures they dislike, as they fear a change of ministers and a dissolution, from the enormous expense they are likely to incur, whereas if elections were inexpensive they would be independent.

The newspapers announce this morning the death of one of Nature's unthroned kings and high priests of humanity,

Charles Dickens, one that can be badly spared from among us when so much remains to be done, and one whose equal for good to society will not I fear be readily found. Fortunately Mr. Dickens was a man whose kindly heart beat in unison with a keen intellect and a well-furnished head; so that while his searching perception left few things to escape his glance, his noble sense of duty led him to expose everything corrupt, unjust, mean, or hypocritical. In his own inimitable way he has perhaps done more to expose wrong and injustice and to improve society socially and politically than any other worker or writer of the present century; at least he had few to equal him in the good work. His happy description of the *Circumlocution Office* and "how not to do it," was a blistering application that the thickest official hide could not but have felt severely; and the scathing doubtlessly did much good as an official stimulus to action and as a corrective of many abuses; although great numbers of *the barnacle tribe* still stick very tightly to our state vessel. His lucid expositions, too, of our vast social misery and wretchedness in close contact with luxury, waste, and superfluous grandeur, and his kindly and graphic pictures of the heroes and worthies of humble life have done much to arouse people to a sense of duty and to a great amelioration of the evil, although not to the extent desired; for so great is our social misery, and so indifferent to it are so many people, that the lessons of duty need to be as frequently repeated and as earnestly enforced as they were by Charles Dickens. Nor was he forgetful of the higher duties of morality and the duties of true religion, for scattered through his numerous works may be found moral lessons and practical sermons, more truly religious, pathetic, and heart-piercing than ever bishop devised or priest delivered.

In 1870 I was requested by the Secretary of the Alliance to write a few articles for their paper. Having been a member of that body from the first, and believing the drink traffic to be one of the greatest of our social and political evils, I complied with his request, and several of my articles appeared in their paper. One of them they sent to the Social Science Congress then sitting at Newcastle. In this article I endeavoured to show my working-class brethren that no general permanent increase of their wages can possibly take place without a general increase of capital, or rather of that portion of it that is paid in wages. That every increase of capital, especially in the hands of the working classes themselves, would give them more employment and better wages ; and that every wasteful diminution of capital would give them less. That were the working classes to economise and save what they now extravagantly waste in intoxicating drinks—consisting of nearly a hundred millions annually, besides the annual expenditure necessitated by drink-made paupers and criminals—there would soon be employment for all, and a great increase of wages. That a very little reflection must convince them that, if this immense sum were saved and annually added to the capital of the country and employed, as most of it would be, over and over again in the work of production, instead of being drunk and wasted year after year, that our unemployed would speedily find work at good wages, and the cost of most necessaries and comforts greatly cheapened by reason of their increase and abundance To this state of things, coupled with the increased intelligence, the economical habits, and improved tastes that sobriety would be certain to engender, there would soon be abundance of capital flowing from the ranks of labour, as well as the knowledge to make a wise application of it.

Alas! there is now another terrific war raging between Germany and France, and is rendered more terrible and destructive by the new inventions and improvements recently made in this accursed art. This war, originating in the restless ambition and jealous feelings of the Emperor of the French, and urged on by the mercenary tools dependant on his will, made an unprovoked attack upon the German people, with the object doubtless of preventing that unity of their conflicting elements which patriots of all opinions among them have so long desired. This unjust interference with the rights of a people very naturally called forth the whole warlike power of the nation to repel it, and so rapid and successful were their movements that

27

the tide of war, which was sought to be carried on to their capital, was speedily rolled back upon the soil of France. Battle after battle soon proved the power and superiority of the German armies ; and after a series of bloody contests, marked by the destruction and misery of thousands upon thousands of lives, the Emperor of the French and a great part of his army were obliged to capitulate, and one town and fortress after another yielded to the victor, till at last Paris itself was surrounded by German armies. The chief originator of the war having been captured, and a provisional government formed in Paris, of men who opposed the Emperor and repudiated the war from the beginning, they naturally wished to put an end to the contest. But here again the ambition of kingly power came in to thwart it: the king of Prussia and his nobles, not content with having driven the enemy from their soil, and to have proved their warlike superiority in many battles, but they now wanted a large portion of the territory of France, in addition to an enormously large indemnity in money—and that without regard to the wishes of the inhabitants, and in opposition also to a considerable portion of the German people, whose leaders and organs were despotically silenced for declaring against the injustice. In this predicament the French people have resolved to defend themselves to the last, and the German Government would seem resolved to crush them ; what will be the result time must show.*

But, pending the settlement of this destructive contest, is there no lesson to be derived from it ? Is there none that the people of Europe can learn from it that may be profitable for their future welfare ? Seeing the misery and wretchedness that one ruler has originated and another is perpetuating, will they still content themselves with placing royal and despotic rulers at their head, to be continually involving one country or another in war, misery, and ruin ? when, if their own *free Parliament, composed of freely chosen representatives, were alone the supreme head of the country,* the

---

* An heroic resistance on the part of some, defiance by others, and a sad and reckless ending, after great sacrifice of life ; and to be conquered, after all !

just interests and welfare of the whole people would soon lead them to devise the peaceful settlement of every national quarrel. Will the productive classes of Europe still continue to keep up the competitive race their rulers have been so long pursuing, in providing more and more expensive armies and navies, and more and more destructive means of killing one another? And that, too, while they talk of Christian brotherhood and advancing civilisation? These *standing armies* and *powerful navies* are not only standing menaces to incite nations to war, and ready tools in the hands of any unprincipled ruler, but are a profligate waste of the productive capital of the people of the various countries—perpetuating a state of poverty and misery among them. During the present century there have been upwards of fifty of those terrible wars among the so-called " Christian nations of the world," people whose professed creed is one of peace, brotherhood, love, and charity among all mankind ; and, during these horrible contests, who can estimate the number of lives that have been sacrificed, the millions of money that have been wasted, the multitude of children that have been made fatherless, the homes that have been rendered desolate? The armies of Europe alone at the present time are said to be composed of *seven millions and a half of men,* and to cost about *two hundred and sixty millions annually*—an amount of men and money which, if employed productively, would bring joy and happiness to millions of homes, where poverty and misery now crush down their inmates.* And for whose benefit and advantage is all this expense, profligacy, and waste? Why, to support a few royal or imperial families in pomp and power ; to give them and their aristocratic satellites military toys to play with and boast of ; to keep up titled and privileged orders, to the exclusion of worth and merit ; and to *keep the toiling millions in subjection.* Rulers and statesmen, as well as legislators, are undoubtedly needed in all countries for the maintenance of order, and for securing, as far as

---

* The " Times " of Feb. 21st, 1859, said that the cost of our own army is just £10,000 a day. Think, working men, what this sum would do for the improvement of our country.

possible, life, property, and freedom ; and who is better to do this than *representatives freely chosen by the whole people*, together with the *ministers* or the heads of departments and the chief officers that they may appoint, and who should be responsible to them?   And this without the useless expense of royal cyphers or despots, to sign their names to public documents ; to appoint pliant tools to suit their purposes, in every important office ; to thwart by intrigues and vetoes the laws and wishes of the people's representatives ; and to embroil their people in war and misery, through their pride, ambition, or dynastic relations. War, I believe, will never cease in the world till the rule and destinies of nations are placed in the hands of the people's representatives.

The great want in the present day is, I conceive, to do that *for all the Nations of the World*, that has been done for *the individual people of all civilized countries* : namely, to bring *all nations*—as individuals have been brought—within the influence and operation of *Law*, and of a superior authority to control them, whether the nation be great or small, strong or weak.   The first requisite to this end would seem to be a Congress of Nations, composed of Representatives from all civilized countries, to devise a *Code of International Law*, which, without interfering with the Constitution, Law, or Government of any country, should *declare war to be a crime*, which all nations hereafter will unite to prevent, as well as to punish its instigators. Such Code should also provide laws for the peaceful intercourse of the people of all nations, by sea and land ; and, while accepting the present boundaries of nations, should declare against all aggressions of any one nation on another ; also to provide for the peaceable settlement of all disputes by arbitration ; and should also determine what force should be retained as a police, available for the enforcement of their decisions. In connection with this Code should be established a *Standing Court of Adjudication*, composed of representives from every civilized nation ; who should arbitrate on all national quarrels that may be brought before them, according to the Code agreed to, as well as to enforce their decisions should it be found necessary—an act that is never likely to happen, as any rebellious nation would know that all nations would unite to punish it for violating the Code of Nations.

My old friend Mr. Howitt has just sent me a very interesting letter from Rome, where he is now residing. He gives a graphic account of the old city and its environs, and of its walks, sites, and curious things. He tells me also that the obstinate old Pope is silly enough to believe that the Queen of Heaven will yet work a miracle in his favour, and restore him to his former temporalities and power.

I have also had a very pleasing visit this day from my friend Miss Meteyard. I had a long and interesting conversation with her on books, as well as on the present state of things—for she is a keen politician, as well as a clever biographer and imaginative writer, and possesses a great variety of knowledge on most subjects. She is also one of the most worthy, industrious, and persevering of women; and has had a very struggling and anxious battle to maintain herself and her old aunt in respectability and comfort, for the last quarter of a century, since I first made her acquaintance. She is the well-known author of the Life of Wedgewood, a Group of Noble Englishmen, Sacred Spots of Ancient London, and very many tales and imaginative works.

My friend, Mr. Maughan, has just called to inform me of the sudden death of my old friend, Mr. John King, of Eden Grove, Barnsbury, one of the oldest of my acquaintances, and one of the staunchest to principle and truest of men. Poor man, it was only on my last birthday, I being then seventy-one, that he reminded me that I " was getting near the end," without suspecting that his own was so near, or would be so sudden.

The sudden death of my friend King has been immediately followed by the sudden illness of another old friend, Mr. Matthew Allen, of Tabernacle Walk, the clever designer and builder of the "Improved Homes for the People." The first of these he built for Sir Sydney Waterlow, and since then a great number for the Company for Building Improved Homes. Mr. Allen has a genius for designing and constructing; for, in addition to his Improved Buildings of various kinds, he has made great improvements in the heating of places by means of hot water, and was the first to construct an over-house telegraph. The homes he has designed and constructed are not only better adapted, more convenient, and more ornamental than those that were first erected under the name of " Model Lodging Houses;" as, from his flat roofs, his mode of construction, and a patent kind of stone which he uses, they are made much cheaper than those previously built, and pay from five to ten per cent. on the capital invested in them: a great incentive to builders and capitalists to build improved dwellings for the people, which are very extensively needed. Mr. Allen has raised himself by his genius, and by his industrious straightforward conduct, from a journeyman bricklayer to his present comfortable position; and I hope that his health will be preserved for many years.

Not wishing to be idle this winter, for I could not venture out from my cough, I amused myself in making for my friend Allen a little model of his Improved Dwellings situated in Leonard Street, Shoreditch.

We seem now to be approaching a crisis in our parliamentary affairs, for retrograde Whigs and Tories seem resolved to thwart and delay every effort made in favour of progress, by speaking against time, and wasting the sessions in useless obstructive talk, so much so that Mr. Gladstone has been obliged to give them a serious lesson.

As, however, these tactics are almost sure to be renewed, it will be well for the liberal majority to legislate so as to prevent the evil. Let them adopt the wise and simple measure of *timing their speakers*, and in making the House one for legislative business instead of vain talking and party squabbles. With the exception of time for the exposition of a budget, or for any important explanation from a minister, or for any member introducing a motion, *an hour* would seem to be ample, and a *quarter of an hour* for other members speaking for or against it; and when in committee a far shorter time. Members should also begin their work early in the morning, like other men of business, and should be impressed with the necessity of concluding at a reasonable time. As for the obstruction the Lords are often making—the best remedy, short of doing away with hereditary legislation altogether, is for the Commons to declare that any Act *passing twice*, in the usual way, though the House of Commons shall be the law of the land, whatever obstruction may be pursued by any other branch of the Legislature.

On calling, to day, on my friend, Mr. Serjeant Parry, he saw that old age had deprived me of my teeth, when he was kind enough to give me a letter to his dentist requesting him to make some for me. This great kindness of his I cherish with grateful feelings, although it is only one of numerous other generous acts I have received from him during the many years I have shared his friendship; for during thirty years or more he has invariably sent me a turkey, or a pair of fowls, for my Christmas dinner, and has otherwise shown the greatest generosity and kindness towards me, both in sickness and health.

I have lately been induced to join the Land Tenure Reform Association, of which Mr. John Stuart Mill is chairman; also the Working Men's Peace Association; and the Anti-Game Law League: all admirable Associations, and well deserving of support. I regret, however, that I am now too old and feeble to render them any personal service, and I am too poor to aid them with money, unless to an infinitesimal extent.

My friend, Mr. Thomas Beggs, to whom I am indebted for many acts of kindness, invited me and my wife this summer to visit him at his very pretty residence at Short-lands, in Kent—where we had often been before—to meet our respected friends from Birmingham, Alderman Goodrick and his wife. We passed a pleasant time there, for Mr. Beggs is not only a hospitable host but is also a man of considerable intellectual abilities and much information, and our friends, the Goodricks, are also very pleasing intellectual people; Mrs. Goodrick especially, being a lady of rare acquirements. She is also a member of the Society of Friends.

A Member of Parliament having given notice of his

intention to propose the extension of the use of the *Cat* for certain offences, and my outspoken and courageous friend, Mr. Peter Taylor, having given notice of a motion for doing away with that torturing instrument altogether, I was induced, at the request of friends, to put forth an Address to Social and Political Reformers on the subject. In this I endeavoured to show that the re-introduction of brutal punishments was a retrograde step, injurious to social progress. That all punishments should be free from vindictiveness, and such as are calculated *to deter or reform* (and in the spirit of that Christian charity we profess); and that, as flogging in Army and Navy has greatly been abolished, and that with benefit; and as flogging—and even death-punishment—have failed to deter persons from the commission of heinous crimes, our legislators should direct their attention more to the sources of our social evils, *with a view of preventing them*, than in devising modes of brutalizing and torturing punishments. I also endeavoured to show that brutal punishment only excites and strengthens the *animal propensities* of our people, which we should aim at keeping in abeyance, and at the same time seek the more general cultivation of the *intellectual and moral faculties* by the adoption of a wiser system of education; and also by the removal of temptations from among them, especially of intoxicating drinks, which, according to our Judges and Magistrates, form the chief source of crime and misery.

Hearing lately that my old acquaintance, Mr. Stansfeld, was about to bring forward a measure for *Improving the Sanitary Condition of the People*, I wrote a letter to him containing a plan which I had put forth in the Beehive about three years before. It was to this effect: that as the chief and greatest obstacles to the sanitary improvement of our towns and cities are the large number of miserable streets, courts, and alleys that abound in them—places often of the filthiest description, where the lowest of our population crowd and often pay high rents—places where their health and morals are injured—where disease is constantly being engendered, and from which it spreads its contagion everywhere around—that as these places mostly belong to town authorities, the magnates of the parish, or persons of great local importance, Sanitary Inspectors very generally fear to meddle with them. Therefore, in order to remedy so great an evil, an Act of Parliament is necessary, to empower capitalists, bodies of philanthropists, or working men, to obtain leave to erect on those sites lofty, spacious, and healthful homes for the people, on making a fair compensation to the owners of such property according to the decision *of a jury*, in a manner *similar to what is now done by Railway Proprietors.* And in order that no inferior or improper building should be erected on those sites, the persons willing to build (before they obtained power to take possession) should deposit with the Board of Works, or other recognized authority, plans and drawings of the buildings they intend to erect. Mr. Stansfeld wrote to me, requesting me to call on him, and in going through the matter he quite agreed with me regarding the desirability of removing those wretched places, but he thought that Parliament would not be disposed so far to interfere with the rights of property. So it would appear that the "rights of property" extend to the right of poisoning our people, and of preventing real improvement in our towns and cities, and erecting dwellings for those that most need it, and Parliament, as at present constituted, will not interfere. But a remedy will surely come, some day.

And now, as the end of my story is approximating, let me say a few last words to my working-class brethren. Persevere then, I would entreat you, in all peaceful efforts for the reform and perfection of your Social and Political Institutions, and reckon no labours nor sacrifices too great for the attainment of your objects; for on these will depend the prosperity and happiness of yourselves and country. Those who would divert your minds away from politics, and from lending your aid—however humble—to reform, or to do away with extravagant, useless, and corrupt institutions, and to secure just government, aiming at the happiness of all classes, you may safely regard as the *enemies of progress*; as you may, also, all those who would urge you on to the attainment of those objects by violence and deeds of blood; for not only are men's hearts hardened and brutified by such barbarous process, but changes thus effected are, in most cases, only changes of one set of oppressors for another. Not that I would urge you to be silent and passive under great wrong and injustice ; for, if the enemies of progress seek to block up every avenue through which the people may peacefully obtain the reforms needed, or to stay our national progress by the sword, or to get enemies to invade our country in the interests of party or faction, then your duty to your children and your country demands that you link yourselves together like a band of brothers to repel them—not by tumult, threats, and fury, but by calm heroic resistance, and a resolute determination to achieve your country's freedom or perish in the attempt. Do not, however, be led away from pursuing a peaceful and just course by any foolish fears of invasion, which those who profit by war are so anxious to excite ; but should an enemy approach your shores, think no sacrifice too great to repel him.

Examine also, coolly and deliberately, all social and political questions before you espouse them or try to create a public opinion in their favour ; for when so much remains to be done for the upraising of our people, you should not waste your energies on vain theories, impractical measures, nor in empty threats or denunciations. All such doings, therefore ; and all talk about the condemnation of capital— which is the heart's blood of an industrial nation—all denunciations of property ; or foolish threats of confiscation, tend to social discord and alarm ; and to cause all those who possess property to place it if possible beyond the reach of danger and to flee to despots for protection, as the least of evils ; and it should also be remembered that, in all social commotions, it is the poor and innocent that first suffer. Large accumulations of capital, and a vast amount of wealth, have doubtless, in many instances, been acquired by injustice ; but in seeking a remedy we should be wise as well as just, for the stability of our whole social fabric would be greatly endangered by any attempts to interfere with *the just rights of property*. The true remedy will lie in such peaceful and efficient reforms as shall prevent such *unjust* accumulations in future, and to prevent such masses of wealth from being made instruments of oppression and injustice.

One of the most prominent of our national evils—productive of exclusive legislative power, great social injustice, poverty and misery—is the vast accumulation of that land, which God gave as a common heritage to all his children, in the hands of a few persons; and these few claiming the right to regard it as their own absolute property; to cultivate it or not as they think proper; to convert vast portions of it into deer runs and game preserves; and to sweep away the human occupants thereon as so many vermin. We have recently had many modes proposed for dealing with this monstrous injustice, which it behoves us coolly to examine; but evidently the most simple, as well as the most just, is to do away with those laws and usages which have chiefly led to this unjust accumulation, such as *the laws of primogeniture and entail;* and, at the same time, legally to compel landowners and others, at death, to divide their land and other property equally among their children. But in order to prevent the extreme division of land—which might lead to the wretched cottier system—provisions should be made that no division of land should be made less than   acres, or a moderate workable farm which one family could cultivate. In addition to which long leases should be given to tenants; the land should be made to contribute, by taxation, a far larger amount than at present to meet the national expenditure, as one of the conditions for holding it;* and the waste lands cultivated, or given up to the State for the employment of our criminal and pauper population. Joined to which should be a law for the register of all landed and household property, and a simple and unexpensive transfer of estates; and for selling off all such as are greatly encumbered. By such just and peaceful mode our land would, in compara-

---

* While France pays in land tax £23,509,000, out of a general taxation of about £41,509,000, England only pays land tax to the amount of £2,350,000, out of a general taxation of £76,617,000— a convincing proof that the landowners of this country have had the making of the laws.

tively a few years, be divided into small or moderate-sized farms; a larger number of persons would be interested in the defence of our country; our waste lands would be utilized, our landed aristocracy would be more usefully employed, and the stimulus afforded by security of possession would cause the land of our country to be more highly cultivated than it is. Under such a system we should have a free trade in land, and co-operative or individual farming might take place as either might be found most advisable. The *nationalization*, or ownership of the land by Government, which some persons suggest, would, I conceive, be attended with great evils; for the present landholders could not be justly dispossessed without fair indemnification, which would necessitate an enormous addition to our debt; in addition to which the State would make but a very indifferent landlord, and the vast revenues, power, and influence it would derive from the land would make it independent of the people, and would give it a host of land surveyors, collectors, and other officials to support its power. If too *communistic views* were acted on—that the land should belong to, and be administered solely by, the *Commune*—it would only be a reduction of the evil within narrower limits; and, from what we have hitherto experienced of municipal and parochial government in minor affairs, it does not augur much in favour of communal government for such a purpose. And this brings me to the subject of *co-operation*, about which so many conflicting notions are entertained: some of them rational, and all important as remedies for our social evils, and some very unwise, and projects no ways to be hoped for, even if practical. The useful and desirable kind of co-operation is *to combine capital and labour in the work of production*, so that there shall be *a unity of interests*, instead of the present conflicting ones, which at present lead to so much social contention and such waste of capital and labour. This may be carried out in various ways; either in the cultivation of the land, in mining, in the establishment of manufactories, the carrying on of trade and commerce, the building of houses, ships, railroads, and other objects. Unhappily, the great obstacles at present in the way of those achievements are, selfish, unwise, and despotic feelings on the one hand, and ignorance, unthrift, jealousy, and disunion on the other. The holders of land and the possessors of capital are, for the most part, too proud of their position and their wealth to interest themselves in striving to solve the great social question—how shall all the resources of our country be best applied so as to administer to the happiness of all our brethren? and a large mass of our people are so intent in obtaining bread from day to day, or intoxicating drink, or a few sensual enjoyments, as to be apathetic to the social and political reforms required, such as the most active and intelligent portion of their brethren are zealously seeking to obtain for them. For this ignorance and apathy, *the most dangerous of social evils*, as have been often seen in revolutions on the Continent, our clergy and exclusive rulers are mainly responsible; the former for having been intent on teaching creeds and catechisms to our people in place of their moral and religious duties, individual, social, and political; and the latter for legislating mostly for party interests, for wasting our country's resources in war and war establishments, for the support and aggrandisement of the few; while they have left the mass of the people in ignorance, and every temptation in their way to allure them the downward road to poverty, vice, and crime.

The kind of co-operation which I conceive would be productive of great social evil, is that known as *socialism:* a species of co-operation founded on a community of property. I have, in an earlier part of my story, stated that I was formerly prepossessed in favour of this notion, and I have there given my reasons for abjuring it. I had much to do with co-operation in former years, and have known and conversed with persons who have been connected with most of the experiments made to establish communities. both in Europe and America; and the result has been to convince me that their general establishment would produce a kind of social despotism far worse than any that now exists; and that it would be a sacrificing of the highest intellect, of the greatest inventions and discoveries, and of the best capacities and powers of the most industrious, to the least competent, the selfish, the careless, and the indolent. In addition to which, I regret to say that many of the socialists of a former day entertained very loose opinions on the subject of the sexes and of marriage; and many cases of separation, and great unhappiness occasioned thereby, fell under my own observation. Our present marriage system is bad enough as it is: for the state and condition of women under our present laws is a kind of social slavery, binding them in complete subjection to men, with no property they can call their own; nor, *if poor*, any escape from the most savage brutes, the most drunken spendthrifts, or the most wily of domestic persecutors. But while this system needs great reform, or the doing away with such laws as sanction *inequality*, or which gives man any unfair advantage over woman, any alteration in law or opinion that would tend to weaken that most sacred of all agreements and obligations would, I believe, be one of the greatest of all social calamities. And here let me advise you, that no reform that *law can effect*, to strengthen this holiest of social ties, will be equal to that which is in the power of the husband alone to achieve. That is, to endeavour to cultivate in his wife a concord of mind, of hopes and aspirations in his pursuits, as he would seek to secure her heart and affections. This is a work that should commence as soon as their faith is plighted, and may often require much patience, labour, and sacrifice; but the man who has resolved to make his home his haven of happiness, and to secure the best and truest of friends to advise and counsel with him, as well as to sympathise with him in his cares and troubles as no others will, will not spare his labour to cultivate, as far as he is able, the mind of his wife; to strive to interest her in his business or pursuits, and to allow her to share in all his pleasures.

Another most important subject, that should engage the serious attention of working men, is the employment of *married women* in our factories; which I think reflects anything but credit on our manufacturing population, masters and men. For every reflecting person must perceive that children cannot be properly brought up without the careful nurture and superintendence of the mother; nor can a man's home—in which his chief happiness should be centred—be much other than a mere resting place or nightly refuge when the wife is taken from it to labour, too often to supply the man with mere sensual enjoyments. It is a folly therefore for such men to talk pompously of right and justice for themselves, while their wives and mothers of their children are thus treated; nor indeed, until they are placed upon a footing of equality, socially and politically, with themselves, and to occupy the station for which they are best fitted. Women, however, unmarried, or without husbands to support them, should be at liberty, equally with men, to earn their living in any business they choose.

Aim also, I would beseech you, to secure a proper education for your children; either by seeking to improve the present system, or, failing in that, by taking the matter in your own hands, and to establish a just system by co-operative effort. The education you should aim at is not merely the old routine of reading, writing, and arithmetic, or such mere technical knowledge as shall enable your children to become more efficient tools of production; but such as shall serve to prepare them to stand on a footing of equality with all others; and possessed of such knowledge, and such moral training, as shall fit them for a life of industry and usefulness, so as to be a blessing to themselves and their country. To this end they must not only be able to read and write and cipher, but to acquire some knowledge of their own nature; of the world they inhabit; of the existences they are surrounded by; a knowledge of the conditions of social and political life, and rules of conduct on which their well-being chiefly depends; together with the outlines and rudiments of science, which form the foundation of those arts and manufactures that contribute to the prosperity and happiness of our country. In the pursuit of those attainments there should be little difference made between boys and girls, seeing that women are destined to have the first and chief hand in moulding the minds and character of our people; excepting that girls should be taught at school to make and mend their own clothing, and to cook their own food : qualifications of the first importance to promote the well-being of a family.

Another great essential you should aim at, is the establishing of libraries and reading-rooms, in sufficient numbers, in different districts of your towns and villages, to which the young and old of both sexes should have free access after the labours of the day; as well as to borrow books from them to take to their homes; as also to have some share in the management. In addition to which, you should aim at establishing halls of science, where the young might extend the knowledge they acquired at school or obtain a more extensive knowledge of any particular science. Our museums and galleries of art should also be freely accessible to the people; and at such times, too, when they may best be able to attend them; and if large halls were connected with them, and men of science and art employed to give daily lectures on their contents, they would form schools of instruction of the first importance to our people.

Seeing, also, the great deterioration that is fast going on among the rising generation owing to most of their recreations and amusements being connected with public-houses, which have spread so extensively within these few years throughout the length and breadth of the land; and seeing, too, the great obstacles in the way of progress which the drinking habits of our people occasion, you should above all things aim to remedy this monstrous evil; and to secure rational and healthful amusements for the young, apart from the means of intoxication. Taking into account the physical and mental injury produced by the poisonous intoxicating compounds drank by our people, the vast amount of social misery they occasion, and the great extent of vice and crime that can be clearly traced to their use, you should not fail to consider and weigh the consequences of this great evil, socially and politically, and the great waste of capital it occasions. You have been making great efforts for a number of years past to improve your social position by obtaining higher wages, or a larger share of the productions your labour helps to create; but while you have been carrying on these contests, you have been spending the largest portion of *a hundred millions annually* in intoxicating drinks, exclusive of the great amount of capital you have frequently been obliged to waste in your efforts to obtain a rise of wages, or to prevent a fall of them. Now, as no labour can be put in motion *without capital*, or, in other words, without materials, tools, and the means of subsistence for the labourers, every waste of it will diminish the employment of labour, and every increase of it, especially *in the hands of the producers themselves*, will occasion an increased demand for labour. The most obtuse among you may perceive that if the hundred millions of capital that is thus annually wasted could be added *year after year* to the present amount that is now paid our labourers in wages, that a vast change would soon be produced in their favour. You can readily perceive what a vast demand for productions of various kinds would take place if the money now spent in drink were only spent in decent furniture, comfortable clothing, good food, and the necessary requisites for housekeeping, among the working millions of our country. But far beyond this benefit, for giving employment and better wages, there are many others of greater importance. The great social want in the present day is the union of capital and labour in the work of production, with *a unity of interests*, and this great saving would soon enable you to effect it ; or if you prefer to put your savings in some savings bank, you could enjoy the interest thereof, and have the best security against ever needing the miserable workhouse, when slackness of work, sickness, or old age, come upon you. Who can fail to perceive that drunkenness is a great obstacle in the way of progress, socially and politically? In your trade associations and unions, tipplers and drunkards are the first to shirk their payments, to mar your peaceful objects by their brawls and misconduct ; the first to desert your cause and go over to the enemy ; and otherwise by their drunken conduct, and neglect of home and children, to bring disgrace upon the general body. *Politically*, they are even worse enemies to progress, as their love of drink drowns all regard for the welfare of their country; causes them to seize with avidity the bribe of the enemy, and to be ready tools to fight, or drown by noisy clamour, the best efforts for the improvement of their country, for a paltry modicum of drink. These evils should awaken the most thoughtful among you to a sense of duty, and should induce you to band yourselves together to discountenance in your fellows this love of drink, and to join in all efforts for removing this great temptation from among you. For you must remember that this is a growing and spreading evil at home and abroad; that publicans, gin-sellers, and brewers are all powerful for evil; and that while you and the well-disposed of other classes are making strenuous efforts to reform abuses, remove evils, and to build up your liberties, these men and their drinking tools are doing all in their power to mar or prevent all social and political progress. It is an evil, however, that sooner or later must be coped with, and the longer it is postponed the more difficult will be its solution. Year after year it is eating deeper and deeper into the heart of the nation, producing its annual crops of pauperism, vice, and crime; and paralysing the best efforts of all those who are seeking to enlighten and improve mankind. Every year adds new victims to the seductions of the drink traffic; gives increased wealth and legislative power to those who flourish by it; and enables them to defy all efforts for the mitigation or removal of this great and intolerable curse from among us.

On the subject of Religion I have already given my opinions, and therefore shall confine myself to a few last words. I regard, then, as *true religion* that teaching which is based on the great and broad principle of human brotherhood, of reciprocal Christian duty, of mental freedom in the pursuit of truth, of love and kindness for the whole human family, and of the necessity for each and all of us doing all in our power for the mental, moral, and physical elevation of our race. Such a religion—founded on the great commandment of love to God and man—would, in my opinion, be one of the most efficient means for building up society upon the foundations of right and justice; for calling forth, promoting, and disseminating the love of knowledge; for purifying and elevating mankind by pure morality and ennobling aspirations; and for being a faithful friend and guide to the erring children of humanity; helping so to improve and direct their conduct in this life, as shall render them more worthy of the next.

You may be assured, then, that all teachers of religion who neglect those great and truly Christian principles of man's elevation and improvement are *not truly Christian.* Those who, banded together as a church, or as a Christian community of any kind, who seek to dominate and subject to their will the minds and consciences of men; who seek to amuse and interest them with gaudy ceremonials, vain repetitions, creeds and catechisms; who preach to the multitude eternal patience under wrong and injustice; side with their oppressors in the perpetuation of the evil, and wink at wickedness in high places, are not true Christian teachers, whatever name they may assume. But those who aim at the mental and moral elevation of our race, and at the same time use their power and influence for the physical improvement of all, *are worthy of all honour;* they being the true imitators of the Great Teacher, who in His day laboured for the poor and oppressed, who went about among them doing good, and who denounced wickedness, hypocrisy and injustice.

Remember that the highest *Christian duty*, the highest *moral duty*, as well as the highest of our *political duties*, all point to the same great end—that of improving and perfecting our fellow-creatures intellectually, morally, and physically, so that they may be enabled to enjoy the highest amount of happiness in this world, and be better prepared for the enjoyment of the next. The Christianity, morality, and political philosophy that fall short of this great aim are only delusive shams, upheld by cant, special pleading, and hollow promises, and which can only end in perpetuating the reign of ignorance, demoralization, and wrong, and in consigning the vast majority of our toiling millions to a life of poverty, care, and anxiety, in order to support and pamper a comparative few in the excesses of luxury and extravagance. It surely cannot be religiously or morally right that mostly all the means of enjoyment in this world shall be monopolised by a few, and that chiefly by "those who toil not, neither do they spin;" that the land of a country which God gave in common to all should be held by a few great families; and that because their ancestors were great buccaneers, who stole it from our ancestors a few hundred years ago, and the possession of which they have secured as far possible by laws of their own making. Nor can it be a satisfactory state of society when the mass of our people are held in a kind of social bondage by a few great capitalists, against whom they are always warring for subsistence; as they must, in most cases, do their bidding or starve, and more especially when trade is bad, and markets over-glutted. It is surely time to put an end to this social strife in the work of production, and not to allow of a state of things to which we are fast hastening, when all the great capitalists will swallow up all the little ones, and when all the machinism and inventive powers of our age shall be engrossed and used chiefly for their benefit; with the lamentable results of making a few great millionaires on the one hand, and a nation of toiling, poverty-stricken slaves on the other. For the competition between labourers, with their continually increasing numbers, will always give a power to capitalists to keep down wages to the lowest subsistence point, and especially of unskilled labour. Even among skilled workmen the strife of competition is fast producing similar results, notwithstanding their unions to prevent it. We have seen the operation of this system in our day, and how the swarms of Irish labourers—driven from their country by their landowners—have brought down the wages of Englishmen, in field or factory, or wherever unskilled labour is needed. In America the same system is producing similar results, although somewhat retarded by their great extent of land, and demand for labour. There they have not only the cheap labour of Ireland, Germany, France, and other countries, to keep down a fair rate of wages, but have recently added to these swarms of Chinese and Coolies from other countries. And we, too, have been lately threatened by our capitalists with an importation of Chinese labourers.

Some pious defenders of this state of things will doubtlessly tell you that this world is only intended by God as a place of toil and trial, in which your chief duty is to prepare yourselves for a future state. This specious doctrine, my friends, is not genuine Christianity; nor do those who preach it practise it themselves, for they generally manage to get the lion's share of good things *in this world*. A true Christian regards his fellow-man as a brother, to whom he wishes to act as he would be done by; and as he would not, if possible, permit a brother to be kept in ignorance, and to be placed in such wretched circumstances as are almost certain to mar the good within him, and consequently to blight, if not destroy, his chance of enjoying the future they talk about, so will he labour with all earnestness to improve his brother's lot, and to make this earth more in accordance with heaven. In fact, the present state of society, with its mere money-getting and sensual aspirations—with its adulterations, trickery, and cheating in trade and commerce—the constant strife and contentions of its labouring classes to obtain a subsistence—its recklessness, drunkenness, and waste—its mass of squalid misery —and the callous indifference of our legislators to provide a remedy, demand with trumpet voice that all earnest, thoughtful men should seriously begin to look beyond the professions of Churches, Sects, and Parties, to the GREAT RELIGION OF DUTY; this being the only religion that can build up the moral man to subdue his animal nature; that can awaken his duties to his brethren; that can form the great cementing power to unite man to man in social fellowship; that can cause nations to prosper by the establishment of justice at home and abroad; and above all, by its being the religion that Christ enjoined for promoting the happiness of man.

Remember also, I implore you, that all just and efficient government must depend *on the intelligence and virtues of the great mass of our people,* as on the possession of these qualities will depend the kind of men that will be chosen for representatives and rulers; and on these will depend the liberty and prosperity of our country. For if the wisest and best are neglected, and the mere shams of wealth, title, and pretensions, are elevated to place and power, whatever changes we may have, or whatever name our Government may assume, it will be fruitless of benefit to the mass of the people. And although ignorance, improvidence, and vice still unhappily pervade the ranks of our population to a lamentable extent, it yet greatly lies in the power of the most intelligent of our working and middle classes to enlighten and improve that unhappy portion of their brethren. For let them but organize and band themselves together for the purpose of their instruction, social and political; let them but exhibit examples of sobriety and orderly conduct, in their own persons, their homes and families, and sternly set themselves against the demoralizing influences that surround them, and the work of reformation will be gradually, but surely, effected. Unhappily we live in an age when the vast accumulations of wealth, which our new discoveries and productive powers have conferred upon our race—but which, hitherto, have chiefly been monopolised by the upper and middle classes—are for the most part spent in luxury and excess, and in administering to mere sensual gratifications; the one class of them striving to ape the other in all their extravagance and folly, and each striving to outvie his neighbour in his finery, equipages, and profusion. This state of things has, unhappily, a corrupting and deteriorating influence on society, not merely by the force of pernicious example on all classes, but by wasting means that ought morally and religiously to be applied to the rescuing of millions from a life of poverty and misery, and for the social and political improvement of our people. To stem this current of pernicious example must be the one great aim of Reformers; for while they should urge on their brethren the necessity of having healthful, tasteful, and neatly-kept homes, and well-clad and well-instructed families, they should urge on them at the same time the virtues of temperance, frugality, and the saving of present means for the time of sickness, accident, old age and infirmity; and for enabling them to lend an efficient hand in the social and political reformation of their country.

Another point to which I would direct the attention of my brethren, is the necessity of their acquiring *equal electoral rights in all matters* with that of others. The people at large, I conceive, in any part of the country, who have a fixed habitation, and help to support the State, should be allowed equal electoral rights with those of housholders and landlords. Not only in the election of Members of Parliament, but in that of School Boards, and of all Municipal and Parochial Officers. The giving of electoral power exclusively to householders (for the difficulties in the way of Lodger Suffrage have rendered that a nullity), because they pay rates and taxes, is a manifest injustice; as those who occupy a habitation and pay rent for it help the householder or landlord to pay his rates and taxes. In most cases, too, they contribute more largely; for they often help to keep him as well as help him to pay his rates and taxes. Justice therefore demands that all who contribute, *directly* or *indirectly*, to the support of our social or political institutions, should have an equal right in choosing the persons who are to direct or manage them.

As also the ultimate cost of every kind of waste and extravagance must be borne by the industrious and saving part of the community; and as the ultimate results of every kind of vice and profligacy help to create burthens for them to support; it becomes the duty of the industrious classes, above all others, to raise their voices against gambling, horse-racing, betting, and all kinds of vicious extravagance; not only as a waste of the capital necessary for giving them profitable employment, and for promoting their happiness, but for their demoralizing influence on those they are striving politically and socially to improve and elevate. Unhappily, those annual saturnalian revels of horse-racing, betting, gambling, and drunken disorder— which had their origin in the low pursuits and gambling propensities of the idle and demoralized portion of our titled and wealthy aristocracy—have, like a foul and muddy torrent, flowed downwards to create a moral pestilence

among the unreflecting of all classes of society. Nay! so
contagious has been the evil, that even among those who
pride themselves on their "respectability," are found persons who take their wives and daughters to witness "this
racing and betting frenzy;" where, in close contact with
drunken roughs, slangy sportsmen, showy courtesans, and
fighting, roaring, and rampant brutality, they cannot help
witnessing scenes and sounds repugnant to all female
delicacy and moral propriety. So much so has this attractive vice of horse-racing, with all its vile accompaniments
of betting and gambling, taken possession of the public
mind, that even in the Legislature its wealthy and aristocratic patrons have influence enough to stay all legislative
proceedings while they go to that carnival of vice and
profligacy, the Derby—"A time," says Goldwin Smith,
"when men, women, and boys are invited to gratify the vile
delights of gambling; mostly to their demoralization, and
often to their ruin." Thus "from high to low the demoralizing influence spreads, contaminating in its course the
sporting nobleman, the turf-bitten manufacturer, the
gambling shop-keeper, and betting publican, down to the
stableman, costermonger, and pot-boy, who foolishly club
their five shillings or half-crowns, in imitation of their
betters, to risk upon a horse-race." Our aristocracy and
wealthy classes pride themselves on being the *élite* of the
nation, and on the refinement and improvement they effect
in society by their high culture, superior manners, worthy
deeds, and noble examples; but they cannot suppose that
those whom they call "the vulgar herd" are so blinded by
the glitter of wealth or title as to believe that racing, betting, gambling, battues and pigeon-shooting, are evidences
of culture or merit; or that such doings are very bright
examples for the multitude to imitate. That many thoughtless and weak-minded ones among them do this, however,
is greatly to be regretted; and therefore to the reform of
those social vices the most intelligent of our brethren
should divert their attention. They must not, however,
rely on this or any other great measure of reformation
coming from, or being achieved by, the classes above them,
for they are generally the opponents of all reform; and

that often from the most mistaken notions. Most of the reforms that have taken place in my day have been won rather in despite of the wealthy and titled classes, than owe to them their origin; though they might at last have been made the unwilling instruments for carrying them into effect. So long, therefore, as those who are aiming at cheap and just government, help by vote or voice to place persons who have neither interest nor sympathy with them in the position of representatives or rulers, so long will they be *putting obstacles in their own path.* The industrious classes, therefore, would do well to remember the wise fable of " The Lark and her Young Ones," and resolve to do their own work themselves; and that by choosing representatives from their own ranks, or from those of other classes who like themselves are seeking the removal of social and political evils, and the establishing of freedom, peace, and plenty in our land; and by otherwise aiding the great cause of human progress by every intellectual and moral effort in their power, and to work onward till their labours are crowned with success. And my working brethren should also remember, that *ignorance and superstition* are the two chief crutches which prop up and support every species of despotism, corruption, and error in every part of the world; and against these, all who wish for the advancement and happiness of mankind *should ever war.* And they would also do well to reflect that, from the past history of this race, little or no improvement can possibly take place in *their social position* under the strife that is continually waging between capital and labour, until all persons interested in the prosperity and happiness of their country and their race unite to put an end to this strife, by establishing a system of co-operation for the production of wealth, founded on the mutual interests of capital and labour, and such distributed according to each person's industry, capacity, and intelligence—the whole based on mutual right and obligation, the highest principles of morality, and the religion of doing unto all as they could wish to be done by.

Having referred to my wife and children in the early part of my story, I deem it advisable to say a few concluding words respecting them; as those who have felt any interest in what I have said, might wish to know something more about those who were dearest to me. And first of my dear Mary, whom I earnestly hope will outlive me, for the sake of my poor daughter and grand-daughter, knowing that the same watchful care and anxiety she has ever shown for them will ever be extended towards them while any mental or bodily powers remain with her. For though I would do my best, if unhappily they were left to my charge, I should be but a poor substitute for my over-anxious wife. To me my dear wife has ever been a second self; always my best adviser and truest friend; ever interesting herself, and sympathising with me in all my pursuits, toils, and troubles; and ever diffusing the sunshine of kindness and good temper in our humble home. I know not indeed what kind of man I should have been, if I had not met with such a noble help-mate; and this I often think of with grateful feelings. She has borne to me two children, named Mary and Kezia. The latter—called after my dear mother—died in infancy; her death, we believed, occasioned by a fall off the lap of a sleepy nurse. Mary, my surviving daughter, was born on the 9th of June, 1827, and married, at the age of twenty-two, Thomas C. Hytch, the son of a London carpenter. He is a compositor by trade, but having worked at Novello's for upwards of twenty years, in setting up the very small type used in music-printing, his eye-sight became so weakened in consequence, that he was obliged to abandon his trade; and for several years past has maintained his family by keeping a tobacconist's shop. My daughter—having only one child —with a view of improving her position, devoted herself for some years to teaching, and to the keeping of a school, and very recently has taken to the stage; a step very much against her mother's wishes and my own, although I have no prejudice against the profession. She is an intelligent and clever woman, and is very sanguine of success in her new calling, but I would much rather she had devoted herself to her home. My grand-daughter Kezia, was born in London, on July 24th, 1857, and has lived with us a great portion of her time, although she attends also to her father's shop when needed. She is a well-grown girl, fond of music, drawing and reading, and is not deficient of intelligence. I hope therefore that she will do well in life ; that she will seek to acquire useful knowledge as a means of happiness, will always strive to be pure and good, and will aim at diffusing happiness around her.

During last winter—1875—I had another severe attack of my horrible bronchial complaint ; and so severe was it, that I was not able to leave my bed for about eight weeks. During this illness I have to record, with grateful feelings, the kindness and generosity of friends, who not only supplied me with everything they thought would administer to my recovery, but unitedly subscribed money to supply me monthly with extra comforts in my old age. I have therefore abundant reasons to be thankful to kind friends, and I hereby record my grateful acknowledgments to them.

APPENDIX A.

PETITION AGREED TO AT THE " CROWN AND ANCHOR " MEETING, FEBRUARY 28th, 1837.

" To the Honourable the Commons of Great Britain and Ireland. The Petition of the undersigned Members of the Working Men's Association and others sheweth—

" That the only *rational use* of the institutions and laws of society is justly to protect, encourage, and support all that can be made to contribute *to the happiness of all the people.*

" That, as the object to be obtained is mutual benefit, so ought the enactment of laws to be by mutual consent.

" That obedience to laws can only be *justly enforced* on the certainty that those who are called on to obey them have had, either personally or by their representatives, a power to enact, amend, or repeal them.

" That all those who are excluded from this share of political power are not justly included within the operation of the laws; to them the laws are only despotic enactments, and the legislative assembly from whom they emanate can only be considered parties to an unholy compact, devising plans and schemes for taxing and subjecting the many.

" That the universal political right of every human being is superior and stands apart from all customs, forms, or ancient usuage; a fundamental right not in the power of man to confer, or justly to deprive him of.

"That to take away this sacred right from the *person* and to vest it in *property*, is a wilful perversion of justice and common sense, as the creation and security of property *are the consequences of society*—the great object of which is human happiness.

"That any constitution or code of laws, formed in violation of men's political and social rights, are not rendered sacred by time nor sanctified by custom.

"That the ignorance which originated, or permits their operation, forms no excuse for perpetuating the injustice; nor can aught but force or fraud sustain them, when any considerable number of the people perceive and feel their degradation.

"That the intent and object of your petitioners are to present such facts before your Honourable House as will serve to convince you and the country at large that you do not represent the people of these realms; and to appeal to your sense of right and justice as well as to every principle of honour, for directly making such legislative enactments as shall cause the mass of the people to be represented; with the view of securing *the greatest amount of happiness to all classes of society.*

"Your Petitioners find, by returns ordered by your Honourable House, that the whole people of Great Britain and Ireland are about 24 millions, and that the males above 21 years of age are 6,023,752, who, in the opinion of your petitioners, are justly entitled to the elective right.

"That according to S. Wortley's return (ordered by your Honourable House) the number of registered electors, who have the power to vote for members of Parliament, are only 839,519, and of this number only 8½ in 12 give their votes.

"That on an analysis of the constituency of the United Kingdom, your petitioners find that 331 members (being a *majority* of your Honourable House) are returned by *one hundred and fifty-one thousand four hundred and ninety-two registered electors !*

"That comparing the whole of the male population above the age of 21 with the 151,492 electors, it appears that 1-40 of them, or 1-160 of the entire population, have the power of passing all the laws in your Honourable House.

"And your petitioners further find on investigation, that this majority of 331 members are composed of 163 Tories or Conservatives, 134 Whigs and Liberals, and only 34 who call themselves Radicals; and out of this limited number it is questionable whether 10 can be found who are truly the representatives of the wants and wishes of the producing classes.

"Your petitioners also find that 15 members of your Honourable House are returned by electors under 200; 55 under 300; 99 under 400; 121 under 500; 150 under 600; 196 under 700; 214 under 800; 240 under 900; and 256 under 1,000; and that many of these constituencies are divided between two members.

"They also find that your Honourable House, which is said to be exclusively the people's or the Commons House, contains *two hundred and five persons who are immediately or remotely related to the Peers of the Realm.*

"Also that your Honourable House contains 1 marquess, 7 earls, 19 viscounts, 32 lords, 25 right honourables, 52 honourables, 63 baronets, 13 knights, 3 admirals, 7 lord-lieutenants, 42 deputy and vice-lieutenants, 1 general, 5 lieutenant-generals, 9 major-generals, 32 colonels, 33 lieutenant-colonels, 10 majors, 49 captains in army and navy, 10 lieutenants, 2 cornets, 58 barristers, 3 solicitors, 40 bankers, 33 East India proprietors, 13 West India proprietors, 52 place-men, 114 patrons of church livings having the patronage of 274 livings between them; the names of whom your petitioners can furnish at the request of your Honourable House.

"Your petitioners therefore respectfully submit to your Honourable House that these facts afford abundant proofs that you do not represent the numbers or the interests of the millions; but that the persons composing it have interests for the most part foreign or directly opposed to the true interests of the great body of the people.

"That perceiving the tremendous power you possess

over the lives, liberty and labour of the unrepresented millions—perceiving the *military* and *civil forces* at your command—*the revenue* at your disposal—the *relief of the poor* in your hands—the *public press* in your power, by enactments expressly excluding the working classes alone —moreover, the power of delegating to others the whole control of the *monetary arrangements* of the Kingdom, by which the labouring classes may be silently plundered or suddenly suspended from employment—seeing all these elements of power wielded by your Honourable House as at present constituted, and fearing the consequences that may result if a thorough reform is not speedily had recourse to, your petitioners earnestly pray your Honourable House *to enact the following as the law of these realms,* with such other essential details as your Honourable House shall deem necessary :—

"A LAW FOR EQUALLY REPRESENTING THE PEOPLE OF GREAT BRITAIN AND IRELAND.
EQUAL REPRESENTATION.

" That the United Kingdom be divided into 200 electoral districts; dividing, as nearly as possible, an equal number of inhabitants; and that each district do send a representative to Parliament.

"UNIVERSAL SUFFRAGE.

" That every person producing proof of his being 21 years of age, to the clerk of the parish in which he has resided six months, shall be entitled to have his name registered as a voter. That the time for registering in each year be from the 1st of January to the 1st of March.

"ANNUAL PARLIAMENTS.

" That a general election do take place on the 24th of June in each year, and that each vacancy be filled up a fortnight after it occurs. That the hours for voting be from six o'clock in the morning till six o'clock in the evening.

"NO PROPERTY QUALIFICATIONS.

"That there shall be no property qualification for members; but on a requisition, signed by 200 voters, in favour of any candidate being presented to the clerk of the parish in which they reside, such candidate shall be put in nomination.   And the list of all the candidates nominated throughout the district shall be stuck on the church door in every parish, to enable voters to judge of their qualification.

"VOTE BY BALLOT.

"That each voter must vote in the parish in which he resides.   That each parish provide as many balloting boxes as there are candidates proposed in the district; and that a temporary place be fitted up in each parish church for the purpose of *secret voting*.   And, on the day of election, as each voter passes orderly on to the ballot, he shall have given to him, by the officer in attendance, a balloting ball, which he shall drop into the box of his favourite candidate.   At the close of the day the votes shall be counted, by the proper officers, and the numbers stuck on the church doors.   The following day the clerk of the district and two examiners shall collect the votes of all the parishes throughout the district, and cause the name of the successful candidate to be posted in every parish of the district.

"SITTINGS AND PAYMENTS TO MEMBERS.

"That the members do take their seats in Parliament on the first Monday in October next after their election, and continue their sittings every day (Sundays excepted) till the business of the sitting is terminated, but not later than the 1st of September.   They shall meet every day (during the Session) for business at 10 o'clock in the morning, and adjourn at 4.   And every member shall be paid quarterly out of the public treasury £400 a-year. That all electoral officers shall be elected by universal suffrage.

"By passing the foregoing as the law of the land, you will confer a great blessing on the people of England; and your petitioners, as in duty bound, will ever pray."

APPENDIX B.

"THE PEOPLE'S CHARTER.

"BEING A BILL TO PROVIDE FOR THE JUST REPRESENTATION OF THE PEOPLE OF GREAT BRITAIN AND IRELAND IN THE COMMONS HOUSE OF PARLIAMENT. REVISED AT A CONFERENCE OF THE PEOPLE, HELD AT BIRMINGHAM, DECEMBER, 1842.

"Whereas, to insure, in as far as it is possible by human forethought and wisdom, the just government of the people, it is necessary to subject those who have the power of making the laws to a wholesome and strict responsibility to those whose duty it is to obey them when made.

"And, whereas, this responsibility is best enforced through the instrumentality of a body which emanates directly from, and is itself immediately subject to, the whole people, and which completely represents their feelings and their interests.

"And, whereas, the Commons House of Parliament now exercises, in the name and on the supposed behalf of the people, the power of making the laws, it ought, in order to fulfill with wisdom and with honesty the great duties imposed on it, to be made the faithful and accurate representation of the people's wishes, feelings, and interests.

"BE IT THEREFORE ENACTED :—

"That, from and after the passing of this Act, every male inhabitant of these realms be entitled to vote for the election of a member of Parliament; subject, however, to the following conditions :—

"1. That he be a native of these realms, or a foreigner

29

who has lived in this country upwards of two years, and been naturalized.

" 2. That he be twenty-one years of age.

" 3. That he be not proved insane when the lists of voters are revised.

" 4. That he be not undergoing the sentence of the laws at the time when called upon to exercise the electoral right.

" 5. That his electoral rights be suspended for bribery at elections, or for personation, or for forgery of election certificates, according to the penalties of this Act.

" ELECTORAL DISTRICTS.

" I. Be it enacted, that for the purpose of obtaining an equal representation of the people in the Commons House of Parliament, the United Kingdom be divided into 300 electoral districts.*

" II. That each such district contain, as nearly as may be, an equal number of inhabitants.

" III. That the number of inhabitants be taken from the last census, and as soon as possible after the next ensuing decennial census shall have been taken, the electoral districts be made to conform thereto.

" IV. That each electoral district be named after the principal city or borough within its limits.

" V. That each electoral district return one representative to sit in the Commons House of Parliament.

" VI. That the Secretary of State for the Home Department shall appoint three competent persons as Commissioners, and as many Sub-Commissioners as may be necessary for settling the boundaries of each of the 300 electoral districts, and so on from time to time, whenever a new decennial census of the people be taken.

" VII. That the necessary expenses of the said commissioners, sub-commissioners, clerks, and other persons employed by them in the performance of their duties, be paid out of the public treasury.

---

* There are, say, 6,000,000 of men eligible to vote. This number, divided by 300, gives 20,000 to each member.

" REGISTRATION OFFICERS.

" Be it enacted, that for the purpose of procuring an accurate registration of voters, for finally adjudicating in all cases of objections made against persons claiming to be registered, for receiving the nominations of Members of Parliament and Returning Officers, and declaring their election ; as well as for conducting and superintending all matters connected with registration, nomination, and election, according to the provisions of this Act, the following officers be appointed :—

" 1. Returning Officers for each electorial district.

" 2. Deputy-Returning Officers for each district.

" 3. A Registration Clerk for every parish containing   number of inhabitants, or for every two or more parishes if united for the purpose of this Act.

" RETURNING OFEICER, AND HIS DUTIES.

" I. Be it enacted, that at the first general election after the passing of this Act, a Returning Officer be elected for every electoral district throughout the kingdom, and so in like manner at the end of every year.

" II. That, at the end of every such period, the returning officer for each district be nominated in like manner, and elected at the same time as the Member of Parliament for the district ; he shall be eligible to be re-elected.

" III. That vacancies occasioned by the death, removal, or resignation of the returning officer, shall in like manner be filled up as vacancies for Members of Parliament, for the unexpired term of the year.

" IV. That every returning officer shall appoint a deputy-returning officer, for the day of election, for every balloting place within his district, and in all cases be responsible for the just fulfilment of the duties of such deputies.

" V. That it be the duty of the returning officer to appoint a registration clerk for every parish within his district containing   number of inhabitants, or for every two or more parishes if united for the purposes of this

Act; and that in all cases he be responsible for the just fulfilment of the duties of such clerks.

"VI. That he also see that proper balloting places, and such other erections as may be necessary, be provided by each parish (or any number that may be united) and that the balloting-boxes be made and provided according to the provisions of this Act.

"VII. That he receive the lists of voters from all the parishes in his district, in which lists shall be marked or specified the names of those persons who have been objected to by the registration clerks or any other persons.

"VIII. That between the first of April and the first of May in each year, he shall hold *open* Courts of Adjudication at such a number of places within his district as he may deem necessary, of which courts (place and time of meeting) he shall cause due notice to be given in each parish of the district, and at the same time invite all persons who have made objections and who have been objected to. And, after hearing the statements that may be made by both parties, he shall *finally adjudicate* whether the voters' names be placed on the register or not.

"IX. That the returning officer shall then cause to be made out alphabetical lists of all the registered voters in all the parishes within his district; which lists, signed and attested by himself, shall be used at all the elections for the district. Such lists to be sold to the public at reasonably low prices.

"X. That the returning officer receive all nominations for the member of his district, as well as for the returning officer of his district, and shall give public notice of the same according to the provisions of this Act; he shall also receive from the Speaker of the House of Commons the orders for any new election, in case of the death or resignation of the member of the district, as well as the orders to superintend and conduct the election of any other district, in case of the death or resignation of the returning officer of such district.

"XI. That the returning officer shall also receive the

returns from all the parishes within his district, on the day of election ; and on the day following the election he shall proclaim the state of the ballot, as directed by this Act, and perform the several duties appertaining to his office, as herein made and provided.

" XII. That the returning officer be paid for fulfilling the duties of his office, the sum of   per annum, as hereinafter mentioned.

" XIII. That, upon a petition being presented to the House of Commons by at least one hundred qualified electors of the district, against any returning officer of the same, complaining of corruption in the exercise of his office, or of incapacity, such complaints shall be inquired into by a committee of the House, consisting of seven members ; and, on their report being read, the members present shall then determine whether such returning officer be or be not guilty, or he be or not be incapacitated.

" XIV. That, for conducting the first elections after the passing of this Act, a returning officer for each district be temporarily appointed by the Secretary of State, to perform the duties prescribed by this Act. He shall resign his office as soon as the new one is appointed, and be paid as hereinafter mentioned. *See Penalties.*

" DEPUTY RETURNING OFFICER, AND HIS DUTIES.

" I. Be it enacted, that a deputy returning officer be appointed by the district returning officer to preside at each balloting place on the day of election, such deputy to be subject and responsible to his authority, as well as to the provisions of this Act.

" II. That it be the duty of the deputy returning officer to provide a number of competent persons, not exceeding   , to aid him in taking the ballot, and for performing the necessary business thereof.

" III. That the deputy returning officer shall see that proper registration lists are provided, and that the ballot begin at six o'clock in the morning precisely, and end at six o'clock in the afternoon of the same day.

" IV. That the deputy returning officer, in the presence

of the agents of the candidates, examine and seal the balloting-boxes previously to the commencement of the balloting ; he shall in like manner declare the number of votes for each candidate, and shall cause a copy of the same, signed by himself, to be forwarded to the returning officer of the district, and another copy to the registration clerk of the parish.

" V. That the deputy returning officer be paid for his services as hereinafter mentioned. *See Penalties.*

" THE REGISTRATION CLERK, HIS DUTIES.

" I. Be it enacted, that a Registration Clerk be appointed by the district returning officer for every parish within his district containing   inhabitants ; or for every two or more parishes that may be united for the purposes of this Act; such clerk to be responsible to his authority, as well as to the provisions of this Act.

" II. That for the purpose of obtaining a correct registration of all the voters in each electoral district, the registration clerk of every parish as aforesaid throughout the kingdom shall, on or before the 1st of February in each year, take or cause to be taken round to every dwelling-house, poor-house, or union-workhouse, in his parish, a printed notice of the following form :—

> " *Mr. John Jones, you are hereby required, within six days from the date hereof, to fill up this list with the names of all male inhabitants of your house, of 21 years of age and upwards ; stating their respective ages, and the time they have resided with you ; or, in neglect thereof, to forfeit the sum of one pound for every name omitted.*
>
> " A. B., *Registration Clerk.*

Name.	Address.	Age.	Time of residence.
John Jones.	6, Upper North Place.	21 years.	3 months.

" N.B.—This list will be called for at the expiration of six days from this date.

"III. That, at the expiration of six days, as aforesaid, the registration clerk shall collect, or cause to be collected, the aforesaid lists, and shall cause to be made out from them an alphabetical list of all persons who are of the proper age and residence to qualify them as voters, according to the provisions of this Act.

"IV. That if the registration clerk shall have any just reason to believe that the names, ages, or time of residence of any persons inserted in the aforesaid list are falsely entered, or not in accordance with the provisions of this Act, he shall not refuse to insert them in his list of voters, but he shall write the words 'objected to' opposite such names; and so in like manner against the names of every person he may have just reason to consider ineligible, according to the provisions of this Act.

"V. That on or before the 8th of March in each year, the registration clerk shall cause the aforesaid alphabetical list of voters to be stuck against all church and chapel doors, market-houses, town-halls, session-houses, poor-houses, union-workhouses, and such other conspicuous places as he may deem necessary, from the 8th of March till the 22nd. He shall also cause a copy of such list to lie at his office, to be perused by any person without a fee, at all reasonable hours; and copies of the said list shall be sold to the public at a reasonably low price.

"VI. That, on or before the 25th of March, the registration clerk shall take, or cause to be taken, a copy of the aforesaid list of voters to the returning officer of his district, which list shall be signed by himself, and be presented as a just and impartial list, according to his judgment, of all persons within his parish who are eligible according to their claims, as well as of all those who have been objected to by himself or other persons.

"VII. That the registration clerk shall attend the Court of Adjudication, according to the notice he shall receive from the returning officer, to revise his list, and shall perform all the duties of his office as herein provided.

"VIII. That the registration clerk be paid for his services in the manner hereinafter mentioned.

" ARRANGEMENT FOR REGISTRATION.

"I. Be it enacted, that every householder, as well as every person occupying or having charge of a dwelling-house, poorhouse, or union-workhouse, who shall receive a notice from the registration clerk as aforesaid, shall cause the said notice to be correctly filled up with the names, ages, and time of residence of every male inmate or inhabitant of his or her house, of twenty-one years of age and upwards, within six days of the day of the date of such notice, and shall carefully preserve the same till it is called for by the registration clerk, or his proper officer.

" II. That when the list of voters is made out from these notices, and stuck on the church doors and places aforesaid, any person who finds his name not inserted in the list, and who believes he is duly qualified as a voter, shall, on presenting to the registration clerk a notice in the following form, have his name added to the list of voters :

" *I, John Jones, carpenter, residing at——in the district of——being twenty-one years of age, and having resided at the above place during the last three months, require to be placed on the list of voters as a qualified elector for the said district.*

"III. That any person who is qualified as a voter to any electoral district, and shall have removed to any other parish *within the said district*, on presenting to the registration clerk of the parish he then resides in, his voter's certificate as proof of this, or the written testimony of any registration clerk who has previously registered him, he shall be entitled to be placed on the list of voters as aforesaid.

" IV. That if an elector of any parish in the district have any just grounds for believing that any person disqualified by this Act has been put upon any parish register within the said district, he may, at any reasonable hour, between the 1st and the 20th day of March, cause the following notices to be delivered, the one at the residence of the registration clerk, and the other at the residence of the person objected to ; and the registration clerk shall, in like manner, send notice of the grounds of objection to all persons he may object to, as aforesaid:—

"To the Registration Clerk.

"*I, William Smith, elector of the parish of———in the district of———object to A.B. being on the register of voters, believing him to be disqualified.*

"To the person objected to.

"*Mr. A.B. of———I, William Smith, elector of the parish of——— in the district of———object to your name being on the register of voters for the following reasons:—(here state the reasons) and I will support my objections by proofs before the Returning Officer of the District.*

"Dated this   day, &c.

"V. That if the person thus objecting neglect to attend the court of the returning officer at the proper time, to state his objections, he shall be fined ten shillings for every such neglect, the same to be levied on his goods and chattels, provided he is not prevented from attending by sickness or accident ; in which case his medical certificate, or a certificate signed by ten voters certifying such fact, shall be forwarded to the returning officer, who shall then determine whether the claim to be put on the register be allowed or not.

"VI. That if the person objected to fails to attend the court of the returning officer at the proper time, to substantiate his claim, his name shall be erased from the register, provided he is not prevented by sickness or accident ; in which case a certificate shall be forwarded, and the returning officer shall determine as before directed.

"VII. That if it should be proved before the returning officer, in his open Court of Adjudication, that any person has frivolously or vexatiously objected to any one being placed on the list of voters, such person objecting shall be fined twenty shillings and expenses, the same to be levied on his goods and chattels, and paid to the person objected to.

"VIII. That, as early as possible after the lists are revised as aforesaid, the returning officer shall cause a copy of the same to be forwarded to every registration clerk within his district.

"IX. That the registration clerk of every parish shall then correctly copy from such lists the name, age, and residence of every qualified elector within his parish or parishes, into a book made for that purpose, and shall place a number opposite each name. He shall then, within ——days, take, or cause to be taken, to all such electors, *a voter's certificate* of the following form, the number on which shall correspond with the number in the aforesaid book :—

"*No. 123. This is to certify that James Jones, of —— is eligible to vote for one person to be returned to Parliament (as well as for the Returning Officer) for the district of ——for one year from the date hereof.*

"Dated.

"Registration Clerk.

"X. That if any person lose his voter's certificate by fire, or any other accident, he shall not have a new certificate till the next registration ; but on the day of any election, if he can establish his identity on the testimony of two witnesses, to the satisfaction of the registration clerk, as being the qualified voter described in the registration book, he shall be allowed to vote.

"XI. That the returning officer is hereby authorised and commanded to attach any small parishes within his district for the purposes of this Act, and not otherwise ; and in like manner to unite all extra-parochial places to some adjacent parish. *See Penalties.*

"ARRANGEMENT FOR NOMINATIONS.

"I. Be it enacted, that for the purpose of guarding against too great a number, who might otherwise be heedlessly proposed, as well as for giving time for the electors to inquire into the merits of the persons who may be nominated for Members of Parliament, as well as for Returning Officers, that all nominations be taken as hereinafter directed.

"II. That for all general elections of Members of Parliament a requisition of the following form, signed by at least one hundred qualified electors of the district, be delivered to the returning officer of the district between the first and tenth day of May in each year; and that such requisition constitute the nomination of such person as a candidate for the district:—

> "*We, the undersigned electors of the district of recommend A. B. of   as a fit and proper person to represent the people of this district in the Commons House of Parliament, the said A. B. being qualified to be an elector according to the provisions of this Act.*
>
> "Dated, &c.
>
> "Signed.

"III. That the returning officer of every electoral district shall, on or before the 13th of May in each year, cause a list of all the candidates thus nominated to be stuck up against all church and chapel doors, market-houses, town-halls, session-houses, poor-houses, and union-workhouses, and such other conspicuous places within the district as he may deem necessary.

"IV. That, whenever a vacancy is occasioned in any district by the death, resignation, or other cause, of the Member of Parliament, the returning officer of that district shall, within three days after his orders from the Speaker of the House of Commons, give notice thereof in all the parishes of his district in the manner described for giving notices, and he shall at the same time request all nominations to be made as aforesaid, within ten days from the receipt of his order, and shall also appoint the day of election within eighteen days from the receipt of such order from the Speaker of the House of Commons.

"V. That if, from any circumstances, no person has been nominated as a candidate for the district on or before the 10th of May, persons may then be nominated in the manner described as aforesaid at any time previous to the 20th of May, but not after that date.

"VI. That, at the first election after the passing of this Act, and at the expiration of every year, the nomination of candidates for the Returning Officer be made in the same manner as for Members of Parliament, and nominations for vacancies that may occur in like manner.

"VII. That if two or more persons are nominated as aforesaid for members to serve in Parliament for the district, the returning officer shall, at any time, between the 15th and 31st of May, (Sundays excepted) appoint such times and places (not exceeding   ) as he shall think most convenient to the electors of the district for the candidates to appear before them, then and there to explain their views and solicit the suffrages of the electors.

"VIII. That the returning officer see that the places above described be convenient for the purpose, and that as many such erections be put up as may be necessary; the same to be paid for by the returning officer, and charged in his account as hereinafter mentioned.

"IX. That, for the purpose of keeping good order and public decorum, the returning officer either take the chair at such meetings himself, or appoint a deputy for that purpose.

"X. That, provided only one candidate be proposed for Member of Parliament for the district by the time herein before mentioned, the returning officer do cause notice to be given, as hereinafter mentioned, that such a candidate is elected a member for the district; and if only one candidate be proposed for the Returning Officer, he shall in like manner be declared duly elected.

"XI. That no other qualification shall be required than the choice of the electors, according to the provisions of this Act; providing that no persons, excepting the cabinet ministers, be eligible to serve in the Commons House of Parliament who are in the receipt of any emolument derivable from any place or places held under Government, or of retired allowances arising therefrom.

" ARRANGEMENT FOR ELECTIONS.

"I . Be it enacted, that a general election of Members of Parliament, for the electoral districts of the United Kingdom, do take place on the first Monday in June in each year; and that all vacancies, by death or otherwise, shall be filled up as nearly as possible within eighteen days after they occur.

" II. That a general election of Returning Officers for all the districts take place at the expiration of every three years on the first Monday in June, and at the same time Members of Parliament are to be elected; and that all vacancies be filled up within eighteen days after they occur.

" III. That every person who has been registered as aforesaid, and who has a voter's certificate, shall have the right of voting in the district in which he has been registered, and in that only; and of voting for the Member of Parliament for that district, and the Returning Officer for the district, and for those only.

" IV. That, for the purpose of taking the votes of the qualified electors, the parish officer in every parish of the district (or in every two or more parishes if united for the purposes of this Act) shall cause proper places to be provided, so as to admit of the arrangements described in Schedule A, and so constructed (either permanently or temporarily as they may think proper) that the votes may be taken with due despatch, and so as to secure the elector while voting from being inspected by any other person.

" V. That the parish officers of every parish in the district provide a sufficient number of balloting-boxes, made after a model described in Schedule B (or made on one plan by persons appointed to make them, as was the case with weights and measures), and none but such boxes, duly certified, shall be used.

" VI. That, immediately preceding the commencement of the balloting, each ballot-box shall be opened by the deputy returning officer (or otherwise examined as the case may be), in the presence of an agent appointed by each candidate, and shall then be sealed by him and by the agents of the candidates, and not again be opened until the balloting has finally closed, when notice shall be given to such of the agents of the candidates as may then be present, to attend to the opening of the boxes and ascertaining the number of votes for each candidate.

" VII. That the deputy returning officer preside in the front of the ballot-box, and see that the balloting is conducted with strict impartiality and justice; and that the various clerks, assistants, and parish constables properly perform their respective duties, and that strict order and decorum be preserved among the friends of the candidates, as well as among all persons employed in conducting the election; and he is hereby authorised and empowered to cause all persons to be taken into custody who interrupt the proceedings of the election, seek to contravene the provisions of this Act, or fail to obey his lawful authority.

" VIII. That during the time the balloting is going on, two agents of each candidate may be in the space fronting the ballot-box, and immediately behind the deputy returning officer, in order that they may see that the election is fairly conducted; such persons to be provided by the deputy returning officer with cards of admission, and to pass in and out by the entrance assigned them.

" IX. That the registration clerk of every parish in the disstrict, who has been appointed for the purposes of registration, be at the balloting place, in the station assigned him, previously to the commencement of the balloting, and see that no person pass on to the balloting place till he has examined his certificate, and seen that it corresponds with the registration list.

" X. That the parish constables and the officers stationed at the entrance of the balloting place, shall not permit any person to enter unless he shows his voter's certificate, except the persons employed in conducting the election, or those persons who have proved the loss of their voter's certificate.

" XI. That at the end of every year, or whenever the Returning Officer is elected at the same time as the Member for the district, a division shall be made in the balloting places, and the boxes and balloting so arranged as to ensure the candidates the strictest impartiality and justice, by preventing the voter from giving two votes for either of the candidates.

" XII. That on the day of election, the balloting commence at six o'clock in the forenoon and terminate at six o'clock in the afternoon of the same day.

" XIII. That when any voter's certificate is examined by the registration clerk, and found to be correct, he shall be allowed to pass on to the next barrier, where a balloting-ball shall be given him by the person appointed for that purpose; he shall then pass on to the balloting box, and, with all due dispatch, shall put the balloting-ball into the box of the candidate he wishes to vote for, after which he shall, without delay, leave the room by the door assigned for the purpose. *See Schedules A and B.*

" XIV. That, at the close of the balloting, the deputy returning officer, in the presence of the agents of the candidates and other persons present, shall break open the seals of the balloting-boxes, and ascertain the number for each candidate; he shall then cause copies of the same to be publicly posted outside the balloting place; and immediately forward (by a trusty messenger) a copy of the same, signed by himself and the agents present, to the returning officer of the district; he shall then deliver a similar copy to the registration clerk, who shall carefully preserve the same, and produce it if necessary.

" XV. That the persons employed as assistants, for inspecting the certificates and attending to the balloting, be paid as hereinafter mentioned.

" XVI. That all the expense of registration, nominations and election, as aforesaid, together with the salaries of the Returning Officers, Registration Clerk, Assistants, Constables, and such other persons as may be necessary, as well as the expense of all balloting places, balloting-boxes, hustings, and other necessaries for the purposes of this Act, be paid out of an *equitable district rate*, which a District Board, composed of one Parochial Officer chosen by each of the parishes in the district, or for any two or more parishes if united for the purposes of this Act, are hereby empowered and commanded to levy on all householders within the district.

" XVII. That all expenses necessary for the purposes of this Act incurred within the district be paid by the district board as aforesaid, or their treasurer; that the salaries of all officers and assistants required for the purposes of this Act be fixed and paid by the said board, according to the expenses and duties of the various localities.

" XVIII. That all accounts of receipts and expenditure for electoral purposes shall be kept distinct, and be audited by auditors appointed by the district board, as aforesaid; copies of which accounts shall be printed for the use of the respective parishes in the district.

" XIX. That all canvassing for Members of Parliament, as well as for Returning Officers, is hereby declared to be illegal, and meetings for that purpose during the balloting on the day of election, are hereby also declared to be illegal. *See Penalties.*

" DURATION OF PARLIAMENT.

" I. Be it enacted, that the Members of the House of Commons, chosen as aforesaid, shall meet on the first Monday in June in each year, and continue their sittings from time to time as they may deem it convenient, till the first Monday in June following, when the next new Parliament shall be chosen; they shall be eligible to be re-elected.

" II. That, during an adjournment, they be liable to be called together by the executive in cases of emergency.

" III. That a register be kept of the daily attendance of each member, which, at the close of the session, shall be printed as a sessional paper, showing how the members have attended.

" PAYMENT OF MEMBERS.

" I. Be it enacted, that every Member of the House of Commons be entitled, at the close of the session, to a writ of expenses on the Treasury, for his legislative duties in the public service, and shall be paid   per annum.*

"PENALTIES.

"I. Be it enacted, that if any person cause himself to be registered in more than one electoral district, and vote in more than one such district, upon conviction thereof before any two justices of the peace within either of such districts, he shall incur for the first offence the penalty of three months' imprisonment, and for the second offence twelve months' imprisonment.

"II. That any person who shall be convicted as aforesaid of wilfully neglecting to fill up his or her notice within the proper time, or of leaving out the name of any inmate in his or her notice, shall for the first offence incur the penalty of one pound for every name omitted; and for the second offence incur the penalty of three months' imprisonment, and be deprived of his electoral rights for three years.

" III. That any person who shall be convicted as aforesaid of forging any name, age, or time of residence on any notice, shall for the first offence incur the penalty of three months' imprisonment, and for the second offence three months' imprisonment, and be deprived of his elective rights for three years.

" IV. That any person who shall be convicted as aforesaid, of having in any manner obtained the certificate of an elector other than his own, and of having voted·or attempted to vote by means of such false certificate, shall for the first offence incur the penalty of three months'

---

* The Committee understand that the *daily payment* of Members of Parliament has operated beneficially in Canada; but they fear that such mode of payment holds out a motive for lengthening the sessions unnecessarily; and if the time of sitting is limited by law, it may lead to too hasty legislation, both of which evils are obviated by an annual payment.

imprisonment, and for the second offence three months' imprisonment, and be deprived of his elective rights for three years.

" V. That any person who shall be convicted as aforesaid, of having forged a voter's certificate, or of having forged the name of any person to any certificate ; or having voted or attempted to vote on such forged certificate ; knowing such to have been forged, shall for the first offence incur the penalty of three months' imprisonment, and for the second offence three months' imprisonment, and be deprived of his elective rights for three years.

" VI. That any person who shall be convicted as aforesaid, of having forged, or caused to be forged, the names of any voters to a requisition nominating a Member of Parliament or a Returning Officer, shall for the first offence incur the penalty of three months' imprisonment, and for the second offence three months' imprisonment, and to be deprived of his elective rights for three years.

" VII. That any person who shall be convicted as aforesaid of bribery, in order to secure his election, shall be subject for the first offence to incur the penalty of two years' imprisonment, and for the second offence shall be imprisoned two years, and be deprived of his elective rights for five years.

" VIII. That any Agent of any Candidate, or any other person, who shall be convicted as aforesaid, of bribery at any election, shall be subject for the first offence to incur the penalty of twelve months' imprisonment, and for the second offence twelve months' imprisonment, and be deprived of his elective rights for five years.

" IX. That any person who shall be convicted as aforesaid, of going from house to house, or place to place, to solicit in any way votes in favour of any candidate for Parliament or Returning Officer, after the nomination as aforesaid, shall for the first offence incur the penalty of one month's imprisonment, and for the second offence two months.

" X. That any person who shall be convicted as aforesaid of calling together, or causing an election meeting to be held in any district during the day of election, shall for the first offence incur the penalty of three months' imprisonment, and for the second offence six months.

" XI. That any person who shall be convicted as aforesaid, of interrupting the balloting, or the business of the election, shall incur the penalty of three months' imprisonment for the first offence, and six months for the second.

" XII. That if any messenger, who may be sent with the state of the ballot to the returning officer, or with any other notice, shall wilfully delay the same, or in any way by his consent or conduct cause the same to be delayed, on conviction as aforesaid, shall incur the penalty of six months' imprisonment.

" XIII. That any Returning Officer who shall be convicted as aforesaid, of having neglected to appoint proper officers as directed by this Act, to see that proper balloting places and balloting-boxes are provided, and to give the notices and perform the duties herein required of him, shall forfeit for each case of neglect the sum of £20.

" XIV. That if any Returning Officer be found guilty of bribery or corrupt practices in the execution of the duties herein assigned to him, he shall incur the penalty of twelve months' imprisonment, and be deprived of his elective rights for five years.

"XV. That if any Deputy Returning Officer be convicted as aforesaid of having neglected to perform any of the duties herein assigned him, he shall forfeit for such neglect three pounds.

" XVI. That if any Deputy Returning Officer be convicted as aforesaid of bribery and corrupt practices in the execution of the duties of his office, he shall incur the penalty of six months' imprisonment, and the deprivation of his elective rights for three years.

" XVII. That if any Registration Clerk be convicted as aforesaid of having neglected to perform any of the duties herein assigned him, he shall forfeit for each such neglect five pounds.

" XVIII. That if any Registration Clerk be convicted as aforesaid of bribery and corrupt practices in the execution of the duties of his office, he shall incur the penalty of six month's imprisonment, and the deprivation of his elective rights for three years.

" XIX. That if the Parochial Officers in any parish neglect or refuse to comply with any of the provisions of this Act, they shall forfeit for every such neglect the sum of £50, or in default of payment, twelve months' imprisonment.

" XX. That all fines and penalties incurred under the provisions of this Act be recoverable before any two justices of the peace, within the district where the offence shall have been committed, and in default of payment, the said justices shall issue their warrant of distress against the goods and chattels of the offender ; or in default of sufficient distress, he shall be imprisoned according to the provisions of this Act

" That all Acts and parts of Acts relating to registration, nominations, or elections of Members of Parliament, as well as the duration of Parliament and sittings of members, are hereby repealed."

APPENDIX C.

"NATIONAL PETITION.

" *Unto the Honourable the Commons of the United Kingdom of Great Britain and Ireland in Parliament assembled, the Petition of the undersigned, their suffering countrymen,*

" HUMBLY SHEWETH,

" That we, your petitioners, dwell in a land whose merchants are noted for enterprise, whose manufacturers are very skilful, and whose workmen are proverbial for their industry.

" The land itself is goodly, the soil rich, and the temperature wholesome; it is abundantly furnished with the materials of commerce and trade; it has numerous and convenient harbours; in facility of internal communication it exceeds all others.

" For three-and-twenty years we have enjoyed a profound peace.

" Yet, with all these elements of national prosperity, and with every disposition and capacity to take advantage of them, we find ourselves overwhelmed with public and private suffering.

" We are bowed down under a load of taxes; which, notwithstanding, fall greatly short of the wants of our rulers; our traders are trembling on the verge of bankruptcy; our workmen are starving; capital brings no profit, and labour no remuneration; the home of the artificer is desolate, and the warehouse of the pawnbroker is full; the workhouse is crowded, and the manufactory is deserted.

" We have looked on every side, we have searched diligently in order to find out the causes of a distress so sore and so long continued.

" We can discover none in nature, or in Providence.

" Heaven has dealt graciously by the people; but the foolishness of our rulers has made the goodness of God of none effect.

" The energies of a mighty kingdom have been wasted in building up the power of selfish and ignorant men, and its resources squandered for their aggrandisement.

" The good of a party has been advanced to the sacrifice of the good of the nation; the few have governed for the interest of the few, while the interest of the many has been neglected, or insolently and tyrannously trampled upon.

" It was the fond expectation of the people that a remedy for the greater part, if not for the whole, of their grievances, would be found in the Reform Act of 1832.

" They were taught to regard that Act as a wise means to a worthy end; as the machinery of an improved legislation, when the will of the masses would be at length potential.

" They have been bitterly and basely deceived.

" The fruit which looked so fair to the eye has turned to dust and ashes when gathered.

" The Reform Act has effected a transfer of power from one domineering faction to another, and left the people as helpless as before.

" Our slavery has been exchanged for an apprenticeship to liberty, which has aggravated the painful feeling of our social degradation, by adding to it the sickening of still deferred hope.

" We come before your Honourable House to tell you, with all humility, that this state of things must not be permitted to continue; that it cannot long continue without very seriously endangering the stability of the throne and the peace of the kingdom; and that if by God's help and all lawful and constitutional appliances, an end can be put to it, we are fully resolved that it shall speedily come to an end.

" We tell your Honourable House that the capital of the

master must no longer be deprived of its due reward; that the laws which make food dear, and those which by making money scarce, makes labour cheap, must be abolished; that taxation must be made to fall on property, not on industry; that the good of the many, as it is the only legitimate end, so must it be the sole study of the Government.

"As a preliminary essential to these and other requisite changes; as means by which alone the interests of the people can be effectually vindicated and secured, we demand that those interests be confided to the keeping of the people.

"When the state calls for defenders, when it calls for money, no consideration of poverty or ignorance can be pleaded in refusal or delay of the call.

"Required as we are, universally, to support and obey the laws, nature and reason entitle us to demand, that in the making of the laws, the universal voice shall be implicitly listened to.

"We perform the duties of freemen; we must have the privileges of freemen.

"WE DEMAND UNIVERSAL SUFFRAGE.

"The suffrage to be exempt from the corruption of the wealthy, and the violence of the powerful, must be secret.

"The assertion of our right necessarily involves the power of its uncontrolled exercise.

"WE DEMAND THE BALLOT.

"The connection between the representatives and the people, to be beneficial must be intimate.

"The legislative and constituent powers, for correction and for instruction, ought to be brought into frequent contact.

"Errors, which are comparatively light when susceptible of a speedy popular remedy, may produce the most disastrous effects when permitted to grow inveterate through years of compulsory endurance.

"To public safety as well as public confidence, frequent elections are essential.

" WE DEMAND ANNUAL PARLIAMENTS.

" With power to choose, and freedom in choosing, the range of our choice must be unrestricted.

" We are compelled, by the existing laws, to take for our representatives, men who are incapable of appreciating our difficulties, or who have little sympathy with them; merchants who have retired from trade, and no longer feel its harassings; proprietors of land who are alike ignorant of its evils and their cure; lawyers, by whom the honours of the senate are sought after only as means of obtaining notice in the courts.

" The labours of a representative, who is sedulous in the discharge of his duty, are numerous and burdensome.

" It is neither just, nor reasonable, nor safe, that they should continue to be gratuitously rendered.

" We demand that in the future election of members of your Honourable House, the approbation of the constituency shall be the sole qualification; and that to every representative so chosen, shall be assigned, out of the public taxes, a fair and adequate remuneration for the time which he is called upon to devote to the public service.

" Finally, we would most earnestly impress on your Honourable House, that this petition has not been dictated by any idle love of change; that it springs out of no inconsiderate attachment to fanciful theories; but that it is the result of much and long deliberation, and of convictions, which the events of each succeeding year tend more and more to strengthen.

" The management of this mighty kingdom has hitherto been a subject for contending factions to try their selfish experiments upon.

" We have felt the consequences in our sorrowful experience—short glimmerings of uncertain enjoyment swallowed up by long and dark seasons of suffering.

" If the self-government of the people should not remove their distresses, it will at least remove their repinings.

" Universal suffrage will, and it alone can, bring true and lasting peace to the nation; we firmly believe that it will also bring prosperity.

"May it therefore please your honourable House to take this our petition into your most serious consideration; and to use your utmost endeavours, by all constitutional means, to have a law passed, granting to every male of lawful age, sane mind, and unconvicted of crime, the right of voting for members of Parliament; and directing all future elections of members of Parliament to be in the way of secret ballot; and ordaining that the duration of Parliaments so chosen shall in no case exceed one year; and abolishing all property qualifications in the members; and providing for their due remuneration while in attendance on their Parliamentary duties.

"And your petitioners, &c."

LONDON : WATERLOW AND SONS LIMITED, PRINTERS.

www.ingramcontent.com/pod-product-compliance
Lightning Source LLC
Chambersburg PA
CBHW080602270326
41928CB00016B/2900